J.K. LASSER'S

FACE TO FACE
WITH THE IRS

Robert G. Nath, Esq.

Macmillan Spectrum
an imprint of Macmillan • USA

Disclaimer

The material contained in this book is as accurate and current as possible, but it is intended for general information and educational purposes only and is not to be used as a substitute for competent professional assistance in individual situations. The names and descriptions of persons appearing in examples and case histories in this volume are the product of the author's imagination, and any resemblance to actual persons, living or dead, is entirely coincidental.

Macmillan General Reference
A Simon & Schuster Macmillan Company
1633 Broadway
New York, NY 10019

Copyright © 1997 by Robert G. Nath

A J.K. Lasser Book

J.K. Lasser and Macmillan are registered trademarks
of Simon & Schuster, Inc.

Robert G. Nath
    J.K. Lasser's Face To Face With The IRS
Robert G. Nath
      p.   cm.
      Includes index
      ISBN 0-02-861606-5
Powers of IRS
         IRS Levies
         Federal Tax Lien
    2. Penalties
    3. IRS Audits

Face To Face With The IRS

KF6425.Z9G64   1996
343.7305'24—dc20   95-46623
                        CIP

Manufactured in the United States of America

10 9 8 7 6 5 4 3 2 1

Publisher's Note: Every care has been taken in the preparation of the text to ensure its clarity and accuracy in regard to the subject matter covered. Taxpayers are cautioned, however, that this book is sold with the understanding that the Publisher is not engaged in rendering legal, accounting, investment or other professional service. Taxpayers with specific tax problems are urged to seek the professional advice of a tax accountant, lawyer or preparer.

DEDICATION

This book is dedicated to my wife, Judy, for her patience, her editorial skills, and her managerial skill in juggling the demands of our three children. Judy's invaluable editorial suggestions, refinement, eye for detail, and humor helped to make this book complete.

This book is also dedicated to my three children, Jennifer, Cheryl, and Daniel. Their enthusiastic hugs at the end of the day always gave me the extra energy I needed to burn the midnight oil.

and

To my father, Jack H. Nath, and to the memory of my mother, Claire S. Nath, who were always there when I needed them.

CONTENTS

Preface   xiii

Part I WHEN YOU OWE TAXES BUT CAN'T PAY   *1*

Part II AUDITS *199*

Part III TAX LITIGATION 261

Part IV THE IRS IN YOUR EVERYDAY LIFE 299

ACKNOWLEDGMENTS

Many helped in many ways to bring this book into print. My colleagues James H. Jeffries, III, Esq., and Eric L. Chase, Esq., contributed valuable insights and suggestions to the text. Former revenue officer Deluvina Valdez reviewed many of the chapters and contributed valuable suggestions. R. Sue Williams typed (and retyped) the manuscript. I also received the encouragement of my partners, Dexter S. Odin, Esq., and James B. Pittleman, Esq., and editorial suggestions as well from them, my partner John Dedon, my sister, Barbara Gold, my brother, Ronald Nath, my father, Jack H. Nath, my brother-in-law, Ronald Sussman, and my in-laws, June and Jules Sussman. I also thank my agents Perry Knowlton and Andrew Pope of Curtis Brown Ltd. and Debra Englander and Richard Staron at Macmillan for their efforts to bring this book to the public.

PREFACE

⎯⎯⎯⎯⎯⎯⎯⎯⎯

"The Congress shall have power to lay and collect taxes . . . ."
-U.S. Constitution, Article I, Section 8, Clause 1.

"The Congress shall have power to lay and collect taxes on incomes, from whatever source derived, without apportionment among the several States, and without regard to any census or enumeration."
-U.S. Constitution, 16th Amendment.

From these simple words and humble origins has sprung the one government agency that touches nearly everyone—the Internal Revenue Service. It's also one of the most complex of agencies. That complexity, coupled with the IRS' potent enforcement powers, sometimes generates confusion, fear, and misunderstanding.

As our government's need for money increases (that seems to be every year), this agency is blessed or cursed by Congress with the task of policing a three-thousand-page tax code that intrudes ever more into daily life. Well-meaning efforts by reformers, as in the recent flat-tax debate, rarely slow the system, which always seems to outlast its harshest and most frequent critics. For most of us, the encroachment of the IRS is like background noise, annoying but somehow tolerable. The tax collector's outstretched hand captures part of our paychecks. We file tax returns once a year. We answer the IRS' occasional questions.

For others, the IRS can be a nightmare that never ends. Every year, the IRS:

1. collects more than $1 trillion in taxes and fees;

2. conducts more than one million audits;

3.   tries to find five million to ten million people who have not filed tax returns;

4.   penalizes other millions who did; and

5.   tries to collect more than $200 billion from millions of other tax delinquents.

The IRS is a silent partner in many divorces and marriages. It polices millions of businesses, large and small. It can levy on wages, ruin your credit, get your records by force if necessary, seize assets, even sell your home. In cases of evasion or fraud, these tax police can throw you in jail.

But even as the IRS becomes more powerful, Congress asks it to do more, not less. The IRS now enforces more than 150 civil penalties, collects child-support payments, and polices our vast private pension system. It keeps your tax refund when you owe some other debt to the government. It regulates charities and performs a myriad of other tasks.

Every few years, citizens and their representatives raise a hue and cry about the system's supposed unfairness. The latest effort, the flat-tax debate, followed closely on the heels of other reform proposals such as a consumption tax and value-added tax. So far, all these "abolish the IRS" movements have died a quick death. Like it or not, the tax system is here to stay. We might as well learn to deal with it.

 For the past several years, the IRS has been trying—off and on—to change both its public image and the way it does business. In some important ways, the agency has made real progress. It has become more user-friendly and, on the enforcement side, somewhat kinder and gentler. Part of this change is the happy result of a ten-year program to modernize the tax system with computers. The modernization effort proceeds in fits and starts, but it is gradually making progress. The agency also is training its employees in the art of being more polite, sensitive, and respectful. Even the Collection Division, whose job includes levying on wages and seizing assets, has been trained to be more businesslike and tolerant of payment problems and daily living needs. But change is slow; hardened attitudes persist. The IRS has never wavered from its mission to collect the most money it can. The national office may have put out the welcome mat, but all of us must still watch that next step.

This book is intended to navigate through the most common, most important issues people encounter with the IRS. Many times you simply need to get along with the agency. At other times the IRS becomes a series of traps with frustration all along the way.

Despite the frightening complexity of the tax code, enforced by the one-sided powers the IRS enjoys, *no one* need fear this agency or needlessly lose a tax battle with it. All you need is to understand the system and its people and to take advantage of the many rights at your command.

Part I gives you a battle plan when you go to war with the IRS over collection of taxes. The IRS may have the death rays, but you have star shields and even a few weapons of your own. Understanding how to use them can save you thousands of dollars and oceans of tears. Part II levels the field in that over-feared part of tax life—the tax audit. This part encourages you to face audits head-on, and to appeal unfavorable audit results to get a better deal. Part III explains when and how you can fight the IRS in court—and possibly win. Part IV explores the many ways in which the IRS is part of our everyday lives—from filing returns, to not filing returns, to organizing records, even to many ways of getting money back from the IRS.

In most chapters you will find case examples. Most are drawn from reported court decisions, with the names and places changed, and the facts condensed.

Part I

WHEN YOU OWE TAXES
BUT CAN'T PAY

Chapter 1

THE COLLECTION "MENU"

INTRODUCTION

Picture yourself going out to eat. You sit down in the restaurant; the waiter brings you a menu with many choices. You select an appetizer, main course, and later a dessert. The chef or waiter may regretfully say, "Sorry. That menu choice is not available. Please choose another." With any luck, the choices are to your liking and you leave satisfied.

Dealing with the Collection Division of the Internal Revenue Service is something like dining out, though nowhere near as tasteful or satisfying. Still, it's often a pleasant surprise to discover how wide an array of choices the law and IRS procedures allow to manage your back tax bill. It's simply not the case that you must always pay in full, and immediately, or go to debtor's prison. This tax collection "menu" of powerful choices applies to almost every tax debt, business or personal. You can choose one "course," then another, or a combination. You can start with one, then switch to another.

Sadly, many people resign themselves to no menu at all; they believe that whatever the IRS says, goes. But it's just not so. Knowing the full range of choices, and how and when to make them, can give you true power in an otherwise one-sided contest.

Of course, the IRS also has a menu of choices that *it* wants to impose on *you*. Like you, agents of the IRS can make one or more choices, or select them in combination. (Or, the IRS "chef" may tell you some courses are not available.)

Naturally, your selections may be radically different from the choices the IRS makes. The key to surviving a run-in with the IRS Collection Division and managing your back tax debt to a successful result is to understand your choices and make them wisely. It also is essential to understand the *IRS'* priorities and to prepare to deal with them. True enough, the IRS has great power to back up the choices on its menu, but with some exceptions the Service restrains the use of its own power.

YOUR COLLECTION "MENU"

Now, let's see. . . . What's on the menu today?

1.   *Pay in full within thirty days.* Some people who owe a back tax debt can quickly pay in full, such as by selling a stock or bond or borrowing money. Sometimes they may have to take the painful step of liquidating a retirement account they've been nurturing for many years. When the IRS catches them, they may reason, "OK, you got me; it's worth any price to get you off my back." The stimulus of a single call or letter is often enough to spur the writing of a check. Other times, people may need to sell something quickly to pay in full. The IRS motivates millions to pay simply by asking.

2.   *Pay in full—over time.* If you can't pay in full right away, the installment agreement comes in handy (see chapter 7). The idea is that you can pay in full but just need time to do it. True enough, the accrued interest and penalties will make your payment plan a form of modern financial torture, but at least you'll be able to see the end. While installment agreements can last an extremely long time, the IRS normally looks for full payment in thirty-six months at most. If you stay within that time limit, you'll have lots of room to negotiate the details.

3.   *Pay part now, pay part over time.* This choice means you liquidate some assets, but still can't pay the tax in full. So the Service lets you sell a stock or bond, cash in a retirement account, or borrow $5,000 from a rich and very nice uncle, then pay the rest by installments. This combination may or may not be your best choice to get the IRS off your back, or it may be that the IRS forces it on you, but it's on the menu as an available option.

Sometimes, if it's in your best interest to pay over time, *you* can force the IRS to accept this menu choice. The most important way is through a bankruptcy such as a Chapter 11 or Chapter 13 reorganization. (These names derive from chapters of the Bankruptcy Code.) In these types of bankruptcies, you are essentially asking the bankruptcy court to approve a long-term installment agreement, sometimes up to five years. The IRS will often agree to your plan, or have little realistic choice but to go along. Still, bankruptcy should never be undertaken lightly. It ruins your credit and has other negative effects as well. Chapter 12 of this book details the how and why of tax bankruptcies.

4. *Pay in part, write off the rest.* Does the IRS do this? Actually write off a debt? Yes. It's done through the offer in compromise program. Chapter 6 explains this option. Convincing the Service to accept an offer can be difficult, especially if you try to "do it yourself" without professional help. But if you succeed, you normally end up paying only a fraction of what you owe. The national average is about thirteen cents on the dollar for accepted offers. This means the IRS gives up nearly 90 percent of claims it compromises (on the average). Why not choose this menu option right away? Usually, it's because the IRS thinks you can pay more than you will offer, or you can pay in full now or over time. Its job is to try to collect to the max—quickly! Still, consider whether you may be eligible for an offer in compromise.

5. *Pay nothing.* The expression, "You can't get blood out of a turnip," applies in the world of IRS collections, too. In fact, the IRS classifies so many taxpayer delinquencies as "currently not collectible" it even has a form and a verb (Form 53, as in, "Let's 53 this case"). If you convince the IRS that you can pay nothing whatsoever, now or in the foreseeable future, the agent may classify your account as "currently not collectible." The IRS shelves these accounts for six months, a year, or more. The Service can revisit your account, but often it does not. Whether "currently not collectible" status is desirable is another story. The federal tax lien stays in place. The tax debt can last for up to ten years, sometimes longer. You are also subject to periodic reviews to see whether you are still as poor as before.

6. *Reduce the amount you owe, then deal with the rest from the other menu choices.* Many people do not realize they can actually reduce how much tax they owe. The clearest example is the tax audit. The IRS proposes more taxes in an amount approximating the national debt, but you contest that proposal within the IRS and in court. Another example is "audit reconsideration." (See chapter 15.) Under some limited circumstances, you can ask the IRS to reconsider an unfavorable audit result either because it is wrong or because the agency failed to consider certain evidence. A third type of case involves people who have failed to file federal income tax returns, so-called nonfilers for whom the IRS is authorized to make returns and assessments. These people can always request audit reconsideration if they file true original returns.

You may also reduce the amount you owe by questioning the IRS's computations. True enough, the assessment you receive is often correct; but sometimes there are errors. Has the IRS correctly computed penalties and interest? Has it applied all of your payments? Has it applied them to the right tax periods? You are entitled to an accounting from the IRS simply by requesting it. Any agent can pull your transcripts to to check all of these items. If you don't understand some of the entries, ask. And, if the agent can't explain an entry that you believe is incorrect, that alone may be grounds for asking for further research to be done or for postponing the payment of the tax until the discrepancy is resolved.

Finally, you can resort to bankruptcy to reduce your taxes. It's a widespread and tragic myth that you can never eliminate taxes in bankruptcy. In fact, you can. Income taxes are potentially dischargeable in bankruptcy. Employment taxes, while not generally dischargeable, can be negotiated downward once a bankruptcy is filed. More than one million people file for bankruptcy each year. The IRS is involved in fully one-third of these cases. These statistics give some idea of how popular bankruptcy is, but no one knows how many people are unaware of their right to reduce or eliminate taxes through bankruptcy. Still, filing for bankruptcy is a major step that should never be taken lightly. A host of nontax considerations should be in play.

7.   *Call the boss.* You can appeal any collection agent's decision at least one or two levels. Simply state, "I would like to speak to your supervisor. Please give me his name, title, and telephone number." If two levels of appeal do not work, sometimes you can launch a flanking attack by appealing to the Problem Resolution Office. Chapter 13 discusses this topic in detail.

8.   *Sue.* Usually a last resort, suing the government over taxes can reduce your taxes or delay the day of reckoning. It can be downright thrilling if you win, and ecstatic if you also win attorneys' fees. Chapters 21 and 22 discuss the types of lawsuits available to contest taxes, when they are permitted, and what the chances are of success.

THE IRS' "MENU"

Those are *your* choices. Now let's see what's on the IRS' menu.

1.   *Pay all—now!* First and foremost, the Service wants you to pay in full, right now, on the spot and immediately! In fact, most people can and do pay. Were that not so, the shortfall of revenue would collapse

the government like a punctured tire. The IRS is hugely successful in persuading many taxpayers to pay in full, "voluntarily," even if they owe one or more years of back taxes.

2. *Pay in full now, involuntarily.* Next on the IRS menu is the iron fist inside the velvet glove. The agency has vast enforcement powers by which its agents can seize and sell assets. Few of your assets can elude its grasp. The IRS wants people to pay voluntarily, but does not hesitate to use its enforcement powers in many cases.

3. *Pay in full—soon.* The Service can and will give you extensions of time to pay, within reason (*its* reason). As a rule of thumb, three to four months (usually fewer) is about as long as the IRS will give you to pay in full without making some other arrangement like an installment agreement. Installment agreements of up to three years are common. Often they last even longer.

4. *Pay part now, the rest later.* Here's a cute combination the Service sometimes uses. It asks you to pay as much as you can now, such as by selling assets, borrowing against them, or borrowing from friends and relatives. Then it asks you to pay the rest over time by an installment agreement.

5. *Pay all later: installment agreement.* This one is on your menu, too, but it's way down on the list for the feds. (It may be high or low on your list.) The Service disfavors installment agreements, though a workable one that is paid in full yields the IRS a "profit"—the penalties. Installment agreements stretch out payment to the government and prolong the taxpayer's pain—neither a result the IRS normally enjoys. Moreover, at one time 80 percent of installment agreement payors defaulted before final payment. Why? People lose their jobs, expenses increase, or the installment amount was set too high to begin with. Still, the IRS grants about 2.6 million per year; these agreements raise billions of dollars despite the high failure rate.

6. *Pay part now, write off the rest: offer in compromise.* Officially, the IRS encourages agents to explore offers in compromise, especially if the taxpayer brings up the subject. Officially, the offer is a useful collection tool, that is, an acceptable way for a revenue officer to resolve a case. But in the real world, the wind is shifting against offers. It is hard to

persuade the IRS to accept one. When the revenue officer considers an offer, it's often because she is convinced there is little else she can do.

7. *Pay nothing now or later: "currently not collectible" accounts.* The Service recognizes reality: some people simply cannot now (and maybe never will) pay their past due tax bills. The IRS will not write off the bill, at least not until the statute of limitations on collection expires (normally ten years). Instead, it will shelve the case as "currently not collectible." The IRS may revisit the case in the future.

8. *Sue the taxpayer.* The IRS usually views lawsuits to collect taxes as a last resort. Still, it does not hesitate to use this option in many cases. Chapter 23 explains when and how.

DUELING MENUS

Your goal is to select menu choices that are best for you and make them digestible to the IRS. This can often be done with a minimum of hassle and pain. Other times a struggle is inevitable. The following chapters will guide you on the best way to convince the IRS that your choices of appetizer, entree, and dessert are acceptable.

RULES OF THE RESTAURANT

1. *Read IRS Publication 594, "Understanding the Collection Process."* It's a terrific publication, well-written and evenhanded. It provides an excellent summary of your rights in the collection process. Those rights include the opportunity to reconsider your tax bill, to make an offer, to propose an installment agreement, to engage a representative, and to receive fair and courteous treatment.

2. *Deal with your tax bill; meet any deadline.* Much as *you* may want to forget about your bill, the IRS will not. The faster you respond and the more businesslike you are, the better the outcome usually will be.

3. *Insist on courtesy and confidentiality.* One of your rights is to fair, professional, and courteous treatment. If you don't get it, call the employee's boss. Extend the same courtesy to the agents with whom you deal.

4. *Use the Problem Resolution Program.* If you run into major roadblocks or snafus, often the Problem Resolution Office can help. Appendix II contains a list of Problem Resolution Office numbers and addresses. Also consult chapter 13 before running to the PROs.

5. *Understand your tax bill.* The IRS usually calculates your tax balance correctly. But sometimes it makes mistakes. Ask to see the agency's calculations, but don't use this as an excuse not to pay or otherwise address the back tax bill.

6. *Put it in writing!* Document any significant statements, decisions, or evidence in writing. Send it to the IRS address listed on your tax bill or collection notice. Without fail, keep a copy of whatever you send.

YOUR RIGHTS AS A TAXPAYER

THE FIRST PART OF THIS PUBLICATION EXPLAINS SOME OF YOUR MOST IMPORTANT RIGHTS AS A TAXPAYER.

THE SECOND PART EXPLAINS THE EXAMINATION, APPEAL, COLLECTION, AND REFUND PROCESSES.

DECLARATION OF TAXPAYER RIGHTS

I. Protection of Your Rights

IRS employees will explain and protect your rights as a taxpayer throughout your contact with us.

II. Privacy and Confidentiality

The IRS will not disclose to anyone the information you give us, except as authorized by law. You have the right to know why we are asking you for information, how we will use it, and what happens if you do not provide requested information.

III. Professional and Courteous Service

If you believe that an IRS employee has not treated you in a professional manner, you should tell that employee's supervisor. If the supervisor's response is not satisfactory, you should write to your IRS District Director or Service Center Director.

IV. Representation

You may either represent yourself, or with proper written authorization, have someone else represent you in your place. You can have someone accompany you at an interview. You may make sound recordings of any meetings with our examination or collection personnel, provided you tell us in writing 10 days before the meeting.

V. Payment of Only The Correct Amount of Tax

You are responsible for paying only the correct amount of tax due under the law—no more, no less.

VI. Help From The Problem Resolution Office

Problem Resolution Officers can help you with unresolved tax problems and can offer you special help if you have a significant hardship as a result of a tax problem. For more information, write to the Problem Resolution Office at the District Office or Service Center where you have the problem, or call 1-800-829-1040 (1-800-829-4059 for TDD users).

VII. Appeals and Judicial Review

If you disagree with us about the amount of your tax liability or certain collection actions, you have the right to ask the IRS Appeals Office to review your case. You may also ask a court to review your case.

VIII. Relief From Certain Penalties

The IRS will waive penalties when allowed by law if you can show you acted reasonably and in good faith or relied on the incorrect advice of an IRS employee.

EXAMINATIONS, APPEALS, COLLECTIONS, AND REFUNDS

Examinations (Audits)

We accept most taxpayer's returns as filed. If we inquire about your return or select it for examination, it does not suggest that you are dishonest. The inquiry or examination may or may not result in more tax. We may close your case without change; or, you may receive a refund.

By Mail

We handle many examinations and inquiries by mail. We will send you a letter with either a request for more information or a reason why we believe a change to your return may be needed. If you give us the requested information or provide an explanation, we may or may not agree with you, and we will explain the reasons for any changes. Please do not hesitate to write to us about anything you do not understand. If you cannot resolve a question through the mail, you can request a personal interview with an examiner.

By Interview

If we notify you that we will conduct your examination through a personal interview, or you request such an interview, you have the right to ask that the examination take place at a reasonable time and place that is convenient for both you and the IRS. At the end of your examination, the examiner will give you a report if there are any proposed changes to your tax return. If you do not agree with the report, you may meet with the examiner's supervisor.

Repeat Examinations

If we examined your tax return for the same items in either of the 2 previous years and proposed no change to your tax liability, please contact us as soon as possible so we can determine if we should discontinue the repeat examination. Publication 556, *Examination of Returns, Appeal Rights, and Claims for Refund,* will give you more information about the rules and procedures of an IRS examination.

Appeals

If you do not agree with the examiner's findings, you can appeal them to our Appeals Office. Most differences can be settled without expensive and time-consuming court trials. Your appeal rights are explained in detail in Publication 5, *Appeal Rights and Preparation of Protests for Unagreed Cases.*

If you do not wish to use our Appeals Office or disagree with its findings, you can take your case to the U.S. Tax Court, U.S. Court of Federal Claims, or the U.S. District Court where you live. If the court agrees with you on most issues in your case, and finds that our position was largely unjustified, you may be able to recover some of your administrative and litigation costs. You will not be eligible to recover these costs unless you tried to resolve your case administratively, including going through our appeals system, and you gave us all the information necessary to resolve the case.

Collections

Publication 594, *Understanding The Collection Process,* explains your rights and responsibilities regarding payment of federal taxes. It is divided into several sections that explain the procedures in plain language. The sections include:

1. *When you have not paid enough tax.* This section describes tax bills and explains what to do if you think your bill is wrong.

2. *Making arrangements to pay your bill.* This covers making installment payments, delaying collection action, and submitting an offer in compromise.

3. *What happens when you take no action to pay.* This covers liens, releasing a lien, levies, releasing a levy, seizures and sales, and release of property. Publication 1660, *Collection Appeal Rights (for Liens, Levies and Seizures),* explains your rights to appeal liens, levies and seizures and how to request these appeals.

Refunds

You may file a claim for refund if you think you paid too much tax. You must generally file the claim within 3 years from the date you filed your return or 2 years from the date you paid the tax, whichever is later. The law generally provides for interest on your refund if it is not paid within 45 days of the date you filed your return or claim for refund. Publication 556, *Examination of Returns, Appeal Rights, and Claims for Refund,* has more information on refunds.

Tax Information

The IRS provides a great deal of free information. The following are sources for forms, publications and additional information:

- **Tax Information:**
  1-800-829-1040

- **Forms and Publications:**
  1-800-829-3676
  (1-800-829-4059 for TDD users)

- **IRS FAX Forms:** From your FAX machine dial **703-487-4160**

- **Internet:** World Wide Web - http://www.irs.ustreas.gov
  FTP - ftp.irs.ustreas.gov
  Telnet - iris.irs.ustreas.gov

*U.S. Government Printing Office: 1996 - 411-952

Department of the Treasury
Internal Revenue Service
Publication 1 (Rev. 5-96)
Catalog Number 64731W

Chapter 2

THE POWERS OF THE INTERNAL
REVENUE SERVICE

Most of us realize, at least in a general way, that the IRS has extraordinary powers to collect the taxes people owe. Those who face the agency with an audit or collection problem naturally have a more focused sense of these powers. The agency's full arsenal suggests a range of powers people would not ordinarily think should be given to our government, at least not all at once. But the agency's powers have all been granted by your legislature and mine, the Congress, and the courts have consistently upheld these powers as legal and constitutional. While the IRS usually exercises most of its authority with great forbearance, sometimes bordering on reluctance, its powers are available and ready in any case. In starkest form, the IRS has the power to:

- invade your business and seize its equipment and other assets;

- seize your personal bank accounts without court order;

- make legally binding tax assessments, and enforce them, without court order;

- seize other assets, such as your retirement accounts, insurance policies, even your home;

- sell them to the highest bidder without your consent;

- send information about you to the states, Congress, the president, the Department of Justice, and other government agencies, without your consent;

- adjust your tax accounts, shifting payments among tax years, without your prior knowledge or consent;

- propose new taxes, impose penalties and interest, and make you sue to contest them;

- sue you for back taxes, foreclose on property, and even set aside transfers and conveyances to others;

- get virtually anyone to talk to Service agents about your taxes and financial affairs, and obtain any documents that bear on those financial affairs (with limited exceptions);

- in cases of fraud and evasion, or where collection is in jeopardy, terminate your tax year and issue an instantaneous assessment. If you show an inclination to flee, the agency can even obtain a civil writ of arrest.

Against all of these powers, you have few weapons:

- you can't sue the IRS for an injunction to stop it from assessing or collecting taxes;

- you can't sue the IRS to stop it from gathering information, or from revealing that information about you to other agents, other government agencies, even to customers, clients, and friends;

- you generally can't stop the IRS from seizing your bank accounts or your other assets, or from selling them without your consent and sometimes without your knowledge;

- you can't sue the IRS at all without the consent of Congress, a consent given in only a few (about ten) types of tax cases.

Once again, every one of these IRS powers, and your corresponding legal incapacity to fight them, have been ruled constitutional in case after case. Because of this severe mismatch, if the IRS did not exercise its powers with restraint, in all likelihood Congress would swiftly take them away.

WHERE IT ALL CAME FROM

After the states ratified the Constitution in 1789, Congress created only four cabinet agencies, among them the Department of the Treasury. For most of its life, the Treasury Department simply collected customs duties, administered the sale of public lands, and managed the federal debt, budgets, and other financial matters. Income and employment taxes were not even on the original Treasury's list of chores—there were no such taxes. Indeed, until this century, the Internal Revenue Service did not exist.

Congress enacted the first income tax during the Civil War as a series of special war measures, promptly repealing them when the conflict ended. On July 1, 1862, Congress created the Bureau of Internal Revenue, the IRS' predecessor. Another income tax lasted only from 1870 to 1872. But twenty years elapsed before the next income tax was enacted, in 1894, and after a series of court battles, the Supreme Court declared that tax unconstitutional.

The modern taxing system began only in 1913 when Congress passed and the states ratified the 16th Amendment to the Constitution. Even then, only the rich and famous paid taxes. In 1950, a mere forty-six years ago, Congress brought the modern Internal Revenue Service into being.

What a difference forty-six years makes! The agency now has 110,000 employees serving a national office, four regions, thirty-three districts (subsets of regions), ten service centers, a data center, and a computer center.

This agency orchestrates a tax system that rakes in more than $1 trillion every year, processes more than 2 billion pieces of paper, polices more than 200 million tax returns of 7 main varieties, generates 150 million pieces of correspondence, and performs a host of other functions. The agency has more than fifteen thousand revenue agents (who audit tax returns), nine thousand revenue officers (who collect the taxes), and five thousand special agents (who investigate tax crimes), plus many other employees.

THE IRS PYRAMID

The IRS is organized in a pyramid. At the top, the national office consists of the commissioner and a staff. This office bears overall responsibility for the administration of the Internal Revenue Service. Its various assistant commissioners make broad policy based on national trends in audits, collection, data gathering, freedom of information, criminal investigation, and other areas of national interest.

REGIONS

The next layer consists of four regional offices. These have regional commissioners, regional inspectors, regional counsel, and other functions. These offices generally coordinate all of the districts within their jurisdiction and report to the national office.

DISTRICT OFFICES AND SERVICE CENTERS

The real work of the Internal Revenue Service is done in field offices: the thirty-three IRS districts and the service centers. Each district is headed by a district director who is chiefly responsible for implementing national policy. District directors have wide authority to set procedures within their districts, authority they do not hesitate to exercise.

FUNCTIONS

The IRS is also organized at all three levels into three major functions: examination, collection, and criminal investigation. (There are also taxpayer service and problem resolution functions.)

The examination division audits tax returns. It employs revenue agents and tax auditors. The collection division, staffed by revenue officer groups, collects the taxes. The criminal investigation division, using special agents, investigates tax crimes. The Problem Resolution Office is a taxpayer advocate section that tries to take your side when you are choking on IRS red tape. There is also a taxpayer service function that attempts to smooth out administrative problems within the district.

In almost every case, these revenue agents, tax auditors, revenue officers, special agents, taxpayer service representatives, and problem resolution officers do the real work of collecting taxes, auditing returns, and performing related duties. These are the officers that you will face when you have an audit, collection, criminal, or other tax problem.

HOW THE IRS LEARNS MORE ABOUT YOU

In almost every IRS investigation, of whatever flavor—audit, collection, or criminal investigation—the agency needs to know more about you, your family, your finances, and your tax return. Agents use three classes of sources: (1) you, (2) public records, and (3) third-party records and sources. They gather what seems like 98 percent of their information voluntarily, simply by asking you questions. For example, a revenue agent might ask, "What is your justification for deducting medical expenses on Schedule A of your tax return?" The revenue officer wants to know, "Where do you keep your bank accounts, stocks, and bonds?" These and other agents often make their requests in a more formal fashion, such as by an Information Document Request or a letter. In most cases, it's wise to volunteer the information, because the IRS can get it anyway. Things usually go easier if you cooperate.

The second main source of information is public records. Years ago, the well-known actor Peter Sellers starred in the movie *Being There*. Mr. Sellers played the part of Chauncy Gardener, a childlike housekeeper who had spent his entire life keeping one house. Through a series of errors, Chauncy becomes an adviser to the president of the United States. In the course of investigating Chauncy's background, the president discovers to his surprise that Chauncy has absolutely no history—no tax returns, no military history, no purchase and sale of assets—nothing

There are no Chauncy Gardeners in America. Almost everyone leaves tracks that become public records. It could be buying a home, filing a court case, getting a government check, earning interest on a bank account, or inheriting property. The IRS has access to public records just like anyone else, and its agents comb through these records all the time. And, as chapters 9 and 11 explain, the IRS knows all of these sources of information.

The third source of information is third parties. These could be banks, brokers, mortgage lenders, or insurance companies. Customers, clients, friends, relatives, and employees are also sources.

The law gives IRS agents of whatever job description the widest possible authority to "inquire after and concerning" anyone who may be liable to pay an internal revenue tax. To enforce this authority, the IRS has subpoena power. The IRS' version of this administrative subpoena is called a *summons*, used when someone does not voluntarily testify or supply data. The agency resorts to this summons power five thousand times a year. In almost every case, it gets the information, records, and testimony. In fact, you and the third parties the agency summons can be held in civil contempt of court for refusing to obey a summons. Technically, it's also a crime to disobey a summons, though this crime is rarely prosecuted.

The service's summons power is far-reaching. It extends to any "books, records, papers, or other data which may be relevant" to your tax liability or its collection. That language, straight from the tax code, was deliberately chosen to be all-encompassing. It means the IRS can get any corporate record, deed, bank account, or accountants' records, some lawyers' records (where the attorney-client privilege does not apply), and almost anything with a number on it. In thousands of cases, the IRS has used this summons power to seize all of these types of paper records, notes, telephone records, computer tapes, even guns. Very few defenses exist to the IRS summons. If you are the summoned person, you can plead the Fifth Amendment, but that sometimes does more harm than good and is seldom an effective legal defense. You may invoke a few other privileges, such as the attorney-client or doctor-patient privilege, but these are narrow and easily breached. Beyond these defenses, the IRS can legally force you or some third party to produce virtually any record or document, and to testify about it.

THE TAX COLLECTION OFFICERS

The IRS uses tax collection officers at three different levels. First, there is the "notice" level. If you file a return that shows a balance due or you are audited and owe more tax, you will get a series of up to five notices. Each is of increasing urgency, instructing you in no uncertain terms to pay. The notice cycles vary from as short as a few weeks to as long as twenty-five weeks. It depends on whether you've had past defaults, what type of tax is involved, and other factors. Beginning in 1997, anyone who owes taxes for a back year will also get an annual statement of the amount still due. You will never see the collection officers who issue these notices; they're all done by computer, automatically, and in the millions from various service centers and the national computer center in Martinsburg, West Virginia. The IRS collects billions of dollars simply by sending these past-due notices.

If the notice system fails, your case will then be transferred to the Automated Collection System (ACS). Chapter 5 explains this system in more detail, but basically it's a computerized, paperless accounts receivable system. All delinquent accounts, whether business or personal, appear on the ACS computer screens. ACS has call sites all around the country. The collection officers in ACS will call you, your employer, friends, third parties, and anyone else they can think of to try to contact you and obtain full payment of the taxes. They will also negotiate with you for installment agreements. Failing that, they will automatically generate notices of levy on your wages, bank accounts, and other assets. They will also file notices of federal tax lien. Again, the IRS collects billions of dollars this way.

If the ACS fails to collect the tax in full, or if the case is complicated, ACS will send the case "to the field." That means your case goes to a living, breathing revenue officer in one of the districts around the country.

Revenue officers have many jobs, but first and foremost their task is to collect the most money they can in the shortest possible time. They are thoroughly trained in collection techniques, including how to locate you and your assets, how to interview you, and when to take strong action. They know how and when to seize assets, when not to, and when to negotiate with you. Still, they are terribly overworked. Depending on the amount owed by the taxpayer, revenue officers may have between forty and one hundred cases to pursue at any time. Their inventory is constantly high. And, when they close one case, there are always new cases that flow to them from the Automated Collection System.

Cases are assigned to revenue officers according to the priority of the case. If you owe $500 for one year, that will receive low priority. If you owe $100,000 for five years, that might be a high-priority case.

Revenue officers also investigate nonfilers, that is, people who have not filed one or more tax returns that are now overdue. Chapter 9 discusses the nonfiler in more detail. In cases of nonfilers, revenue officers can persuade you to file the delinquent return, make one for you, or refer the case for criminal investigation.

Revenue officers all go out into the field to collect the taxes. They have the right to investigate your personal and business affairs. Toward that end, they may ask you to complete financial statements, narrative statements about your business, and other documents. They can investigate your business to decide whether your workers are employees rather than independent contractors, making your business liable for the payroll taxes attributable to these workers. In the case of a business that has defaulted on its payroll taxes, they will investigate whether you are personally liable for a portion of those taxes. (Chapter 10 discusses this in more detail.) To collect your back taxes, these revenue officers have the authority to seize any property you or your business owns. The process is easy. They simply send a notice of levy, affix a notice of seizure to the property, or haul it away. They also have the authority to sell noncash assets and apply the money to your back taxes.

It's these powers that make the tax collection system so credible. When you make an offer in compromise, request an installment agreement, or seek relief from a tax lien, you are required to deal with revenue officers. When you have not filed a tax return, revenue officers can recommend that you be prosecuted, or, if not, they can file a return for you, and then file a notice of tax lien to "protect the revenue."

THE TAX AUDITORS

Revenue agents and tax auditors of the examination division audit income and other tax returns of businesses and individuals. Like revenue officers, these agents have the summons power. They can also propose more taxes, penalties, and interest. You are usually stuck with their figures unless you can persuade a higher office in the IRS or a court to change them. And in all of these dealings, the burden of proof is usually on you.

THE CRIMINAL INVESTIGATORS

Special agents of the criminal investigation division investigate eleven main types of tax crimes, and related offenses (about thirty tax and nontax crimes in all). Tax evasion, false statement, and failure to file a return are the most common. Special agents, too, have the summons power. They never hesitate to use it when they meet resistance. Special agents conduct raids, seize records and monies, trace assets, and arrest people who try to interfere with any other agent of the IRS.

THE PROBLEM RESOLUTION OFFICES

Problem resolution officers are appointed in every IRS district to help you when you run into a bureaucratic brick wall. They are like ombudsmen, slashing through the red tape, taking your side in cases of extreme hardship, and performing many other useful, protaxpayer functions. Chapter 13 discusses what they do and how they help.

These are the people you will usually meet when you have an IRS problem. They know their jobs; they know their power and authority. To contend on an equal footing with them, you also need to know your rights and powers and use them wisely.

Chapter 3

―◎◎◎―

HOW THE IRS ASSESSES A TAX

Understanding your tax bill is the first step to dealing effectively with it. Sometimes these bills seem to strike out of the blue. Other times you'll see them coming but be unable to duck. The amounts can be a total surprise, and many people have difficulty comprehending these bills.

THE PLAIN VANILLA BILL

By far the most common type of bill is the one you get if you don't pay the tax due with your return (called a "balance due" return). When you send your return to one of the seven regional service centers, someone opens the envelope, unfolds the return, and scans it manually or by machine into a computer. The agent enters your name, other identifying data, and key income and deduction items. (Electronically filed returns are "entered" automatically.) The agent punches the numbers into a huge data bank called the "master file." Every one of us has an "account" in the master file. More than 140 million accounts track individuals; 40 million accounts track businesses in the "business master file." The master file contains a running balance of all your transactions, plus and minus, year by year. Master file records go back a minimum of ten years. So, when you send in a return, your own individual master file account will record the transaction as "return filed and liability assessed." The IRS codes this and other transactions with a three-digit number, such as "150" for filing a return. The Service has about four hundred different transaction codes in all. Then the computer enters the amount you pay with the return and a code, "payment with return." It will already have noted how much withholding is credited to your account. If you have paid everything, the balance in the year's "module" will be zero. If you have overpaid, the computer generates a refund check. An under-payment generates a notice of tax due. All of this is automatic and electronic. It could not be done any other way, because the IRS keeps track of more than two hundred million tax returns.

If you owe a balance, you'll normally get five notices over as many as twenty-five weeks (sometimes fewer). The first will be a Request for Tax Payment. The second, third, and fourth are more insistent. The fifth, sent by certified mail, is a Notice of Intent to Levy. That legally required notice means the IRS can start seizing your assets thirty days later. And the agency means business. When the thirty days have run out, the next thing you know, your bank account has been seized or your wages levied. It's therefore crucial to check the accuracy of these payment-due notices as soon as you get them. If they're wrong, call *and* write to the IRS to make the corrections or to notify the system of an error. The form itself contains clear, well-written instructions. Don't wait for that last notice. Calling the toll-free number alerts the computer that you believe the bill is incorrect, so the IRS won't seize your property. Your follow-up evidence normally completes the correction process. Always make note of the person(s) to whom you spoke and when.

This balance due notice is the most basic type of bill. There are some per-mutations. If you have a credit or refund on file from a previous year, the IRS will absorb that first, then bill you for the rest or generate a refund. Another variation occurs when a business loses money. The law allows the business to carry that loss back three tax years. But the IRS will not do it automatically. You have to file a special form to carry back your losses three years, a step that already begins to slow down the computer.

Paying even the basic, plain vanilla tax bill can be complex. What if you have moved, as millions of people do every year? There's no way the IRS can keep track of every move. Besides, it is up to *you* to tell the Service where you have moved. Use Form 8822, which the IRS now routinely sends with balance due notices. If you file a tax return from a new residence, the IRS computers log in your new address. But they do not routinely or quickly check back to prior years. There are many slips. You are always better off being proactive: use the official form to notify the IRS of a move. If you don't, calls, notices, and levies may go unanswered, and you will be hard-pressed to undo them. The IRS has complied with the law by notifying you (at the last address it knows) before seizing assets— even if you never receive the notices.

These balance due notices also show accrued interest and penalties. The first may tell you how the penalties and interest are calculated, but after that, other notices just tack "accruals" onto the last balance. You can learn the breakdown of tax, penalty, and interest by asking for a transcript of your account from any IRS office or calling the nationwide toll-free number, 1-800-829-1040. Remember also the magic of daily compounding. Interest on your tax bill is compounded daily on everything: the tax, the penalties, and the interest. You are in fact paying interest on interest, but it's all perfectly legal. Daily compounding raises the effective IRS interest rate by more than 1 percent (to more than 10 percent currently). If you throw in the typical penalties, you're often paying an effective "interest" rate of more than 20 percent.

Everyone knows that the IRS receives billions of documents every year. Its computers now match your forms W-2 to your income tax return. The computers also match dozens of other type of reports. These might include forms 1099 for interest, dividends, and miscellaneous income, and many others. The IRS even matches information from state governments.

If there is a mismatch between one of those forms and your return, the IRS will send you a notice. Even more scary is the case where the IRS finds you have received income, but it does not detect a filed return. That makes you a "non-filer," discussed in chapter 9. This "matching" bill works the same as any other. Either you pay it, or the IRS will assess it and attempt to collect.

THE AUDIT BILL

The second most common type of bill is the one you get following an IRS audit. If you and the agent agree on the audit results, you sign an agreement form and the agency sends you a bill four to six weeks later. These are relatively straightforward, at least if you have understood the audit itself. The bill will usually recite the tax, penalties, and accrued interest to some date near the expected date of payment. Interestingly, these audit-related bills often do not find their way to the master file.

APPLYING YOUR TAX PAYMENTS—THE "VOLUNTARY PAYMENT" RULE

Many times you will get a bill that seems to have no rational connection to what you think you owe. (The only consistent feature is that the bill exceeds what you think you owe.) This can happen because the IRS has applied your payments to some other tax bill, or to interest and penalty first, before applying it to taxes as you intended. Like any other creditor, the IRS applies payments in its own best interest. The IRS manual tells the technicians to apply the money to the oldest liability, first to tax then penalties and last interest.

To avoid this problem, you may "designate" your payment, a simple procedure to tell the IRS where you want the money applied. The agency must honor your request as long as the payment is voluntary, hence the name "voluntary payment" rule. In this context, "voluntary" means you are paying outside bankruptcy, and the IRS has issued no levy on the money you are paying. Designating a payment is straightforward. In the memo portion of the check, write, "Apply to tax year 1996, tax only, Form 1040, SSN: (for example) 123-45-6789," or any other instructions on how you want the money applied. It also helps to send a cover letter with the same instructions. Just be sure your designation is crystal clear and as simple as possible.

Designating your payments can often save you big bucks. Let's say you owe taxes for 1990 and 1995. You intend to file bankruptcy in 1996 to discharge the taxes from 1990 (see chapter 12, "The Bankruptcy Alternative"). You send in the payment, instructing the IRS to apply it to 1995, the tax for which is not dischargeable if you file bankruptcy in 1996. Undesignated, your payment would have been applied to the 1990 tax, leaving the full liability for 1995 unpaid even after you discharge 1990's remaining taxes in bankruptcy.

A variation of the voluntary payment rule is the designation on Form 1040 itself. People who overpay their taxes during the year can check a box to apply the resulting refund to the next year's taxes. But if you owe a back tax, the IRS' computers will offset your overpayment against any other tax you owe regardless of the voluntary payment rule. So far, the courts have sustained the IRS on this issue.

NONFILER ASSESSMENTS

IRS studies estimate that between five million and ten million people have not filed one or more tax returns. (Chapter 9 discusses the nonfiler.) That's an astounding number for a system that supposedly depends on voluntary compliance, but it rings true in actual experience. While nonfilers come in from the cold all the time, each year's filing deadline creates new ones or extends the delinquency of others. It is not unusual to see three to six years of nonfiling; ten to fifteen years is not unknown.

When the IRS catches a nonfiler, it can (1) prosecute, (2) assess and collect, or (3) both prosecute and assess and collect. Mostly, the agency just wants people to file and pay, so usually it won't prosecute. Instead, the agent opens a case file for you for each year of nonfiling. Then, if you don't file quickly on your own, the agent makes a Substitute for Return rather than a true return. She starts with a blank Form 1040 for the year involved. She fills in your name, address, and Social Security number, then opens an account in the individual master file for that tax year. The agent then "audits" the blank return. Gross income will consist of anything the agent can find that you received. Usually the income figures come from bank accounts, W-2 and 1099 forms, or any other source of income. How about deductions? The IRS will give you one exemption—yourself—that's all. It will also give you a standard deduction, but nothing for itemized deductions, even if it knows you have some.

In other words, the IRS makes all assumptions against you and in its favor, then generates a proposed tax bill from the result. You have the right to contest that bill, but you must go to court to do so (or request audit reconsideration—see chapter 15 and below). If you don't—and most people don't—the computer generates the tax assessment and the IRS comes after you to collect.

Despite the apparent arbitrariness of such a bill, you can still fight it. To do so, file true returns, request reconsideration of your bill, and make arrangements to pay the true tax. You'll not be excused from penalties unless you show reasonable cause (see chapter 18), but at least your tax bill will be lower than the one the agent generated.

THE UNKNOWN "ASSESSMENT FROM HELL"

Sometimes, the IRS sends a bill no mortal can decipher. The dates are wrong, the amounts are wrong. It gives little clue as to what the IRS is really upset about. For these bills, rare as they are, you must take action right away. Spend no time thinking about it or questioning whether you might have owed some tax in a past life; analyzing the "Tax Bill from Hell" should not be an out-of-body experience. Immediately call the nationwide toll-free number (1-800-829-1040), identify yourself, and ask what the bill is all about. Get as much information as you can. If you can figure out why the IRS sent the bill, you can deal with it. But if you can't, take the next step. Call the Problem Resolution Office. They're on your side in cases like this; they help willingly.

The goal with this or any other tax bill is to determine whether you in fact owe all of the tax, penalties, and interest for which you have billed. If you don't, you'll need to assemble any evidence you have and send it to the IRS for reconsideration. If you do, the IRS will force you to make arrangements to pay it.

Chapter 4

THE FEDERAL TAX LIEN

The federal tax lien is no more and no less than a legal charge or encumbrance on a taxpayer's property to secure the eventual payment of the tax debt. It's like a mortgage on your house or a lien on your car. You can think of the tax lien as a legal ball and chain that attaches to each piece of property you own. The more you owe, the heavier the ball and chain.

As we will see, the federal tax lien does not usually cause problems until the IRS files public notice of it. Once filed, that notice can hurt. It can damage your credit, cause you embarrassment, and hamper your efforts to sell property. The IRS is fully aware of this impact. Agents know the tax lien filing is a big club they carry around and use from time to time. If the tax you owe is large enough, and if you pay slowly enough, the IRS will almost always file a Notice of Federal Tax Lien to "protect the revenue." Translation: The agency will file the notice to make sure you do not sell property out from under its claim. Once the IRS files notice of the lien, generally there is little you can do with your properties unless you get the IRS' input and consent. Later on, this chapter will tell you how to deal effectively with the federal tax lien even when notice of it has been filed.

HOW THE LIEN ARISES

When you file a tax return of whatever the type—income, employment, estate, or other—the IRS enters the tax you report as an assessment on its computer system in the master file. The IRS keeps track of individual master files by Social Security number, business master files by employer identification number. This assessment is simply the official recording of your tax liability on the IRS' computers, signed by a specifically delegated person. At the point of signing, you officially have a tax assessment. The computer also logs in payments. Since most people pay their taxes in advance (with payroll deductions) or at the latest when they send in their return, the self-assessment on the return is considered fully paid when it is made.

Tens of millions of people, however, file returns with a balance due. These are usually income, employment, or estate tax returns. Of course, the IRS immediately assesses the taxes on these "balance due" returns and sends notice and demand for payment. If ten days pass with no payment, the federal tax lien arises—automatically by law—and the IRS need do nothing further at this time. At this point, you don't actually see that the lien has arisen, since notice of it is neither filed publicly nor sent to you; but that's what the law provides. It's a secret lien, known only to the IRS and the taxpayer (who is presumed to know the law).

If you still do not pay, the IRS sends a series of notices demanding payment in ever more threatening tones. Individuals typically suffer through five notices; businesses, sometimes only two. It's then that the IRS really gets rough. Agents call; they threaten to file a notice of lien, seize assets, or levy on wages. They give you a fighting chance, but if you can't pay it in full or by an acceptably short installment agreement, at this point the IRS files a Notice of Federal Tax Lien. The notice is a one-page form filed in the land records of your city or county and also sometimes in another office that state law requires (for example, the Office of the Secretary of State in your state). At the end of this chapter, you will find a blank Notice of Federal Tax Lien. It lists your name and address, the tax periods involved, the type of tax involved (by form number), and the amounts owed.

WHAT THE LIEN ENCUMBERS

The federal tax lien is not a laser-guided smart bomb, zeroing in on a precise piece of property. It's more like nerve gas, contaminating everything in its path. By law, it attaches to everything you own: all of your right, title, and interest in every piece of property, wherever located throughout the world. This is a surprising feature about the tax lien, a feature that makes it different from every other creditor's rights to your property. Sometimes a taxpayer will say, "The IRS has put a lien on my house." Yes, it has, and everything else the taxpayer owns—automatically. Your mortgage and other liens attach to specific pieces of property; the federal tax lien is universal. The best way to conceptualize the reach of the lien is this: Whatever you own, that's what the lien attaches to. Many a sad businessperson has discovered this fact after buying the assets of a failing business. She thought she got a bargain, only to find that the federal tax lien followed the assets right into her hands.

Some important examples of the federal tax lien's reach are these: it encumbers real property, including every home you own, wherever located. (But the IRS has to file public notice of the lien in the city or county where the property is located to make it enforceable against third-party claims. If it does not, the tax lien will not attach to that property when it is sold.)

The lien also attaches to money you might have on deposit as escrow with a court, a real estate agent, or elsewhere. The lien reaches your bank account, brokerage account, insurance policies, and other near-cash property. It also attaches to lawsuits or claims you may have against other people, licenses (such as liquor licenses), certain property you transfer in a divorce, property you transfer to third parties, stolen property held by the police, partnership interests, and interests held in trust. The lien also attaches to your retirement plans such as a pension plan or IRA, and to your vested share of a profit-sharing plan. The IRS may not be able to get at that money right away (if you can't), but it's still valuable property, and, as such, the lien attaches to it.

> *Example:* James, John, and Joseph went into business together as Jim's Boutique. Joseph was the silent partner who supplied start-up money. Everything went great until they didn't pay some payroll taxes. The IRS filed a notice of lien and levied on the partnership's bank account. The partners went straight to court, screaming that the money belonged to them individually. "You're right, guys, that's not the partnership's money," said the court. "It belongs to James and his silent partner, Joseph." But, no matter. The lien still attaches to it, because the partners were personally liable for the debts of their partnership.

Example: Jordan and his wife, Jodie, were happily married for many years. Unfortunately, their financial life was not as blissful. Jordan had to file for bankruptcy. At the time, the couple owed $13,000 in back taxes, and the IRS had filed a Notice of Federal Tax Lien. Jodie had filed a claim for disability compensation with the Social Security Administration, then unfortunately passed away. Five days after Jordan filed his bankruptcy petition, Social Security granted Jodie's claim and issued a check for $14,000, payable to Jordan and Jodie. The money was exempt from all normal creditors' claims. Twenty days later, the IRS levied on it, claiming the funds were subject to the federal tax lien.

So here's the picture: Jordan's wife had died; Jordan was destitute and had to file for bankruptcy; and, to add insult to injury, the IRS claimed Jodie's disability money. Who won? The IRS, of course. By law, the tax lien attached to "after acquired" property, including Jodie's disability windfall.

Example: Chad was merrily driving along a Kentucky road one day. Then, out of nowhere came a monster eighteen-wheeler, which plowed into him. The inevitable lawsuit followed. The trucking company set up a settlement fund for Chad. That's the good news. The bad news is that at the time Chad owed federal taxes, and a lien had arisen. Who got the money? The IRS, of course.

Examples like these litter the casebooks. Time after time, the government has enforced the federal tax lien against all types of property: alimony payments, accounts receivable, loans, condemnation awards, military pensions, reserve accounts, trust accounts, and just about anything else that has value reducible to cash.

Still, despite its pervasiveness, the lien filing does not steamroll everything in its path. The "first in time, first in right" principle applies, and the IRS respects it. So a properly recorded first mortgage on your home takes precedence over the federal tax lien. The same is true for personal property subject to a prior lien. So the lien filing poses no problem for your lender, who almost always records its interest first.

If you don't borrow against property but simply sell it before the tax lien is recorded, that lien does not attach to the property because it is not yours when the lien notice is filed. This important principle is really common sense: If you don't own property at the time the tax lien arises (because you have sold it, transferred it, made a gift of it) there's nothing to which the lien can attach. But if you conveyed it in an effort to defeat the government, that's fraud. The long arm of the IRS can then reach the property in the hands of your transferee.

OVERCOMING THE FEDERAL TAX LIEN

In the real world, the tax lien causes people major heartburn in two main ways: (1) It ruins your credit and (2) it sabotages the sale of your property. If you want to refinance or sell property, any title search will reveal the lien. Many mortgages contain "no lien" clauses, which trigger technical defaults if you allow a lien to be recorded in the chain of title, even if you are up to date in your payments. The same is true for many security interests in personal property.

Credit Rating. Lien filing or not, your credit rating usually remains intact until you try to borrow more money or the credit reporting agency has some other reason to check your debts. Credit rating companies are private corporations. They store millions of data files. But, they do not sit down each month and say "OK, this month let's check ten thousand people to see if a tax lien has been filed." They check only when one of their clients, like a mortgage or title company, asks them to check. Only then will they discover the notice of lien. Even then, they may not always check every place the lien has been filed.

Still, if your goal is to borrow more money, or to sell or refinance an asset, it does not matter whether the credit reporting agency finds out about the lien. You must disclose your tax debt on any financial statement you prepare in connection with the application.

A Drag on Selling Property. The second biggest complaint people make about the federal tax lien is that it undermines their ability to sell their property. Unquestionably, that is true in some cases. Lenders get nervous at a minimum, and sometimes run far and fast, when they discover you have a federal tax lien on file.

One thing the IRS could *not* do (until 1996) to solve this problem was to "unfile" the notice of lien. Under prior law, once a notice was filed, that was it. Like a fire-and-forget missile, it could not be recalled once launched. (But you could do many things to avert its worst effects.) Many people complained about this apparent inequity. So, in 1996, as part of the Taxpayer Bill of Rights,

Congress gave the IRS the authority to withdraw a Notice of Federal Tax Lien. But, it's all up to the IRS. The agency can withdraw the notice if the filing was premature or against agency procedures, or if you entered an installment agreement. It can withdraw to "facilitate the collection" of the taxes or promote the best interests of you and the government. These rules leave it mostly up to the IRS, and no one should expect wholesale withdrawals of liens. The IRS views the filing of a notice of lien as one of its most powerful weapons. Still, the new authority is there, and you may ask for it, particularly in the case of sales of property. Even the presence of a filed notice that is not withdrawn should still never prevent a sale. Within limits, the law gives you flexibility to get around this lien.

RELEASING THE LIEN IN FULL

In most cases, outright release of the filed notice of lien is next to impossible. However, you can still ask for a release, and the IRS must give it, if (1) you pay the full liability (including penalties and interest), (2) the statute of limitations on collection expires, or (3) you give a bond to secure payment of the taxes. In real life, few people can buy these bonds. If they could, they would have paid the tax. This option is so rarely used that most revenue officers don't even know where to send you to buy a tax payment bond acceptable to the IRS.

The first two possibilities, full payment and expiration of the statute of limitations, are more realistic. Some people outwait the tax collector, usually a ten-year wait from the first assessment. If you haven't signed an extension of the time for collection or taken some action that extends it by law (such as filing for bankruptcy or making an offer in compromise, among other things), you can ask for a certificate of release of the federal tax lien once it expires.

If you think you are beyond the ten years, call your local IRS office or the toll-free number (1-800-829-1040) and ask for a "literal transcript" of your account to be sent to you. Ask the technician whether the liens in your name have expired. (Discussing your liens with the technician rather than simply asking for a transcript carries some danger that the agent will wake up and refer your case for more collection, but that danger is not great. Still, if you want to play it safe, ask solely for a transcript.) The transcript will tell you how old the assessment is. Once you are sure the assessment is more than ten years old and its life has not been extended, write the district director (the chief IRS official in your IRS district), asking for a certificate of release to be filed. The IRS is normally prompt about filing these releases. If it delays, you can appeal the delay within the IRS and even sue for damages if the delay is too long. Chapter 22 discusses whether and when you can sue the government for its failure to release a notice of lien.

The third way to get a release is to pay the liability. Usually this is not an option for most people; if they could have paid, they would have. But circumstances change. People borrow money, they come into an inheritance, or they make more money and decide they want to pay the taxes. The problem with this "solution" is that by the time they decide to pay, the taxes come loaded down with megapenalties and interest.

> *Example:* Sudden Sam had a federal tax lien going back to 1977; the life of the lien had been extended into 1994 for various reasons. The IRS was threatening to sell his property. After all that time, he had made some money and bought valuable property. Now he was in a position to borrow against the property and liquidate some retirement accounts to fully pay the liability. In that way, he protected the value of his major properties against the discount that would have resulted from a forced tax sale.

There is one other, minor, way you can have a lien released. If you don't owe taxes in the first place but the IRS erroneously files a notice of lien in your name, it must issue a certificate of release stating that the lien filing was erroneous.

DISCHARGING SPECIFIC PROPERTY FROM THE LIEN

Short of a release, there are still plenty of ways to sell your property out from under that federal tax lien. Some creditors understand this process; unfortunately, many do not.

1. Let's say you want to sell a crane you have been using in your construction business for five years. The crane is worth $100,000. You've paid down the debt on it to $20,000, but you owe the IRS $50,000. If the IRS seized and auctioned the crane, it might get $60,000. After the IRS paid the $20,000 debt, $40,000 would be left for the government. You would still owe $10,000 in taxes. But in the open market, you could get $100,000, fully paying the IRS and the old debt, and leaving you with $30,000 to lease a new crane. If you can get the revenue officer to agree, the two of you can sign a contract to allow you to sell the

property free and clear of the lien. The revenue officer issues a certificate that "discharges" the crane from the federal tax lien so the buyer can have it free and clear. The proceeds of sale are then put in a special fund subject to the lien, usually at a bank. Then that money is divided, with $20,000 going to the first lienholder, $50,000 to the IRS, and $30,000 to you.

2. A variation of this scenario is even more common. You find a buyer for the crane, call the revenue officer, and schedule a settlement. The revenue officer attends, bringing a certificate discharging the crane from the federal tax lien in exchange for a certified check for $50,000. Again, no muss, no fuss.

The same technique works, every day, in real estate sales. In fact, if you want to sell a house, a building, or land and a federal tax lien is on file against you as the owner, you *can't* sell unless you give the IRS its share of the equity at settlement. The process is the same. Put the property up for sale, get your best price, and insert a line for the IRS at the settlement table. It does not even have to be for the full amount you owe. As long as the IRS gets all your equity (after paying the superior liens), it will be happy.

> *Example:* Tim owes the government $70,000 in taxes. His house is worth $110,000. The first mortgage is $40,000. He sells it, and, after commissions, the amount available for distribution is $100,000. The settlement agent pays $40,000 to the First Mortgage Bank and $60,000 to the IRS. Even though Tim will still owe $10,000 in taxes, the revenue officer will come to the settlement armed with a certificate of discharge of property from the federal tax lien.

This type of release makes economic sense to the IRS. After all, by releasing the property the Service gets every last dime out of it. If it didn't let the sale proceed, it would get nothing. So it's in the agency's interest to issue the release, and it normally does.

3. In the above example, what if the first mortgage were $150,000, not $40,000. That scenario happened depressingly often in the 1980s, when the value of people's homes went through the roof and they merrily borrowed—also through the roof—against that value. Then the recession set in, plunging values through the floor. In such a case, the IRS' lien is valueless because the first mortgage exceeds the market value. There's nothing in the sale for the IRS, so the agent might as well let it go. The agent will therefore still issue the release.

4. Another way to get a discharge of property is extremely rare, but it has

probably occurred somewhere in the universe. The government can, in its discretion (read: if it wants to), discharge one piece of property if all the other property you own is worth at least twice the unpaid taxes plus all other liens on that property.

> *Example:* You own two pieces of land, the first worth $10,000, the second worth $100,000. There is a $5,000 mortgage on the second piece. You owe $10,000 in taxes. The IRS can discharge the first piece of property from the tax lien so you can sell it, because it has plenty of equity in the second piece. Specifically, that second piece is worth $100,000, but two times the other debts on it, including the tax debt, comes to only $30,000 (two times $5,000 plus $10,000). Will the Service release the first piece? Maybe not. After all, the release is discretionary; it goes against a revenue officer's training and experience to release your valuable property without getting something for it. But the law does allow this remedy.

To get these property discharges in motion, send for Publication 783, Certificate of Discharge of Property from Federal Tax Lien (reproduced at the end of this chapter). This publication tells you what you'll need. Make the application for the discharge by letter. In general, you need to include a description of the property, how you will be divested of your ownership, and who the buyer and seller are. Also include information on the tax liens, the amount of federal taxes, costs of sale, value of the property, and the holders of prior liens. You will also have to certify that you are selling the whole property, or at least all of your interest in it.

5. Sometimes, there is a fifth way to deal with the lien: You can ask the IRS to subordinate its lien to some other claim. The Service will normally subordinate if it can make more money in the long run. As an example, let's say a builder owes taxes. He is in the middle of a construction project that will net a big profit. But the bank won't release the money necessary for completion because the revenue officer has filed a notice of lien. Here, the IRS can subordinate its lien to the bank's fresh capital. To get this subordination, ask or write the revenue officer, providing the information specified in Publication 784 (Application for Certificate of Subordination of Federal Tax Lien). The revenue officer will consider the application, and, if she agrees, sign a certificate of subordination, which is filed in the same office as the lien notice. Publication 784 is also reproduced at the end of this chapter.

WITHDRAWAL OF NOTICE OF LIEN

6. The 1996 Taxpayer Bill of Rights allows the IRS to withdraw the notice of lien if such withdrawal will "facilitate the collection" of the taxes. Let's say you want to sell some property to which the lien has attached. The new law allows you to request the IRS to withdraw the notice of lien. It will certainly be in the IRS' interest to do so if the agency will be included at the settlement table. Probably, this will work as follows: You negotiate the deal and arrange for the settlement. At the settlement table, the settlement agent draws a check to the IRS, in exchange for which the IRS will supply a formal withdrawl of lien. The settlement agent will then file the lien withdrawal in the land records, so that clear title to the property may be transferred.

SUPERPRIORITIES

Despite the power of the tax lien, sometimes you don't have to worry about it even if it is filed. There are eight types of property sales that can go through without a second thought about the lien. A special law declares that the lien simply does not attach to the asset you are selling no matter when the lien is filed. The rationale is that in each of these cases commerce would grind to a quick halt if every buyer had to conduct a lien search before buying property from a seller.

The first of these "superpriorities" is securities. When you buy and sell stocks, bonds, notes, and other securities, you don't have to worry about the seller's tax debts. The financial markets would clog quickly if you did.

The second type of sale involves a motor vehicle. This exception protects the buyers of new and used vehicles from the tax lien, unless they in fact know that the tax lien exists. Unaware of the lien, they should not have to check in advance of the sale.

A third exception is property you buy at retail. No one checks to see whether the Big Pricebreak Store has a tax lien on file before buying a television or refrigerator, nor should they have to. But if you buy the store's inventory in bulk, or if you buy to help someone evade or hinder the collection of taxes, then the tax lien does attach to what you buy. That's rare, but it occasionally happens.

The fourth exception is a casual sale such as a garage or yard sale, but the property has to be sold for less than $250 and the buyer must not actually know there is a lien on file.

The remaining exceptions protect repairpeople, mechanics' liens, some attorneys' liens, and some commercial and real estate financing. Also protected are some insurance, endowment, and annuity contracts. Finally, banks that give passbook loans are also protected.

You are always better off convincing the IRS not to file a notice of lien. But if you own realty, or if you owe more than $10,000, the IRS will almost always do so. Still, don't lose hope. Working to discharge property from the lien is the solution to selling the property.

Department of the Treasury - Internal Revenue Service

Notice of Federal Tax Lien Under Internal Revenue Laws

District	Serial Number	*For Optional Use by Recording Office*

As provided by sections 6321, 6322, and 6323 of the Internal Revenue Code, notice is given that taxes (including interest and penalties) have been assessed against the following-named taxpayer. Demand for payment of this liability has been made, but it remains unpaid. Therefore, there is a lien in favor of the United States on all property and rights to property belonging to this taxpayer for the amount of these taxes, and additional penalties, interest, and costs that may accrue.

Name of Taxpayer

Residence

IMPORTANT RELEASE INFORMATION: With respect to each assessment listed below, unless notice of lien is refiled by the date given in column (e), this notice shall, on the day following such date, operate as a certificate of release as defined in IRC 6325(a).

Kind of Tax (a)	Tax Period Ended (b)	Identifying Number (c)	Date of Assessment (d)	Last Day for Refiling (e)	Unpaid Balance of Assessment (f)

Place of Filing

Total | $

This notice was prepared and signed at _____ , on this,

the _____ day of _____ , 19 _____ .

Signature	Title

(**NOTE:** Certificate of officer authorized by law to take acknowledgments is not essential to the validity of Notice of Federal Tax lien Rev. Rul. 71-466, 1971 - 2 C.B. 409)

Form **668 (Y)** (Rev. 1-91)

Instructions on how to apply for

Certificate of Discharge of Property From Federal Tax Lien

Department of the Treasury

Internal Revenue Service

Publication 783 (Rev 9-91)
Cat. No. 46755I

Since there is no standard form available for an application for a certificate of discharge of property from a Federal Tax Lien, a typewritten request will be considered as an application. Submit your typewritten request and all accompanying documents in duplicate to:

District Director of Internal Revenue
(Address to District in which the property is located)

Attention of: Chief, Special Procedures Staff

Give Date of Application

Information required on application

Please give the name and address of the person applying, under section 6325(b) of the Internal Revenue Code, for a certificate of discharge. See the reverse of this publication for applicable Internal Revenue Code sections. Give the name and address of the taxpayer, and describe the property as follows:

1. Give a detailed description, including the location of the property for which you are requesting the certificate of discharge. If real property is involved, submit a legible copy of the title or deed to the property, and the complete address (street, city, State). If the certificate is requested under section 6325(b)(1), also give a description of all the taxpayer's remaining subject to the lien.

2. Show how and when the taxpayer has been, or will be, divested of all rights, title and interest in an to the property for which a certificate of discharge is requested.

3. Attach a copy of each notice of Federal tax lien, or furnish the following information as it appears on each filed notice of Federal tax lien:

a. The name of the Internal Revenue District;

b. The name and address of the taxpayer against whom the notice was filed;

c. Serial number shown on the lien;

d. Taxpayer's identification number shown on the lien;

e. The date and place the notice was filed;

f. In lieu of the above, a preliminary title report may be substituted listing the required information.

4. List the encumbrances (or attach a copy of the instrument that created each encumbrance) on the property which you believe have priority over the Federal tax lien. For each encumbrance show:

a. The name and address of the holder;

b. A description of the encumbrance;

c. The date of the agreement;

d. The date and place of the recording, if any;

e. The original principal amount and the interest rate;

f. The amount due as of the date of the application, if known (show costs and accrued interest separately);

g. Your family relationship, if any, to the taxpayer and to the holders of any other encumbrances on the property.

h. In lieu of the above, a preliminary title report may be substituted listing the required information.

5. Itemize all proposed or actual costs, commissions and expenses of any transfer or sale of the property.

6. Furnish information to establish the value of the property for which you are applying for a certificate of discharge. If the certificate is requested under **section 6325(b)(1)** furnish an estimate of the fair market value of the property which will remain subject to the lien. In addition,

a. If private sale—Submit written appraisals by two disinterested people qualified to appraise the property, and a brief statement of each appraiser's qualifications.

b. If public sale (auction) already held—Give the date and place the sale was held, and the amount for which the property was sold.

c. If public sale (auction) to be held—Give the proposed date and place of the sale, and include a statement that the United States will be paid in its proper priority from the proceeds of the sale.

7. Give any other information that might, in your opinion, have bearing upon the application, such as pending judicial actions.

8. The District Director may request you to furnish additional information.

9. If you are submitting the application under the provisions of **section 6325(b)(3)**, dealing with the substitution of proceeds of sale, attach a copy of the proposed agreement containing the following:

a. Name and address of proposed escrow agent;

b. Caption, type of account, name and address of depositary for the account;

c. Conditions under which the escrow fund is to be held;

d. Conditions under which payment will be made from escrow, including the limitation for negotiated settlement of claims against the fund;

e. Estimated costs of escrow;

f. Name and address of any other party you and the District Director determine to be a party to the escrow agreement;

g. Your signature, and those of the escrow agent, District Director and any other party to the escrow agreement;

h. Any other specific information the District Director requests.

10. Give a daytime telephone number where you may be reached.

11. Give the name, address and telephone number of your attorney or other representative, if any.

12. Make the following declaration over your signature and title: "Under penalties of perjury, I declare that I have examined this application, including any accompanying schedules, exhibits, affidavits, and statements, and to the best of my knowledge and belief it is true, correct, and complete."

Additional Information

Please follow the instructions in this publication when applying for a Certificate of Discharge of Property From Federal Tax Lien.

The District Director has the authority to issue a certificate of discharge of a lien that is filed on any part of a taxpayer's property subject to the lien. The following sections and provisions of the Internal Revenue Code apply:

Section 6325(b)(1), a specific property may be discharged; if the taxpayer's property remaining subject to the lien has a Fair Market Value (FMV) which is double the sum of the balance due a) all Federal Tax Liens b) all other liens. $(FMV=(a+b) \times 2)$

Section 6325(b)(2)(A), if there is paid in partial satisfaction of the liability secured by the lien an amount determined to be <u>not less than the value of the interest</u> of the United States in the property to be discharged.

Section 6325(b)(2)(B), if it is determined that the interest of the United States in the property to be discharged <u>has no value.</u>

Section 6325(b)(3), if the property subject to the lien is sold and, under an agreement with the Internal Revenue Service, the proceeds from the sale are to be held as a fund subject to the liens and claims of the United States in the same manner, and with the same priority, as the liens and claims on the discharged property.

1. No payment is required for the issuance of a certificate under **section 6325(b)(1)** or **section 6325(b)(2)(B)** of the Code. Payment is required for certificates issued under **section 6325(b)(2)(A).** Do not send the payment with your application, however. The District Director will notify you after determining the amount due.

2. The District Director will have your application investigated to determine whether to issue the certificate, and will let you know the outcome.

3. A certificate of discharge under **section 6325 (b)(2)(A)** will be issued upon receipt of the amount determined to be the interest of the United States in the subject property under the Federal tax lien. Make remittances in cash, or by a certified, cashier's, or treasurer's check drawn on any bank or trust company incorporated under the laws of the United States or of any State, or possession of the United States, or by United States postal, bank, express, or telegraph money order. (If you pay by uncertified personal check, issuance of the certificate of discharge will be delayed until the bank honors the check.)

4. If application is made under **section 6325(b)(2)(A)** or **6325(b)(2)(B)** because a mortgage foreclosure is contemplated, there will be a determination of the amount required for discharge or a determination that the Federal tax lien interest in the property is valueless.

Within 30 days from the date of the application, the applicant will receive a written conditional commitment for a certificate of discharge. When the foreclosure proceeding has been concluded, a certificate of discharge will be issued in accordance with the terms of the commitment letter. Also see, Application Requesting the United States to Release Its Right to Redeem Property Secured by a Federal Tax Lien, Publication 487.

5. If application is made under the provisions of **section 6325(b)(3),** the District Director has the authority to approve an escrow agent selected by the applicant. Any reasonable expenses incurred in connection with the sale of the property, the holding of the fund, or the distribution of the fund shall be paid by the applicant or from the proceeds of the sale before satisfaction of any claims and liens. Submit a copy of the proposed escrow agreement as part of the application.

Publication 783 (Rev. 9-91)

*U.S. GPO: 1994-301-643/12155

Date: _____

District Director
Internal Revenue Service

Att: Special Procedures Staff

Re: Application for Discharge of Property from Federal Tax Lien: John J. Smith, SSN _____, 1 Main Street, Anytown, USA 11111

Ladies/Gentlemen:

Under the authority of IRC Section 6325( )( ), application is hereby made for a certificate of discharge of property from federal tax lien. The name and address of the taxpayer are as shown above. The following additional information is supplied in support of this application.

1.   Description.   The property is a single family home located at 1 Main Street, Anytown, USA 11111, and is shown by the enclosed deed.

2.   Divestment of Interest.   The taxpayer will be divested of all right, title, and interest in and to the property, since the property will be sold to an unrelated third-party buyer and the net proceeds, after payment of prior liens and encumbrances, will be paid to the IRS.

3.   Federal Tax Liens.   The federal tax liens are as follows:

See enclosed copies of tax liens.

4.   Encumbrances.   The encumbrances with priority over the federal tax lien are as follows:

Holder:	Big Bank
Description:	First Mortgage
Date:	1/2/96
Recording date:	1/3/96

Original principal, interest rate: $100,000; 7%
Amount now due: $ 75,000
Relationship to taxpayer: unrelated

5.   <u>Costs of Transfer.</u>   The estimated costs of transfer are as follows:

Recording fees $1,000
Commissions $6,000

6.   <u>Value of Property.</u>   The property has a fair market value of $95,000, as shown by the enclosed appraisal.

7.   <u>Other Information.</u>

8.   <u>Point of Contact.</u>   Further information may be obtained by contacting the undersigned, whose telephone number is shown above.

Thank you for your attention.

Sincerely yours,

John J. Smith

DECLARATION

Under the penalties of perjury, I declare that I have examined this aplication, including any accompanying schedules, exhibits, affidavits, and statements, and to the best of my knowledge and belief it is true, correct, and complete.

_____
Date

_____
Applicant

Department of the Treasury
Internal Revenue Service
Publication 784 (Rev. 9-91)

How to Prepare

Application for Certificate of Subordination of Federal Tax Lien

(Since there is no standard form available for an application for certificate of subordination of Federal tax lien, a typewritten request will be considered an application. Submit your typewritten request and all accompanying documents in duplicate to):

Address application to: District Director of Internal Revenue
(Address to District in which the property is located.)

Attention of: Chief, Special Procedures Staff

Give date of application:

Please give the name and address of the person applying, under section 6325(d)(1) or section 6325(d)(2) of the Internal Revenue Code, for a certificate of subordination. See the reverse of this publication for applicable Internal Revenue Code sections. Give name and address of the taxpayer, and describe property as follows:

1. Give a detailed description, including the location, of the property for which you are requesting the certificate of subordination. If real property is involved, give the description contained in the title or deed to the property, and the complete address (street, city, State).

2. Attach a copy of each notice of Federal tax lien, or furnish the following information as it appears on each filed notice of Federal tax lien:

  a. The name of the Internal Revenue District;
  b. The name and address of the taxpayer against whom the notice was filed;
  c. The date and place the notice was filed.

3. Describe the encumbrance to which the Federal tax lien is to be subordinated, including:

  a. The present amount of the encumbrance;
  b. The nature of the encumbrance (such as mortgage, assignment, etc.);
  c. The date the transaction is to be completed.

4. List the encumbrances (or attach a copy of the instrument that created each encumbrance) on the property which you believe have priority over the Federal tax lien. For each encumbrance show:

  a. The name and address of the holder;
  b. A description of the encumbrance;
  c. The date of the agreement;
  d. The date and place of recording, if any;

  e. The original principal amount and the interest rate;
  f. The amount due as of the date of the application for certificate of subordination, if known (show costs and accrued interest separately);
  g. Your family relationship, if any, to the taxpayer and to the holders of any other encumbrances on the property.

5. Furnish an estimate of the fair market value of the property for which you would like a certificate of subordination.

6. If you are submitting the application under the provisions of section 6325(d)(1), show the amount to be paid to the United States.

7. If you are submitting the application under section 6325(d)(2), attach a complete statement showing how the amount the United States may realize will ultimately increase and how collection of the tax liability will be made easier.

8. Furnish any other information that might help the District Director decide whether to issue a certificate of subordination.

9. The District Director may request you to furnish additional information.

10. Give a daytime telephone number where you may be reached.

11. Give the name, address and telephone number of your attorney or other representative, if any.

12. Make the following declaration over your signature and title: "Under penalties of perjury, I declare that I have examined this application (including any accompanying schedules, exhibits, affidavits, and statements) and to the best of my knowledge and belief it is true, correct, and complete."

Additional information regarding

Application for Certificate of Subordination of Federal Tax Lien

Please follow the instructions in this publication when applying for a Certificate of Subordination of Federal Tax Lien.

The District Director has the authority to issue a certificate of subordination of a lien that is filed on any part of a taxpayer's property subject to the lien. The following sections and provisions of the Internal Revenue Code apply:

Section 6325(d)(1), if you pay an amount equal to the lien or interest to which the certificate subordinates the lien of the United States.

Section 6325(d)(2), if the District Director believes that issuance of the certificate will increase the amount the United States may realize, or the collection of the tax liability will then be easier. This applies to the property that the certificate is for, or any other property subject to the lien.

1. No payment is required for the issuance of a certificate under section 6325(d)(2) of the Code. Payment is required for certificates issued under section 6325(d)(1). Do not send the payment with your application, however. The District Director will notify you after determining the amount due.

2. The District Director will have your application investigated to determine whether to issue the certificate, and will let you know the outcome.

3. A certificate of subordination under section 6325(d)(1) will be issued after approval and upon receipt of the amount determined to be the interest of the United States in the property under the Federal tax lien. Make remittances in cash, or by a certified, cashier's, or treasurer's check drawn on any bank or trust company incorporated under the laws of the United States or of any State or possession of the United States, or by United States postal, bank, express, or telegraph money order. (If you pay by uncertified personal check, issuance of the certificate of subordination will be delayed until the bank honors the check.)

4. Instead of the description required in item (3) on the other side of this publication, you may submit a copy of each instrument under which you believe an encumbrance exists.

5. In certain cases the District Director may require additional information such as written appraisals by disinterested third parties, a list of all the taxpayer's property, or other information needed to make a determination.

Publication 784 (Rev. 9-91)

Chapter 5

———⊶⊷———

IRS LEVIES: CAN THEY REALLY DO THAT?

THE NATURE OF A TAX LEVY

Imagine buying a television or a new suit, but, if you don't pay, the seller can almost immediately seize your bank account or paycheck, or even sell your house. Imagine also that the seller needs no court order, no hearing, no judge, and no jury to do this. In its starkest form, that's the power the Internal Revenue Service has to seize your property when you fail to pay your taxes. The IRS almost never uses this seizure power in such an arbitrary fashion, but the authority is solidly entrenched in the law. In fact, in 1994, the IRS issued three million levies and made ten thousand additional property seizures.

A levy is simply the act of seizing your property to pay a back tax. Often it is confused with its collection cousin, the federal tax lien. When you fail to pay a tax for which the IRS has billed, a lien—that is, a legal claim—arises by law automatically and attaches to all your property. That lien is secret at first—no one knows about it except you and the IRS. Only when the IRS files notice of the lien in the local courthouse or land records does the public "know" that you owe taxes and that the IRS has a lien on your property to secure payment. This notice of lien is not a levy; it seizes nothing. It merely encumbers your property with a legal charge, somewhat like a mortgage.

The levy is the actual seizure. In fact, the IRS does not even have to file a notice of lien before seizing your property. All it must do is bill you for the taxes, demand payment, and wait thirty days.

The IRS levy comes in three main varieties. The first is a wage levy, which captures most of your paycheck, the commissions you've earned, and just about any other compensation due to you. The second is a nonwage levy, a one-time seizure of specific property such as your home, car, real estate, bank account, or insurance policy. The third type, rarely used, is a jeopardy or termination levy, a hurry-up version of the nonwage levy. Reserved mostly for gambling, drug, and money-laundering cases, the jeopardy or termination levy is almost instantaneous. In fact, sometimes IRS officials will authorize revenue officers by telephone to make these levies.

If the IRS' levy power sounds ominous to you, it should. Many people have challenged this power in court; few have succeeded. In case after case for the past sixty years, the Supreme Court and dozens of lower courts have rejected challenges to the levy power, ruling that this power to seize property without a court order or judgment is completely constitutional, indeed necessary to the proper functioning of government.

> *Example:* Abelard had a habit of violating the tax laws and accumulating back tax bills. In fact, he owed the government $925,000. Then, as luck would have it, he violated his state's criminal laws as well and was arrested and thrown in jail. Heloise, his good friend, came to the rescue by lending him $5,000 for bail money. The IRS found out about it and immediately levied on the clerk of court for the bail money. "You can't do that," screamed both Heloise and Abelard's lawyer (who also claimed the money for his legal fees). "Yes, they can," said the court. Once Heloise loaned the money to Abelard, it became his, and the court bailiff was holding it only in trust. So the IRS got it.

This levy power stands a world apart from a private creditor's rights to collect money. Normal creditors have to obey dozens of state and federal laws that regulate and restrict their right to dun you by telephone, write you nasty letters, and otherwise take steps to collect their money. Not so the IRS (though it too must obey the Fair Debt Collection Practices Act). Ordinary creditors must also go to court to get a judgment if all else fails. They must give the judgment to a sheriff to be served on you to seize your wages or your property in others' hands. Not so the IRS. You can usually file bankruptcy to foil most creditors, but bankruptcy often merely slows down the IRS. In short, there's very little shelter from this nuclear bomb of collection once it is dropped.

Example: Frank ran afoul of the IRS, which made a quick assessment of taxes, interest, and penalties for more than $100,000. The IRS quickly levied on money that Joe was holding in trust for Frank, but Joe refused to hand over the money. What did the IRS do? Nothing. It sat around until eight years later, and *then* sued Joe for the money. The result? The IRS won.

Example: Andrew certainly had his problems with the U.S. government. One arm of the Department of Justice filed a multimillion dollar claim against him and sued him for it. That division threatened to seize his assets, so Andrew agreed to escrow some money, awaiting the outcome of the suit. In the meantime, the IRS filed a notice of lien against Andrew and levied on the account. It levied again three years later, and again the following year. Andrew threatened the bank. The Justice Department threatened Andrew, and the IRS threatened everyone. Naturally, a lawsuit followed. The bank ran to federal court, asking for protection. Who won? The IRS, of course. What about the agreement between the Justice Department and Andrew to keep the money in escrow? "That was another division," said the judge. "That's not bind-ing on the *Tax* Division; and besides, the agreement doesn't say that the money *must* be held, only that the division would use its 'best internal efforts' to make sure no other government agency levies on the funds." So, the IRS won the money.

Example: Theodore bought an annuity contract from the Big Umbrella Life Insurance Company. For years, he dutifully made contributions of more than $13,000. In the meantime, four years into the contract, the IRS made an assessment against Theodore totaling $55,000. Then the IRS levied on the insurance company. "No go," said the insurance company. "The annuity is not in our possession or custody." The court disagreed. The insurance company had to cut a check to the IRS for the cash with-drawal value of the annuity. To add insult to injury, the court held the insurer liable for a 50 percent penalty as well. Congress intended that the IRS should be able to reach "every interest in property a taxpayer might have," said the court. The right to withdraw the cash value is itself a valuable property right, so the IRS could reach it by levy.

BEFORE THE IRS LEVIES

Because the levy is so powerful, the IRS restrains its use except when collection is deemed to be in jeopardy. So, in almost every case, you get plenty of warning before a levy hits. Like an oncoming freight train, you can see it and hear it, often in time to get out of the way. For example, you get a bill from the IRS if you file your tax return with a balance due, or if you owe more tax after an audit, or if you fight the IRS in tax court and lose. All of these bills are called "assessments," and they tell you to pay, or else. The "or else" includes the threat of a levy.

The IRS normally sends five notices of tax due to individuals, and two to businesses. Each new notice is more urgent than the one before. The final notice arrives by certified mail. After waiting thirty more days, the IRS is legally free to seize any property it can find. This final notice is entitled Final Notice of Intent to Levy, to resolve any lingering confusion about the agency's intentions.

> *Example:* Your worst nightmare: A husband and wife come into the office, both in tears. The boss has fired the husband. Why? The IRS levied his wages, and he hadn't told his boss he owed taxes, much less that he was having trouble paying them. (The firing is illegal under federal law, but it happens in the real world.) As the story unfolded, the IRS had matched a Form 1099 with the husband's return and found an error. The Service sent a bill, but this was two years after the couple had filed their return and had moved, as millions of Americans do every year. Because of that move, the IRS didn't know where they lived. Then they moved again. Notice after notice went unclaimed, including the Final Notice of Intent to Levy.

"You mean we don't actually have to *receive* that final notice for the IRS to have the right to levy?" asked the husband. That's right. The Service only has to *send* it to the last known address.

An extreme example? Yes, but it does happen from time to time. In most cases, people know they owe taxes. They get the notices, or at least some of them, but they stick their heads in the sand. In fact, the IRS sometimes issues so many notices that people feel intimidated by the volume of paper itself. So they stack the envelopes in the corner, hoping the paper will grow legs and walk away. They don't claim certified mail, figuring it's bad news from the Internal Revenue Service and will fade like morning fog if they ignore it. No matter. The IRS freight train continues to chug inexorably toward them, gaining speed with each new notice.

IRS LEVY POLICY AND PRACTICE

Because the levy is so powerful, the Services uses it sparingly. The Internal Revenue Manual in fact requires this restraint. So as an institution, the IRS does not *want* to seize your wages, your car, or your other property. What the IRS really wants is your attention and commitment to face up to your tax problem and deal with it. "Dealing" with a tax debt means filing an offer in compromise, making an installment agreement, borrowing money, or crafting other solutions. So think of the levy as an abrupt wake-up call. After the IRS chases you around, the levy finally says, "Gotcha." Having obtained your attention, the Service will typically release most levies if you begin to cooperate. Surprising as this sounds, in the real world it holds true, and confirms the IRS' policy not to use the levy power unless it sees no other choice.

You also have certain rights when the IRS levies. For example, you may request expedited review if the IRS seizes personal property that you need for your business. You also have the right to request that property be sold within sixty days. Note that these "rights" do not automatically grant you the relief you seek. They are dependant on the discretion of the IRS. You also have the right to a preseizure review using the Collection Appeals Process. This is a fairly new mechanism by which a proposed action, such as the filing of a notice of lien or the issuance of a levy, can be reviewed through the agent's group manager, and then to the Office of Appeals.

You also have the right to a release of any levy if the equity in the property is not enough to warrant its sale. This might occur even if the property seems to be worth little more (but is actually worth less) than the debt attached to it. For example, a home worth $100,000, with a debt of $90,000, has no equity for IRS purposes, because the IRS discounts the market value for the hypothetical forced sale condition of the property.

The IRS' internal policy, as well as the law, also require the release of the levy if certain conditions are met. For example, if the tax is paid or it expires, the levy must be released. If you enter an installment agreement, or if releasing the levy will facilitate tax collection, it may be released. Also, if the levy is creating an undue economic hardship, it must be released. This last condition, in fact, is the one most often relied on to obtain a release of a levy.

AVOIDING OR RELEASING THE LEVY

What to do when the revenue officer's threat to levy seems real, or if in fact she has levied? Before the levy, by far the most important tactic is: Communicate! Never let a notice go unanswered. Write and call the IRS every time it notifies you or every time it asks for information. Stay in touch with the revenue officer or the Automated Collection System representative. Ask that no seizure action take place. Consider getting help from a tax professional, and ask for time from the IRS if you need it.

Consider also appealing the proposed seizure, either to the Problem Resolution Office or to the revenue officer's group manager, and from there to the Office of Appeals.

If the IRS has just levied your bank account, your car, or your business property, you must obviously take immediate action. The most extreme form of action is to file an emergency bankruptcy petition. Such a petition will usually result in the release of tangible property and real property, but not cash or cash equivalents. Still, filing for bankruptcy ought to be a last resort, never done lightly or without careful consideration. Short of bankruptcy, you may call the revenue officer and ask for release of the levy. Of course, if the revenue officer is willing to do this in the first place, there will be conditions. These may include entering an installment agreement, providing updated financial information, or anything else the revenue officer deems appropraite. If the levy is creating a true hardship, you may seek a taxpayer assistance order (see chapter 13), or simply go up the chain of command through the group manager, branch chief, and chief of collection in your district. It's all a matter of negotiation, and in such negotiations, the less hostile you are, the more businesslike and cooperative, the better things usually go.

WHAT CAN THE LEVY CAPTURE?

Almost nothing is out of reach of the levy. Bank accounts, wages, commissions, accounts receivable, stocks, bonds, the cash value of insurance policies, jewelry, even homes can be seized and sold by the IRS. The law excepts only eleven narrow categories of property from the levy power. The exceptions include books, tools of your trade, and some parts of salary, among other things. Everything else is fair game.

Of course, the IRS goes for the easy kills first: bank accounts, cars, stocks, bonds, and wages. Its second set of targets are items such as insurance policies and accounts receivable. Third, the agency really hits home: it can seize your retirement accounts and your home (with some restrictions). Seizing a retirement account is a triple problem: first you lose the money, and then the seizure triggers the income tax *and* the penalty for early withdrawal.

BANK ACCOUNTS

These assets are easy marks. The Service sends a one-page form entitled Notice of Levy to your bank. From the instant the levy is received, by law the collected balance in your account is frozen. Note that the "collected balance" is not your checkbook balance but the balance you have at the bank. Then the bank waits twenty-one days, after which it sends that frozen balance to the IRS. (Of course, the bank also deducts the usual processing fees.) The twenty-one-day grace period was added by the 1988 Taxpayer Bill of Rights as a window for you to work things out with the IRS. But you're certainly bargaining from a position of weakness. Many revenue officers, knowing they have the money, will simply refuse to release that first bank levy.

The IRS uses names and Social Security numbers to find and identify bank accounts. A levy to the First Patriotic Red-Blooded American Bank will recite your name, Social Security number, and a description of the tax due according to the IRS. It also contains a demand to pay the account balance. What if you have a joint account and you are not the owner, or you own only part of the funds? Examples would include a bank account in trust or a joint account where a non-delinquent taxpayer like a child or spouse puts in some of the money. If so, the IRS has no right to those funds. But quite often the account does not reflect someone else's ownership. So, convincing the IRS to release this levy is roughly equivalent to pulling teeth from an alligator. If it's in your name, or bears your Social Security number, the IRS will try to take it all on the legal presumption that it's all yours because you have the right to withdraw it all. You then have to prove someone else owns the funds in the account in whole or in part. Normally, that's done by showing who deposited the money, but this can be difficult. In fact, such seizures of joint accounts in parent-child names prompted Congress to expand the freeze period to twenty-one days from the original ten.

Example: Abe was a good and dutiful father. He opened a bank account for his children and began putting money in it, all as gifts. Unfortunately, only Abe could sign on the account, and the account card did not show that the money was property of his two sons, Todd and Tim. He also got a passbook for his savings account (banks issued passbooks in those days) with his name on it, but not the children's. Abe put the passbook in an unlocked drawer in his living room. Years passed. Abe got into tax trouble, and the IRS levied on the bank accounts. The bank sent the money to the IRS. Abe got notice, and nine days later went to withdraw the balance. The bank refused. A month later, the children went to the bank and tried again to withdraw the money. "Gone," said the bank, "sent off to the feds." So Abe and his children sued the bank. The bank won. Had there been any evidence that the money belonged to the children, the bank might have lost the case. But absent such evidence, the money belonged to Abe, and the bank was perfectly right and duty-bound to send the money to the IRS.

To add insult to injury, after the IRS applies the money to taxes, then penalties and interest, you may still end up owing a substantial sum. The bank can do absolutely nothing to help you. It's not the bank's problem; the bank is a mere stakeholder.

The IRS knows where you bank from many sources: your last several tax returns, a Form 1099 the bank may have filed for you, a Collection Information Statement you gave to the IRS the previous year, or simply good detective work on the agent's part in the computer system. Revenue officers will sometimes loose a flurry of levies, at random, to see what targets they hit. Often they strike gold.

In the meantime, since your bank account funds have been frozen, your checks will begin to bounce. Each bounced check results in another modest bank charge, which can quickly add up, as well as the damage to your reputation in the eyes of your payees. So those twenty-one days are precious time in which to beg the IRS to release the levy. The price is usually an interim agreement to begin paying the taxes in installments. (See chapter 7.)

WAGES AND SALARIES

A wage levy is "continuous," meaning the IRS has to levy only once to get your wages, salaries, or commissions week after week, month after month. It differs from other one-time levies, which seize only the property in the possessor's hands when the levy hits.

The wage levy is probably the IRS' most effective attention-getter. It instantly clarifies the thinking of all but a few reluctant taxpayers. Out of $100 of wages, the IRS' take is typically $70 to $90. The exact amount depends on the number of exemptions you have claimed on your W-4. The IRS has a formula for this calculation that is set out in the levy notice to your employer.

> *Example:* James and Jackie, husband and wife, did their best to make it in the farming business. They had a good company and did just fine for many years. But then they got into trouble and didn't pay more than $200,000 of payroll taxes. What to do? James came up with the idea of selling some property at auction, so they put up the property and told the IRS about it. Naturally, the IRS levied on the $50,000 check from the auction company. To add insult to injury, the IRS also made an assessment against Jackie (not James) personally for $100,000, a portion of the unpaid payroll taxes. (The agency can personally assess corporate officers who are deemed responsible for the company's failure to pay payroll taxes.) So the government then had half its money, but it needed the other half. It couldn't levy on Jackie's wages, because she appeared to be destitute. Instead, it levied on James's pay, even though he had not been assessed for these taxes. Could it do this? Yes. The IRS took advantage of the state's community property laws, which make one spouse's community property like wages vulnerable to satisfy the other spouse's separate debt. (In addition to the powerful enforcement measures available only to the IRS, the government enjoys the ordinary rights available to any creditor.)

Not many people can live on the paltry sum a wage levy leaves, so you need to act instantly when that happens. In many cases, the IRS will release a wage levy. However, in many cases the agent will insist on taking one paycheck and require full financial disclosure and an installment agreement. To get the release, call the toll-free number on the levy form itself and explain the situation. Note that you need your wages to live on, that you won't be able to pay the rent, mortgage, or feed or clothe your family if your wages are seized. Of course, your statements must be truthful, but it's almost self-evident in the case of a wage levy. Also tell the agent that you intend to pay attention now and work out your collection problem.

You have several choices. You can sell assets or borrow money, not usually a realistic option if the case has gone so far as to require a levy. You can "deal with" the tax collection problem by filing for bankruptcy, which will in fact require the

IRS to release the levy as to future wages (but not as to funds seized or frozen before you file). Bankruptcy is not always a permanent solution, though in many cases it can be. (See chapter 12.)

You can also ask the IRS to stop collecting completely because you can't pay *anything.* That situation is so common the IRS even has a form for it, Form 53. When you use Form 53, the Service concludes that your account is "currently not collectible." The Service shelves currently not collectible accounts for six months, one year, or longer. It reviews your case from time to time to see whether you are doing better. In the meantime, an agent will file at least one Notice of Federal Tax Lien, protecting the IRS' position against the claims of other creditors and preventing the sale of your home or other property (including property you acquire after the lien is filed). This gives you some immediate relief from the levy. "Currently not collectible" status is like a cancer in remission: it doesn't cure the problem, and the symptoms could reappear at any time.

Another choice is to ask the IRS for an installment agreement, a method of paying your taxes slowly, over time. (See chapter 7.)

Finally, you can suggest that you will never be able to pay your taxes in full, but you may be able to pay 10 percent, 20 percent, or some other fraction. This condition calls for filing an offer in compromise, a deal in which the Service permanently forgives some part of the taxes as long as you pay the rest. See chapter 6 for discussion of offers in compromise.

Those are your choices. Select one, or a combination, and propose it, if you're hoping for any chance of the Service releasing the levy.

RETIREMENT ACCOUNTS

That nest egg you were incubating for retirement is definitely *not* exempt from IRS levy. This fact surprises many people because the law bars ordinary creditors from seizing retirement accounts. In fact, if you file bankruptcy, retirement monies are exempt from the claims of your ordinary creditors.

The IRS is no ordinary creditor. It has in fact seized retirement accounts. In one well-known case, the IRS levied the entire IRA of a retired judge! Seizing a retirement account is a last resort; the agency will usually exhaust almost every other source of collection. So if you can arrange an installment agreement or an offer in compromise, the IRS may leave your retirement account intact.

But when a retirement account is seized, there's triple trouble: (1) You lose the whole thing; (2) you owe the 10 percent penalty for early withdrawal; *and* (3) you trigger the income taxes due because of that withdrawal. So while the IRS has paid all or part of your old liability with the IRA, it has also created a fresh new one for the tax year in which the seizure occurs.

INSURANCE POLICIES

The IRS can seize the cash surrender value of any whole life policies you own or any other type of insurance policy that has cash value in it, such as universal life or a retirement annuity. Term life policies, which have no cash value, are of no interest to the IRS. The IRS seizes the equity in the policy by sending the levy to the insurance company. By law, the carrier is then required to send a check for the cash value, less loans, fees, or penalties.

YOUR HOME

The IRS seizes homes, cars, and other big-ticket items by physically slapping a preprinted sticker, called a Notice of Seizure, on the property. Things the IRS can haul away, it will. In fact, the IRS seizes so many cars and trucks that the local collection office often has standing arrangements with towing companies and storage lots. Physically putting that sticker on a car, home, or other property is an act that legally seizes the property for the IRS. That means it's a felony to sell, remove, or damage it. Agents record all seizures in a central notebook and then schedule the properties for sale.

Any time the IRS seizes assets on private property, it needs either your consent or a court order. This rule stems from the Fourth Amendment's restriction on unreasonable searches and seizures. The IRS' warrant to enter business or personal premises is called a Writ of Entry. A taxpayer who refuses to consent to entry only delays the inevitable by a few days or weeks. The revenue officer obtains the writ by asking the U.S. Attorney's Office to go to court, usually a formality. Normally you won't even know that the agent has asked for this Writ of Entry. The U.S. attorneys can obtain it without your knowledge or consent, and you would have no legal standing to contest its issuance even if you knew it was being sought from a judge.

COMMUNITY PROPERTY

Nine states are "community property" states: Arizona, California, Idaho, Louisana, Nevada, New Mexico, Texas, Washington, and Wisconsin (which has a form of community property). Figuring out what the IRS can reach in a community property state is very difficult, because each of these states has its own peculiar twists and turns on the community property laws. And, since the IRS' liens and levies can reach only what you, the taxpayer, own under the law of your state, the issues become quite muddled and complex.

Still, people who live in these states should note a few general principles about community property and how the IRS' rights might apply in those states. In general, and subject to your particular state's law, community property is property that comes into a marriage. Separate property is property each spouse has before marriage, or which is acquired by gift or inheritance. Community and separate property generally retain their character, but people who commingle separate property can, in effect, make it community property. Transmutation agreements can also convert separate property to community property.

As a broad general rule, community property is liable for the debts of either spouse or both spouses. That means the IRS can levy on one spouse's income for the other spouse's tax debt. This indeed has happened many times in many cases. If you are faced with such a threat where only one spouse owes taxes, several options are available. First, you and your spouse may keep completely separate property accounts, including separate bank accounts. Remember that this works only for property that is not "community property." Also, some states allow you to "transmute" community property into separate property by a simple written agreement. Where that device applies, it can often give you protection against the IRS.

The IRS is often careful about enforcing its claims in community property states. The agents are cautioned to ask for a legal opinion on what is liable for the tax debts and what is not.

EXEMPTIONS FROM LEVY

By law, eleven types of property are exempt from levy. But don't hold your breath; even if your property fits one of these categories, it usually won't feed the children.

Workers' compensation payments are exempt, including any amounts payable to dependents.

Wages, salary, and other income are exempt, but only a small fraction figured according to a formula. The formula is linked to the standard deduction and personal exemptions, prorated on a weekly basis. Figure only 10 percent to 30 percent of your net paycheck will remain yours.

Clothes and schoolbooks are exempt, but only to the extent "necessary" for you or members of your family. In practice, the IRS rarely levies on clothing or schoolbooks. (It might if you had an expensive fur coat.)

Fuel, provisions, furniture, and personal effects in your home, arms for personal use, and livestock and poultry, are exempt. So your guns, chickens, cows, and firewood are exempt from IRS levy. Even so, the limit is $2,500 in value.

Unemployment benefits, including amounts for dependent care, are exempt from levy, but again, that's not much. Since disability benefits are not unemployment compensation, they can be seized.

Annuities or pensions payable under the Railroad Retirement Act and the Railroad Unemployment Insurance Act, special payments to Medal of Honor winners, and annuities for armed forces members are exempt. Again, the amounts are not large. Social Security benefits? Government pensions? These can be seized. It happens all the time.

Judgments for the support of minor children are exempt up to the amount of salary, wages, or other income necessary to comply with the court order for support. And, they are exempt only if the judgment was entered before the levy was issued. You bear the burden to show how much is necessary to comply with the court order, and the Service does not have to release the money until shown that the money will in fact be used to support the child.

Welfare and Job Training Partnership Act payments and books and tools necessary for the taxpayer's trade, business, or profession are also exempt.

Finally, your home is exempt from seizure, except where the local district director personally approves the sale of your home.

THE AUTOMATED COLLECTION SYSTEM

Most wage and nonwage levies originate in the IRS' Automated Collection System (ACS). ACS is the Service's mighty reserve army, activated after the service center's computer nudges you to pay, and you don't. Normally, the IRS' service center will send out five notices of tax due for income tax cases, or two for businesses or repeat offenders. Large-dollar cases also receive only two notices. In all of these cases, the last notice is called a Notice of Intent to Levy. The IRS is required by law to give you thirty days from that notice before it issues any levies. Beware of any of these notices, particularly the last one. If it expires and you've done nothing, you can expect the Automated Collection System to spring into action and immediately issue levies to whatever levy sources it can find. In fact, most problems that occur with the IRS' collection arm result from the taxpayer's failure to heed these warnings or to cooperate in giving information to the IRS. In most cases, no levy action is "out of the blue." You get plenty of opportunities to work things out. In fact, the sooner you respond to any of these notices, the better off you usually will be.

As its name implies, the Automated Collection System collects automatically by machine-generating levies and notices of lien. ACS also has a staff of real people. They work in large rooms at seven regional service centers around the country, calling taxpayers to convince them to pay or receiving your calls. The ACS people work in teams. They have a number of interrelated goals. First, they will demand full payment of the tax. At the same time, they want to interview you to determine if you can pay, and how much. This interview will also establish sources on which they can levy in the future. They will set deadlines for paying or filing returns, and they will warn you that collection action will follow swiftly if you fail to meet any of these deadlines. Also, if your case is complex, they will research it for you. All day, ACS employees talk to taxpayers like you who call trying to get a break or make a deal on their taxes. When you call, the agent is trained to note in the computer everything you say, including your promises to file an offer in compromise, make installment payments, or take other action. When you call back again, you will usually get another agent, but that agent will have the institutional memory at her fingertips. In most cases, a mere contact by the Automated Collection System is enough to wake you up about your past taxes. So, even though you have received multiple notices from the service center and a Notice of Intent to Levy, you still have some credibility if you respond quickly and forthrightly to the ACS representative. True enough, that representative will pump you for information, exposing your financial neck. But you really have no choice, and, in any event, an attitude of cooperation is the only way you can hope to avoid levies and possibly avoid notices of federal tax lien.

Sometimes, however, liens are unavoidable. The cutoff point is usually taxes of $5,000 or more. Where the tax is between $2,000 and $5,000, and an installment agreement is for more than twelve months, a lien must also be filed. ACS will warn you that notices of lien are routinely picked up by credit bureaus, a fact you probably already knew.

Calling the Automated Collection System can sometimes be a terribly frustrating experience. The agents are trained to collect taxes and to be tough. Also, they are usually lied to ten times between breakfast and lunch. And they've heard enough sob stories to keep Ann Landers supplied for years.

When you call, remember a few rules. First, have all your information ready. This includes complete financial data on your assets and liabilities, income, and expenses. The agents will usually ask for all of this, plus addresses, phone numbers, and so on, even before you discuss how you're planning to deal with the back taxes. Second, be friendly and businesslike with the agent, and always tell the truth. Third, explain exactly the hardship the levy is causing and why you need relief from it. The agents already know the levy is painful, but you may have to explain the details. Fourth, propose a realistic, sensible plan of action to resolve the delinquent taxes. To do this, prepare—in advance—all your monthly income and expense figures. ACS will usually take these over the phone. Use the checklist in chapter 6 as a guide. Fifth, your attitude, and that of the ACS agent, are crucial. If you antagonize the agent, you can expect no breaks. But if you are cordial, cooperative, and meet your deadlines, you may win over the agent and distinguish yourself from others who do not. And, be sure that the tax bill you are discussing is correct. The IRS usually gets it right, but not always. Check the bill. Is it for the right tax period? Are penalties and interest properly calculated? It never hurts to be sure. Finally, if you don't like the result you get with ACS, appeal to the agent's supervisor. Then, appeal again if you must. You can also appeal to the Problem Resolution Office if you believe that the installment agreement that ACS insists on is too burdensome. Chapter 13 discusses this in more detail.

The ACS agents will then set deadlines depending on what the next step is, such as thirty days to submit a financial statement, or, if the amount you owe is small, ten to thirty days to submit a signed installment agreement. If you cannot meet the deadline, call before the deadline expires to get an extension or to tell the agent you cannot meet the deadline, and why. Despite the IRS' resort to a levy, you do in fact have credibility when you call the Automated Collection System to request relief. But you lose it fast if you miss even one deadline. And remember, *the IRS* has most of the power; you have little.

Normally, the agent will release a levy if you face your collection problem squarely and propose an acceptable solution. You need to ensure that the release gets to your employer in time for your next paycheck; otherwise, you may lose that, too.

SELLING SEIZED PROPERTY

The Service conducts no "sale" when it seizes your wages, tax refunds, bank accounts, cash value of insurance policies, and other cash assets. It simply takes the money and pays your tax bill. But other property, such as homes, stocks, bonds, and cars must be converted to cash. Here's how they do it.

The IRS gives formal notice (usually one to two pages) of the seizure to you, the owner of real property, or to the possessor of personal property. That notice, required by law, must recite the taxes owed and describe the property seized. The notice gives you the chance to work things out with the IRS, or, if not, to attend the sale and bid for the property. Notices of seizure and everything else having to do with property sales are strictly construed against the IRS. If the assigned agent makes a mistake and realizes it, he will usually back off and redo the process, knowing that he can't give clear title if any minor detail is wrong.

After sending or delivering the Notice of Seizure, the revenue officer makes sure that the title to the property is in the taxpayer's name. The revenue officer wants to be sure that the property is really yours and that the prior liens or mortgages are taken into account. After all, the IRS wants cash. If the mortgage or lien exceeds the value of the property, there will be no cash for the IRS, so selling it makes no sense. Selling property that has no equity for the IRS is also a violation of the IRS manual.

Next, the revenue officer prepares a Notice of Sale on an IRS form. Normally, the agent issues this notice within thirty days after the Notice of Seizure, mailing a copy to all lienholders and to you, the taxpayer. Then he publishes the Notice of Sale in the local newspaper or posts it at the post office nearest the property. The revenue officer will also typically post the notice on or outside the property to be sold, such as on a business property or a home. The notice sets the conditions of sale, such as date and time.

The sale must occur between ten and forty days after the notice. But agents often postpone these sales. The most common reasons are that they don't think they'll get enough money from it or the taxpayer is finally working on the collection problem.

Sometimes the IRS hires an auctioneer to sell property. This happens often with cars, particularly if there are many to sell. But the IRS is perfectly capable of holding its own auction, either by "sealed bid" or public auction. In public auction, the revenue officer stands up, calls the bidding to order, recites a statement of his authority, and opens the bidding at a minimum amount. Then, as in any auction, he tries to get the highest price and declares the property sold to the highest bidder.

In a sealed bid sale, people submit sealed bids in advance. The revenue officer opens them at the appointed time and place and declares the winner.

The IRS calculates a "minimum bid" for all property it sells. Essentially, the minimum bid is the least someone would have to pay to get title to the property. For example, let's say a home is worth $100,000, and the first mortgage is $40,000. An IRS formula reduces the $100,000 fair market value of the home to account for the forced sale condition of the auction. While this formula varies, a typical discount would fix the forced sale value at $68,000. The minimum bid would then be $28,000, the forced sale value of $68,000 minus the mortgage of $40,000. So a successful bidder could get a $100,000 property for $28,000, subject to the first mortgage of $40,000. What about the $32,000 of "value" that was somehow "eliminated" by the IRS' formula? The taxpayer can protest long and hard, but that value is lost.

The IRS can sell property that two people own together, even if only one of the owners owes taxes. The nondelinquent owner is paid his share. That doesn't normally happen with homes, which are usually owned as "tenants by the entirety" by a husband and wife in states that recognize this form of ownership. The IRS cannot seize and sell such a home where only one spouse owes taxes, nor can it get a court order to sell that home unless both spouses owe taxes or agree to the sale. Tenancy by the entirety is one of the few safe havens against a forced sale of property.

REDEMPTION OF PROPERTY

In theory, you can reclaim your property even if the IRS has seized it. If it's real property such as a home, you have 180 days to "redeem" the property after sale by paying the amount the purchaser paid, plus interest at 20 percent per year. It's a tough rule, but many taxpayers have used it. Watch out: the law says 180 days, not six months.

What about personal property? That cannot be redeemed once it has been sold.

Here is a summary of the important rules about levies.
1. Pay attention to them. The levy exists to get your attention, and failing that, to take your property for back taxes.

2. The IRS uses the levy sparingly.

3. Quickly develop an overall plan of action to solve your tax collection problem if you are hit with a levy.

4. Tell the truth to the IRS. Agents are human beings, too. They listen and pay attention to life stories, especially after levies are issued.

5. Consider getting the help of a tax professional to handle a levy or your collection problem in general.

Form **668-A(c)** (Rev. August 1994)	Department of the Treasury — **Internal Revenue Service** **Notice of Levy**

DATE:

REPLY TO:

DISTRICT:

TELEPHONE NUMBER OF IRS OFFICE:

NAME AND ADDRESS OF TAXPAYER:

TO:

IDENTIFYING NUMBER(S):

THIS ISN'T A BILL FOR TAXES YOU OWE. THIS IS A NOTICE OF LEVY WE ARE USING TO COLLECT MONEY OWED BY THE TAXPAYER NAMED ABOVE.

Kind of Tax	Tax Period Ended	Unpaid Balance of Assessment	Statutory Additions	Total

THIS LEVY WON'T ATTACH FUNDS IN IRAs, SELF-EMPLOYED INDIVIDUALS' RETIREMENT PLANS, OR ANY OTHER RETIREMENT PLANS IN YOUR POSSESSION OR CONTROL, UN-LESS IT IS SIGNED IN THE BLOCK TO THE RIGHT. ——————————➤

Total Amount Due ▶

We figured the interest and late payment penalty to _____

The Internal Revenue Code provides that there is a lien for the amount that is owed. Although we have given the notice and demand required by the Code, the amount owed hasn't been paid. This levy requires you to turn over to us this person's property and rights to property (such as money, credits, and bank deposits) that you have or which you are already obligated to pay this person. However, don't send us more than the "Total Amount Due."

Money in banks, credit unions, savings and loans, and similar institutions described in section 408(n) of the Internal Revenue Code <u>must be held for 21 calendar days</u> from the day you receive this levy before you send us the money. Include any interest the person earns during the 21 days. Turn over any other money, property, credits, etc. that you have or are already obligated to pay the taxpayer, when you would have paid it if this person asked for payment.

Make a reasonable effort to identify all property and rights to property belonging to this person. At a minimum, search your records using the taxpayer's name, address, and identifying numbers(s) shown on this form. Don't offset money this person owes you without contacting us at the telephone number shown above for instructions. You may not subtract a processing fee from the amount you send us.

To respond to this levy:
1. Make your check or money order payable to Internal Revenue Service.
2. Write the taxpayer's name, identifying number(s), kind of tax and tax period shown on this form, and "LEVY PROCEEDS" on your check or money order (not on a detachable stub.).
3. Complete the back of Part 2 of this form and mail it to us with your payment in the enclosed envelope.
4. Keep Part 1 of this form for your records and give the taxpayer Part 3 within 2 days.

If you don't owe any money to the taxpayer, please complete the back of Part 2, and mail that part back to us in the enclosed envelope.

Signature of Service Representative	Title

Part 1 - FOR ADDRESSEE

123456789

FORM **668-A(c)** (Rev. 9-94)   16740V

Form **668-W(c)** (Rev. August 1994)	Department of the Treasury — **Internal Revenue Service** ## Notice of Levy on Wages, Salary, and Other Income

DATE:

DISTRICT:

TELEPHONE NUMBER
OF IRS OFFICE:

IRS ADDRESS:

NAME AND ADDRESS OF TAXPAYER:

TO:

IDENTIFYING NUMBER(S):

Kind of Tax	Tax Period Ended	Unpaid Balance of Assessment	Statutory Additions	Total
			Total Amount Due ▶	

We figured the interest and late payment penalty to _____

THIS ISN'T A BILL FOR TAXES YOU OWE. THIS IS A NOTICE OF LEVY WE ARE USING TO COLLECT MONEY OWED BY THE TAXPAYER NAMED ABOVE.

The Internal Revenue Code provides that there is a lien for the amount that is owed. Although we have given the notice and demand required by the Code, the amount owed hasn't been paid. This levy requires you to turn over to us: (1) this taxpayer's wages and salary that have been earned but not paid yet, as well as wages and salary earned in the future until this levy is released, and (2) this taxpayer's other income that you have now or for which you are obligated.

We levy these monies to the extent they aren't exempt, as shown on the instructions. Don't offset money this person owes you without contacting us at the telephone number shown above for instructions.

If you don't owe money to this taxpayer, please complete the back of part 3. Attach part 3 as a cover to the rest of this form. Return all of the parts to IRS in the enclosed envelope.

If you do owe money to this taxpayer, please see the back of this page for instructions on how to act on this notice.

Signature of Service Representative	Title

Part 1 - FOR EMPLOYER OR OTHER ADDRESSEE

FORM **668-W(c)** (Rev. 8-94)   16748F

REVISED

Form **668-B**

Department of the Treasury — Internal Revenue Service

Levy

Taxpayer Name/Address

Originating Internal Revenue District *(City and State)*

Kind of Tax	Tax Period Ended	Date of Assessment	Taxpayer Identification Number	Unpaid Balance of Assessment	Statutory Additions	Total
				$	$	$
				Total amount due ▶		$

The Internal Revenue Service (IRS) is using this levy to seize assets owned by the taxpayer named above.

Although IRS has given the required notice and demand for payment, the taxpayer named still owes the federal tax amounts shown. The Internal Revenue Code (IRC) provides a lien for the unpaid tax and statutory additions. IRC section 6331 authorizes IRS to collect taxes by levy on all taxpayer property or rights to property, except property exempt under IRC section 6334.

Therefore, IRS levies (seizes) under IRC section 6331, as much property or rights to property, real or personal needed to pay the total amount due, with additions provided by law, including fees, costs, and expenses of this levy.

Dated at _____ _____ , 19 _____ .
                                   (Place)   *(Date)*

Signature of Revenue Officer	Telephone Number	Date
Concurrence — Signature of Group Manager		Date
Signature of District Director or Asst. District Director if taxpayer's principal residence is to seized, unless Collection is in jeopardy		Date

_____ **was asked to be present during inventory.** _____
    (Taxpayer's Name)   *(Revenue Officer Signature)*

_____ **was present at inventory.**
(Taxpayer or Taxpayer's Representative's Name)   ☐ Yes   ☐ No

Part 1 - SPf Seizure File

Form **668-B** (Rev. 1-95)
Cat. No. 20440G

Chapter 6

"LET'S MAKE A DEAL"
(OR, "AN OFFER YOU CAN'T REFUSE")—
OFFERS IN COMPROMISE

OFFERS ARE IMPORTANT

This chapter describes probably the single most effective way anyone can nullify a big tax bill—the offer in compromise. It is no surprise that the IRS is willing to compromise back taxes. About thirty million Americans owe up to $200 billion in back taxes (the estimates depend on whose numbers you use), and that's only the part the IRS knows about. The total does not include the underground economy, where megabillions more flow unnoticed and untaxed.

Every couple of years when Congress feels like smacking the IRS around a bit, it hauls the commissioner of Internal Revenue before one of its committees to blame the agency for not collecting the billions it has on the books. The IRS then recognizes, publicly, that it will never collect all of that money, but says that it's "doing the best it can." Besides, even with increased collections, the dollars it collects this year are often replaced by fresh accounts receivable next year.

For decades, the agency has had the statutory authority to settle any tax debt for less than full payment, but the authority was seldom used. In February 1992, this offer in compromise program woke up from a deep coma and became a real, honest-to-goodness alternative for settling tax debts. In short, the IRS got serious about cleaning up its accounts receivable; it advertised a new willingness to take less than one hundred cents on the dollar.

Still, even today, the program is definitely not the Filene's Basement of tax collection. The IRS' philosophy and goal is to give you a fresh start by accepting an offer, but only after it has squeezed out the last dollar it can get from you now or in the near future. If that's 90 percent of what you owe, so be it. If that's 10 percent, so be it.

Nationwide, the IRS received about fifty-seven thousand offers in fiscal 1996 and accepted about half. Astoundingly, the average accepted offer was thirteen cents on the dollar. Few other creditors in this world would make you that generous of a deal (when they make a deal at all). In 1996, the IRS became more reluctant to grant offers, but if your facts fit the guidelines, it's still worth a try.

This chapter guides you on how the compromise program works and how to make an offer. To make a successful offer you do not always need professional tax help such as that of a lawyer, accountant, or enrolled agent. Many taxpayers make their own offers; many are successful. But tax professionals can make the difference between success and failure, and they can often save you thousands of dollars on the amount you eventually have to pay.

HOW THE IRS THINKS ABOUT OFFERS

Here is the logic behind the rejuvenated offer program. The IRS generally has three years (from the time you file a tax return) to assess a tax and ten years to collect the assessment. In other words, it has three years to send you a bill and ten years to collect that bill. The IRS could choose to hound you for ten years—levy your bank accounts, file notices of lien, sell your property, levy your wages—but the agency knows people can not live that way. Politically it is also unacceptable, and in any event, the IRS is just not that efficient in keeping the pressure on you all the time. Rather than suffer that slow agony for both sides, the IRS reasons that if you will never be able to pay the full amount in the ten years, the agency is better off taking what it can get now and forgetting the rest. In this sense, the IRS is like any other creditor with good business judgment.

When the IRS looks at your finances to evaluate how much you should offer, it focuses on two sources of value or payment: (1) your current assets and (2) your future income potential (the money you might expect to pay the IRS in the future, using a five-year rule). Logically, those two baskets of assets are all anyone has to offer. *An acceptable offer must equal or exceed the total of these two baskets of assets.* Still, even if you meet these financial tests, you are not guaranteed an offer. The IRS also looks at your age, health, employment history, and any other factor that might bear on whether it can collect more in the future. Is the tax liability fresh, giving the IRS up to ten years? Are you young, with potential earning capacity, even if the IRS can't exactly pinpoint your future success? If the answer to these and similar questions is "yes," your offer may be refused even if it is acceptable on paper. But it still may be worth a try because of the big tax break you may get with an accepted offer.

Current Assets. You must offer an amount equal to the equity in your current assets. Details will follow below, but as an example let's say Tom Taxpayer owns a car worth $10,000, with a first lien of $6,000. In theory, the IRS could seize the car, sell it, pay the $6,000 first lien and pocket the difference of $4,000 toward Tom's back taxes. But the sale would never yield $10,000. As a rule of thumb, the IRS would net only $2,000, because the forced sale value of a $10,000 car might be only $8,000. After paying off the first lien of $6,000, that leaves $2,000 for Tom's taxes. So, in this example, the "equity" for offer purposes is $2,000. Similar reasoning applies to other assets, with varying discounts. Liquid assets such as bank accounts merit no discount. Extremely unsaleable assets such as household goods and furniture are subject to deeper discounts.

Future Income Potential. The second source of equity is your future earning power. Here, the theory goes, the IRS asks hypothetically, "If Tom paid us a fixed amount of money per month, how much could we get over the remainder of the ten years we normally have to collect?" Since some tax debts have only a few years left for collection and others are more fresh, the IRS uses a five-year average. Then it calculates a one-time, lump-sum payment amount that represents the present value of what it could hope to get over five years.

> *Example:* Tom Taxpayer makes an offer to compromise a $10,000 tax bill. Looking to the future, he can afford to pay the IRS $100 per month after paying his necessary living expenses. If he paid that for five years (sixty months), he would pay $6,000. Instead of putting Tom on a payment plan for sixty months, he could offer a discounted lump sum, now, that would equate to the present value of that stream of sixty $100 payments. The IRS has a formula for this. The present value in this case turns out to be $4,857 at 9 percent. So, for this part of Tom's offer, he must offer to pay a lump sum of $4,857.

Putting It All Together. Now let's add up the two baskets. The equity in Tom's car for offer purposes is $2,000. The present value of his future earning potential is $4,857. So Tom must make an offer of at least $6,857.

Apply the same logic to all other assets you own, add them up, and you have your offer amount.

It sounds simple, but, in the real world, there is plenty of room for maneuver, negotiation, and slippage. And, like any other smart creditor, the IRS won't always take the first offer that comes along. Remember, the agency's job is to find every dollar it can. Also, if it is prepared to give up an average of 80 percent of its claim, it wants to be sure there is no more.

OFFERS AND BANKRUPTCY

As you will see in chapter 12, you can often use the bankruptcy laws to discharge some, or even all, of your taxes. It's a complex subject; some taxes are dischargeable, others not. Some are dischargeable if certain time frames are adhered to, others not. And, there are exceptions to all of the bankruptcy rules. The IRS knows that everyone has the right to file bankruptcy. You can also file an offer either before or during bankruptcy. In theory, if you are actually threatening to file a bankruptcy that would discharge taxes, the offer examiner is supposed to take that into account in negotiating the proper offer amount. In the real world, most do not. They take bankruptcy threats with less than full seriousness, and if you actually file bankruptcy to discharge some or all of your taxes, they rarely care. They simply ship the case to a different office for processing of the IRS' bankruptcy claim. They rarely consider the threat of bankruptcy in making a "calculated business decision."

So, offers during bankruptcy are not favored, but again they are possible. It all depends on the type of bankruptcy and the type of tax involved.

LOOK BEFORE YOU LEAP

Offers sound good, so what's the catch? Actually, there are at least eight "catches." Some you may be able to live with, others may be too onerous.

1. *Statute of limitations on collection.* When you make an offer, you also agree to suspend the IRS' ten-year statute of limitations on collection. This suspension lasts for the time the offer is pending, plus one year. So if your offer is rejected, you've accomplished nothing but add a year plus the offer time to the IRS' already-long collection period.

2.   *Timing and results vary around the country.* An offer can be processed in as few as sixty days in some districts; in others, it can take as long as a year. Also, some districts have higher acceptance rates than others. The range is from 15 percent to 75 percent, raising the question of whether it might be wise to move. Naturally, the generosity of offer examiners (or revenue officers where they work the offers) also varies widely. Some are lenient, some strict, depending on the IRS district and their own personalities. The official IRS offer guidelines restrain this variability, however. The best course is to ask the revenue officer with whom you are dealing whether an offer is possible, or likely, and whether he or she will help. If the answer is, "Forget it. Not in this century," you have your answer. The party line you will almost always hear is, "Well, every taxpayer has the right to file an offer." Don't settle for that—you already know *that* much. Ask the Revenue Officer whether her or she really believes there is a chance to make a successful offer in *your* case.

3.   *You've shown your cards.* You must disclose your finances completely to make a successful offer in compromise, and that disclosure must be truthful. If your offer fails, look what you've voluntarily revealed: your entire financial picture. Now, agents can go out and collect to their hearts' content. So, by making an offer, you take a real chance that the IRS will use the information against you if the offer is rejected.

People sometimes ask whether revenue officers invite an offer just to get you to open up about your assets, then lower the boom on you. Such cases must surely be extremely rare. One reason is that the revenue officers can get all the information anyway, either by asking you directly or using their summons (subpoena) power to drag you into their office to complete an interview about your finances. So they really have no need to use the offer program as a subterfuge to discover your assets. Moreover, their oath, training, and personal integrity would normally dissuade them from such a course.

Also, if you do not make an offer and still refuse to cooperate, a revenue officer has ways of rearranging your attitude—a wage levy here, a seizure there. These steps often make the most reluctant taxpayer suddenly eager to get the revenue officer off his back by disclosing finances and working out a deal.

4.   *The IRS keeps refunds and credits.* If the IRS owes you a refund or you have a tax credit due from a past year, the IRS keeps these as a condition to accepting any offer. So do not count on making an offer using a $5,000 refund from last year's taxes. The IRS figures it's got that money anyway; you need to offer more.

5.   *Five-year compliance.* You must agree to be a model tax citizen for five

years after the offer is accepted. That means filing your returns on time and paying your estimated and any other taxes on time. If you don't, the Service can revoke the offer, keep the money you've paid, and collect the rest of what you originally owed. This condition does not mean that after five years you're free to default again. The Service reasons that if you can obey the law for five years, you have a reasonable chance of remaining a taxpaying citizen.

6. *Collateral agreement.* You may have to sign a "collateral agreement." This is a side agreement, not something to do with collateral on your tax debt. A collateral agreement is part of the offer; when it's used, it binds you to pay more money in the future if you strike it rich. The IRS reasons that it can accept an offer for the most money it can get right now, but if your income suddenly and unexpectedly goes way up, the Service wants a piece of it. These collateral agreements are not favored, but some offer examiners demand them. When used, they usually last for five years and take only certain percentages (usually up to 45 percent) of your net income above your current level.

7. *Bankruptcy impact.* Making an offer can also disarm one of your main weapons against taxes—bankruptcy. One of the many rules for discharging taxes in bankruptcy is the requirement to file the bankruptcy petition more than 240 days after the IRS bills you. Making an offer in compromise during that 240-day period suspends that rule for the time the offer is pending, plus thirty days. Filing bankruptcy also suspends the IRS' period of limitations on collection for the entire bankruptcy, plus six months. If you are thinking about making an offer, it is critical to get accurate legal advice about the bankruptcy alternative. See chapter 12.

8. *Public record.* An accepted offer is a public record. That means your wife, husband, partner, local newspaper, and so on, can find it and publish it. Every once in a while you run across a newspaper feature about some prominent citizens who compromised their taxes. A famous example is the singer Willie Nelson, who literally saved millions of dollars by making a successful offer.

ON THE GOOD SIDE

So much for pessimism. There is good news, too.

1. *Easy to do.* The paperwork to make an offer is relatively easy. You need only a few forms, and these are well-designed, understandable, and easy to complete.

2. *Collection suspended.* When you make a serious offer, in some districts the IRS sometimes suspends its collection efforts (except for installment payments you are making) while the offer is being considered. If it is rejected, collection does not resume right away. The IRS waits to see if you appeal the rejection. If you do, it will continue holding off while the appeal is being considered. This gives much-welcome peace of mind to many taxpayers. And, while there are some slipups, generally the IRS is as good as its word about suspending collection.

3. *An accepted offer wipes out the debt.* This is the best news of all. The threat of the IRS sword hanging over your head, impacting your job, your marriage, your livelihood and other important things, is totally relieved by an accepted offer. The debt simply fades away—you pay the offer amount and the IRS releases the lien and forgets about you. Moreover, the amount of an acceptable offer can be very little. As noted above, nationally, on average, it is thirteen cents on the dollar— a terrific deal in anyone's book.

MAKING AN ACCEPTABLE OFFER

The process is straightforward: get the forms, fill them out, mail them in, and when the IRS contacts you, answer its questions. Work with the offer examiner to see if your original offer is acceptable or what other amount might work. Try in every possible way to come to an agreement. If you can't, and the offer is rejected, consider whether to appeal the rejection. You can also withdraw an offer at any time before it is accepted or rejected.

You need at least two forms: Form 656 (Offer in Compromise) and Form 433-A (Collection Information Statement for Individuals). If you own all or part of a business, you also need a financial statement for that business, Form 433-B. Samples of these forms are found at the end of this chapter.

The offer is made on Form 656. This is a one page form in a two-part carbon assembly, one for you, one for the IRS. It is actually one of the easiest of all IRS forms to understand and fill out. Complete all parts that apply except for the offer amount. You will not know this until you complete your financial statements.

On line 4, fill in all the tax periods for which you owe (example: income taxes for 1994, 1995). This means *everything*—even taxes that you may owe but for which you have not yet been billed. It's in your interest to be complete anyway, because the offer is a contract. If you do not list a tax debt, the IRS hasn't compromised it. It can still collect. Nor is the IRS "scared off" by how much you owe, or for what tax periods. You may be making a $10,000 offer on a $100,000 liability, but in theory, if the IRS concludes that this is all you can pay, it should not matter whether you owed $100,000 or $1,000,000. So list every tax period for which you owe or may owe taxes, assessed or not. The IRS checks its computer records anyway and will make you refile the offer if you have omitted any tax.

If you don't know exactly how much you owe, or for what periods, call the IRS at 1-800-829-1040. IRS representatives are always pleased to remind you of how much you owe. If your case is already being handled "in the field," that is, by a living, breathing revenue officer at the local IRS office, you may be sure that she will tell you exactly what you owe. In fact, the revenue officers and other collection personnel are required to help you make your offer, if you ask.

Line 5 asks when you want to pay. People typically ask for 30 to 120 days after the offer is accepted. This means that from the time you make the offer, you may have as long as one year to come up with the money: one to two months for the IRS to log the offer in and assign it to an agent, two to six months to negotiate the offer, another one to two months to process the acceptance, and two to four months to pay after acceptance.

> *Hint:* If you know you'll have trouble coming up with the offer amount, the time to start lining up resources is when you make the offer. Then they are ready when it comes time to pay. The IRS wants you to pay from sources it can't otherwise access. These would include family, friends, relatives, and other lenders.

> *Another hint:* The offer amount starts to accrue interest on the day it is accepted, not when it is made. So the amount you offer is free of interest until the offer is accepted.

Line 6 of the form asks whether you are offering to compromise because you don't owe the taxes (doubt as to liability) or because you can't pay them (doubt as to collectibility). Logically and legally, these are the only two ways in which a tax can be compromised. Liability offers are rare, collectibility offers common. So in almost every case, check the box marked "doubt as to collectibility."

Then sign the offer in the bottom right corner box (line 8) and date your signature. The offer is officially made only when the IRS signs its part of the form (lower left). Also, the Service will enter your offer on its computer system, so you'll have a firm "offer made" date. That could become important when you calculate how long the collection statute of limitations has to run.

FILLING OUT THE COLLECTION STATEMENT— FORM 433-A

Now comes the heart of the offer process—filling out your personal financial statement.

> *Hint:* Remember that you are making this statement under the penalties of perjury. You cannot lie. But the offer rules allow you to present the facts in the most favorable light—and you should not hesitate to do so.

Page 1 (sections I and II) asks for personal and employment information (lines 1 through 12). The IRS will check its computers to see whether you are current in your tax payments and filing requirements. It makes no sense to discuss your past defaults if you can't even keep current. And if you can't agree to stop the tax bleeding now, the IRS reasons, there is no point in settling the past by an offer. Inevitably, you will be back again.

Sections III, IV, and V are the heart of this form, the places where your offer sinks or swims. List all assets at their "forced sale value," not their current market value. The discounts this rule allows are crucial; the IRS wants you to offer only the equity it could get by forcibly selling your assets.

Section III calls for your bank accounts, including savings and loans, credit unions, IRAs and retirement plans, certificates of deposit, and similar items. Consider each of these separately and differently when you calculate the equity in them for offer purposes.

Checking Accounts. This one seems easy. After all, we all spend everything we make, so, if you're a normal American, you'll have a checkbook balance of zero or close to it. But that is not how the IRS thinks. It goes by "average daily collected balance," the average amount the bank shows in your checking account. The average daily balance reflects the checks that have cleared into your account minus the checks you have written that have "cleared" (been paid). The average daily balance is usually higher than your checkbook balance. The IRS reasons that if it seized your bank account, it would get that collected balance, not your checkbook balance. So list what the IRS could get anyway—the average daily balance. If your checkbook reads "$100" but your bank balance is "$1,000," list $1,000 for this asset in your offer calculation. Offer examiners will typically ask for three months of bank statements (from all banks), from which they will figure the average daily balance. Of course, calculating this figure for the examiner adds credibility to your financial statement. Just indicate in the "balance" column that you have figured the average daily balance.

> *Hint:* The more homework, substantiation, backup, and analysis you do on these forms, the more credible is your offer. This also means less work for the offer examiner to perform, and increases the chances of acceptance.

Savings and Loans, Credit Unions. These types of accounts are usually less active than your checking account, but the same principle applies. List the average collected balance in these accounts.

Certificate of Deposit. Here list the face amount minus early withdrawal or other bank fees, and minus any federal and state taxes that would be due if you withdrew the money.

IRAs, Retirement Plans. State and offer the face amount, minus the premature withdrawal penalty and minus the federal and state taxes inherent in this asset.

> *Example:* Your retirement plan has $10,000. The penalty for early withdrawal is $1,000. The federal and state taxes that will be due on withdraw total $3,000, for an overall total of $4,000. Include $6,000 ($10,000 minus $4,000) for this asset.

Add up the balance column in the lower right-hand corner, and you are done with that page.

Page 2, line 14 asks for your charge cards and lines of credit. In most cases, that's charge cards only, but if you also have an unsecured line of credit, list it here. If your line of credit is secured, such as by a home equity loan, list that on line 28 (section IV) or on line 50 (section V).

Once you list all credit cards and lines of credit, add the four columns marked Monthly Payment, Credit Limit, Amount Owed, and Credit Available, as shown on the form. The key item is the Monthly Payment column. The offer examiner looks at this and says, "I see you are paying $533 per month to VISA, MasterCard, and Discover. That is money you could be paying to us, and, after all, we are ahead of those credit card companies because we are a secured creditor (we have a lien on file)." The examiner might allow some payments for necessary living expenses, calculated in section V. Otherwise, the IRS sees those charge card payments as available for the "future income potential" calculation.

Examiners also reason that you might be able to work out a deal with the card companies to pay less, or to stretch out the payments. Even if you can't, the IRS reasons, "Well, you tried your best to work something out with VISA, but were unsuccessful. Too bad, but that doesn't mean we have to roll over and give you an offer just because VISA was tough with you."

> *Major concern:* Often people have "credit available" on their charge cards. A big worry, usually justified, is that offer examiners will ask you to borrow up to the hilt immediately, pay that amount down on your past taxes, and then talk about an offer. Try to resist this unless it's clearly in your best interest. Instead, suggest borrowing the credit available as a down payment on the offer, rather than to reduce the tax you are trying to compromise. If the offer fails, the IRS must send back your down payment. But it won't return preoffer money you've paid on your past-due taxes. Also, do a little trading. If the offer examiner insists that you borrow to the max, counter that the extra monthly payments you will be forced to make are an allowable expense for future income potential calculations. After all, the IRS is insisting you borrow the money, and for a clearly "necessary" expense—the back taxes. The same reasoning applies if the offer examiner insists you take out a home equity loan or other loan.

Line 15 asks about safe deposit boxes. The IRS can inspect these boxes with your permission, but it rarely does so. After all, if you are so far in debt that you have to make an offer, you've probably used all the money in that safe deposit box anyway. Still, you must describe the location, box number, and contents.

Line 16 asks about your real property. This is the place to list your home and the type of ownership, but not its value. State something like this: "Personal residence—single-family home, owned as tenants by the entirety." The right-hand column asks for the address.

Line 17 calls for life insurance. For offer purposes, the IRS is interested only in policies with cash or loan value, not term policies. Still, list all policies. After all, one day term policies will ripen into real proceeds. If you still owe taxes, the IRS can make a claim against your estate if the estate receives the proceeds.

List the loan value of each policy. For example, a $10,000 policy may have $1,000 of loan value. Include $1,000 for this asset in your offer amount.

Line 18 asks you to list securities, including stocks, bonds, mutual funds, money market funds, government securities, and others. You can easily find the value of publicly traded stocks from newspapers, brokers, or on-line services (as of a certain date). The form expects you to list and offer the net equity in those stocks, that is, their market value minus any sales fees or other charges. If the value declines substantially between the time of the offer and its acceptance, bring that to the IRS' attention and ask for a reduction in the offer amount.

Stocks that are not publicly traded pose a very different and troublesome problem. Stock in a closely held corporation such as a family business normally has a limited market, or no market at all. Tight rules restrict its sale; the net worth of the company may be zero or negative if you owe back taxes. Sometimes, the balance sheet will show a positive number for "retained earnings" (generally the business's accumulated profit from its start). Some offer examiners calculate the value of this stock at the amount of retained earnings multiplied by your owner-ship percentage. If you own all or part of such a business, you are in any case required to complete Form 433-B (Collection Information Statement for Businesses), so the IRS can evaluate your small business from that financial state-ment, too.

> *Example:* Wonder Widget, Inc., has been in business eight years. It made money in the first three years and lost money in the last five. At the end of the eighth year, when the offer is made, it had an accumulated profit of $100,000. Willy Wonder owns 40 percent of the stock. The IRS may require Willy to include $40,000 ($100,000 times 40 percent) in his offer for his interest in Wonder Widget. This may not reflect the true forced sale value of Willie's stock.

Often, businesses have zero or negative retained earnings. On this ground, you may think that nothing should be offered for the stock, but the IRS' guidelines usually require you to offer *something* for small business stock. The manual takes into account such factors as the net worth of the business's assets, its record of earnings, dividend policy, current financial condition, future prospects, and value as a going concern. But if you can show you have a truly minimal interest in the business, no control over its affairs, and your stock can't be liquidated, the IRS considers your stock to have no value.

If you own an unincorporated business (a sole proprietorship) or a partnership, list the assets elsewhere on this form or on Form 433-B, the business collection statement.

Line 19 asks for information about court proceedings, bankruptcy, asset transfers, repossessions, and anticipated increases in income. It also asks whether you have a source of income from a trust, estate, or profit-sharing plan. If you check "yes" for any of these, explain in the Additional Information or Comments box on page 4 or on a continuation page.

Section IV (page 3) summarizes the information you have just given and adds more detail. Remember that for making an offer the column named Current Market Value does *not* mean fair market value between a willing buyer and seller. It means "forced sale value," sometimes known as "liquidation value."

Line 20 (cash) means the greenbacks in your pocket when you sign the form.

Lines 21 and 22 are carryovers from lines 13 and 18. *Line 23* carries over the cash value of insurance from line 17.

Line 24 asks about your vehicles. As a rule of thumb, the liquidation value of a car, truck, van, or similar asset is at least 20 percent less than fair market value. Take this discount on the form itself, listing the net number.

> *Example:* Tina Taxpayer owns a car worth $10,000. For offer purposes, its current market value is $8,000. If the car has body damage, rust, broken glass, and so on, the discount may be even deeper. If the car loan is $3,000, Tina would have to offer $5,000 for this car.

The form also asks for the lienholder, the date the asset was pledged, and the payoff date.

Line 25 deals with real property. You may discount the fair market value of your home by 20 percent as a general rule, more if the local real estate market is weak. If you own other real property, such as rental property, you may discount that as well. Note the level of discount you are taking and your reasoning. Then list all secured debts against the property, including the date pledged and the payoff date. List the monthly payment in the appropriate column.

How much to offer for these real estate assets? If you have borrowed against them to the maximum, and they have no equity after you have taken the 20 percent (or more) discount, then offer nothing. But if they have equity after this analysis, something must be offered. If you own the home or rental property by yourself (not jointly with anyone else), the equity for offer purposes is simply the debt minus the (discounted) fair market value.

What if you own the property jointly with others? If Tom Taxpayer and his wife, Tina, own their home as tenants by the entirety and both owe income taxes (or other federal taxes), the equity is equal to forced sale value minus the secured debt. If only Tom owes taxes, the offer guidelines require some amount even though the IRS legally can not sell the property. Unfair? Possibly, and a violation of the spirit of the offer guidelines. After all, if the idea is to offer only what the IRS could forcibly collect, then Tom should offer zero for a home owned as tenants by the entirety where only he owes taxes. But the IRS guidelines still require *something*. The amount is usually between 20 percent and 50 percent of the net equity.

> *Example:* Tom and Tina's house is worth $100,000. The mortgage is $20,000. Only Tom owes taxes. Tom discounts the market value to $80,000, making the total equity for offer purposes $60,000 ($80,000 discounted value minus $20,000 debt). Of that $60,000 of potential equity, Tom must offer somewhere between $12,000 and $30,000 (20 percent and 50 percent).

The lower figure applies if Tina paid the mortgage over many years, the higher one if Tom paid it.

What about other properties, such as rental properties? Here again, the rules allow a discount from fair market value to arrive at current market value for offer purposes. Subtract the debt on the property. Then figure your share of the net equity, and that is the offer amount for that asset.

Line 26 calls for "other assets." This includes household goods, rings, jewelry, art, and anything else of value. It is also the place to list your interest in a partnership, whether general or limited. If you are doing business as a partnership, also complete Form 433-B, Collection Information Statement for Businesses.

Line 27 transposes the bank revolving credit figure from line 14.

Line 28 asks for other liabilities. List every other debt you owe (except the federal taxes, which go on *line 29)* . Some of it may be secured, some unsecured.

But the IRS wants to know about it all. It may not allow any payments on these debts as "necessary" living expenses, but list all debts anyway.

Monthly Income and Expense. The fun continues in section V, Monthly Income and Expense Analysis. This section determines the future income potential portion of the offer. The IRS reasons that if you can afford to pay, say, $100 a month after allowing for these expenses, that's $6,000 in its pocket over five years. Instead of that dragged-out solution, it will take the present value of that stream of payments in a lump sum immediately.

> *Hint:* As a rule of thumb, for every $100 of net positive income per month, you must offer to pay $5,000. Because of this multiplier effect, section V scuttles many offers in compromise. So it is to your advantage to argue for every expense dollar as being "necessary." What the IRS considers necessary, and what you consider necessary, can be quite different. And when the Service gets finished reducing "necessary" living expenses, many taxpayers sadly discover that they suddenly have hundreds or thousands of hypothetical "extra" dollars per month. Because of that, they never make an acceptable offer.

Still, it's worth a try. Bear in mind that offer examiners in every part of the country follow formal and informal guidelines on how much of each expense is "necessary" for living. The IRS has also developed national and regional guidelines for three major expense categories.

Basically, the left side of the page asks for all sources of money, the right side for necessary living expenses. The difference between the two is the amount of disposable income that you could theoretically pay the IRS each month. It's that amount from which the IRS figures your future income potential.

Let's look at each item. As we do, you'll find a handy summary and fill-in chart on the following pages. Your expenses must meet two overall rules: (1) they must be within the IRS' guidelines, and (2) they must be necessary for health and welfare, or for the production of income.

INCOME SOURCES

Wages (spouse) _____

Wages (other spouse) _____

Interest-Dividends _____

Net Business Income _____

Rental Income _____

Pension _____

Child Support _____

Alimony _____

Other _____

_____

Total

NECESSARY LIVING EXPENSES

National Standard Expenses

Clothing _____

Clothing Services _____

Food _____

Housekeeping Supplies _____

Personal Care Products
and Services _____

Miscellaneous _____

_____

Subtotal

Housing and Utilities

Rent or Mortgage
(principal residence only) _____

Property Taxes _____

Homeowners or Renters
Insurance _____

Parking _____

Necessary Maintenance
and Repair _____

Homeowner Dues _____

Condominium Fees   _____

Utilities   _____

    Gas   _____

    Water   _____

    Fuel Oil   _____

    Coal   _____

    Bottled Gas   _____

    Trash Collection _____

    Wood Fuel   _____

    Other Fuel   _____

    Septic Cleaning   _____

    Telephone   _____

    Electric   _____

    Other   _____   _____
                                                Subtotal

Transportation

    Lease or Purchase Payments   _____

    Insurance   _____

    Registration Fees   _____

    Normal Maintenance   _____

    Fuel   _____

    Public Transportation   _____

    Parking   _____

    Tolls   _____   _____
                                                        Subtotal

Health Care

    Health Insurance   _____

    Medical Services   _____

    Prescription Drugs   _____

    Medical Supplies   _____   _____
                                                Subtotal

Taxes

    Income   _____

    FICA/Medicare   _____

    Past Due Taxes (incl. state)   _____

    Other Taxes   _____   _____

                                                          Subtotal

Court-Ordered Payments

    Alimony   _____

    Child Support   _____

    Other   _____   _____

                                                          Subtotal

Child/Dependent Care

    Elderly   _____

    Invalid   _____

    Handicapped   _____

    Baby-sitting   _____

    Day Care   _____

    Nursery   _____

    Preschool   _____   _____

                                                           Subtotal

Life Insurance   _____   _____

                                                           Subtotal

Secured or Legally Perfected Debts   _____

                                                           _____

                                                           Subtotal

Other Expenses

    Accounting/Legal Fees   _____

    Charity   _____

    Other   _____   _____

                                                           Subtotal

                     GRAND TOTAL   _____

The first item is national standard expenses (line 42). National standard expenses are expenses for:

- apparel and services (shoes, clothing, laundry, dry cleaning, and shoe repair)

- food (all meals, home or away)

- housekeeping supplies (postage, stationery, laundry and cleaning supplies, household products, cleansing and toilet tissue, paper towels and napkins, lawn and garden supplies, and miscellaneous household supplies)

- personal care products and services (including hair care, hair cuts, oral hygiene products, shaving needs, electric personal care products and repairs of these, and similar items)

- miscellaneous expenses

Add these up, and you have your national standard expenses. How much is "necessary" depends on your gross income and the number of people in your household. The chart at the end of this chapter gives the details. For example, a single person earning less than $830 per month is allowed $315. A family of four earning $5,830 per month or more is allowed $1,397. Households with more than four get more of an allowance. To find the amount you qualify for, consult the chart.

You can usually allocate the expenses within this category without much problem. For instance, if you spend a little more on clothing and a little less on food, that is OK, as long as the totals are within the overall limit.

The second big expense is housing and utilities (line 43). This includes almost everything you would associate with housing: the rent or mortgage payment, insurance, parking, necessary maintenance and repair, homeowner or condominium dues, and utilities. Utilities means gas, electric, water, fuel, trash, and telephone, and similar items. Again, if you are within the government's limit, the amounts are usually accepted. Here, the IRS sets a local, not national, limit, because these expenses vary so widely around the country. Call your local IRS office to find out what the limits are. An agent may even send you a list of them.

> *Example:* Tom and Tina have a first mortgage of $1,400 per month. This is at the high end of what the IRS will allow as "necessary" in their part of the country. They took out a second mortgage for a new wing, making their total monthly payments $2,500. Then Tom incurred a separate

$50,000 tax liability. Even though the second mortgage is superior to the IRS' tax claim (because it was recorded before the lien arose), the IRS will allow only $1,400 per month. This limit is enforced even though in theory the IRS can not legally sell the home or force the couple to move. The IRS reasons, "We may not be able to sell your home and force lower monthly mortgage payments with a smaller home, but we don't have to accept your offer, either."

The third big expense item is transportation (line 44). Again, the local IRS districts set the limits. This category includes car payments (either lease or purchase), insurance, maintenance, fuel, registration fees, inspection fees, parking fees, tolls, license fees, and public transportation. But, like anything else, if you spend money on transportation that does not produce income or ensure health and welfare, the expense is not "necessary." So you can have two cars as long as you meet this test and don't exceed the local standard.

After these three big expense categories, the IRS does not set national or local standards, but the expense still has to be necessary for health or welfare or for the production of income. Otherwise, it's a "conditional" expense and not normally allowable for offer purposes.

Line 45 lists your health care expenses. This category includes health insurance, doctor and dentist visits, prescription drugs, and medical supplies (including eyeglasses and contact lenses). It also means special items such as guide dogs, and probably also includes stair climbers and other medical devices necessary for health and welfare. The copay part of your medical bills is included here.

Line 46 makes taxes a necessary expense. (What a relief!) Here, the IRS has in mind your current federal, state, and local tax payments (including FICA and Medicare). If you owe taxes to a state or local government for past periods and are paying them, these can also be "necessary," but you must work this out with the IRS.

Next come court-ordered payments (line 46). These can certainly be necessary for the production of income, such as a judgment that a supplier has against you. They may be necessary for health and welfare, such as suit by a doctor for past fees. Court-ordered payments also include alimony and child support. It is up to you to prove that the expense meets the "necessary" test.

Child and dependent care expenses go on *line 48*. Day care and babysitting are certainly included, as are nursery and preschool expenses. But they must still meet the health and welfare or production of income tests. For instance, a mother who drops "little rascal" at day care so she can work would incur "necessary" day care or sitters' fees. But only "reasonable" amounts are allowed. The IRS knows children are costly, but it also warns that costs can vary greatly. The examiner will ask if there are alternatives to private tutors or one-on-one day care.

Line 49 lists your life insurance as a necessary expense. Again, only the premiums on term policies are deemed necessary (or the term component of a whole life policy). Some IRS districts restrict this to small policies only.

Line 50 allows for secured or legally perfected debts as an expense. This means judgments other people have against you, or other secured debts such as secured lines of credit. Once again, the debt must meet the health, welfare, or production of income tests.

Finally, there are the "other expenses" (line 51) that life always throws your way, and this is where to list them.

How about education? For your children, the IRS seems to draw the line at private schools. It's unclear whether the "extras" many people pay, even in public schools, would be included, but you can certainly argue the extras are necessary for *your* health and welfare.

For handicapped children, expenses would normally be allowable, but prepare to show that no public school or other public alternatives are available.

How about adults? Education expenses are "necessary" if they help your production of income. Examples would be real estate courses for real estate brokers or continuing professional education courses.

What else might the IRS allow? *Accounting and Legal Fees.* (Did you think the IRS would forget the struggling tax professional trying to help you out of all this?) The IRS lets you pay your tax lawyer, accountant, or enrolled agent for representing you before the IRS. Other legal or accounting fees must meet the health and welfare or production of income tests.

Charitable Contributions. The IRS does not consider these necessary unless they promote your health and welfare, or that of your family, or unless they are required for your job.

Other Expenses. Do not bother calling some expenses necessary since the IRS will disallow them almost automatically. For instance, in some districts, the IRS disallows all entertainment expenses ("Go read a book."). It usually disallows college tuition payments, private school payments, and pet expenses.

That completes section V. Then sign the agreement and date it.

Summary: The total from line 30 (equity in asset column) plus the present value of your net monthly income (from line 53) will dictate the amount of your offer. That's where to start and, you hope, end.

PROVING YOUR FINANCES

Would you like to gain instant and impressive credibility with the offer examiner> It's easy. Anticipate his or her request for proof of your financial statement, and supply it with the offer itself. Here are some guidelines on what to supply with your Form 433-A.

1. *Bank statements.* Last six months, for all accounts over which you have signature authority or control (business or personal).

2. *Investments.* Current statement, such as IRA account statement, brokerage statement, and so on.

3. *Credit card debt.* Last statement.

4. *Insurance.* Copy of the face of each policy of any kind (life, health, disability, and so on), plus statement of premium. Also include latest statement of cash value, if that applies.

5. *Home.* The deed, mortgage, evidence of recordation, monthly mortgage coupon, or other evidence of payment, and latest statement of equity. Also, if you have it, include a statement of the market value of the home, such as from the county land records or an appraisal.

6. *Other real estate.* The deed, the mortgage, and current statement of fair market value and amount owed. If you own real estate in a partnership, supply the same information.

7. *Cars.* Copy of title, latest statement of the amount of the lien, copy of payment coupon, copy of the "blue book" page on which your car is listed (actaully, the NADA Used Car Guide has an orange cover).

8. *Household goods.* Make an informal list of your furniture, by room. Do not include every stick, but be sure to cover all the main items, including any artwork. Make an estimate of the value of each on a forced sale basis. You need not engage an appraiser or some other expert to evaluate the items unless the IRS requests.

9. *Other debts.* Any documentation, such as promissary notes, for other debts you owe. If your uncle loaned you $10,000 and there is no note, see if you can get the check. If not, write up a statement for the uncle

to sign that demonstrates that he loaned you the money, the date of that loan, and the terms of repayment.

10. *Income items.* Three latest pay stubs for you and your spouse, and other evidence of income such as bank interest, brokerage statements, distributions from estates or trusts, and so on.

11. *National standard expenses.* These normally do not have to be proved, unless the IRS requests. Be prepared to prove any unusual items.

12. *Housing expenses.* Be prepared to prove utility bills, telephone bills, repair bills, and other housing type expenses, in addition to rent or mortgage payment. Sometimes, the offer examiner will not ask for proof if the amount you state on Form 433-A is within the IRS' guidelines.

13. *Transportation expenses.* Aside from showing title to the cars, be prepared to prove expenses, such as lease payments, repair bills, gas, and so on.

14. *Court-ordered payments or secured debts.* Copy of the court order, such as alimony or child support order. Supply a copy of any judgments against you, and executions on those judgments, or security instruments you gave to others.

15. *Safe deposit box.* Provide an inventory of the contents.

16. *Other.* Consider supplying three years of back tax returns for yourself and your spouse.

IF YOU OWN A BUSINESS

If you own a business that you operate as a proprietor, partner, or corporation, complete and submit Form 433-B (Collection Information Statement for Businesses). For a sole proprietor, the IRS will simply look at net assets, which legally *you* own, and increase your offer by the equity in those assets, discounted for forced sale value. But if you are a partner or a shareholder in a corporation, legally you do not own those assets as an individual. The partnership or corporation owns them, and *it* does not owe taxes. (If it does, see below.) The IRS usually respects the existence of the corporation or partnership, but still makes you offer something for your ownership interest in those entities because it considers you the true owner of assets in a family business even if, technically, you own only the stock. Also, it looks carefully at how much you are being paid and whether you are hiding gross income inside the corporation or partnership. This is important if you have many partners unrelated to you, or if your corporation or partnership documents restrict your authority to sell your shares or interest.

OFFERS FOR BUSINESSES

Corporations, partnerships, and sole proprietors that owe back business taxes, principally employment taxes, can also qualify for an offer. Here, the process is usually easier than with an individual who seeks to compromise income taxes. *Paying* is not easier, only making the offer. The same number of forms are involved, but there is normally less debate over which expenses are "necessary."

A "C" corporation commonly owes income or employment taxes. Partnerships and "S" corporations do not owe income taxes since their profits pass through to the owners individually. But these enterprises can owe payroll taxes. Also, an unincorporated proprietor can have employees and owe payroll taxes.

For all these business taxes, use Form 433-B, Collection Information Statement for Businesses.

The IRS looks at the business the same way it looks at an individual: What is the business's maximum ability to pay? Businesses are different from individuals in that their assets are directly involved in production and the business may not be able to borrow against or sell them. Moreover, they often need a cash flow cushion, particularly if they have seasonal ups and downs. Many times the IRS takes this into account; other times you may need to argue for it.

Form 433-B asks for typical introductory information: the owners, partners, officers, and major shareholders. Section I then asks for the latest tax return information, bank accounts, bank credit available, safe deposit boxes, real property owned, life insurance, and accounts and notes receivable. The IRS wants this information to see if the business can liquidate assets to pay the taxes, or for future reference if the IRS decides to force a liquidation. List all accounts and notes receivable, and in the "status" column indicate whether they are collectible.

Section II of Form 433-B (lines 16 through 27) summarizes the assets and liabilities of the company. *Line 16* (Cash on Hand) is the amount of money in the cash register. Lines 17 through 20 carry over information on bank accounts, receivables, life insurance loan value, and real property from section I.

Lines 21 through 24 require a list of all other assets, including vehicles, machinery, and merchandise inventory. State the market value, the debt on the asset, the equity in the asset, and the monthly payment if there is one. As with offers for individuals, you may discount the market value to forced sale value. Also, list the lienholder or noteholder and the dates the debts are due.

Section III, the Income and Expense Analysis, is the most important part of this form. *Lines 28 through 32* require listing the gross receipts of the business from all sources. *Lines 34 through 44* call for the expenses. The IRS usually assumes that all business expenses are "necessary." But if an expense is personal, out it goes. For example, if the company pays for your personal Cadillac, the IRS may not see that expense as "necessary."

The form also asks for a period of time covering the income and expenses. Many businesses choose one year. Others use six months. Pick a range in which income and expenses are typical, especially if you have a seasonal business. And try to choose a time period that ends within two to three months of the date you sign the statement.

If all of the income and expenses check out, the IRS totals them. The income minus the expenses is a net number, which the Service uses for the future income potential calculation.

Can the business afford it? Often it cannot, because of problems related to cash flow or seasonal fluctuations. You must argue these points to the offer examiner.

PROVING YOUR BUSINESS EXPENSES

Be prepared to prove your business expenses, as with offers for individuals. Normally, this is easy. You have your checkbook and your canceled checks. But you should consider supplying other information to the offer examiner, such as:

1. *Inventory.* A detailed statement of your inventories, including date of purchase and liquidation value.

2. *Accounts receivable and notes receivable.* Copies of these, including an aging report, may be helpful to your offer.

3. *Machinery and equipment.* These are easily obtained from your depreciation schedule. Otherwise, make a list, including date or year of purchase, description of the item, and fair market value (including the debt on any equipment).

APPEALING A REJECTED OFFER

You've negotiated. You've dug up and produced reams of supporting data. You've argued, cajoled, even begged. Still, the offer examiner wants $50,000, not the $10,000 you offered nor the $20,000 you could possibly pay if you robbed a bank. What happens then? You can either withdraw the offer or appeal the anticipated rejection. Tell the offer examiner that you want to appeal, and she will be more than happy to accommodate you. You'll soon receive a rejection letter that gives you either thirty or sixty days to appeal. Those deadlines are hard and fast. If you miss them, you lose your appeal rights.

The rejection letter instructs you how to prepare a protest and where to send it. But it does not give many details. For instance, you may have discussed five or more items, assets, and expenses with the offer examiner. But the rejection was based on two. You may not know which two items were the basis for being turned down, and the rejection letter may not specify. This is a defect in the system that may one day be fixed. Still, try to guess, and include those items in your appeal. You can be assured that the appeals officer will have the complete file and will know each ground on which the offer examiner rejected your offer.

A timely appeal is soon followed by a letter from the office of appeals telling you who is assigned to the case and letting you know if a conference date has been scheduled. To prepare for the appeal, assemble as much supporting data as you can, or review what you've already sent. Prepare to argue each point (or at least each point you can think of). It might help to call the appeals officer two weeks before the conference. Ask her exactly what items the offer examiner changed to reject the offer, then address those points. Often months will have elapsed between the rejection and the appeals conference. Use that time to gather more data. For example, suppose you told the offer examiner that you were about to be downsized, that is, lose your job or take a cut in pay, but he did not believe you. By the time of the appeals conference, you may be on unemployment. Or, suppose that your health insurance went up by $200 per month *after* the rejection. That is new evidence the appeals officer can consider. The worst the appeals officer can do is to sustain the rejection, so there is little downside to appealing a rejected offer. The only legal downside is that the ten-year statute of limitations on collecting your tax remains suspended. The upside is that collection may also be suspended.

LIFE AFTER APPEALS

If the appeals officer sustains the rejection, you are back to square one. The Collection Division regains a live account receivable it is required to try to collect. Sometimes you can then work out an installment agreement. Offer examiners will sometimes suggest that alternative in their rejection letter. But you are still back at the beginning.

On the other hand, the appeals officer could overturn the offer examiner's finding, or suggest some other figure for a compromise. If you agree, the appeals officer will write this up and send it forward for final review. Statistically, the chances of a reversal are small, but again it is often worth a try.

THE BANKRUPTCY OPTION

What if you threaten the IRS with bankruptcy? In theory, the offer guidelines require bankruptcy to be considered and "negotiated" if some or all of your taxes can be discharged in a Chapter 7 liquidation. The same is true for a reorganization proceeding such as Chapter 11 or Chapter 13 bankruptcies, where the taxes are not immediately discharged but could be if the case were converted to a liquidating bankruptcy. In the real world, however, offer examiners are reluctant to take bankruptcy into consideration at all. This is unfortunate, but it is their attitude. They don't take these threats seriously enough. Actually, if you file bankruptcy, offer examiners and revenue officers may be secretly relieved—it's a case off their inventory; they send it to another unit, the special procedures function. So, do not count on a bankruptcy threat to help your offer, even though it should.

The subtleties and permutations in taxpayers' offers are many and varied, as varied as people's personal and business affairs. No one chapter can address all of them, but every taxpayer who owes taxes owes it to himself or herself at least to consider making an offer to resolve—permanently—a nagging tax problem.

Form **433-A**
(Rev. September 1995)

Department of the Treasury — Internal Revenue Service

Collection Information Statement for Individuals

NOTE: **Complete all blocks, except shaded areas, Write "N/A"** *(not applicable)* in those blocks that do not apply.
Instructions for certain line items are in Publication 1854.

1. Taxpayer(s) name(s) and address	2. Home phone number ( )	3. Marital status
County _____	4.a. Taxpayer's social security number	b. Spouse's social security number

Section I.   Employment Information

5. Taxpayer's employer or business *(name and address)*	a. How long employed	b. Business phone number ( )	c. Occupation
	d. Number of exemptions claimed on Form W-4 _____	e. Pay period: ☐ Weekly ☐ Bi-weekly ☐ Monthly ☐ _____ Payday: _____ (Mon - Sun)	f. *(Check appropriate box)* ☐ Wage earner ☐ Sole proprietor ☐ Partner
6. Spouse's employer or business *(name and address)*	a. How long employed	b. Business phone number ( )	c. Occupation
	d. Number of exemptions claimed on Form W-4 _____	e. Pay period: ☐ Weekly ☐ Bi-weekly ☐ Monthly ☐ _____ Payday: _____ (Mon - Sun)	f. *(Check appropriate box)* ☐ Wage earner ☐ Sole proprietor ☐ Partner

Section II.   Personal Information

7. Name, address and telephone number of next of kin or other reference	8. Other names or aliases	9. Previous address(es)

10. Age and relationship of dependents living in your household *(exclude yourself and spouse)*

11. Date of Birth ▶	a. Taxpayer	b. Spouse	12. Latest filed income tax return *(tax year)*	a. Number of exemptions claimed	b. Adjusted Gross Income

Section III.   General Financial Information

13. Bank accounts *(include savings & loans, credit unions, IRA and retirement plans, certificates of deposit, etc.)* Enter bank loans in item 28.

Name of Institution	Address	Type of Account	Account No.	Balance
		Total *(Enter in Item 21)*		

Cat. No. 20312N

Form **433-A** (Rev. 9-95)

14. Charge cards and lines of credit from banks, credit unions, and savings and loans. List all other charge accounts in item 28.

Type of Account or Card	Name and Address of Financial Institution	Monthly Payment	Credit Limit	Amount Owed	Credit Available
Totals *(Enter in Item 27)* ▶					

15. Safe deposit boxes rented or accessed *(List all locations, box numbers, and contents)*

16. **Real Property** *(Brief description and type of ownership)*	**Physical Address**
a.	
	County _____
b.	
	County _____
c.	
	County _____

17. **Life Insurance** *(Name of Company)*	Policy Number	Type	Face Amount	Available Loan Value
		☐ Whole ☐ Term		
		☐ Whole ☐ Term		
		☐ Whole ☐ Term		
	Total *(Enter in Item 23)* ▶			

18. Securities *(stocks, bonds, mutual funds, money market funds, government securities, etc.):*

Kind	Quantity or Denomination	Current Value	Where Located	Owner of Record

19. Other information relating to your financial condition. If you check the yes box, please give dates and explain on page 4, Additional Information or Comments:

a. Court proceedings	☐ Yes ☐ No	b. Bankruptcies	☐ Yes ☐ No
c. Repossessions	☐ Yes ☐ No	d. Recent sale or other transfer of assets for less than full value	☐ Yes ☐ No
e. Anticipated increase in income	☐ Yes ☐ No	f. Participant or beneficiary to trust, estate, profit sharing, etc.	☐ Yes ☐ No

Section IV.   Assets and Liabilities

Description	Current Market Value	Current Amount Owed	Equity in Asset	Amount of Monthly Payment	Name and Address of Lien/Note Holder/Lender	Date Pledged	Date of Final Payment
20. Cash							
21. Bank accounts *(from Item 13)*							
22. Securities *(from Item 18)*							
23. Cash or loan value of insurance							
24. Vehicles *(model, year, license, tag#)*							
a.							
b.							
c.							
25. Real property *(From Section III, item 16)* a.							
b.							
c.							
26. Other assets							
a.							
b.							
c.							
d.							
e.							
27. Bank revolving credit *(from Item 14)*							
28. Other Liabilities *(Including bank loans, judgments, notes, and charge accounts not entered in Item 13.)* a.							
b.							
c.							
d.							
e.							
f.							
g.							
29. Federal taxes owed (prior years)							
30. **Totals**			$	$			

Internal Revenue Service Use Only Below This Line

Financial Verification/Analysis

Item	Date Information or Encumbrance Verified	Date Property Inspected	Estimated Forced Sale Equity
Personal Residence			
Other Real Property			
Vehicles			
Other Personal Property			
State Employment *(Husband and Wife)*			
Income Tax Return			
Wage Statements *(Husband and Wife)*			
Sources of Income/Credit *(D&B Report)*			
Expenses			
Other Assets/Liabilities			

Form **433-A**   **page 3**   (Rev. 9-95)

Section V. Monthly Income and Expense Analysis

Total Income		Necessary Living Expenses		
Source	**Gross**		**Claimed**	*(IRS use only)* **Allowed**
31. Wages/Salaries *(Taxpayer)*	$	42. National Standard Expenses[1]	$	$
32. Wages/Salaries *(Spouse)*		43. Housing and utilities[2]		
33. Interest - Dividends		44. Transportation[3]		
34. Net business income *(from Form 433-B)*		45. Health care		
35. Rental Income		46. Taxes *(income and FICA)*		
36. Pension *(Taxpayer)*		47. Court ordered payments		
37. Pension *(Spouse)*		48. Child/dependent care		
38. Child Support		49. Life insurance		
39. Alimony		50. Secured or legally-perfected debts *(specify)*		
40. Other		51. Other expenses *(specify)*		
41. **Total Income**	$	52. **Total Expenses**	$	$
		53. *(IRS use only)* Net difference *(income less necessary living expenses)*	$	

Certification **Under penalties of perjury, I declare that to the best of my knowledge and belief this statement of assets, liabilities, and other information is true, correct, and complete.**

54. Your signature	55. Spouse's signature *(if joint return was filed)*	56. Date

Notes

1. Clothing and clothing services, food, housekeeping supplies, personal care products and services, and miscellaneous.

2. Rent or mortgage payment for the taxpayer's principal residence. Add the average monthly payment for the following expenses if they are *not* included in the rent or mortgage payment: property taxes, homeowner's or renter's insurance, parking, necessary maintenance and repair, homeowner dues, condominium fees and utilities. Utilities includes gas, electricity, water, fuel oil, coal, bottled gas, trash and garbage collection, wood and other fuels, septic cleaning and telephone.

3. Lease or purchase payments, insurance, registration fees, normal maintenance, fuel, public transportation, parking and tolls.

Additional information or comments:

Internal Revenue Service Use Only Below This Line

Explain any difference between Item 53 and the installment agreement payment amount:

Name of originator and IDRS assignment number:	Date

*U.S. Government Printing Office: 1995 — 387-109/21883

Form **433-B**
(Rev. June 1991)

Department of the Treasury — Internal Revenue Service

Collection Information Statement for Businesses

(If you need additional space, please attach a separate sheet)

NOTE: Complete all blocks, except shaded areas. Write "N/A" *(not applicable)* **in those blocks that do not apply.**

1. Name and address of business	2. Business phone number ( )

3. *(Check appropriate box)*

☐ Sole proprietor   ☐ Other *(specify)*
☐ Partnership
☐ Corporation

County_____

4. Name and title of person being interviewed	5. Employer Identification Number	6. Type of business

7. Information about owner, partners, officers, major shareholder, etc.

Name and Title	Effective Date	Home Address	Phone Number	Social Security Number	Total Shares or Interest

Section I.   General Financial Information

8. Latest filed income tax return ▶

Form	Tax Year ended	Net income before taxes

9. Bank accounts *(List all types of accounts including payroll and general, savings, certificates of deposit, etc.)*

Name of Institution	Address	Type of Account	Account Number	Balance
		Total *(Enter in Item 17)* ▶		

10. Bank credit available *(Lines of credit, etc.)*

Name of Institution	Address	Credit Limit	Amount Owed	Credit Available	Monthly Payments
Totals *(Enter in Items 24 or 25 as appropriate)*		▶			

11. Location, box number, and contents of all safe deposit boxes rented or accessed

Form 433-B (Rev. 6-91)

Section I - *continued*   General Financial Information

12. Real property

Brief Description and Type of Ownership	Physical Address
a.	County _____
b.	County _____
c.	County _____
d.	County _____

13. Life insurance policies owned with business as beneficiary

Name Insured	Company	Policy Number	Type	Face Amount	Available Loan Value
		Total *(Enter in Item 19)*		▶	

14a. Additional information regarding financial condition *(Court proceedings, bankruptcies filed or anticipated, transfers of assets for less than full value, changes in market conditions, etc.; include information regarding company participation in trusts, estates, profit-sharing plans, etc.)*

b. If you know of any person or organization that borrowed or otherwise provided funds to pay net payrolls:

a. Who borrowed funds?

b. Who supplied funds?

15. Accounts/Notes receivable *(Include current contract jobs, loans to stockholders, officers, partners, etc.)*

Name	Address	Amount Due	Date Due	Status
		$		
	Total *(Enter in Item 18)* ▶	$		

Form 433-B (Rev. 6-91)

Section II.   Asset and Liability Analysis

Description (a)		Cur. Mkt. Value (b)	Liabilities Bal. Due (c)	Equity in Asset (d)	Amt. of Mo. Pymt. (e)	Name and Address of Lien/Note Holder/Obligee (f)	Date Pledged (g)	Date of Final Pymt. (h)
16. Cash on hand								
17. Bank accounts								
18. Accounts/Notes receivable								
19. Life insurance loan value								
20. Real property (from Item 12)	a.							
	b.							
	c.							
	d.							
21. Vehicles (Model, year, and license)	a.							
	b.							
	c.							
22. Machinery and equipment (Specify)	a.							
	b.							
	c.							
23. Merchandise inventory (Specify)	a.							
	b.							
24. Other assets (Specify)	a.							
	b.							
25. Other liabilities (Including notes and judgments)	a.							
	b.							
	c.							
	d.							
	e.							
	f.							
	g.							
	h.							
26. Federal taxes owed								
27. **Total**								

Form **433-B** (Rev. 6-91)

Section III.   Income and Expense Analysis

The following information applies to income and expenses during the period _____ to _____	Accounting method used

Income		Expenses	
28. Gross receipts from sales, services, etc.	$	34. Materials purchased	$
29. Gross rental income		35. Net wages and salaries Number of Employees _____	
30. Interest		36. Rent	
31. Dividends		37. Allowable installment payments (IRS use only)	
32. Other income (Specify)		38. Supplies	
		39. Utilities/Telephone	
		40. Gasoline/Oil	
		41. Repairs and maintenance	
		42. Insurance	
		43. Current taxes	
		44. Other (Specify)	
33. Total Income ▶	$	45. Total Expenses (IRS use only) ▶	$
		46. Net difference (IRS use only) ▶	$

Certification   Under penalties of perjury, I declare that to the best of my knowledge and belief this statement of assets, liabilities, and other information is true, correct, and complete.

47. Signature	48. Date

Internal Revenue Service Use Only Below This Line

Financial Verification/Analysis

Item	Date Information or Encumbrance Verified	Date Property Inspected	Estimated Forced Sale Equity
Sources of Income/Credit (D&B Report)			
Expenses			
Real Property			
Vehicles			
Machinery and Equipment			
Merchandise			
Accounts/Notes Receivable			
Corporate Information, if Applicable			
U.C.C. : Senior/Junior Lienholder			
Other Assets/Liabilities:			

Explain any difference between Item 46 (or P&L) and the installment agreement payment amount:

Name of Originator and IDRS assignment number	Date

Form **656**
(Rev. Sept. 1993)

Department of the Treasury—Internal Revenue Service
Offer in Compromise

▶ **See Instructions**
Page 5

(1) Name and Address of Taxpayers	**For Official Use Only**	
	Offer is *(Check applicable box)* ☐ Cash *(Paid in full)* ☐ Deferred payment	Serial Number *(Counter's stamp)*
(2) Social Security Number (3) Employer Identification Number	Alpha CSED Ind.	
To: **Commissioner of Internal Revenue Service**	Amount Paid $	

(4) I/we (includes all types of taxpayers) **submit this offer to compromise the tax liabilities plus any interest, penalties, additions to tax, and additional amounts required by law (tax liability)** for the tax type and period checked below: (Please mark "X" for the correct description and fill-in the correct tax period(s), adding additional periods if needed.)

☐ Income tax for the year(s) 19_____ , 19_____ , 19_____ , and 19_____

☐ Trust fund recovery penalty (formerly called the 100-percent penalty) as a responsible person of _____
_____(enter business name) for failure to pay withholding and Federal Insurance Contributions Act taxes (Social Security taxes) for the period(s) ended _____ /_____ /_____ , _____ /_____ /_____ , _____ /_____ /_____ , _____ /_____ /_____ (for example - 06/30/92)

☐ Withholding and Federal Insurance Contributions Act taxes (Social Security taxes) for the period(s) ended _____ /_____ /_____ , _____ /_____ /_____ , _____ /_____ /_____ (for example - 06/30/92)

☐ Federal Unemployment Tax Act taxes for the year(s) 19_____ , 19_____ , 19_____ , and 19_____

☐ Other (Be specific.) _____

(5) I/we offer to pay $ _____ .

If you aren't making full payment with your offer, describe below when you will make full payment (for example – within ten (10) days from the date the offer is accepted): See the instructions for Item 5.

_____

_____

_____

As required by section 6621 of the Internal Revenue Code, the Internal Revenue Service (IRS) will add interest to the offered amount from the date IRS accepts the offer until the date you completely pay the amount offered. IRS compounds interest daily, as required by section 6622 of the Internal Revenue Code.

(6) I/we submit this offer for the reason(s) checked below:

☐ Doubt as to collectibility ("I can't pay.") You must include a completed financial statement (Form 433-A and/or Form 433-B).

☐ Doubt as to liability ("I don't believe I owe this tax.") You must include a detailed explanation of the reason(s) why you believe you don't owe the tax.

IMPORTANT: SEE REVERSE FOR TERMS AND CONDITIONS

I accept waiver of the statutory period of limitations for the Internal Revenue Service.	Under penalties of perjury, I declare that I have examined this offer, including accompanying schedules and statements, and to the best of my knowledge and belief, it is true, correct and complete.	
Signature of authorized Internal Revenue Service Official	(8a) Signature of Taxpayer-proponent	Date
Title Date	(8b) Signature of Taxpayer-proponent	Date

Dispose of prior issues.　　　　**Part 1 IRS Copy**　　　　Cat. No. 16728N　　Form **656** (Rev. 9-93)

(7) By submitting this offer, **I/we understand and agree to the following terms and conditions:**

(a) I/we voluntarily submit all payments made on this offer.

(b) IRS will apply payments made under the terms of this offer in the best interests of the government.

(c) If IRS rejects the offer or I/we withdraw the offer, IRS will return any amount paid with the offer. If I/we agree in writing, IRS will apply the amount paid with the offer to the amount owed. If I/we agree to apply the payment, the date the offer is rejected or withdrawn will be considered the date of payment. I/we understand that IRS will not pay interest on any amount I/we submit with the offer.

(d) I/we will comply with all provisions of the Internal Revenue Code relating to filing my/our returns and paying my/our required taxes for five (5) years from the date IRS accepts the offer.

(e) I/we waive and agree to the suspension of any statutory periods of limitation (time limits provided for by law) for IRS assessment and collection of the tax liability for the tax periods checked in item (4).

(f) IRS will keep all payments and credits made, received, or applied to the amount being compromised before this offer was submitted. IRS will also keep any payments made under the terms of an installment agreement while this offer is pending.

(g) IRS will keep any refund, including interest, due to me/us because of overpayment of any tax or other liability, for tax periods extending through the calendar year that IRS accepts the offer. This condition doesn't apply if the offer is based only on doubt as to liability.

(h) I/we will return to IRS any refund identified in (g) received after submitting this offer. This condition doesn't apply if the offer is based only on doubt as to liability.

(i) The total amount IRS can collect under this offer can't be more than the full amount of the tax liability.

(j) I/we understand that I/we remain responsible for the full amount of the tax liability unless and until IRS accepts the offer in writing and I/we have met all the terms and conditions of the offer. IRS won't remove the original amount of the tax liability from its records until I/we have met all the terms and conditions of the offer.

(k) I/we understand that the tax I/we offer to compromise is and will remain a tax liability until I/we meet all the terms and conditions of this offer. If I/we file bankruptcy before the terms and conditions of this offer are completed, any claim the IRS files in the bankruptcy proceeding will be a tax claim.

(l) Once IRS accepts the offer in writing, I/we have no right to contest, in court or otherwise, the amount of the tax liability.

(m)The offer is pending starting with the date an authorized IRS official signs this form and accepts my/our waiver of the statutory periods of limitation. The offer remains pending until an authorized IRS official accepts, rejects, or withdraws the offer in writing. If I/we appeal the IRS decision on the offer, IRS will continue to treat the offer as pending until the Appeals Office accepts or rejects the offer in writing. If I/we don't file a protest within 30 days of the date IRS notifies me/us of the right to protest the decision, I/we waive the right to a hearing before the Appeals Office about this offer in compromise.

(n) The waiver and suspension of any statutory periods of limitation for assessment and collection of the amount of the tax liability described in item (4), continues to apply:

(i)   while the offer is pending (see (m) above),

(ii) during the time I/we haven't paid all of the amount offered,

(iii) during the time I/we haven't completed all terms and conditions of the offer, and

(iv) for one additional year beyond the time periods identified in (i), (ii), and (iii) above.

(o) If I/we fail to meet any of the terms and conditions of the offer, the offer is in default, and IRS may:

(i)   immediately file suit to collect the entire unpaid balance of the offer;

(ii) immediately file suit to collect an amount equal to the original amount of the tax liability as liquidated damages, minus any payments already received under the terms of this offer;

(iii) disregard the amount of the offer and apply all amounts already paid under the offer against the original amount of tax liability;

(iv) file suit or levy to collect the original amount of the tax liability, without further notice of any kind.

IRS will continue to add interest, as required by section 6621 of the Internal Revenue Code, on the amount IRS determines is due after default. IRS will add interest from the date the offer is defaulted until I/we completely satisfy the amount owed. IRS compounds interest daily, as required by section 6622 of the Internal Revenue Code.

Financial Analysis Total: Monthly National Standards

(Reference: IRM 5323)

Total Gross Monthly Income	Number of Persons				
	One	Two	Three	Four	Over Four
Less than $830	315	509	553	714	+120
$830 to $1,249	383	517	624	723	+130
$1,250 to $1,669	448	569	670	803	+140
$1,670 to $2,499	511	651	731	839	+150
$2,500 to $3,329	551	707	809	905	+160
$3,330 to $4,169	590	840	948	1,053	+170
$4,170 to $5,829	665	913	1,019	1,177	+180
$5,830 and over	923	1,179	1,329	1,397	+190

Expenses include: Housekeeping supplies
Apparel & Services
Personal care products & services
Food
Miscellaneous

For each person in a family with more than four persons, add the amount in the "Over Four" column to the amount in the "Four column.

Normally, expenses should be allowed only for persons whom can be claimed as exemptions on the taxpayer's income tax return.

Dollar amounts are derived from Bureau of Labor Statistics (BLS) Consumer Expenditure Survey, 1992-93, Tables 1, 3, 4, and 5.

A complete breakdown by expense item of these total monthly necessary expenses is in Exhibit 5300-49.

Exhibit 5300–49

Financial Analysis—Monthly National Standards

(Reference: IRM 5323)

ONE PERSON Item	less than $830	$830 to $1,249	$1,250 to $1,669	$1,670 to $2,499	$2,500 to $3,329	$3,330 to $4,169	$4,170 to $5,829	$5,830 and over
Housekeeping supplies	15	20	28	29	30	33	48	49
Apparel & services	41	68	85	112	126	145	146	240
Personal care products & services	12	17	20	24	27	29	38	44
Food	147	178	215	246	268	283	333	490
Miscellaneous	100	100	100	100	100	100	100	100
Total	315	383	448	511	551	590	665	923

TWO PERSONS Item	less than $830	$830 to $1,249	$1,250 to $1,669	$1,670 to $2,499	$2,500 to $3,329	$3,330 to $4,169	$4,170 to $5,829	$5,830 and over
Housekeeping supplies	25	29	33	36	40	51	52	71
Apparel & services	67	69	86	127	134	173	208	314
Personal care products & services	23	24	30	31	37	39	47	63
Food	269	270	295	332	371	452	481	606
Miscellaneous	125	125	125	125	125	125	125	125
Total	509	517	569	651	707	840	913	1,179

THREE PERSONS Item	less than $830	$830 to $1,249	$1,250 to $1,669	$1,670 to $2,499	$2,500 to $3,329	$3,330 to $4,169	$4,170 to $5,829	$5,830 and over
Housekeeping supplies	26	30	34	37	42	52	60	74
Apparel & services	83	108	109	128	138	200	238	316
Personal care products & services	24	28	36	37	40	54	55	74
Food	270	308	341	379	439	492	516	715
Miscellaneous	150	150	150	150	150	150	150	150
Total	553	624	670	731	809	948	1,019	1,329

FOUR PERSONS Item	Less than $830	$830 to $1,249	$1,250 to $1,669	$1,670 to $2,499	$2,500 to $3,329	$3,330 to $4,169	$4,170 to $5,829	$5,830 and over
Housekeeping supplies	27	31	48	49	50	56	67	82
Apparel & services	143	144	147	151	170	209	239	346
Personal care products & services	26	29	37	38	42	55	57	75
Food	343	344	396	426	468	558	639	719
Miscellaneous	175	175	175	175	175	175	175	175
Total	714	723	803	839	905	1,053	1,177	1,397

Chapter 7

THE INSTALLMENT AGREEMENT

A big IRS bill can be unnerving at best, paralyzing at worst. Sometimes you see it coming, like a bill following a three-year audit. Other times, the IRS bill can be a total shock, leaving you with the terrifying question—"How am I ever going to pay this?"

That's what the installment agreement is for. The IRS has long had the legal authority to allow past-due taxes to be paid in installments. The installment agreement is not a legal right you can enforce, but the Service can and does grant these agreements—about 2.6 million last year, covering $12 billion in back taxes.

The installment concept seems salutary on the surface; the tax bill is too big to swallow all at once, so you pay in digestible chunks. And in fact, most parts of an installment agreement are negotiable: the time period, the amount per month, the date of payment. Its biggest advantage is to allow you breathing room to pay a bill you cannot pay in full right away.

But it has drawbacks, too. First, the effective "interest" rate of some installment agreements is more than 20 percent. That 20 percent combines the normal interest rate on back taxes, in recent years 9 percent to 10 percent, plus a late-payment penalty of up to 12 percent a year (1 percent a month). The magic of daily compounding can really run up that total. So if you can possibly borrow the money to pay the IRS, even from a high interest credit card issuer, you are at least even and maybe better off.

Second, the IRS may file a Notice of Federal Tax Lien while you are paying. That notice is like a mortgage on all your property, a legal charge or encumbrance to secure the tax debt. The lien ties up almost everything you own until the debt is paid. However, sometimes you can discharge certain property from the lien. See chapter 4. The 1996 Taxpayer Bill of Rights also allows you to ask the IRS to withdraw the notice of lien if you agree to installment payments. But don't hold your breath on this one: the IRS will be very reluctant to withdraw its lien, and that decision is in the agency's sole discretion.

Third, the IRS often asks you to "voluntarily" extend the period of limitations on collection as the price for an installment agreement. The agent may not insist on this extension if you can pay in a relatively short time such as three years. But if your agreement stretches longer than that, especially past the ten years the IRS normally has to collect, the IRS may demand a waiver, or else no installment agreement. Sometimes this waiver can last for five more years, sometimes ten. It all depends on how long the computer calculates it will take to pay the tax debt in full, including interest and penalties. (Official policy calls for no more than a five-year extension at a time.) The IRS will also file a Notice of Federal Tax Lien for such long-term agreements. So if your choice from the tax collection "menu" is the installment agreement, watch out for the aftertaste.

The IRS' menu also includes the installment agreement, but it's way down on the Service's list. First on the list is always: Pay in full, and now! Sell assets if you have to. Borrow money if you can. But pay now, and in full. The IRS manual explicitly emphasizes collecting the back taxes from "available assets," a phrase that contemplates forced sales of your valuable properties. Other methods such as installment agreements are considered only if the IRS cannot collect in full, quickly.

So, when you propose to pay with an installment agreement, bear in mind it is not the IRS' first choice. In fact, the default rate on installment agreements at one point hovered around 80 percent. No wonder the agency is reluctant to grant them.

THE INSTALLMENT AGREEMENT MENU

There are five main types of installment agreements. Ask for the one that is right for you. The first is a regular installment agreement, nothing more or less than a monthly payment plan. Once the agreement is in place, the IRS sometimes even sends you a payment coupon each month; you send it back with a check.

The second type is a Direct Debit Installment Agreement. Here, you give the IRS the authority to debit your bank account each month for the payment. (Don't play the bank float on this one!)

The third type is the Payroll Deduction Installment Agreement. Here, the money is deducted directly from your paycheck, just like current taxes.

A fourth type is Form 433-F, reserved for small delinquencies of short term. The qualifying amounts are not generally known, so ask if you qualify for this type of agreement.

Finally, there is the "name your own," or "streamlined," installment agreement. The IRS established this one in 1994 for people who owed less than $10,000. If you qualify, use Form 9265 and put down the amount you think you can pay per month. As long as you pay within thirty-six months, the IRS automatically accepts it.

Some agents use informal installment agreements, requiring a fixed monthly payment but without the formality of a written agreement.

WHERE TO GET AN INSTALLMENT AGREEMENT

If you qualify for the "name your own" agreement, all you need is Form 9265. You can find this from an on-line computer service, the IRS' Web site, a local IRS office, some libraries, or by dialing 1-800-TAX-FORM. Fill out the form, attach it to your tax return, and send it in. (Keep a copy!) That should be the end of the matter.

The more complicated agreements, involving more than $10,000 or several years of taxes, usually find their way to the IRS' service centers or the Automated Collection System (ACS). Still more complex ones are referred to revenue officers "in the field."

Here's how the process generally works at any of these levels. The IRS computers catch up with you for past taxes by sending a number of letters. Starting in 1997, you will also get an annual update of your tax bill. Most people take the hint and respond to the letters. You can propose an installment agreement by return mail in this way.

At whatever level you discuss an installment agreement within the IRS, you will be interviewed. This is known as the "TDA Interview," standing for

"Taxpayer Delinquent Account." Remember that the IRS is after the most money in the shortest possible time. So the Automated Collection System representative, or the revenue officer, will demand full payment up front. That's step one. Failing that, in step two you will be quizzed on all of your assets and liabilities. If the agent sees that you can sell something quickly, such as a stock, bond, or savings account, he or she will demand that this be done. He may also demand that you liquidate a retirement account, despite the penalty for early withdrawal and the income tax you have to pay on it. He will look for sources of borrowing—credit cards, home equity loans, family loans, you name it. Often the agent will ask you to apply for one or two loans, and to send evidence that you have done so, even if you know you can't qualify and are sure to be rejected.

When all of these "quick money" sources are exhausted, in step three the agent moves on to review your monthly income and expenses to arrive at an installment amount.

An agent will ask many questions in interview form to see how much you can pay. Figure on spending up to two hours on the telephone. Essentially, the agent goes through the same financial data, verbally, that she would have asked you to put in writing. This includes verifying your name, address, employment, family circumstances, where you bank, assets and liabilities, income, and expenses.

The agent first asks how much you earn from all sources, taxable or not. She then catalogs your necessary living expenses. Review pages 110 through 117 of this chapter and the checklist in chapter 6 before responding, so you are prepared when the IRS calls. Often that IRS call scares people. As a result, they underestimate their living expenses. This mistake is as costly an error as if you overestimated them. Be accurate. That accuracy depends on thinking through your expenses, item by item, category by category, in advance of the IRS' call. Later, this chapter provides a guide to this process.

At the end of the interview, the IRS adds up your "necessary" living expenses (according to its standards) and subtracts these from your pay and other income. If the result is a positive number, the agency will expect you to pay that amount or close to it.

Example: Tanya Taxpayer works at Churner Stockbroker as a salaried stockbroker. Her gross pay is $6,000 per month. She has necessary living expenses of $1,500 for taxes, $1,000 for rent, $1,000 for food, $1,000 for child care, and $1,000 for all other items. These total $5,500, so she has $500 left. The IRS will expect Tanya to pay $500 per month. Possibly it may shave that to $450 or $400 if it's near Christmas.

The agent must also decide whether to file a Notice of Federal Tax Lien (chapter 4 discusses this lien). If you owe less than $5,000 generally a lien will not be filed. Between $5,000 and $10,000, a lien is not required if you use the streamlined installment agreement. In all other cases, the IRS will almost always file a Notice of Federal Tax Lien. The actual rules for lien filing are somewhat more convoluted and complex, but these may be your general guides.

Ignoring the Service's past-due notices is usually futile. Agents will begin calling either from the service center where you filed your returns or from the automated collection system if the case has been transferred to that function after the service center gives up. The representative goes through the same interview process described above. She enters the information on the computer screen and proposes an installment agreement based on your net monthly income.

You can agree or disagree, and you can even appeal, but normally the figures will not change much.

The third way you can get an installment agreement is to delay, hide, or stall long enough to prompt "the field" into action. This means your case has merited the personal attention of a revenue officer of the Collection Division. Millions of people adopt this "head in the sand" attitude toward paying their past taxes, only making things worse. After all, when an ostrich sticks its head in the sand, what part is then exposed to a kick?

Revenue officers have the same menu as the other collectors. They call, visit, or otherwise find you. They are out to get the taxes, so they also demand full payment, up front. But they, too, recognize that you may not be able to pay in full right away. Certainly they will ask you to borrow from lines of credit or credit cards, refinance assets, or liquidate assets, before an installment agreement can be granted. In other words, they will try to get the most money in the shortest time and save the installment agreement for any balance.

Finally, you also ask for an installment agreement simply by walking into your local IRS office. The same interview process will occur, and often you get quick, one-stop service in this way.

If you negotiate with the Automated Collection System representative, you can often obtain a short-term payment of sixty days or less. It's often in your best interest to look around everywhere for those dollars, because interest and penalties mount up very quickly.

TIPS ON NEGOTIATING THE AGREEMENT

Tip Number 1: Know your finances; don't guess. The IRS agent, at whatever level, will usually try to keep you on the phone (or in an interview) to get as much personal and financial information as she can on the first contact. If you are nervous or unsure about information, say so: you do not know, you need to verify, or you are unsure. Don't guess, and don't try to please the agent by stabbing at a number you think the agent might want to hear. Most people know what they pay for rent or mortgage, but few know the figure for transportation, food, or medicine without looking at bills and receipts. Official Service policy allows this breathing room if you ask for it. In fact, it is perfectly acceptable to tell the agent (if true), "Please let me know all the categories of expense you want me to research. I will call you back with the exact figures, which I can't recall now." Then be certain you call back on or before the next deadline. Otherwise, the IRS will feel free to collect, such as by levying your wages, filing a Notice of Federal Tax Lien, or seizing other assets. Try to ask for a date far enough ahead that you know for sure you can have all the information.

This leads us to *Tip Number 2: Meet all deadlines.* If you cannot, call the agent back anyway before the deadline and say you cannot meet the deadline. Then set another one. If the case is in ACS, you get a different agent each time you call, but all have access to the same computer screen and data bank. Each agent notes what you say every time you call. So the first agent notes that you promised to call back on November 1. The second agent sees that deadline, and checks whether you met it.

Tip Number 3: Appeal. Let's say that at the end of the interview the agent proposes $1,000 per month, a figure you just can't meet. You can afford only $200. You don't have to accept $1,000, at least not right away. You can appeal. Tell the agent you want to appeal to her supervisor. Ask what the process is and how long it takes. In the meantime, show good faith by sending in what you think you can afford. Often such appeals take several weeks. In the meantime, you have generated a track record of paying what you think you can afford. This good-faith pattern can work in your favor when you try to negotiate a lower number.

Tip Number 4: If you decide to borrow money against an asset, get credit for the repayments. Borrowing means your monthly expenses go up, which should reduce your installment agreement.

> *Example:* You owe $15,000 in taxes. At the IRS' request, you borrow $10,000 against your home, leaving $5,000 for the installment agreement. The IRS wants you to pay $500 per month, but because of your new home equity loan, you can pay only $250. The IRS should give you credit for that new loan payment as an additional "necessary" living expense, and ask for only $250 per month. The same reasoning should apply if you borrow on your credit cards, even though the credit card debt is not "secured" as a home loan would be. But the Internal Revenue manual is silent on this point.

Tip Number 5: Stay current. The agent *always* looks at your compliance and tax history before granting you an installment agreement. If you have defaulted once or more in the past, if you are behind on your current taxes, if your expenses have recently increased without justification or explanation, she may be reluctant to let you pay over time.

Tip Number 6: Ask for lien withdrawal. Ask the IRS to withdraw any Notice of Federal Tax Lien it has filed against you. Since the agency will be reluctant to do this, you need to have a solid, business or personal reason for asking for the withdrawal. This withdrawal must be considered a long shot, but may be worth a try. In theory, you can ask the Problem Resolution Office to intervene for you to obtain this withdrawal, but you will probably be required to show substantial hardship. If the IRS agrees to the withdrawal, you may also write the agency, asking it to notify your credit reporting agencies and banks and other creditors of the withdrawal of the notice.

Tip Number 7: Request nonfiling of Notice of Federal Tax Lien. If you believe the filing of a notice of lien will hurt your credit, or otherwise damage your finances, you can always request that one not be filed. The IRS always has discretion to file a notice of lien, though only if you owe more than $5,000 can you be relatively sure this discretion will not be exercised. But even in cases in which the lien appears "mandatory," it doesn't hurt to make the argument, and you can always appeal to the Problem Resolution Office if the agent says that the lien notice must be filed. See chapter 13. Note that even if the notice of lien is filed, the 1996 Taxpayer Bill of Rights allows the lien to be withdrawn if you enter into an installment agreement. This is not a right, but it certainly rises to the level of a strong congressional suggestion.

FILLING OUT THE COLLECTION INFORMATION
STATEMENT

The heart of the installment agreement is the Collection Information Statement, Form 433-A for individuals, 433-B for businesses. (There is also a short version of Form 433–A, called Form 433–F.)

You will find both forms at the end of chapter 6. Completing them is relatively easy as IRS forms go, but heed an old expression, "The devil is in the details." Remember also that you sign both forms under the penalties of perjury.

Let's start with Form 433-A. *Section I* asks for employment information. *Section II* lists personal and tax information, including the adjusted gross income from your last-filed federal tax return.

Starting with *Section III*, the form gets serious. *Line 13* calls for your bank accounts, including savings and loans, credit unions, IRAs, retirement plans, and certificates of deposit. List all, even if some are held jointly with your spouse or children. As long as you have the authority to withdraw from the account, it must be listed. Explain on page 4 if the account belongs to someone else under the law of your state.

The "balance" column means the checkbook balance on your last statement. (If this were an offer in compromise, you would list the average daily collected balance. See chapter 6.) Revealing your accounts of course gives the IRS valuable information about assets it can then more easily seize. But experience shows that agents do not use this form as a subterfuge. They genuinely try to work out an installment agreement or other arrangement to pay or compromise your taxes. If all else fails, however, they can certainly use the information. Still, you're only making their job easier; they could get the financial information by other means anyway.

Line 14 asks for your charge cards and lines of credit. This is the place to list all charge accounts, the monthly payments, the total amount owed, and available credit. Most of these types of cards are *unsecured,* meaning the card issuer has no security for the debt. The IRS gives credit for those components of your monthly payments that are for "necessary" living expenses. The general test is whether the payment is for your or your family's health and welfare or for the production of income. So, most credit card payments will not qualify. But food is a necessary living expense (within the IRS' limits), so if you charge your groceries, that amount would qualify. You bear the burden to show that a charge card payment is for a necessary expense. List the necessaries that you pay by plastic in part IV, discussed below.

If you have credit available, the IRS will sometimes ask you to borrow against it before allowing you to pay the rest of the tax in installments. Many people have already maxed out their credit cards or other credit sources, but often there is some room for further borrowing. It is not pleasant, but you're no worse off by essentially exchanging one debt (the taxes) for another (the credit card debt). Which is easier to bear? In most cases, it's easier to deal with the credit card company than with the IRS. Credit card loans usually cost 18 percent to 20 percent more than the 9 percent to 10 percent the IRS typically charges these days for interest, but if you include the tax penalties as well, the effective IRS interest rate starts to climb.

Line 15 asks for the location and contents of your safe deposit boxes, the valuables in which the IRS may ask you to sell. It can also ask you to inventory the box. You can refuse, but the Service can get a court order to seize the box. This doesn't often happen, but the power is there. The agency might even *want to* if you refuse to say what's inside the box.

Line 16 discusses your real estate. This category includes your home, land, rental property, and other real property you own. It does not mean partnership interests that invest in real estate, nor any corporations. These go on a different line. On line 16, describe the real estate, such as in the following two examples.

> *Example 1:* "Single family home, 123 Main Street, Anytown, USA, owned as tenants by the entirety."

> *Example 2:* "Townhouse in Breezy Acres Subdivision, 3 floors, owned as joint tenant with my brother."

Don't fill in the values or the mortgages here. These go in section V.

Line 17 asks about life insurance. The IRS considers only term life premiums a necessary expense, and then only if the premium is not "excessive." Experience varies on what is excessive. In some districts, the IRS will allow the premiums on $500,000 of face value. In others, it can be as low as $10,000.

If you have whole, universal, or some other investment-type policy, the extra premiums over a comparable term policy are not "necessary" in the IRS' view.

Line 18 asks for your securities, including stocks, bonds, mutual funds, money market funds, and government securities. State what they are, how much you have, who owns them, where they are located, and their current value.

Publicly traded stocks are easy enough. Call your broker or look in the paper. But stock in a small, closely held corporation like a family business is also a "security." Often such stock has no value, either because the company is not doing well (after all, that's why you owe back taxes), or because there is no market. Still, the form requires you to list *some* value, even if it's zero. Whatever value you list, be prepared to back it up. Chapter 6 summarizes the factors that influence the valuation of closely held stock for this purpose.

On *Line 19,* the IRS wants to know about court proceedings, that is, whether you have been sued or are suing anyone. If you are the plaintiff, your claim may be valuable. For example, suppose you owe $100,000 in taxes, and yesterday your lawyer filed suit against Big Burger because you spilled their scalding coffee on your lap. Your claim for $1 million for pain and suffering, plus actual damages of seventy-five cents for the coffee (hold the cream) is a valuable asset. Check the "yes" box and explain the details in the Additional Information section on page 4.

The Service also wants to know about repossessions and bankruptcies. Do you anticipate getting a raise? Check the "yes" box. Do you participate in a trust, estate, or profit-sharing plan? The IRS wants to know about that. All these are sources of collection either now or at some time in the future.

That completes section III.

Section IV, Assets and Liabilities, summarizes the data you have given and adds a few more details.

Line 20, "Cash," means the actual greenbacks you have in your pocket on the day you sign the statement.

Lines 21 and 22 carry forward the totals from *lines 13 and 18.*

Line 23 asks for the cash or loan value of insurance, a figure you carry over from *line 17.*

Line 24 calls for vehicles, including cars, trucks, and anything else with wheels. List the current market value, the amount owed, the equity (the difference between market value and amount owed), as well as the monthly payment and data on the lienholders.

The IRS wants this information for two reasons. On the helpful side, it may ask you to borrow against your car. If it's a clunker, the Service may conclude the car is not worth the debt. On the other side, it now knows what to look for if it wants to seize your car.

Line 25 sets out the numbers on your real property. List current market value, the amount you owe, and the equity. This is the place to list your mortgage payments and the payments on your rental and commercial properties. Real estate is often the first place the Service looks when it asks you to borrow against assets. Still, the IRS knows borrowing is hard even when you have good credit. And many lenders run for cover when they find you owe taxes. Still, some lenders lend against solid assets, such as a home, despite the IRS lien.

The IRS agents who look at these statements are human, too. They have mortgages; they pay bills. They understand your difficulties. They also know about things like loan-to-value ratios and second trusts. So don't be worried if line 25 seems to show a large "equity" in your home. In the real world, all of that equity may not be available to pay your taxes.

Line 26 asks for other assets. Here list jewelry, furniture, and anything else of value you own. Be conservative in your estimates. Most of these assets have a value to you that is greater than to others on the open market.

Line 27 carries over bank revolving credit from *line 14.*

On *line 28,* list other debts you owe such as bank loans, judgments, notes, and charge accounts not otherwise stated. Note the monthly payments and the name of the lender. Listing the monthly payment doesn't mean the IRS will allow the payment as "necessary," but the agency wants to know about it anyway. And if the expense is for health and welfare, or to produce income, it may well qualify as "necessary." Finally, list your delinquent federal taxes on *line 29,* and take the column totals on *line 30.*

That finishes section IV and brings you to the heart of the installment agreement process, the Monthly Income and Expense Analysis (section V). Remember that the agent will start with your gross income and subtract the expenses he thinks are "necessary" (therefore allowable for this purpose). The difference is what he will expect you to pay, every month, until your taxes are down to zero. So it is important to argue for every possible allowable expense.

Lines 31 through 40 ask you to list all income, including wages and salaries, interest and dividends, rentals, pensions, child support, alimony, and "other." This includes loans and gifts, even if nontaxable. List the gross amounts, without any deduction for taxes or anything else withheld from your paycheck.

LOOKING AT "NECESSARY" LIVING EXPENSES

Divide your expenses into two categories: necessary and conditional. Every expense on your financial statements is analyzed according to these two categories. The IRS typically allows only "necessary" expenses to be paid in the ordinary course of living, but it may allow conditional expenses if the taxes can be fully paid within three years. The guidelines also call for allowing one year to eliminate the expenses the IRS considers unnecessary.

An expense is "necessary" if it promotes the health and welfare of you and your family or if it is necessary for the production of income.

Lines 42 through 51 cover necessary living expenses. Your expenses for these categories are preapproved for allowance within certain limits. In chapter 6 you will find a chart of the expenses included in these categories. The IRS has established upper limits for three of these categories, depending on household income and size. The first is National Standard Expenses (line 42). National Standard Expenses are expenses for these items:

- apparel and services (shoes, clothing, laundry, dry cleaning, and shoe repair)

- food (all meals, home or away)

- housekeeping supplies (postage, stationery, laundry and cleaning supplies, household products, cleansing and toilet tissue, paper towels and napkins, lawn and garden supplies, and miscellaneous household supplies)

- personal care products and services (including hair care, hair cuts, oral hygiene products, shaving needs, electric personal care products and repairs of these, and similar items)

- miscellaneous expenses

Add these up, and you have your National Standard Expenses. How much is allowable depends on your gross income and how many people are in your household. The chart at the end of chapter 6 gives all the details. (It's based on Bureau of Labor Statistics numbers for 1992 through 1993.) For example, a single person grossing less than $830 per month is allowed $315 for these expenses. A family of four earning $5,830 per month or more is allowed $1,397. People sometimes chafe at these limits; after all, how can the IRS tell you how much to spend for your family's food? Agents respond that they do not, that you may spend as much as you like, but only certain amounts are "allowed" for purposes of calculating the monthly installment agreement.

You can usually allocate the expenses within this category without much problem. For instance, if you spend a little more on clothing and a little less on food, that's OK, as long as the totals are within the overall limit.

The second big expense is housing and utilities (line 43). This includes almost everything you would associate with housing: rent or mortgage, insurance, parking, necessary maintenance and repair, homeowner or condominium dues, and utilities. Utilities include such items as gas, electric, water, fuel, trash, and telephone. Again, if you are within the government's limits, the amounts should be accepted. But here, the limits are locally set because these expenses vary so much around the country. So call your local IRS office; an agent will let you know the local limits and may even send you a list.

The third big expense is transportation (line 44). Again, the local IRS districts set the limits. This category includes car payments (lease or purchase), insurance, maintenance, fuel, registration fees, inspection fees, parking fees, tolls, license fees, and public transportation. But like anything else, if you are spending on transportation that does not produce income or ensure health and welfare, it's not a "necessary" expense. So you can own two cars as long as you meet this test and don't exceed the local standard. Within that limit, the IRS does not care how you spend the money.

After these three big expense categories, the IRS sets no national or local standards, but the expense still has to be necessary for health or welfare, or for the production of income. Otherwise, it's a "conditional" expense, allowable only if the IRS will get all its money within three years.

Line 45 states health care expenses, clearly a necessary item for everyone. This category includes health insurance, doctor and dentist visits, prescription drugs, and medical supplies (including eyeglasses and contact lenses). It also means special items such as guide dogs, and probably also includes stair climbers and other medical devices that are necessary for health and welfare. The copay part of your medical bills is also included here.

Line 46 makes taxes a necessary expense. Here, the IRS has in mind your current federal, state, and local tax payments (including FICA and Medicare). If you are paying past-year taxes to a state or local government, these can also be "necessary," but you must work out the amount with the IRS.

Next come court-ordered payments (line 46). These can certainly be necessary for the production of income, for example a judgment a key supplier has against you. They may also be necessary for health and welfare, such as suit by a doctor for past fees. Court-ordered payments also include alimony and child support. It is up to you to prove the expense meets the "necessary" test. It always helps if the court-ordered payments are in place *before* the IRS files a notice of its tax lien.

Child and dependent care expenses go on *line 48.* The IRS is usually understanding about these. Day care, baby-sitting, nursery and preschool expenses are certainly included, but they must meet the health and welfare or production of income tests. For instance, a father who drops "little rascal" off at day care so he can work would have "necessary" day care or sitters' fees, if they are "reasonable" in amount. The IRS knows children are costly, but also warns that these costs can vary greatly. An agent will often ask if there are alternatives to private tutors or one-on-one day care.

Line 49 lists life insurance as a necessary expense. Only term policies are deemed necessary, and only for premiums the IRS does not consider excessive.

Line 50 allows an expense for "secured or legally perfected debts." This means judgments other people have against you, or other secured debts such as secured lines of credit. A secured charge card, or even a second mortgage, might fit here. Once again, the debt must meet the health, welfare, or production of income tests.

Finally, there are the "other expenses" (line 51) that life always throws your way, and here is where to list them.

How about education? For your children, the IRS seems to draw the line at private schools. It's unclear whether the "extras" we all pay for schooling our children, even in public schools, are "necessary." You can certainly urge that these extras are necessary for *your* health and welfare, as well as that of the kids.

Adult education expenses are necessary if they help you produce income. Examples would be real estate courses for real estate brokers, or continuing professional education courses for others. Master's or doctorate program expenses to train you for a new profession or field would also seem to fit this test, but the IRS has not said so publicly.

Expenses to care for handicapped children would normally be allowable, but be prepared to show that no public school or publicly available alternatives exist.

What else might the IRS allow? It can permit "conditional" expenses if you will still be able to pay in full within three years.

Accounting and legal fees. (Did you think the IRS would forget the poor, struggling tax professional trying to help you out of all this?) The IRS lets you pay your tax lawyer, accountant, or enrolled agent for representing you before the

IRS. Other professional fees must meet the health and welfare or production of income tests.

Charitable contributions. The IRS sees these as unnecessary unless they promote your health and welfare or are required for your job.

Education. Private school and college tuition are viewed as not necessary.

Voluntary retirement payments. These are allowable if your taxes can be paid within three years.

Other. Almost any other expense can be considered conditional. These might include family debts, other unsecured debts, credit card payments above the minimums, life insurance premiums that have an investment component (for example, whole life or universal life), boats, second or third cars, and so on.

That completes section V. You then sign and date the agreement (if the agent has asked for a signed agreement). Remember that the IRS can, in theory, still allow a conditional expense, as long as the numbers show you can pay the full tax within three years.

REVISING THE INSTALLMENT AGREEMENT

What if circumstances change? What if you default? If your income goes down or necessary expenses increase, call *and* write the IRS immediately. Ask for a lower installment agreement. Send whatever information the agent requests. If your income goes up or your expenses decline, you are not legally required to let the IRS know you can pay more. But you may want to. Paying more sometimes makes sense because of the high penalty and interest charges that accrue on your tax bill. In any event, the IRS has the right to review your agreement periodically, and often does.

The worst course is to default. Eighty percent of these agreements in fact default, with dire consequences. A default opens the door to full collection by the IRS, with its levy and seizure powers. True enough, you may reinstate a defaulted installment agreement at least once without much problem (cost: $24), but probably not more often than once.

You get a small break on these defaults, courtesy of the 1996 Taxpayer Bill of Rights. The IRS must give you thirty days' warning before terminating or changing your installment agreement. The agency routinely did this even before the new law. In fact, the default notice invites you to reinstate the agreement.

IF ONLY ONE SPOUSE OWES TAXES

It's quite common for either a husband or wife, but not both, to owe taxes. If both list their income on Form 433-A as the IRS requires, it looks like the IRS is collecting from the spouse who does not owe taxes by making one earner pay part of the other's tax bill. Still, the Service requires both earners to list total household income and expenses. The only exception occurs where you and your spouse handle and track expenses separately. Note that fact on Form 433-A and separate your income and expenses as best you can.

INSTALLMENT AGREEMENTS FOR BUSINESSES

Corporations, partnerships, and sole proprietors that owe back taxes (usually employment taxes) can also qualify for an installment agreement. The process is usually much simpler than with an individual. *Paying* is not easier, only the process. The same number of forms must be completed, but there is less debate over which expenses are "necessary."

A "C" corporation can owe income or payroll taxes. Partnerships and "S" corporations normally have no income taxes since their profits pass through to the owners individually. But they can owe payroll taxes, as can an unincorporated proprietor.

All these businesses must complete Form 433-B, the Collection Information Statement for Businesses.

The IRS looks at the business the same way it looks at an individual: what is the business' maximum ability to pay? But businesses in tax trouble are different from individuals in that they cannot always or easily sell assets to pay back taxes and still operate. Borrowing against business assets may also be hard. Moreover, a business often needs a cash flow cushion, especially when it has seasonal ups and downs. Many times, the IRS takes this into account; other times, you must argue long and hard for it. Also, the Service often pressures a business by investigating the officers and directors for their personal liability for payroll taxes. As a corporate officer, you may feel somewhat more motivated to find those past-due payroll taxes if the Service is reaching for your own wallet at the same time.

Form 433-B asks for typical introductory information: the owners, partners, officers, and major shareholders. *Section I* then calls for the latest tax return information, bank accounts, bank credit available, safe deposit boxes, real property, life insurance, and accounts and notes receivable. The IRS wants this information to see if the business can liquidate assets to pay the taxes, or for future reference if the IRS forces a liquidation. List the accounts and notes receivable, and in the "status" column indicate the extent to which they are collectible.

Section II of Form 433-B (lines 16 through 27) summarizes the assets and liabilities of the company. *Line 16* (Cash on Hand) is simply the money in the cash register. *Lines 17 through 20* carry over information on bank accounts, receivables, life insurance, loan values, and real property from section I.

Lines 21 through 24 require the listing of all other assets, including vehicles, machinery, and merchandise inventory. List the market value, the debt, the equity, and the monthly payment. Also show the lienholder or noteholder, as well as the due dates for the debts.

Section III, the Income and Expense Analysis, is the most important part of this form. *Lines 28 through 32* show the gross receipts of the business from all sources. *Lines 34 through 44* show all expenses. The IRS usually assumes that all business expenses are "necessary." But wave good-bye to personal expenses. For example, if the company pays for your personal Mercedes, that's not "necessary."

The form also requires a time period for which the income and expenses are stated. Many businesses choose one year; others, six months. Select a range that is typical, especially if you have a seasonal business. And try to choose an ending date within two to three months before the date you sign the statement.

If all of the income and expenses check out, the IRS totals them. The income minus the expenses is a net number that the Service will ask for every month.

Can the business afford it? Sometimes not, because of problems related to cash flow or seasonal fluctuations. Argue these points to the agent and ask for a lower amount for the installment agreement, possibly to be reconsidered when business picks up.

RULES OF THE ROAD

Installment agreements can be like slow medieval torture, or they can be a real blessing. It depends on your particular circumstances, the total to be paid, and the amount of the monthly payment. The big advantage of such an agreement is the peace and quiet it gives you. You know exactly how much you will have to pay, and when. As long as you comply, the IRS will leave you alone. That itself is worth a lot in terms of daily living and mental stability. But whether *you* want an installment agreement or the IRS forces you into one, remember these rules:

1. *Be prompt.* Don't miss deadlines. If you run up against a deadline, call and write the IRS in advance to request an extension. Give the IRS the data it wants *on time.*

2. *Be truthful.* You are signing these financial statements under the penalties of perjury. You can go to jail for a false statement. You'll rarely get away with falsehoods anyway, since the IRS knows all the tricks. Be complete in the data you provide.

3. *Don't take no for an answer.* Don't let one agent pressure you into an agreement you can't fulfill. Consider an appeal, or signing on for a short time, then appealing or asking for a reduced payment.

4. *Request courtesy and respect.* And give the same to the agents you deal with. Try not to be intimidated by threats that the agency will immediately start collection if you don't agree to the number it wants.

5. *Be patient.* These agreements can take weeks or months to negotiate, and years to pay.

6. *Prepare for tax lien filing.* If you owe more than $5,000 or you will take more than sixty days to pay in full, the IRS will likely file a Notice of Federal Tax Lien. Be prepared for this. If it will cause hardship, tell the agent why and ask for a delay. Under the 1996 Taxpayer Bill of Rights, you may request that the agent withdraw the notice of lien in exchange for an in-place installment agreement. It's not mandatory; but give it a try.

Form **433-D**
(Rev. February 1995)

Installment Agreement

check box if installment agreement fee was paid ☐

Name and address of taxpayer(s)	Social security or employer identification number
	(primary) *(secondary)*

Telephone number
(home)   *(business)*

Kinds of taxes *(form numbers)*   Tax periods

Amount owed as of _____   Earliest CSED
$

Employer *(name and address)*   Financial institutions *(names and addresses)*

For assistance:
Call 1-800-829-1040 or write:

_____ Service Ctr.

City, State and Zip Code

I/We agree that the federal taxes shown above, **PLUS ALL PENALTIES AND INTEREST PROVIDED BY LAW,** will be paid as follows:

$ _____ will be paid on _____ and $ _____ will be paid

no later than the _____ of each month thereafter until the total liability is paid in full. I/we also agree that the above

installment payment will be increased or decreased as follows:

check box if pre-assessed modules included ☐

				AGREEMENT LOCATOR NUMBER: ___ ___ ___ ___
Date of increase *(or decrease)*	/ /	/ /		*(circle)*
Amount of increase *(or decrease)*	$			0 No future action is required

New installment amount	$			5 Financial review date: ___ ___ / ___ ___
				       m m y y
				 6 SCCB — Monitor ES compliance:
				       Amount per quarter $ _____
				       (If amount(s)/quarters will vary, provide details.)

Conditions of this agreement:
- We must receive each payment by the date shown above; if you have a problem, contact us immediately.
- This agreement is based on your current financial condition. We may change or cancel it if our information shows that your ability to pay has changed significantly.
- We may cancel this agreement if you don't give us updated financial information when we ask for it.
- While this agreement is in effect, you must file all federal tax returns and pay any taxes you owe on time.
- We will apply your federal or state tax refunds (if any) to the amount you owe until it is fully paid. (This includes the Alaska Permanent Fund dividend for Alaska residents.)
- You must pay a $43 installment agreement fee.
- If agreement defaults, you must pay a $24 reinstatement fee if agreement is reinstated.

Additional Conditions: *(To be completed by IRS)*

- If you don't meet the conditions of this agreement, we will cancel it, and may collect the entire amount you owe by levy on your income, bank accounts or other assets, or by seizing your property.
- We will cancel this agreement at any time if we find that collection of the tax is in jeopardy.
- We will apply all payments on this agreement in the best interest of the United States.
- This agreement may require managerial approval. If it is not approved, you will be notified.
- **A NOTICE OF FEDERAL TAX LIEN** *(check one)*
  - ☐ **HAS ALREADY BEEN FILED**
  - ☐ **WILL BE FILED IMMEDIATELY**
  - ☐ **WILL BE FILED WHEN TAX IS ASSESSED**
  - ☐ **MAY BE FILED IF THIS AGREEMENT DEFAULTS**

Your signature	Title *(if corporate officer or partner)*	Date	Originator's name, title and IDRS assignment number *(or district):*
Spouse's signature *(if a joint liability)*		Date	
Agreement examined or approved by *(signature, title, function)*		Date	Originator Code:

YOU MAY HAVE YOUR INSTALLMENT AGREEMENT PAYMENT DEDUCTED FROM YOUR CHECKING ACCOUNT EACH MONTH (DIRECT DEBIT); IF YOU CHOOSE THIS OPTION, FOLLOW THE DIRECTIONS ON THE BACK OF YOUR COPY OF THIS FORM.

If you agree to Direct Debit, initial here:

_____

and attach a blank voided check.

- I (we) authorize the IRS and the depository (bank) identified on the attached voided check to deduct payments (debit) from my (our) checking account or correct errors on the account. This authorization remains in effect until I (or either of us) notify IRS in writing to stop or until the liability covered by this agreement is satisfied.
- I (we) understand that if the depository is unable to honor IRS's request for payment due to insufficient funds in my (our) account on the payment due date I (we) will be charged a penalty of $15 or two percent of the payment request, whichever is greater. If the payment request is for less than $15, the penalty is the amount of the request.

CAT. NO. 16644M   **Part 1 — IRS Copy**   Form **433-D** (Rev. 2-95)

Chapter 8

≈≈≈

JEOPARDY AND TERMINATION
ASSESSMENTS

One of the most frequent complaints people make about the IRS is how grindingly slow it is to act. Don't tell that to anyone who has looked down the barrel of a jeopardy or termination assessment. Jeopardy and termination assessments are like nuclear weapons delivered by a stealth bomber. The damage is devastating, and you rarely see it coming. True enough, the IRS doesn't use these weapons very often, mostly reserving them for criminal cases or cases of illegal or unreported income. Still, the Service resorts to jeopardy and termination assessments hundreds of times each year, and won't hesitate to use these powerful weapons in any case where it feels collection is at great risk. Even normal folks must sometimes look over their shoulder when they owe back taxes and try to plan the sale of their assets.

A jeopardy or termination assessment is simply an assessment made very quickly because the IRS has officially determined that collection of the tax is in jeopardy. Termination assessments are so called because the IRS "terminates" your current tax year immediately, makes the assessment, and proceeds to collect it. Jeopardy assessments are for past years where the taxes have not yet been assessed. In a normal, nonjeopardy case, the Service cannot begin to collect until it has taken these steps: audited your tax return, proposed a tax bill, allowed your appeal rights, allowed you to go to court, and, after the resolution of the court case, assessed the tax and issued a bill. That assessment process takes months or years. In a jeopardy case, all the in-between steps are eliminated. It takes only hours. Even after the agency assesses you, court rights are preserved, but, in the meantime, the IRS has protected the revenue by seizing everything in sight.

> *Example:* Horace was in the marijuana production business. One day, the local police raided his digs and found fifty pounds of the stuff, $18,000 in currency, and drug paraphernalia. One police officer was courteous enough to call the IRS during the search at Horace's house (law enforcement authorities often cooperate by tipping each other off). The IRS agent headed out to watch the search in progress. Then he checked to see if Horace had filed tax returns (he had not), found another house he owned, and located other cash transactions. He also checked with experts, learning that the wholesale value of the marijuana was between $250 and $400 per pound. Finally, the agent found that Horace had bought an Audi. That was enough for the IRS, which jeopardy-assessed $52,000 against Horace. He challenged it in court, but the court sustained the assessment in full.

Legally, the agency can make a jeopardy assessment if it officially decides that (1) you are about to leave the United States; (2) you are hiding your assets, transferring them, or otherwise putting them beyond the reach of the government; or (3) your financial solvency is in peril.

As you might expect, drug busts often generate jeopardy assessments. So do gambling raids where gambling is illegal. Noncitizens of the United States who appear ready to flee the country can be the subject of jeopardy assessments, and it would not be surprising if the government jeopardy-assessed people who planned to give up their citizenship to avoid taxes.

The Service determines you are about to flee the country by looking for a number of signs: your citizenship, whether you have a passport, and previous criminal convictions indicating that you might leave. It also checks whether you are liquidating assets, whether some other jurisdiction has warrants out for you, and even whether you have bought airline tickets. The Service knows you are concealing assets when you transfer ownership, use aliases, destroy or conceal records, or use a lot of cash.

In a jeopardy case that arises from a drug bust, police officers usually find cash and drugs. The experts estimate the purchase value of the drugs, add that to the cash, and advise the IRS. IRS special agents check for filed tax returns. If there are none (and not many drug dealers file true returns, or *any* returns), the agents make a termination or jeopardy assessment by telephone, swoop down, seize the cash, and apply it to the assessed taxes. In short order, the government has $100,000. Theoretically, the suspects could contest the assessment in tax court or federal district court, but the IRS counts on them to be otherwise occupied.

> *Example:* Karl and his sister lived in a small house in Denver. The police became interested in this location, and watched it, watched it, watched it. One sunny morning, Karl left the house. A short time later, the police raided the place. They found pounds of cocaine and more than $500,000 in cash. Documents found at the house bore Karl's name and referred to many sales of cocaine, with some transactions valued at more than $2 million. But Karl was not a U.S. citizen, only a resident alien who had been to the United States three other times. The police also had a confidential informant who told them where else to look. That search turned up a safe deposit box with more cash.

The IRS terminated Karl's tax year and assessed $1.6 million based on the street value of the cocaine. Karl ran to federal court for relief, but the court found that it was reasonable to assume he would quickly leave the country unless the assessment were made. The assessment stood.

Jeopardy assessments are not exclusive for people who always operate outside the law. Let's say you anticipate a huge tax bill and you begin to put property in the names of your children, friends, or relatives, or you transfer property overseas. Absolutely nothing prevents the IRS from determining jeopardy exists, and it might well be justified in doing so.

> *Example:* Archibald, a surgeon practicing in a major city for many years, had a wife, five children, and a dog. From time to time, he made trips to a European country to visit his elderly, infirm mother and to pay tribute to his deceased father. There was only one little problem. The IRS thought he evaded paying taxes on millions in medical fees over three years, and that he used company money for personal expenses, hiding them as "business expenses" on his return. Also, while the IRS was investigating him, he sold all the real estate he owned and hid the nearly $1

million in sales proceeds. Now, you might ask, what tipped off the IRS? Apparently, it had something to do with the agent's obtaining copies of canceled checks, endorsements, notes on the checks, irregular second endorsements, and bank deposits, as well as the real estate liquidations. These problems, plus the trips abroad and the disappearance of funds, all showed that the making of these assessments was reasonable.

If Archibald had managed to get all his assets out of reach and appeared about to depart the United States, the IRS could resort to a writ *ne exeat republica,* a writ of civil arrest that could have held him until his taxes were paid or a suffficient bond posted.

FIGHTING A JEOPARDY OR TERMINATION ASSESSMENT

You can rarely see a jeopardy assessment coming, so it's hard to fight one before it explodes. But afterward, you have some limited rights. Within five days after the IRS makes the assessment, it sends an "information statement" outlining its reasons. Within thirty days, you can ask for the IRS to review the assessment, usually a useless act. Within sixteen days after the request, you can sue the government in federal district court to review the jeopardy assessment. The court has jurisdiction to determine whether (1) the making of the assessment is reasonable and (2) the assessed amounts are appropriate. Almost every case results in a victory for the government, so they are rarely seen these days. Here is an example of this type of case.

> *Example:* Curtis led a double life. Publicly, he was a low-profile citizen. Privately, he had a small "business on the side," conducted in a secret room behind a fiberboard wall covered by tennis rackets, snow shovels, and tools. The room remained secret until the local police somehow learned of it and arrested Curtis for gambling, specifically, running a bookmaking operation. He pleaded guilty to a state-level charge. The IRS then woke up. Based on Curtis's secret journals, betting slips, and other evidence, the IRS said that he had been in business for more than two years and took in $10,000 in bets every week. The average for one sixteen-day period the IRS examined was $5,100 *per day.* The agents multiplied that figure by 365 (no vacations for Curtis?), and the resulting figure by

4.5 percent, as Curtis's reasonable profit margin, coming up with unreported income on which the taxes, penalties, and interest totaled $150,000. Curtis challenged all of this in court, and was able to get a reduction because the IRS had selected his "busy season," fall football time, on which to extrapolate the assessment. Still, the court sustained most of the assessment.

Where the government's jeopardy assessment springs from such a drug or gambling raid, little if anything will undo the government's action. But if the government has jumped the gun and unfairly jeopardy-assessed anyone else, there are remedies even besides the court suit described above. You can always file Form 911, requesting a Taxpayer Assistance Order. Chapter 13 describes how to do this. You can also go up the chain of command, all the way to the district director of Internal Revenue for your district. That official must personally review the circumstances to approve any jeopardy assessment in advance, so he has already said no to you once. But maybe the agents got the facts wrong or there are mitigating circumstances. It does not hurt to place these phone calls and write letters, unless doing so would incriminate you. (This type of action always assumes truthful statements to the government. Any false statement to a government official, oral, written, or by demonstrative conduct, is punishable as perjury.)

Finally, there are more leisurely remedies, such as the normal tax court suit filed to contest the government's assessment.

The jeopardy and termination assessment provisions remain among the most powerful of IRS collection weapons. You can rarely anticipate them, and more rarely still can you fight them. But you can contest them after they are made. If the IRS has truly erred and you can prove it, you may be able to recover your money and property.

Chapter 9

〜∞〜

YOUR WORST (TAX) NIGHTMARE, PART 1—THE NONFILER

DOES IT REALLY HAPPEN?

Every year, around April 15, five million to ten million Americans are reminded of a nagging headache: they have not filed or will not file federal and state income tax returns.

Most nonfilers think they are alone, or at worst members of a small, private club. After all, nonfiling is not something you brag about. There's no Nonfilers Anonymous. The numbers involve some guesswork, but the IRS is fairly confident about the five million to ten million figure.

For several years before 1991, the IRS studied nonfiling at many levels. A national task force investigated the problem and recommended action. The result was a national nonfiler program that began on October 1, 1992, and continues today. More on this program later.

The IRS discovered that nonfilers come in all shapes and sizes. They are blue collar and white collar, real estate brokers and computer executives, wage earners and independent contractors. Nonfilers count among their ranks many doctors, lawyers, even accountants. The only apparent common factor is that most nonfilers are men, but even that "rule" has many exceptions.

The average delinquency period was three years. But tax professionals have seen nonfiler cases of up to twenty years, and more. Four, five, or six years of nonfiling is quite common in cases where nonfilers seek the help of a tax professional.

"THEY'LL NEVER FIND ME! WILL THEY?"

Everyone has heard a story of "Joe" or "Jane," who failed to file tax returns in three, four, five, or more years and has "gotten away with it." Sometimes the story is absolutely true. Other times the number of nonfiling years seems to grow with the number of people who pass the story on. True enough, there *are* flagrant violators out there, even people who brag about nonfiling. Sooner or later, the IRS is bound to catch up with you. No one can hide forever. In these days when everyone's vital statistics seem to be on the Internet, the IRS particularly has many ways to find you. The Form W-2 from your employer tells the IRS who you are and where you work. Form 1099 tells them who paid you money, where your mortgage is placed, and whether you received barter income. It says where and how much you received in dividends or interest, whether you received a state tax refund, and many other things. Each of these reporting devices can be tracked back to find you.

Even if you don't file a tax return for one year, the IRS will look at the last one you did file to try to find you.

But they don't give up if these sources run dry, Do you have credit cards? These may often be canvassed by Social Security number. The IRS simply asks the credit card agency, "Give me the name and address of anyone with a Social Security number 000-00-0000."

The IRS can also try to locate you through other agencies: the military, the Social Security Administration, the Immigration and Naturalization Service, even the telephone directories. In fact, there are at least three varieties of telephone and geographic directories it can use. One is the familiar "white pages." Another is a "criss-cross directory," which is indexed by street. There are others. The Service can also use information from credit reporting agencies and consumer reporting agencies, all of which track their clients and customers by name and sometimes by Social Security number.

For these reasons, anyone who had not filed a tax return is sitting on a ticking time bomb.

REASONS OR EXCUSES?

Why do people not file? The reasons range from the absurd to the heartrending. Nonfilers clearly have a capacity for denial, taking quick and easy refuge in self-deluding excuses. Let's look at some of the most common ones that cover most cases.

> *Excuse Number 1:* "Filing can wait—the government owes *me* money." This nonfiler is saying that more than enough money was withheld from paychecks, or was paid in estimated payments, to cover his taxes. Sometimes that's true. But the nonfiler can't possibly know this unless he goes through the complex calculations on a tax return to the bottom line, finding he owes nothing or is owed a refund.

On top of that, the IRS often has a nasty surprise for the nonfiler who thought the government owed *him:* the agency has the legal authority to file a return for you if you don't file one. The IRS would much rather *you* file, but it won't hesitate to file a return for you if you don't. Then, watch out! You thought you were married? The IRS assigns you "married filing separately" status, the worst possible assumption in terms of the tax rates. You thought you had five dependent children? The IRS assumes none. At most it gives you one exemption—yourself. (That is, it grudgingly admits you are alive.) Did you pay megabucks in mortgage interest? Did you have huge deductible medical expenses? Did you pay real estate and state income taxes? Maybe, but the IRS will assume you did not. In short, it makes every assumption against your interest and in its favor.

The result: a Substitute for Return on which your W-2 withholding comes nowhere near the amount necessary to cover the taxes—as calculated by the IRS. Moreover, many nonfilers are paid as independent contractors, or have other "Form 1099" income on which nothing was withheld. Either way, you get a whopping bill, topped off by a 25 percent late-filing penalty, a late-payment penalty, and interest. These bills are major shocks to taxpayers who hid their heads in the sand, mumbling, "*They* owe *me.*" True enough, with much pushing and shoving, you can get the IRS to reconsider the Substitute for Return, but it's heavy lifting, and in the meantime, bad things happen. The IRS won't wait around for your answer. Agents will go out and collect! They will file notices of federal tax lien, levy on your bank accounts, sell your assets, or garnish your wages. You could even lose your job if the IRS contacts your employer and the boss sees your problem as a terminable offense.

"But I can file for bankruptcy and discharge these taxes," the nonfiler says.

Possibly. Income taxes can indeed be discharged in bankruptcy if you meet certain tests. Chapter 12 covers this in detail. But under current law, you cannot discharge income taxes that the IRS bills you on a Substitute for Return. Even if you file a true return, you must wait at least two years before filing for bankruptcy; otherwise, no discharge.

> *Excuse Number 2:* "I didn't have the money to pay." Many taxpayers who owe money on April 15 in fact don't have enough to pay. They reason that bad things will happen immediately if they file a "balance due" return. Some even think they're not legally required to file if they can't pay, a cruel myth. Years ago, if you filed but didn't pay, the IRS was somewhat slow to act. Even now, nothing bad happens right away. Instead, a series of notices issues requesting payment of the tax, interest, and penalties shown on the return. The tone of these notices gets progressively nastier, and if you do nothing, eventually the IRS collectors move into action.

But a delinquent taxpayer may take many steps to avoid enforced collection, even if he owes money on April 15. By far the worst choice is not to file, because, among other things, you will automatically be subject to the late-filing penalty (5 percent per month up to 25 percent) for every month or part of a month a return is late. That penalty is easy to avoid—simply file on time—but hard to abate. (Chapter 18 explains this and other penalties, and how to avoid or abate them.)

Filing a balance due return does mean the late-payment penalty will be imposed, but that's only .5 percent to 1 percent per month. It defies common sense to risk criminal prosecution and a 25 percent late-filing penalty when you can opt for the 1 percent late-payment penalty. True enough, the day of reckoning for the balance due is advanced somewhat if you file on time, but that's preferable to having the extra lead weight of a late-filing penalty around your ankles.

> *Excuse Number 3:* "I'm getting my records together." Variations are: "I never got my W-2," or "I'm waiting for a Form 1099," or "I have all my records, I just haven't organized them, or "The dog ate them." If records truly are missing, you can always file for an extension; the first one, to August 15, is automatic. But these are *your* records, and the law says you have a duty to keep them in sufficient shape so you can file on time. (It's not that hard. Chapter 28 gives you a guide)

These are only some of the excuses. Dozens of others have been used, limited only by the nonfiler's imagination.

REASONS THAT WORK

Good excuses for late filing, what the law calls "reasonable cause," do exist. You are not relieved of the legal duty to file and pay the tax and interest. It just means that there was a good enough reason to excuse some of the penalties. Chapter 18 lists the most common, "IRS approved," reasonable causes. In the real world, it's rare to encounter most of them. The one that comes up most often is the serious illness of the taxpayer or a member of his immediate family.

The IRS in fact understands and accepts the plight of some nonfilers. Its own studies have mirrored the experience of tax practitioners, finding that many people don't file because some terrible, traumatic event or series of events so debilitated them that it caused the nonfiling. Chronicles of these events read somewhat like a soap opera, but they are the stuff of real life, and the IRS understands them if you document them properly and in detail.

> *Examples:* A nonfiler suffered through a terrible youthful marriage, a bitter separation, mental and physical abuse. The other spouse also extorted money over a period of years because of the nonfiler's infidelity. All of this culminated in a bitter divorce. This nonfiler had reasonable cause to abate the late-filing and late-payment penalties.

Another successful case might be the nonfiler who became addicted to drugs or alcohol, sliding into ever deeper states of dependence and depression leading almost to suicide, before turning her life around through a support group such as Alcoholics Anonymous. A third example might be the struggling salesperson who was the sole support of his mother and father. The parents came down with simultaneous cases of terminal, inoperable cancer, and died within one year of each other. A fourth example is a business disaster: the nonfiler had put heart, soul, and all of his money into a venture, to the neglect of family and friends, only to have the entire business collapse in a period of several months.

In each case, the IRS ruled there was "reasonable cause" for late filing.

These types of reasons for nonfiling are often buried deep, with roots in childhood. Events from early life often show illness or personality traits that, combined with more recent causes, resulted in the nonfiling. When events like these overwhelm someone, even the IRS seems to understand why filing a tax return becomes of secondary importance.

THE IRS' NONFILER PROGRAM

On October 1, 1992, the IRS launched a nationwide campaign to entice non-filers back into the ranks of the taxpaying and return-filing public. Spearheading that effort was a nationwide task force of two thousand revenue agents and tax auditors who looked for the nonfilers and tried to bring them back into the system. The IRS mandated each of its local districts to begin the program, and publicized the program in speeches and news releases. This program continues today.

For whom is the IRS searching? Ideally, everyone who hasn't filed for one or more years. But realistically, the IRS targets only "highly productive" nonfilers. Congress used the term "high income" in hearings on this topic, but the IRS is not necessarily looking for high income, only high taxes. It's going for the gold. While high income often means high taxes, the IRS casts the nonfiler net more widely. It is fishing in affluent neighborhoods and professional groups and among categories of expense such as mortgage interest to target returns that will yield the most money. In its first six months of operation, the nonfiler program brought in about six hundred thousand delinquent returns.

The IRS' own studies and its manual name these callings as most likely to harbor nonfilers and produce the most tax:

1. manufacturing apparel

2. trucking and warehousing

3. wholesale groceries and related products

4. legal services

5. wholesale dry goods and apparel

6. manufacturing and machinery (excluding electrical)

7. mining and quarrying

8. general construction

9. retail automotive dealers

10. laundry and dry cleaning

11. automobile repair

The agency's computers augment the effort. For many years, IRS computers have matched information reports such as forms W-2 and 1099 to filed returns. That's one of the ways the IRS checks whether you have reported all income and taken the correct credit for withheld taxes. So, if the computer checks a W-2 or 1099 against your account and finds no return on file, it generates a notice and several follow-up notices if you don't respond to the first. These notices mean you have been discovered.

When you totally fail to respond, the computer concludes, "You just don't get it," and refers your case to an agent on the task force. The agent or another IRS representative will call, write, or visit—and begin the process of getting you to file willingly, or not.

When the IRS representative catches up with you, he or she will make a judgment as to whether your case should be referred for criminal investigation and possible prosecution. Statistically, few of these cases are referred for prosection, but you never know if yours will be the unlucky one. The agent will typically look for "badges of fraud," that is, illegal sources of income, the hiding of assets, a complete refusal to cooperate, transfers of property, and the like. High-dollar cases, and taxpayers who deal in cash, are prime targets for criminal investigation. But everyone, whether prosecuted or not, will then enter the nonfiler system.

The assigned revenue officer also will look for a pattern of delinquency. That is, are more than two years involved? Is the taxpayer well educated, so that it is reasonable to presume he or she fully understood the obligation to file? Does the taxpayer appear to owe substantial tax? The revenue officer will also consider these in deciding whether to refer your case for criminal investigation.

The nonfiler program has clear benefits if you come forward voluntarily. By official policy, the IRS will not recommend criminal prosecution of a nonfiler who comes forward on his own. Of course, full payment of any tax due will stop the running of interest and penalties. The agency is also more open to working with voluntary confessors on agreements to pay any tax due in installments. It may even forgive some of the tax, penalties, or interest under the offer in compromise program discussed in chapter 6. Most nonfilers don't end up owing a hopeless amount, even for very old tax years. In fact, among all tax delinquents (including those who filed on time but simply owe money), fully 97 percent qualify to pay their taxes in installments over a reasonable time, usually six to thirty-six months.

This is all part of the new look that the IRS wants the public to accept: firm, no-nonsense, businesslike attempts to get taxpayers back into the system. The IRS' new businesslike attitude toward overdue accounts means it will take steps within the law to make it easier for you to pay, file returns, and pay taxes now and in the future. In short: compliance, not compulsion.

Also, for voluntary confessors, the IRS has said it would go easier on the penalties, perhaps more readily concluding that your reasons for not filing are credible and reasonable. But if you have to be dragged, kicking and screaming, into compliance, the IRS will skeptically eye any excuses you may offer.

If you have already received a phone call, a letter, or other notice from the IRS, it's not too late to comply voluntarily. But you must respond immediately to be considered a "voluntary" filer.

IF YOU DON'T FILE

When the IRS catches you, you'll either go to jail, possibly pay big penalties, or both. In most cases, the agency doesn't really want to throw you in jail, only to prompt you to file and pay. So it will content itself with making a Substitute for Return and collecting the resulting tax. It's rare that the IRS totally throws the book at someone for nonfiling, but the agency is quite satisfied with several big penalties.

The agent will, of course, try his best to get you to file. If you snub your nose, the agent may also issue a summons to you, requiring your appearance and the production of your business and personal books and records. Failure to obey the summons can result in civil or criminal contempt charges, with the usual and customary jail sentences. Finally, the agent can file a return for you and sign it himself, though in most cases, the Substitute for Return is used.

The strongest IRS weapon, criminal prosecution, is the biggest fear of many repeat nonfilers. Nonfiling is a federal misdemeanor (not a felony) punishable by up to one year in prison and/or a fine of up to $25,000 plus prosecution costs, for *each year* that you willfully failed to file. All states that impose income taxes have analogous criminal penalties. Sometimes, if a nonfiler persists for a number of years, the IRS will prosecute the case as "attempted tax evasion," a felony carrying a maximum fine of $100,000, five years in prison, or both (plus prosecution costs), for each year involved. Even a willful failure to pay any tax is, in theory, a criminal offense, though that's rarely prosecuted.

The IRS' approach to prosecution is both carrot and stick. Most years, around April 15, the agency announces a list of about one hundred "chosen" individuals who have been or will be indicted for failure to file. In all, the Service prosecutes about one thousand nonfiling cases each year. That's small compared to the estimated 5 million to 10 million nonfilers nationwide. So the IRS prefers to prosecute only the most flagrant cases.

To add to your incentive to file, Congress in 1989 enacted the "fraudulent failure to file" penalty, equal to 15 percent of the tax due per month, up to a maximum of 75 percent. This penalty applies in cases where there are indications of fraud or attempted evasion, but not quite enough to merit criminal prosecution.

WHAT'S A NONFILER TO DO?

It's April 15. You sit there, mired in records and paralyzed in the third year of nonfiling. The IRS has not *yet* caught you. But every day the newspaper features another story about the IRS, the filing deadline, the filing season, or something else to remind you of your secret. Your nerves are shot. You sweat. So, you make up your mind. The time has finally come. You are going to catch up. How to start?

Beyond question, the first step is: Get help. You can't do it yourself. You may need anything from a gentle nudge to a major transfusion of courage, but you need *something*. The mild encouragement of a spouse or friend, a few wise words from a tax professional, or assistance from a tax attorney or even from the IRS itself may be enough. But you've procrastinated too long—someone else needs to know about your problem, and ride herd on you until you get the job done.

A five-part filing program like this may ease the way:

1. prompt and full disclosure to a lawyer or other tax helper

2. preparation of the returns quickly and accurately—by a lawyer, accountant, enrolled agent, or other professional tax return preparer

3. a plan to pay or settle any taxes the returns show are due

4. if necessary, a full and powerful statement of reasonable cause for nonfiling

5. luck (but sometimes you can make your own)

Many nonfilers find they need a team composed of a return preparer (such as an accountant or enrolled agent) and an attorney. The preparer's task is to prepare the returns. If necessary, the attorney can review them from a legal perspective and present them effectively to the IRS. A useful rule of thumb is: If three or more years are involved, first see a lawyer experienced in tax matters. Three or more years of nonfiling increases the chances of criminal prosecution, so you may need criminal defense work or legal advice on the civil penalties in addition to accounting help.

Also, the attorney-client privilege shields most discussions you have with an attorney. Nonattorneys, such as CPAs, enrolled agents, and other preparers, lack that shield against the ears of the federal government. The IRS can force these non-lawyer professionals to reveal anything you say to them, and you may be sure what you say can and will be used against you. Therefore, route all discussions through an attorney at least until it's clear that the likelihood of prosecution is small and a client privilege unnecessary. But beware: Even if you go first to an attorney, not all communications will be privileged. Your lawyer can advise you on this point.

Your lawyer can also explain in detail the civil and criminal penalties and discuss the likelihood of criminal prosecution (small if the returns are filed quickly and before the IRS catches you). However, civil penalties for late filing and late payment are certain to be imposed if you owe taxes. Sometimes the IRS will suspect fraud and assess additional tax penalties unless you can prove reasonable cause for the nonfiling.

Once this disclosure process is under way, keep it on track, a task often harder than it sounds. The nonfiler excels at procrastinating. Sure, you are very motivated when you first come forward. You make ironclad promises about quickly gathering far-flung records, filing the returns, and fully cooperating. But once the nonfiler is into the process, almost invariably he becomes complacent and reassured—the very syndrome that caused him not to file in the first place. Delay ensues. Sometimes it never ends.

After you evaluate the danger of criminal prosecution, the next step is to prepare and file the returns. Those returns must be accurate the first time and totally defensible if they are audited. But they must also be prepared quickly, especially where your lawyer advises prosecution is likely if the IRS catches you before you file. The preparer should lean toward conservatism, taking all lawful, provable deductions but avoiding those for which there is inadequate proof. Above all else, every penny of gross income must be reported. The attorney or preparer will often check behind the client by performing one or more indirect analyses of the correctness of the return and the gross income reported.

Even as you prepare the returns, it's important to develop a plan to pay or compromise any back taxes. That's because the IRS will demand payment a short few weeks or months after the returns are filed. (If there is no balance due, this is not a problem. But often, and unexpectedly, there *is* a tax due.) Addressing the collection problem up front helps persuade the IRS that you are sincere and committed. That perception, in turn, may limit civil penalties and ease the pain of payment.

Also, remember state returns, which normally follow and parallel the federal returns. The state tax liability can also be large, so include it in your thinking.

The nonfiler for three or more years can also discuss the reasons the returns were not filed. In many cases, exploring those reasons in depth unearths traumatic events that caused the nonfiling. If the penalties are large enough, it may be cost-effective to prepare a detailed affidavit explaining the reasons, with any supporting documentation and statements you can find. So, make a judgment about how far to go and how much effort and money to spend on a showing of reasonable cause.

WHAT'S "REASONABLE" CAUSE FOR NOT FILING?

Officially the IRS will accept eight reasons for filing a late return. These are:

1. the post office delayed your return;

2. you filed the return in the wrong IRS office;

3. you relied on erroneous information given to you by an IRS officer or employee;

4. the taxpayer died or was seriously ill, or there was death or serious illness in the immediate family;

5. the taxpayer was unavoidably absent;

6. the taxpayer's business or business records were destroyed by fire or other casualty;

7. the IRS didn't supply the right forms in enough time to file; and

8. you tried to get help or information to prepare your return from the IRS, but its representative didn't meet with you.

Of these reasons, the first two, postal delays and filing in the wrong office, are self-explanatory, but you must prove the postal delay. It's easier to prove filing in the wrong IRS office because that office sends the return back to you. (Keep the envelopes!)

If the IRS gave you the wrong tax information and you relied on it, that's reasonable cause. Even the IRS makes mistakes. Millions of people call in for advice every year (usually between January 2 and April 15). Studies consistently show error rates in this advice of more than 10 percent. But the excuse, "I relied on the IRS," is very narrow. The IRS has to have given you advice that you "reasonably" relied on. So if the advice is totally off base, you won't have reasonable cause even if you relied on that advice. Also, the information on which the advice was based must have been accurate and adequate. And the burden to prove all of this is on you!

The fourth reason—death or serious illness—is one the IRS and practitioners see often. As noted above, it can be mental or physical illness, addiction to drugs, mental trauma caused by life events such as a business disaster, divorce, or separation. Serious illness has to be proved, credibly and completely. It must also cover the periods of nonfiling.

Unavoidable absence is also narrow. Very few absences are deemed "unavoidable" for this purpose. Records destroyed? Be prepared to prove date, time, and place, furnish police, fire, or insurance reports, and tell what efforts you made to get copies or recreate them.

IN THE END

When all is said and done and you are back in the tax-filing and tax-paying system, you may find to your relief that you owe no back taxes. You and the IRS simply have a newfound relationship, and life goes on.

But if you owe money, you then have to deal with the Collection Division. It's not as bad as it sounds, even though the IRS has many weapons at its command and you have limited defenses. In the last five years, the IRS, without in any way getting soft on collection, has definitely made paying taxes less painful by many different programs and techniques. These include forgiving some taxes altogether if the IRS concludes you will never be able to pay them.

Chapter 10

⎯⎯⎯⎯ ⬿⬾ ⎯⎯⎯⎯

YOUR WORST (TAX) NIGHTMARE, PART 2— PERSONAL LIABILITY FOR CORPORATE PAYROLL TAXES (THE TRUST FUND RECOVERY PENALTY)

SETTING THE SCENE

Nineteen ninety-five had been a banner year for Wonder Widgets, Inc. Sales had finally hit the $1 million mark, an all-time high. The last calendar quarter (October, November, and December) had been exceptionally good, capped by a great Christmas rush. Sure, some of Wonder Widgets' customers were a bit slow to pay, but the money always came in, enough for a great Christmas party and bonuses for Ed Wonder, the president, Ben Bighthard, the controller, and Penny Pencil, the chief bookkeeper.

Early in January, Ed Wonder called a meeting with Bighthard, Pencil, and the sales force. He did this every year. This time, he was feeling good.

"How do we look for this year?" he asked.

"Things look great," said Sam Sellmore, the chief sales representative. "We've just gotten three big orders from the U.S. government for thirty thousand boxes of widgets. You can buy a widget down the street for ten bucks, but ours are so good, they sell for $900! You may have to bring on more workers or order new machines. Certainly, you'll need more steel and other parts."

"Great," said Wonder. "Our slow-paying customers will always pay, and I know that 1996 is going to be a terrific year."

Bighthard jumped in. "Not so fast. You know we have a lot of bank debt to service, and there was that little IRS payroll tax problem last year. We had to pay a 10 percent penalty for late deposit of payroll taxes because we didn't get enough money in to pay anything but net payroll. Let's be careful."

"Nonsense," scoffed Wonder. "That was an exception. In fact, I'll get out in the field myself a lot more this year to help with sales and servicing of our widgets. While I'm gone, you and Penny can mind the store. Go ahead and make the federal tax deposits, but if you're short at the end of a week, don't worry. Just pay our people their net pay. They'll never feel the difference, and we'll always get the money in later."

January began with a record snowfall and the beginning of a severe recession. Wonder was in the field for most of the month. He kept in touch with Bighthard, Pencil, and Sellmore by telephone. In the third week, one big check they were expecting never came through. Another came through, but bounced. So money was short.

"I told you," said Wonder, "pay our employees their net pay. We have to keep the doors open, and they simply won't work, nor should they, if we don't pay them."

"What about paying Soomee Supply Company, which just shipped us a trailer load of widget parts?" said Bighthard. "They'll just have to wait," said Wonder. He told Bighthard that if the same situation happened again, he and Pencil should use their own judgment as to whether to pay Soomee or other suppliers.

January became February. February rolled into March. At the end of the quarter, the company owed $10,000 in payroll taxes.

"What do we do now?" lamented Bighthard.

"Don't worry," said Wonder. "Things will get better." But they did not. In April, May, and June, the company fell another $15,000 behind in payroll taxes. Now Ed Wonder was harder to reach. He called in less often. Bighthard and Pencil, following Wonder's request, began to use their own judgment, paying this bill here and not paying that bill there, just to keep the doors open. They always paid the employees their net wages, and Bighthard always filled out, signed, and filed the payroll tax returns (Form 941) on time. But he and Pencil were worried. What if things didn't get better? What if Wonder gave up? What about the state withholding taxes? State sales taxes?

In September, Bighthard had had enough. "You have to do something, Ed. I can't go on like this. I'm afraid the IRS will catch up with us, and we've got all those penalties to pay, too."

"I know, I know," moaned Wonder. "But we have to keep the doors open. We have to pay our people. We have to keep making widgets. I know some of our customers are even slower paying now than they were before, but they'll catch up.

I've just put another $10,000 of my own money into the company, and that should hold us for a while."

But it didn't. The company fell behind another $10,000 in September. Money was tighter than ever. The recession was biting deeply.

Then came the notices. Some IRS computer had awakened to the company's $35,000 tax debt. The first notice came to Bighthard. It was polite but firm. He called Wonder.

"Ed, we just got a notice from the IRS for $35,000. There's a penalty in there as well. What do we do?"

Wonder wondered and pondered. "Pay what you can," he finally said, "but if we can't pay it all, we'll just have to tough it out. I know that the money will be there. Just use the net incoming checks to pay the IRS."

"But we promised that money to Soomee Supply, remember? And also to Cold Steel for more parts."

"I know," said Wonder. "Just use your own judgment. You and Pencil work it out. You decide who is screaming the loudest, and pay them."

September became October, then November. November rolled into December. On December 15, the knock on the door came. It was an IRS revenue officer, Dan Dollar, there to collect the back taxes.

"Did you know, Mr. Wonder," Dollar said in a firm and sincere tone, "that you can be held personally liable for the withheld taxes that you didn't pay to the government? That's what I'm here to investigate."

Wonder cringed. Acid turned his stomach into a small but growing knot. "I guess so," he sighed, "But I really wasn't making any of the decisions on whom to pay, at least not lately. I've been out in the field. Ben Bighthard and Penny Pencil were doing all of the decision making and all of the check signing."

"Did you know that these taxes were due?" asked Dollar.

"Yes, we all did," said Wonder. "We've had the same problem before, and we fixed it! Nobody meant any harm. Lots of money has come in to the company, more than enough to pay the taxes, but there always seemed to be something that was more pressing. But don't worry, we'll catch up."

"I know you will try, Mr. Wonder," said the revenue officer. "But in the meantime, I'm here to see who should be made personally liable for these back taxes. It's called the Trust Fund Recovery Penalty. Let's start with—you."

Does this scenario sound familiar? Something like it happens hundreds of thousands of times each year. Here's how that company payroll tax problem becomes a personal problem, and what you can do about it.

WHAT IS THIS "PENALTY"?

The Wonder Widgets problem occurs because employers really work for Uncle Sam, collecting the IRS' taxes through the withholding system. Even "sole proprietors," who operate a business but don't organize it as a corporation or partnership, may have employees and therefore an obligation to withhold. States with income tax laws (that's almost every state) also impose wage withholding. If most employers didn't obey the withholding laws, our federal and state governments would grind to a screeching halt. In fact, most employers comply, doing their best to get you the right forms, to withhold the right amount from your pay, and to pay that money over to the federal and state governments.

By law, employers make three kinds of payments to the IRS after each payday. The check (or electronic transfer) they send covers (1) the income tax withheld from your paycheck, (2) the Social Security and Medicare tax also withheld, and (3) the employer's matching Social Security/Medicare payment. The first two items—the withheld portions—are known as the "trust fund" part of the tax because a special statute imposes a trust on those withheld funds until the employer pays them to the IRS. The money doesn't have to be put in a separate bank account, but it's automatically deemed "in trust" from the instant your employer withholds it from your pay.

In a perfect world, the money is there. But the world is far from perfect. What if your employer, like Ed Wonder of Wonder Widgets, just doesn't have the money, or decides to pocket that money? What if he deliberately fails to pay the payroll taxes to the federal and state governments for some other reason? This happens with annoying frequency. The Wonder Widgets example (a company short of cash) is only one example of how it happens in the real world. The federal and state governments lose billions that way every year.

THERE OUGHT TO BE A LAW!

And there is. Actually, there are several laws. (There's a law against everything—except more laws.)

Technically, it's a crime for an employer to fail to pay the payroll taxes. But the IRS rarely invokes that law. Instead, the IRS goes for the wrongdoer's pocketbook. It uses a special weapon about fifty thousand times a year, the Trust Fund Recovery Penalty. (It used to be called the "100 percent" penalty.) This penalty makes the people who were responsible for the nonpayment personally liable for

100 percent of the money that was withheld but not paid over to the IRS. That means 100 percent of the withheld income and Social Security/Medicare tax. The penalty does not apply to the *employer's* share of Social Security/Medicare.

Let's say the employer is strapped for cash, and the payroll for a two-week pay period totaled $92,500. But the net pay to the employees was only $70,000. The other $22,500 was made up of (1) $15,000 of withheld income tax and (2) $7,500 of withheld Social Security/Medicare. (3) The corporation also owes another $7,500 of Social Security/Medicare. If the employer doesn't pay that $30,000 to the IRS, the people responsible for the nonpayment are each personally liable for the $15,000 and the withheld $7,500 (items 1 and 2), though not for the $7,500 of employer Social Security/Medicare. Of course, the corporation is also liable, and the IRS goes after that primary payor first. But the Trust Fund Recovery Penalty makes the responsible persons "guarantee" the corporation's payment, at least in part.

This penalty is a debt that can follow you for at least ten years, or the rest of your life, whichever comes first. The limited liability you personally enjoy from most corporate debts simply does not apply against this federal law. On top of that, you cannot discharge this penalty by filing personal bankruptcy, as you can with most personal debts. Though the debt is enforceable for a long time, many employers either don't realize this or give in anyway to the temptation not to pay the IRS.

Most states have laws like the federal one, holding the responsible officers personally liable for state withholding taxes. They also have laws imposing personal liability for many other types of taxes, sometimes including sales tax and other taxes.

This Trust Fund Recovery Penalty can be a major tragedy for the businessperson. After all, why would any employer not pay these trust fund taxes? For most, like Ed Wonder, it's only because he doesn't have the money. Sure, in some cases the businessperson simply pockets the money and takes a permanent vacation to Tahiti. But those cases are rare. Most business owners want to stay in business and prosper, but when money gets too tight, it seems many of them take a chance by paying the squeaky wheels. And often, they get away with it. An employer, however, might pay the taxes late, after that anticipated big income check arrives. This will cost a federal tax deposit penalty.

Other employers aren't so lucky. As in the Wonder Widgets story, sometimes an employer misses one tax payment, holds his breath, and finds that the world doesn't end. Then another is missed, and another. Many never catch up. Quarter after quarter goes by; the back taxes keep building up. Their accountants, controllers, bookkeepers, lawyers, or other financial advisers warn them of what they already know, that they must pay those taxes. But the cash never seems to come in the door fast enough. There is an unexpected repair on a big machine, the air conditioning system breaks down, or an important customer goes bankrupt. A failing economy or recession can collapse interdependent businesses like dominoes, with the result that withholding taxes seem to be last on the payment list. To such employers, keeping the doors open is paramount. Since the IRS squeaks only later, though louder, many ever-optimistic businesspeople take a chance by hoping that good times are right around the corner.

What about the employees? They've paid their taxes. Despite their employers' failure to pay that money to the federal government, by law they still get credit on their tax returns.

HOW THE IRS HANDLES THESE CASES

The IRS is like a hibernating bear in these payroll tax cases. It wakes up late, sometimes years after the first default, but it also wakes up very hungry and aggressive. Often two or three years have gone by; the employer may owe $50,000, $100,000, $200,000, or more. On top of that, penalties and interest have been assessed by the IRS' computers, so the situation often looks close to hopeless. The IRS is becoming more efficient at catching these defaults earlier; it has made improvements in that department a high priority. If the agency could alert the employer right away, many employers would surely get back on track. In fact, the agency has "FTD Alerts " in place for many businesses that stop depositing payroll taxes. But the longer the default goes on, the easier it is to continue and the harder it is to feel that you can ever catch up.

When the IRS' computers wake up to an employer's default, the service centers first print out a series of notices. These notices have lots of information, but they boil down to this idea: "Hey, Wonder Widgets, you didn't send us your tax deposits. Please do so now, or else." For every calendar quarter the employer doesn't pay in full, normally four such notices go out. The first one is polite ("It seems there may be a problem here, please check and pay."), the last, a declaration of war ("This is your final notice. Enforcement action may be taken immediately against you."). Some repeat offender businesses and large-dollar cases get only two notices. Others get phone calls, too.

When you get one of these notices, the absolute worst course is to ignore it. The computer remembers that it sent you the notice, and that you didn't respond. (The computer is very offended by such impoliteness.) Once the last notice is issued and thirty days pass, the IRS is legally free to start collecting by any means it can. This can include levying on bank accounts and accounts receivable, or even closing down a business where the boss is "pyramiding the payroll taxes."

Sometimes the delinquent accounts are transferred to the Automated Collection System (ACS), the IRS' second-stage collection function. Despite the name, the Automated Collection System employs real people who call you for payment and schedule payment dates or installment agreements. The "automated" part comes into play when ACS automatically files notices of tax lien and issues levies.

The IRS collects a great deal of money by these computerized notices from the service centers and the Automated Collection System. But billions still fall through the cracks. That's when the cavalry, the revenue officers of the Collection Division, charge into action. The computer doesn't give up. It prints out alert notices known as TDAs, or Taxpayer Delinquent Accounts. One TDA form is printed for each reporting period, in this case, a calendar quarter (January through March, April through June, and so on). The computer, having done its best, now sends the TDA to the Collection Division and its frontline employees, revenue officers. The TDA forms for each quarter arrive at the local Collection Division office, where the case is assigned.

The revenue officer's job is to go out and get the taxes. For the most part, revenue officers are well-educated, well-trained, and tough. They use a range of powers. At one end, there is friendly persuasion. At the other, they can impose and carry out a corporate "death sentence," physically closing down a business by locking the doors and changing the locks to prevent more tax defaults.

The revenue officer's first step is to call or visit the employer and have a little "chat." He does not say, "Hello, I'm Revenue Officer Dan Dollar, and I'm here to help you." He is and he's not. At this first meeting, the revenue officer demands full payment immediately of all the taxes. He also explains how much is due—taxes, penalties, and interest. Does Ed Wonder immediately turn around and write out a check, saying, "Gosh, I'm glad you're here. I was just about to give you a call"? Of course not. He doesn't have the money. That's why the company defaulted, and that's why the revenue officer is there in the first place. Revenue officers know that, but they are required to make the demand anyway.

Then the revenue officer and Ed Wonder discuss how the back taxes can be paid (if they can be paid). Paying over time is possible in some cases. While dealing with past defaults, the revenue officer will insist on one absolute, nonnegotiable condition of any deal to pay the back taxes. The bleeding must stop. Wonder Widgets must start paying the current payroll taxes (that is, make federal tax deposits) right away when they are due, and must demonstrate that compliance to the revenue officer. Otherwise, the revenue officer will close the business.

Of course, Ed Wonder agrees. What choice does he have? Between life and death, he'll choose life, even if it turns out to be short.

Wonder then gets down to the nitty-gritty: negotiating with the revenue officer for payment of the rest of the back taxes. Chapters 1 and 7 discuss this process in more detail.

IN THE MEANTIME

In the meantime, Revenue Officer Dollar also begins to investigate the people who might be personally liable for the nonpayment. He reminds Ed that he and possibly others in the company can be held personally liable for the trust fund portion of the payroll taxes. He tells Ed that even if the corporation can pay, the IRS is required to investigate others' personal liability for the Trust Fund Recovery Penalty. As a rule, if a corporation owes $10,000 in taxes, about $6,000 to $7,500 will be the withheld, or trust fund, portion. At least that way, the government can hope to recover about two-thirds of the unpaid taxes (the trust fund portion) if all else fails and the corporation goes under. When your personal assets are on the line because of this potential penalty, it tends to focus your attention. But the Trust Fund Recovery Penalty is not automatic or self-executing. The revenue officer can't just hand you a bill. He has to investigate thoroughly who should be assessed, then make a recommendation based on the facts and the law. That's all he can do—recommend. That recommendation has to be approved and a bill sent out. As we'll see, anyone who is considered for the penalty has an appeal right before the recommendation is made final, and the additional right to fight it afterward in court. The revenue officer's investigation usually lasts several weeks. Often it can stretch into months.

WHO IS A "RESPONSIBLE" PERSON?

The Internal Revenue Code imposes personal liability for the Trust Fund Recovery Penalty on anyone who (1) is a "responsible" person and (2) "willfully" caused the corporation not to pay the payroll taxes or "willfully" failed to ensure that the taxes were paid. You don't even have to be employed by the corporation, or be an officer or director, to be liable for this penalty. Even other corporations have been held liable for this penalty where they took such an active role in the defaulting corporation's financial affairs that they became responsible for the trust fund taxes. But those cases are rare. These days, only the true sources of financial authority inside the corporation will be investigated and held liable. In most cases, it's the officers and directors on whom the IRS first focuses.

So Revenue Officer Dollar will be on the lookout for two issues as to each person he investigates: (1) "responsibility" and (2) "willfulness." The responsible persons are those who truly controlled the finances and made the decisions on whom to pay and when. The revenue officer looks for "badges of authority." Signature authority on the checking account is usually a dead giveaway, especially if the revenue officer finds that the signatory also actually signed checks to creditors. In the Wonder Widgets case, clearly Ed Wonder had enough financial authority. What about Bighthard and Pencil? Not at first; but later, when they began to make decisions on their own and signed checks, they became liable. The revenue officer also looks at the corporate officers, shareholders, and directors. He'll find out who hired and fired employees, a sign of significant authority. Who was responsible for completing the employment tax returns (Form 941)? Who was responsible for signing these returns, for preparing payroll, for cutting the payroll checks? Who negotiated for loans at the bank?

> *Example:* Abel, his two sons, Baker and Charlie, and his wife, Delta, all worked together in the family business, a retail store. While the company had been formally incorporated for more than twenty years, the family ran the shop as informally as their breakfast table. Abel and his sons operated the store; Delta kept the books. In fact, she had the authority to sign checks and signed over ten thousand of them stretching over seven years. Delta was the only one who had training in financial matters, and she used that training to work with the bank, the company's accountant, and the IRS. While she called herself a bookkeeper, in fact she exercised control and made all the decisions on expenses, including paying taxes. She could have stopped the $250,000 of defaulted payroll taxes, but she didn't. So the IRS assessed her for $194,000, and made it stick in court.

> *Example:* Robert formed Fixtures, Inc., to install fixtures in office and commercial buildings. The next year, he hired his brother Gary as controller, treasurer, and chief financial officer. Gary's job was to supervise all account-

ing, prepare financial statements, keep up the books, and supervise an outside payroll service. An outside accountant also helped Robert run the business. On top of this, Robert had signature authority over the checking account. Three years later, things went downhill. Cash flow became very tight, and Gary and Robert fought often over a new computer system that was supposed to help them. Everyone met in October. The accountant recommended a delay in paying the payroll taxes for up to six weeks so the company could save $60,000. "Of course," said the CPA, "there will be interest, and, at worst, the government can make some personal assessments," but it will give the company breathing room. That breathing space turned into a gasp and a choke. The payroll taxes went unpaid, and the IRS assessed—you guessed it—Gary. Who won this case? This time, Gary won. True enough, he had the authority to sign checks, but Robert and the CPA actually decided which checks were to be made out. All financial control was in the hands of Robert and the CPA, not Gary. So despite all his apparent authority, he was found not responsible.

To find these and other badges of authority, the revenue officer hunts for and demands to see paper: corporate minutes, stock records, bank records, bank signature cards, and virtually anything else he can find that tells him who had the true authority to direct the payment of creditors. He'll look at contracts and bills, canceled checks, and receipts. He will interview as many people as seems appropriate, using an interview form, Form 4180, as a guide. When completed, this form tells the revenue officer virtually everything he needs to know about the financial movers and shakers inside the corporation.

The revenue officer then turns to the other issue, willfulness. He has to show that a responsible person willfully caused the corporation not to pay, or stood by while other creditors were paid ahead of the IRS. No fraud or evil intent need be proved. In the Wonder Widgets story, there was no fraud, but everyone knew the taxes were due. So all involved were "willful." The revenue officer needs to show that a responsible person knew the taxes were due at a time when that person could have paid the IRS. Simple knowledge is enough. And even if you didn't actually know, if you should have known, that's enough to make you willful. For example, if you signed a Form 941 payroll tax return showing a balance due, as Ben Bighthard did, you know taxes are due. If you prepared or saw a financial statement for the company showing taxes due, that's enough. If there was a payroll tax problem in the past, as happened in the Wonder Widgets example, that too could be enough to put everyone on notice and make those future defaults willful.

Example: Ed and Boris formed Allover Company, a construction firm. Both were in charge, with full authority to sign checks, determine the payment of creditors, and essentially run the show. Soon after starting, Ed found out that the company owed $5,000 in withholding taxes. The IRS had sent notices, but Boris assured him that the problem would be taken care of and would not happen again. OK, thought Ed, so far so good. Things went along fine for ten years. Then, the company became delinquent again. Eventually, it went out of business. The IRS assessed the two officers, but Ed said, "I didn't know the taxes were due. I can't be 'willful' for those periods." Not so, said the court. You knew about the earlier default, and that put you on notice that the company was in trouble. You had a duty to confirm or ensure that the future taxes were paid. One default, however small, is all it takes.

Example: Omri was a terrific baker, but he lacked a certain finesse as a businessperson. He was operating his business as a proprietorship when the IRS made an assessment against him for payroll taxes. He was able to work out an installment agreement. Seeing the handwriting on the wall, he formed a company with Bill, a longtime friend who had a catering business. Bill did all the book work, including paying expenses and sending checks to the IRS. Still, Omri had his share of check-signing duties. Things began to go downhill. Omri defaulted on his installment agreement and the IRS sent a notice of levy. The power company called about unpaid bills. They also had to pay a key supplier to keep the doors open. The fledgling company downsized by laying off two employees, but, all the time, Bill assured Omri that the taxes were being paid. Omri did not investigate on his own; he relied on Bill's statements. Of course, these assurances were false. The company ended up in bankruptcy, and the IRS assessed both Omri and Bill. Omri's defense: "Bill told me all the taxes were paid. I had a right to rely on him." No, you did not, said the court. You can't watch the financial walls crumbling all around you in every other way and assume that the taxes are also being paid. So, Omri was just as willful as Bill, and had to pay his share of the payroll taxes.

After the revenue officer gathers the evidence, he writes a report as part of a form called Recommendation for Trust Fund Recovery Penalty Assessment. True enough, it's only a recommendation; but once the agent recommends, this part of the battle is usually over.

The revenue officer brings that form and all the supporting documentation to his boss, the group manager. If the group manager approves, as they almost always do, the revenue officer then calls the responsible persons, asking whether they will agree to the liability.

Many people so fear the IRS that they quickly give in when the revenue officer proposes to assert the penalty. This is a major mistake. Often a bookkeeper, or even someone higher up like a corporate controller, was simply following the boss' orders. That subordinate should not be held liable, at least not for *all* the taxes. Just because a revenue officer says you are liable doesn't make it so. Remember that the revenue officer, despite his power, cannot actually make you liable or give you a tax bill. All he can do is recommend. You then have rights you can exercise before any bill is issued, and when you exercise those rights, sometimes the penalty is reduced or not imposed.

Now, let's say the revenue officer has called you, and after careful thought you politely say, "No, thank you" to the suggestion that you agree to a $100,000 tax bill. ("Sorry, can't contribute this year. Not in my plans.") What then? If you have more evidence in your favor, you can send it to the revenue officer. But that's normally a useless exercise. The revenue officer then writes a formal letter to you in which he says he will recommend the assessment. Again, that is not a bill. It's only a notice to you that he wants to make it official, subject to your right to appeal.

That formal letter, now required by law, is known as a "sixty-day letter." It means you have sixty days formally to agree or disagree. If you formally agree or fail to respond, that's the end of the matter. Your tax bill will shortly issue, and you will become even better acquainted with the revenue officer as he pursues your personal assets for collection.

If you disagree, you can fight the recommendation by appealing. Should you? Yes, if you truly believe you are not liable for some or all of the default and you have favorable evidence. To stop the revenue officer's recommendation from becoming a legally enforceable bill, respond to the sixty-day letter by appealing with a document called a "protest." You can protest whenever there is real doubt that you in fact are liable. By right, anyone who is recommended for the Trust Fund Recovery Penalty can demand a formal appeal and a hearing with the IRS. During that appeal time, no interest accrues on the penalty (nor is it assessed). And, appeals can be heard quickly or not, depending on how busy your IRS district is.

Now let's say you want to appeal. At this point, it is essential to get help from a tax professional experienced with this penalty. Appealing a Trust Fund

Recovery Penalty recommendation is complicated. The case law governing who is liable is vast and challenging. You may need only advice. You may need more guidance or reassurance that you're on the right track. Or you may need the tax professional to carry the full burden for you. But do not appeal on your own. You will almost surely lose.

To fight the penalty, send the protest as a letter to the IRS office that proposed the assessment.

These protests are similar in format to protests in income tax cases. In the protest, acknowledge receipt of the sixty-day letter and state that you are now protesting it. The body of the protest has seven parts.

1. *Name and Address*

2. *Date and Symbol of Letter.* State the date of the sixty-day letter, and the symbols of the letter, normally located in the lower-right or lower-left corner on the first page.

3. *Tax Periods Involved.* Here state what calendar quarters are proposed in the assessment. You can take these straight off Form 2751, which is an attachment to the sixty-day letter.

4. *Request for Appellate Conference.* If you want a conference with the office of appeals before a decision is made, say so here. It's almost always in your interest to request a conference.

5. *Findings to Which the Taxpayer Protests.* State the errors you believe the revenue officer made. In Trust Fund Recovery Penalty cases, it is enough to say, "I was not a person responsible for the failure of Wonder Widgets, Inc., to collect, account for, and pay over the withholding and Social Security taxes for the periods stated above." You can also say, if true, that you were either not "responsible" or not "willful."

6. *Statement of Facts and Argument.* This is the heart of your protest. Here you present all the facts you have, describe all the documents you have (providing copies), and make all credible factual and legal arguments to show that you are not responsible at all, or not responsible for all periods, or not willful.

Appeals officers know that many people prepare and file their own protests. So don't worry about how "legal" the protest sounds. Proven facts always speak loud volumes, so just state and support the facts and tie them to the legal standards as best you can. Still, a professional adviser can greatly help. A professional knows the law and knows how to gather or present the facts and law in the most effective way. Also, don't worry about whether facts you state would be admissible in court. The rules of courtroom evidence don't apply to appeals cases. Often hearsay and other inadmissible evidence will be considered. Still, everything you say must be true. It's a criminal offense to lie to a federal official, under oath or not.

Your concluding paragraph should ask for the result you want. That's usually called "nonassertion" of the penalty, but frame this paragraph exactly in the terms of the relief you seek.

DEFENSES YOU MAY USE

People have thought of dozens of defenses to put in protests and in later court cases. Let's take a look at the most important ones.

The "Nuremberg" defense. Maybe you can argue that you were "just following orders." From our Wonder Widgets example, Penny Pencil or Ben Bighthard would say, "President Wonder told me what checks to sign, what checks to write, and I just followed orders. Even though I could prepare and sign checks myself, the reality was that only Ed Wonder told me what to do. Every Friday he would call me into his private office. There he would go over the list of people we had to pay, and sort them out by the ones that we absolutely had to pay and others who could wait. Unfortunately, the IRS could always wait. I told him I thought it was wrong, but he ordered me around anyway. He told me he would fire me if I disobeyed him."

That's a very common defense bookkeepers and controllers use. It works in most parts of the country if it's true and you prove it. But you bear the burden of proof. Very often Wonder will say just the opposite, so try to get other people to back you up, people who have no ax to grind. And put it in writing! Under oath!

The "pointing finger" defense. In this defense, Ben Bighthard points the finger at Ed Wonder and says, "*He* did it, not me." Ben claims that Wonder was the only person authorized to sign checks, even if Ben was on the bank signature card. Ben also tries to get the backing of others by letters or affidavits. This defense also works if you can prove it. If you resigned your corporate office, or went off the company's checking accounts at the bank, show these facts by documents such as new bank signature cards or a corporate resolution demonstrating that you resigned. However, in the real world, corporations often lack such formal documentation.

The "it's been paid" defense. Sometimes all or part of your liability has been paid. The corporation might have paid it by designated payments. Or, some other officer might have paid some part of the liability the IRS now seeks from you. Under IRS policy, you are entitled to credit for those payments. The IRS is also required by law to let you know what efforts it has made to collect from other responsible persons. Insist on that right.

The "your calculations are wrong" defense. Sometimes the IRS makes a mistake in calculating the amount of trust fund taxes. Go back to the corporation's employment tax returns and do it yourself. Make sure that any deposits the company made during the tax period are allocated to taxes, not to penalties and interest.

The "contribution" defense. If the IRS is coming after you for these taxes, and you claim someone else is liable, you may now sue in federal court to have that person "contribute" his or her share. This right did not exist before 1996, when Congress added it through the 1996 Taxpayer Bill of Rights.

FILING YOUR PROTEST

Once you have assembled your documents and have written your protest, send it to the office that sent you the sixty-day letter. Missing the sixty-day deadline is fatal to your appeal. The IRS will quickly process the paperwork for an assessment bill. If you can't meet the deadline, ask for an extension. Call the revenue officer assigned to your case as soon as you know you will need more time. Ask for thirty days at a minimum, but as long as you realistically need. Tell the revenue officer why you need more time. He'll usually grant the request, but make you put it in writing. Sometimes he'll grant it grudgingly, sometimes for fewer than thirty days, but he will usually give you enough time. It is one of the great ironies of tax practice that the IRS will grudgingly grant one extension—usually not more than one—and then wait five to ten times that time period to hear your appeal. But that's the way it is. If the revenue officer won't extend the deadline at all, file a bare-bones protest. That will preserve your appeal rights. You can supplement it later.

Now you are ready to assemble your protest. It should have two main parts: first, a cover letter with all the identifying information that a protest normally requires, as discussed above; second, as much supporting documentation as you can possibly assemble to show you are not liable for the penalty.

While you're preparing the protest, what's the revenue officer doing? Nothing. He's waiting. After he gets your protest, he'll also write a rebuttal. His instincts and training are frustrated because he is forbidden to seize assets or otherwise collect during this sixty-day period (or longer, if extended). He may want to collect, to seize bank accounts, sell your house, but he cannot. It's not a constitutional or statutory right but internal IRS procedures that give you this window, plus the appeal time. While your appeal is pending, the revenue officer generally leaves you alone.

What if your corporation is in bankruptcy? There, too, official IRS policy calls for "no collection" as long as the corporation is current in its payroll taxes and proposes a plan of reorganization that will take care of these taxes. But if the business begins to liquidate assets, or "pyramids" its delinquencies, among other things, the revenue officer can go full speed ahead to recommend the assessment against you.

In the great majority of these proposed assessments, the responsible persons never file protests. They throw up their hands and say, "You got me. I'm guilty." And in most cases, they are. But it's surprising how many times revenue officers propose the Trust Fund Recovery Penalty assessment against persons who are *not* liable, or who have one or more excellent defenses. Even the 100 percent owner, a president and chief operating officer of a corporation, may still have some defenses, usually relating to the proper amount to be assessed. But in most cases, feeling badly about the default or assuming he's absolutely liable, the executive gives up without a fight. In other cases, even if he has a defense, he misses the sixty-day deadline.

It's not possible to overstress the importance of meeting that deadline or any extension. If you do, and file a proper protest, the revenue officer will wait until the protest is resolved. You have exercised a right that the IRS grants you, the right to preassessment reconsideration within the IRS.

THE APPEAL

After you file a timely protest, you wait. And wait. And wait. In busy IRS districts, you can wait up to a year to have your protest considered. Sometime shortly after you file the protest, you will receive a polite letter from the office of appeals. The letter says simply that it has received your protest, it is assigned to Ms. Jones, appeals officer, and you will be hearing from Ms. Jones shortly. Then you wait some more. Sometimes the letter will courageously set up an actual appointment, with a date, time, and place, two to four months in the future. If so, check your calendar immediately. If you can't meet that date, write or call the appeals officer directly to set up a new appointment. Her number and address are on the letter.

WHO ARE THE APPEALS OFFICERS?

The office of appeals is simply an arm of the IRS to which you can appeal the recommendation of the revenue officer without having to go to court. It's the same office that considers appeals from income tax audits. These appeals offices are located in every IRS district. The IRS set up this office in 1925 to try to keep down the volume of court litigation on tax matters, and it has worked. Appeals officers settle a high percentage of income tax and employment tax cases. "Settlement" is even written into their job description. In theory, appeals officers are supposed to be neutral and detached, to consider both sides, and to try to arrive at a fair settlement. They will generally make a good-faith effort to see your side of the case and to consider all your evidence. They are trained to be more objective and detached than the revenue officer. But remember: They get a government paycheck just like the revenue officer who wants to sell your house.

Appeals officers will also candidly tell you that Trust Fund Recovery Penalty cases are tough to settle. Some say they don't like to settle these cases because of the moral component: the taxpayer sitting across the desk from them has been accused of violating a sacred trust, the obligation to hold employees' monies and pay them over to the government. Others confess they find it hard to settle these cases because all the accused are pointing fingers at each other, saying, "He did it, not me." Moreover, in many cases officers even swear that "it was the other guy." So the appeals officer sometimes throws up her hands and sustains the revenue officer's recommended assessments with the comment: "Let them fight it out in court."

In addition to your protest, the appeals officer has the revenue officer's entire case file. That includes everyone else's protests, the interview forms, the revenue officer's written recommendations, and his rebuttal to your protest. The file also contains all of the corporate documents, bank documents, canceled checks, and other evidence. Finally, there are IRS forms that ensure the file gets to the right appeals officer and back to the correct place when she is finished with it. The size of that big administrative file discourages the appeals officer from settling many cases because she typically finds so many contradictory accusations and facts. That is also discouraging to you; it means the appeals officer is less likely to reach any settlement, or a good settlement from your point of view. An appeal in a Trust Fund Recovery Penalty case can therefore be very much an uphill battle. The appeals officer has seen a hundred come and go, many involving taxpayers who lie under oath to try to get a better result.

PREPARING FOR YOUR CONFERENCE

Now you're in the period between the protest and the in-person conference. What can you do? The rule is: Keep moving. Look for more evidence. Find more documents and witnesses. Obtain their statements, preferably under oath, and send them to the appeals officer. She'll always take new evidence, up to the date of the conference and even after. If you made a Freedom of Information Act request for the IRS' administrative file, continue to comb through that file for holes in the revenue officer's investigation, helpful facts, or leads to other evidence that can help your case. Relentlessly track down those leads and get them on paper. For example, let's say you want to prove that you didn't sign corporate checks to pay bills until six months after you came on the job. (The president has said you did.) You might consider asking for copies of the actual checks from the bank. It is expensive, but the banks have them on microfilm going back a number of years. You can then show the checks to the appeals officer and argue that you were not responsible during that six-month period because you were not a check-signer.

Suppose you were the secretary/treasurer of the corporation, but the president called all the shots. The bookkeeper has moved to Kodiak, Alaska. But you find and call her. By luck, she kept a copy of the corporation's bylaws. Those bylaws say that the president was in charge of everything. So you get the bylaws and send them to the appeals officer.

The idea is to think of any piece of evidence, any fact, any document, that will help prove a negative—that you were not a "responsible" person or that you did not know or should not be expected to have known that the taxes were due.

Now it's time for the conference. An appeals conference is unlike any court proceeding. The appeals officer does not don a Tyrannosaurus rex suit for the occasion, but neither does she greet you with a bouquet of flowers.

The conference usually takes place in her office. You come in, sit across the desk from her, and proceed to the issues.

The discussion can range over the entire history of the corporation, or it may concentrate only on the delinquent periods. Your task is to use the facts in your protest to convince the appeals officer that you are not liable. Have all of your protest firmly in mind, and be prepared to rebut any contrary evidence. If you have prepared well, there should be no surprises. You'll be especially well-prepared if you made a Freedom of Information Act request for the IRS' administrative files. Sometimes the appeals officer will have discussed the case with the other proposed responsible persons, a circumstance for which you cannot fully prepare. She'll tell you about those discussions at the conference and ask for your rebuttal.

If after the conference you need more time to gather evidence, the appeals officer normally allows it. But if the conference goes well and you don't need more time, the appeals officer will begin to discuss settlement. As a general rule, appeals officers will rarely suggest a settlement at less than 20 percent of the full amount of the proposed liability (unless it's crystal clear that you're not liable). The 20 percent is considered a "nuisance" settlement. To go lower, they would have to justify in detail why the IRS should not fully concede the case. So, if some evidence points to your liability, your best result may be 20 percent of the full amount proposed.

Appeals officers have authority to settle if all of the responsible persons get together and agree to chip in an equal amount, or if they pay the full amount, even if somebody pays more than an equal share. But if everyone denies liability and points the finger elsewhere, often the appeals officer will be unable to craft a settlement and may sustain the full penalty against each responsible person. That doesn't mean the IRS collects three or four times. It will collect only once, but it can collect 100 percent from you; 50 percent each from two people; or 10 percent from one, 30 percent from another, and so forth.

If you are able to settle, the appeals officer writes up the settlement for her boss and sends a copy to you for signature. You sign it, send it back, and await the resulting bill.

IS THERE LIFE AFTER APPEALS?

If you try and try but just can't settle, civilization as we know it does not come to an end. True enough, that's your last chance before a formal bill is generated. But it's not your last chance to contest the liability. You can always go to court. Still, fighting the Trust Fund Recovery Penalty in court is difficult and expensive. Attorneys in the Tax Division of the Department of Justice, the government's lawyers in these cases, have a long and consistent winning record. Most of the case law is unfavorable to taxpayers. So, before you decide to go to court, consult an attorney experienced in these cases. Despite these odds, many people choose to litigate, and a government win is by no means a foregone conclusion.

You cannot simply file suit after your appeal is denied. First, to establish the federal court's jurisdiction over your case, pay a portion of the assessment and file a Claim for Refund on Form 843 (Claim for Refund). The idea behind a Claim for Refund is this: You pay the tax first and then sue the government in federal district court for a refund of the tax you have paid. Paying the tax does not mean you agree to it. It simply allows the federal district court to exercise jurisdiction over the case.

In most cases, people cannot pay the full amount of the Trust Fund Recovery Penalty. So, an exception allows you to pay only a small amount for each calendar quarter that you want to place in issue. That amount is equal to the withholding and Social Security/Medicare taxes due for only one employee for each quarter at issue. It could be the lowest paid employee, the highest paid employee, or anyone in between. It can be the same employee for each quarter at issue. If you can't find out how much that amount is, guess. Paying $100 or $200 per quarter will often be enough.

FILING YOUR CLAIMS FOR REFUND

File one claim for each quarter at issue. At the end of this chapter, you will find a sample Claim for Refund. The "memo" section of your personal check for each quarter is earmarked to pay that quarter. Also, send your Claim for Refund forms to the regional IRS service center by certified or registered mail, return receipt requested.

The IRS will process the claim, but since the tax has already been assessed against you, a rejection is inevitable. The rejection letter is your "ticket to court." If the IRS fails to act within six months after you file the claim, you also can sue at that time.

Winning a tax refund suit in a Trust Fund Recovery Penalty case is difficult. If you are serious about suing, always consult a lawyer experienced in such cases. Yes, it is true, some taxpayers sue on their own; some even win. But that's as rare as a surplus in the federal budget.

When you file suit, the Department of Justice will counterclaim for the unpaid balance of the assessment. For example, if you sue for a refund of $500 out of a $25,000 assessment, the counterclaim will be for $24,500. The issues in court are identical to those you and the IRS considered before. The judge or a jury will adjudicate who was a responsible person and who acted willfully. Witnesses will be called, documents will be introduced into evidence, and the trial will follow the usual pattern of trials in federal district courts. Some federal courts will complete these trials quickly; others can take years. While you're waiting for your case to be tried, interest accrues on the assessment.

If you win, there is no more liability. But if you lose, you have a federal court judgment that can be collected either by the IRS or by the Department of Justice. For more information on collection by these agencies, see chapters 1, 2, 4 through 7, and 23.

THE TEN COMMANDMENTS OF THE TRUST FUND RECOVERY PENALTY

1. Keep out of harm's way. Don't take responsibility for paying corporate bills if the boss should really have it.

2. Make early requests under the Freedom of Information Act for the IRS' administrative file.

3. Tell the truth—to yourself, to the revenue officer, to the appeals officer.

4. Meet all deadlines, especially for the protest.

5. Respond to all IRS notices.

6. Keep looking for evidence while you await the appeals conference.

7. Don't fight the penalty alone. Seek professional advice from a tax practitioner experienced in handling Trust Fund Recovery Penalty cases.

8. Be careful what you say to the revenue officer. Anything you say can and will be used against you.

9. Do not fear the revenue officer. Be respectful but not defensive.

10. Stand on your rights. You have them; use them.

Form **843**
(Rev. January 1994)

Department of the Treasury
Internal Revenue Service

Claim for Refund and Request for Abatement

▶ See separate instructions.

OMB No. 1545-0024
Expires 1-31-97

Use Form 843 only if your claim involves one of the taxes shown on line 3a or a refund or abatement of interest, penalties, or additions to tax on line 4a.

Note: *Do not use Form 843 if your claim is for—*
- *An overpayment of income taxes;*
- *A refund of fuel taxes; or*
- *An overpayment of excise taxes reported on Form 720, 730, or 2290.*

Please type or print		
Name of claimant		Your social security number
Address (number, street, and room or suite no.)		Spouse's social security number
City or town, state, and ZIP code		Employer identification number
Name and address shown on return if different from above		Daytime telephone number ( )

1 Period—prepare a separate Form 843 for each tax period
From _____ , 19 ____ , to _____ , 19 ____

2 Amount to be refunded or abated
$

3a Type of tax, penalty, or addition to tax:
☐ Employment   ☐ Estate   ☐ Gift   ☐ Excise (other than excise taxes reported on Form 720, 730, or 2290)
☐ Penalty IRC section ▶ _____

b Type of return filed (see instructions):
☐ 706   ☐ 709   ☐ 940   ☐ 941   ☐ 990-PF   ☐ 4720   ☐ Other (specify)

4a Request for abatement or refund of:
☐ Interest caused by IRS errors and delays (under Rev. Proc. 87-42—see instructions).
☐ A penalty or addition to tax as a result of erroneous advice from the IRS.

b Dates of payment ▶

5 **Explanations and additional claims.** Explain why you believe this claim should be allowed, and show computation of tax refund or abatement of interest, penalty, or addition to tax.

Signature. If you are filing Form 843 to request a refund or abatement relating to a joint return, both you and your spouse must sign the claim. Claims filed by corporations must be signed by a corporate officer authorized to sign, and the signature must be accompanied by the officer's title.

Under penalties of perjury, I declare that I have examined this claim, including accompanying schedules and statements, and, to the best of my knowledge and belief, it is true, correct, and complete.	Director's Stamp (Date received)
Signature (Title, if applicable. Claims by corporations must be signed by an officer.) Date	
Signature Date	

For Paperwork Reduction Act Notice, see separate instructions.

Cat. No. 10180R

Form **843** (Rev. 1-94)

*U.S. Government Printing Office: 1994 — 301-628/00070

Report of Interview with Individual Relative to Trust Fund Recovery Penalty or Personal Liability for Excise Tax	Date of Interview
Notice 609 was furnished during the interview. (Check here) [ ] (See instructions below.)	Name of Interviewer

INSTRUCTIONS TO INTERVIEWER: The questions which follow are to be used as a guide as you conduct the interview. Other questions may be asked. You must prepare this form personally, recording the interviewee's answers. Where a question is not applicable, write "N/A." Do not leave any blocks or lines blank. Attach additional sheets if necessary.

Notice 609, Privacy Act and Paperwork Reduction Act Notice, must be given to persons who haven't received notice of their right to privacy. If furnished during the interview, check the box above. If not, explain in the case history.

IRC 6672, failure to collect and pay tax from *(date)* _____ to *(date)* _____

IRC 4103, failure to pay tax from *(date)* _____ to *(date)* _____

Section I—Background Information

1.
a. Person interviewed *(name)*

b. *(address)*

c. Telephone number *(home)*   d. Telephone number *(work)*

e. Social Security number

2.
a. Taxpayer (Corporation) *(name)*

b. *(address)*

c. Incorporation *(date)*   d. State where incorporated

e. Has the state revoked the corporation franchise?   ☐ yes ☐ no   f. If so, when?

g. Has the corporation ever filed bankruptcy?   ☐ yes ☐ no   h. If so, when?

3. Was any of the property of the corporation sold, transferred, quitclaimed, donated or otherwise disposed of, for less than fair market value, since the accrual of the tax liability?   ☐ yes ☐ no
What happened to the corporate assets?

4.
a. How were you associated with this corporation?

b. Describe your duties/responsibilities.

c. By whom were you hired?

d. What were the dates of your employment with the corporation?

e.	Did you resign from the corporation? ☐ yes ☐ no	f. In writing?		☐ yes	☐ no
g.	When?	h. Is a copy of your resignation available? ☐ yes ☐ no			
i.	To whom was your resignation submitted?				
j.	Did you have your name removed from the bank signature cards? ☐ yes ☐ no			k.	When?
h.	Do you have any money invested in the corporation? ☐ yes ☐ no			m.	Amount $

5.

a.	Have you ever been involved with another company which had tax problems? ☐ yes ☐ no	
b.	If so, explain. *(Corporate name, EIN, etc.)*	

6. With what banks or financial institutions did the corporation have transactions such as checking and other accounts, loans, financing agreements, etc.? *(attach additional sheet, if necessary)*

Financial Institution	Transaction(s)	Address	Date(s)

7. Where are the financial records located?

8. Please indicate the names, dates of service and percentage of ownership for the positions indicated below.

Position	Name	Dates of Service	% Ownership
Chairman of the board			
Other Directors *(list)*			
President			
Vice President			
Secretary			
Treasurer			
Others *(shareholders, owners)*			

		Section II—Ability to Direct			Interviewee		

Please indicate whether you performed any of the duties/functions indicated below for the corporation and the time periods during which you performed them. If another person performed these duties, please list names and time periods.

Did you...	Yes	No	Dates from	Dates to	Did anyone else? (name)	Dates from	Dates to
1. Hire/fire employees							
2. Manage employees							
3. Direct (authorize) payment of bills							
4. Deal with major suppliers and customers							
5. Negotiate large corporate purchases, contracts, loans							
6. Open/close corporate bank accounts							
7. Sign/countersign corporate checks							
8. Guarantee/co-sign corporate bank loans							
9. Make/authorize bank deposits							
10. Authorize payroll checks							
11. Prepare federal payroll tax returns							

Did you...	Yes	No	Dates		Did anyone else? *(name)*	Dates	
			from	to		from	to
12. Prepare federal excise tax returns							
13. Sign federal excise tax returns							
14. Authorize payment of federal tax deposits							
15. Review federal income tax returns							
16. Determine Company financial policy							

17. Please provide the information requested below for each person, other than yourself, listed for the above questions. Also, please provide any additional information indicating their knowledge and/or control over the corporation's financial affairs. *(Attach additional sheets if necessary.)*

Name	Address
Phone Number	Social Security number

Additional information

Name	Address
Phone Number	Social Security number

Additional information

Name	Address
Phone Number	Social Security number

Additional information

Name	Address
Phone Number	Social Security number

Additional information

Section III—Knowledge	Interviewee

1. When and how did you first become aware of the delinquent taxes?

2. What action did you take to see that the tax liabilities were paid?

3. Were discussions or meetings ever held by stockholders, officers or other interested parties regarding the non-payment of the taxes? ☐ yes ☐ no
   Identify who attended, the dates of the meetings, and any decisions reached.
   (Attach additional sheets, if necessary.)

4. Are minutes available from any meetings described in question 3 above? ☐ yes ☐ no

5. Who maintained or has access to the books and records of the corporation? When?
   (Please provide name, address and phone number, if possible)

6. Were financial statements ever prepared for the corporation? ☐ yes ☐ no
   If so, by whom? Who reviewed them and to whom were they submitted?
   (Please provide time periods.)

7. Did the corporation employ an outside accountant? ☐ yes ☐ no
   If so, please provide the name, address and phone number of the person or firm.

8. Who in the corporation had the responsibility of dealing with the outside accountant?

9. Did you personally have discussions with the accountant or bookkeeper of the corporation regarding the tax liability?
☐ yes ☐ no

If so, when?
What was discussed?

10. Who reviewed the payroll tax returns or tax payments?

11. Who reviewed the excise tax returns or tax payments?

12. Who handled IRS contacts, such as IRS correspondence, phone calls from IRS, or visits by IRS personnel?

When?
What were the results of these contacts?

13. During the time the delinquent taxes were increasing, or at any time thereafter, were any financial obligation of the corporation paid?
☐ yes ☐ no
If so, which ones?

14. Which individual or individuals authorized or allowed any of these obligations to be paid?

15. During the time that the delinquent taxes were increasing, or at any time thereafter, were all or a portion of the payrolls met?
☐ yes ☐ no

16. When there was not enough money to pay all the bills, what decisions were made and what actions were taken to deal with the situation? Who made the decisions?

17. Did any person or organization provide funds to pay net corporate payrolls?   ☐ yes ☐ no
If so, explain in detail.

Section IV—Special Circumstances

1. Is the corporation required to file federal excise tax returns?   □ yes □ no
   If so, are you aware of any required excise tax returns which have not been filed?   □ yes □ no
   (If either response is negative, do not complete remaining questions in Section IV.)

2. With respect to excise taxes, were the patrons or customers informed that the tax was included in the sales price?
                                                                                             □ yes □ no

3. If the tax liability is one of the so-called "collected" taxes—transportation of persons or property and communications:

   a. Was the tax collected?   □ yes □ no

   b. Were you aware, during the period tax accrued, that the law required collection of the tax?   □ yes □ no

Continue answers from Sections I through III below. Identify by section and item number.

Section V—Additional Comments

Is there anyone else who may have been involved or who could provide additional information regarding this matter?
☐ yes ☐ no

Please add any comments you may wish to make regarding this matter.

_____

_____

_____

_____

_____

_____

_____

_____

_____

_____

_____

_____

I declare that I have examined the information given in this statement and, to the best of my knowledge and belief, it is true, correct and complete.

Person interviewed *(signature)*	Date
Interviewer *(signature)*	Date

Date copy given to person interviewed

Chapter 11

YOUR WORST (TAX) NIGHTMARE, PART 3—THE CRIMINAL INVESTIGATION

THE FEAR FACTOR

What feeling do you get when you receive a letter with the return address, "Internal Revenue Service"? Many law-abiding citizens with healthy superegos think, "Oh my God, I'm going to jail." The fact is, though you need not fear the IRS' Criminal Investigation Division (CID) unless you have committed a tax crime, the fear factor in tax crimes is pervasive. After all, tax fraud, not bootlegging or murder, sent Al Capone to jail. And it is tax fraud that gnaws at otherwise honest people when they "shave" a little on their returns.

Given the infrequency of tax prosecutions, the Criminal Investigation Division of the IRS generates fear far out of proportion to its actual impact. In part this is due to the high profile of some cases and to the odds: anyone investigated by CID statistically has a 45 percent chance of actually going to jail. In 1994, the Criminal Investigation Division started 5,346 investigations. Fully 70 percent were referred for prosecution. Of those, 92 percent resulted in convictions. More than 2,400 people were sentenced to jail.

There is extraordinarily wide variation in who is prosecuted, and how many. A recent article in the *New York Times* (April 16, 1996) summarized Justice

Department data that showed that the statistical chances of being prosecuted in the Roanoke, Virginia, area were fifty-seven times that of the New Mexico area. But statistics alone do not tell the story. Some areas of the country are more prone to tax evasion than others. The agents may be more or less aggressive in certain areas of the country. The U.S. Attorneys who prosecute these cases may be more interested in one area of the country than another. While it may be desirable to have the criminal tax laws applied uniformly throughout the country, the fact remains that there is wide variation in prosecuting tax crimes.

Each of the thirty-three IRS districts has at least one CID group. A group consists of eight to thirty special agents. Their job is to investigate suspected criminal violations of the tax laws and related offenses, such as assault on a revenue officer or seizure by the taxpayer of levied property. Most criminal cases involve the charge of tax evasion, that is, failing to report all income or overstating deductions with specific intent to evade the tax laws. CID also investigates a fair number of nonfiler cases, about one thousand a year, an occasional failure to pay case, and a variety of other tax crimes. Altogether, CID has authority to investigate about thirty tax and nontax crimes. This chapter tells you how CID works and the defenses you may have to a criminal tax investigation.

CID STARTS A CASE

Most criminal tax cases arise from routine audits, that is, a tax audit of an individual, corporation, partnership, or exempt organization. Sometime during the audit, the revenue agent spots something that does not pass her "smell test." It could be a big bank deposit that somehow doesn't square with the tax return, the *absence* of an expected deposit, an overstated deduction, a business deduction that is grossly wrong, or the use of many or fictitious corporations. It could be a cash horde or anything else that seems to be unaccounted for and untaxed. When the revenue agent spots this, she does not immediately throw the cuffs on. She asks for an explanation. If the explanation does not ring true, she has what is known as an "unexplained indication of fraud." At this point, she pulls out Form 2797 (Referral for Potential Fraud Case), a one-page information report to CID. The form asks CID if it is interested in the case. The agent suspends her audit until CID responds. The special agents do not accept every case; they accept the most promising ones or the ones that have the most potential for publicity. After all, headlines are part of their job of enforcement and compliance.

The winds of case selection blow hot and cold; they also change direction frequently. In the 1970s and 1980s, tax shelters and drug and gambling cases filled CID's plate. The 1990s have seen a shift to money laundering, cash businesses, and traditional tax evasion cases. Every new commissioner seems to bring a different policy slant to CID case selection. Generally though, CID goes for either the most publicity-worthy cases or the ones that will yield the most money or promise the greatest deterrent effect.

If the special agent and her group manager agree, they open, or "jacket," the case, and the agent begins the investigation. Often these cases are investigated jointly with the revenue agent, who acts as the special agent's assistant and works the numbers in detail. That cooperation is critical because the special agent must accumulate evidence beyond a reasonable doubt that a substantial tax was actually evaded. The revenue agent often has more expertise than the special agent in the accounting aspects of this task.

The second big source of cases is information reports. For example, someone may file a Currency Transaction Report showing more than $10,000 in cash deposited into a bank account.

Another source is the confidential informant or tipster. An example could be a fired employee who knew the boss was skimming cash. Other tipsters could be an unhappy wife, husband, or partner, or anyone who has a gripe against an evading taxpayer. CID also often receives information from other law enforcement agencies, such as the Drug Enforcement Agency, the Bureau of Alcohol, Tobacco, and Firearms, the FBI, and local law enforcement agencies.

CID will listen to anyone, anytime, and it can pay rewards—up to 10 percent of the taxes recovered.

INVESTIGATING THE CASE

Both agents then begin to investigate your case. Before you ever know they are around, they have looked high and low for information about you, the "subject."

The first phase is background. They check everywhere—public records, lien searches, military history, postal covers (a request to the post office to record who sends you mail, and when), national computer banks, newspapers, even electronic data sources. They check the Internet and the World Wide Web if those seem a likely source of information. Their special agent's manual gives them more sources of leads than they could possibly use, but they look at every one they can.

The IRS does not engage in court-authorized wiretapping, except for the occasional use of pen registers, which record the numbers of all outgoing calls. These will ordinarily be used only in gambling and other organized crime cases. Very infrequently, CID will resort to search and seizure warrants. Often, however, agents will "piggyback" on other law enforcement warrants if you are the subject of some other agency's attention.

The second phase may well be confidential interviews. They may talk to customers, suppliers, friends, neighbors, and acquaintances. The agents find out all they can about you. They examine your reputation for honesty and look for other problems you may have, such as money, marital, or other personal problems.

In the third phase, they appear at your front door, badge and credentials in hand, demanding an interview. This is almost always a surprise if they've done their job well to that point. It's astounding how many targets will, at that point, invite the agents in, close the door, and confess their tax crimes in a four-hour interview. If the agents successfully do that, in most instances their case is made and the rest is paperwork. It's all over but the sentencing. If not, they have to prove their case out of other evidence.

Caution: If the agents come to your door, stop what you're doing and get legal help immediately. Tell the agents you want to consult a lawyer. Never, ever, try to explain your way out of this problem. Even if you are as innocent as a newborn lamb, something very serious has occurred to cause a Treasury law enforcement agent to appear at your door, and there is no safe way for you to deal with it without immediate, competent legal counsel.

In this third phase, the agents also launch searches for records where the fact they are searching becomes known to the subject. This would include compulsory summonses to the taxpayer, his business, banks, brokers, accountants, and any other third parties the agents think might have knowledge of the taxpayer's finances or tax transactions.

The fourth stage (sometimes the third) is to formulate a method of proof—how to reconstruct your true tax picture to show where and how you cheated.

The final stage is the recommendation for prosecution or nonprosecution. The agents assemble all the data, mark their exhibits, create huge, thoroughly indexed binders of documents, referenced and cross-referenced. These exhibits and the witnesses who will identify them are their case. They forward the case through the group manager. Eventually, it winds up in the hands of the U.S. Attorney's Office for prosecution. There, a case may be further developed by a grand jury investigation.

HOW CID PROVES ITS CASE

To prove you cheated with criminal intent, the special agent typically selects one of three principal "methods of proof." The first is the "specific item method," a so-called direct method of proof. As the name of this method implies, the agents have found one or more specific items you have omitted from a return or specific deductions you have overstated (the "smoking gun"). They could find these from bank accounts, canceled checks, or business deductions for personal expenses or from deductions that are wildly overstated. Special agents love specific item cases because they are easy to make. The agents can assume that the rest of your return is right and still get a conviction.

> *Example:* George was a general practitioner of medicine in Maine. He was a fine doctor but accounted for his fees in a somewhat unconventional way. Many of his patients paid in cash, so each day his receptionist pre-pared a list of cash and checks and put them on a deposit slip. Then the doctor personally went to the bank to make a deposit. Of course, a little of this might have slipped into a safe at home, until it accumulated to a tidy sum. Then he put that money in a separate bank account. The IRS added all of his bank accounts, subtracted out gifts, transfers, and loans, and compared the resulting figure to the doctor's income—as he reported on his tax return. Not enough, according to the IRS. The doctor was con-victed. Although he tried to overturn the conviction by showing that he had previously taxed cash on hand at the start of the year (which the IRS disputed), the court sustained the conviction.

Two other principal methods are called "indirect" methods, where the agents prove, indirectly, that you evaded your taxes. One is the "bank deposits method." In this method, the agents add all your bank deposits for each year and subtract transfers from one account to another. The difference is presumed by law to be taxable. If you have net $200,000 of bank deposits but you reported only $100,000 on your tax return, you've got some explaining to do. In case after case, the courts have sustained that method of proof as valid and constitutional.

The second indirect method is called the "net worth and expenditures method." This one is harder to document, but agents have used it effectively for years. In this method, the agents establish your net worth at the beginning of one year and then prove the level to which it grew at the end of one or more additional years. The increases in net worth, plus your other spending, must have come from somewhere. If they arose because you received loans, bequests, or gifts, no problem. But if you cannot account for these large increases in net worth and expenditures as nontaxable, the law presumes them to be unreported taxable income. Many a conviction has been obtained by this method.

> *Example:* William and Katherine immigrated to the United States. Believers in free enterprise, they engaged in the freest possible enterprise by conducting the oldest possible profession, big time. According to their tax returns, however, things were not very profitable. They reported only $11,500 in each of three years. But according to the IRS, that was slightly below their real income. Why could the IRS think this? It might have had to do with the couple's purchase of a $420,000 home with $135,000 down, plus their depositing more than $250,000 in cash into fourteen separate bank accounts. Based on these and other facts, the IRS concluded that the couple's net worth was largely unaccounted for, so it must be unreported income. "You bet," said the jury and the judge. The cash deposits, their false statements and evasiveness with their hired accountant, and the lack of any other explanation showed that William and Katherine had intentionally violated the tax laws.

DEFENDING AGAINST THE INVESTIGATION

Is there anything you can do to defend against these investigations? Your options are limited, but you can take a few steps.

First and foremost, *never* let the special agents interview you. This first defense is the constitutional privilege against self-incrimination. (However, it is not a defense, in a failure to file case, to plead the Fifth Amendment privilege against self-incrimination.) When they come to the door, you should politely but firmly state, "I do not wish to be interviewed, and I would like to consult my lawyer." Special agents understand this and will rarely press the point. Then immediately drop what you are doing and call your lawyer. In any criminal investigation, particularly a tax investigation, you will need a criminal defense lawyer well-versed in tax matters. Then follow your lawyer's advice!

Another mistake people make is to begin transferring assets. This not only shows a guilty mind, but also probably will do no good. After all, the IRS has full authority to make jeopardy assessments and seize property, even when it's transferred to someone else's name. See chapter 8. And it probably constitutes a new, separate crime. Moreover, good special agents watch for this very thing; it helps prove the element of criminal intent.

A second defense is the "voluntary disclosure" defense. This applies in almost every case of nonfilers. An evader can also sometimes escape prosecution with this defense. It consists of filing original or amended returns and fully paying the taxes, penalties, and interest *before* the special agents make their first contact. The Justice Department's policy of nonprosection in such cases is usually honored.

A third possibility is a grant of immunity. This is more rare, but on occasion taxpayers have negotiated for a grant of "use immunity." This means the Department of Justice will not prosecute you as to documents and information you voluntarily disclose.

Fourth, you may try to attack the agent's method of proof. For example, if the agent finds an extra $50,000 of unexplained bank deposits, explain them by showing that they were a gift, loan, or inheritance (if that is true).

Several other defenses may be available, defenses not reserved to tax cases alone. For example, showing that you relied on a lawyer's or accountant's advice to report a deduction or omit an income item might be a defense. But "advice of counsel" must be proved, and you must show that you disclosed all the underlying facts to your professional adviser. This defense is a variation of the "good faith" defense, in which you argue that for one reason or another, you did not violate a "known" legal duty.

Mental incapacity is also a defense, but that too must be clearly proved. Still, occasionally this defense is successful.

As in any criminal investigation, your maneuvering room is usually limited. After all, CID accepts only the investigations it feels have solid conviction potential. If you are to stop this investigation, it's usually at the agent's level or not at all. Even when the agents fail to make a criminal case, they often recommend the civil fraud penalty—75 percent of the understated tax. The lesson is simple: A criminal investigation can have no happy ending except the rare one of no prosecution or an acquittal.

Chapter 12

THE BANKRUPTCY ALTERNATIVE

Can bankruptcy solve your tax problem? Yes, it *is* possible. But there are more myths, errors, and misconceptions about managing taxes through bankruptcy than there are politicians making election-year promises to lower your taxes.

Bankruptcy is so detailed and complex a subject that it cannot be fully treated in one chapter or even one book. Bankruptcy is not for the fainthearted or the uncounseled. You need an experienced bankruptcy lawyer to advise you whether, when, and how to file a bankruptcy petition. From this chapter you may learn only whether it makes sense to *think* of a bankruptcy to handle all or part of your taxes. If so, the next step would be to see a bankruptcy lawyer.

With this caution, let's start by looking at the most common myths or misconceptions about taxes in bankruptcy.

The first misconception centers on the bankruptcy "discharge," the technical term for legal relief of a debt through bankruptcy. Most normal debts are "dischargeable" by the simple act of filing a petition under Chapter 7, the liquidation chapter of the Bankruptcy Code. The first tax myth is: "Taxes aren't normal debts. You can never discharge a tax in bankruptcy." In fact, taxpayers discharge millions of dollars of taxes in bankruptcy every year. Of the one million or so bankruptcies people file each year, the IRS is involved in fully one-third.

"I can *always* discharge my taxes in bankruptcy—just file and forget." This is another misconception. The technical, detailed bankruptcy rules relating to taxes are monuments to poor writing and confusing syntax. Yes, some types of taxes are in fact dischargeable; others never are. Even if a tax may possibly qualify for discharge, the timing and detail can trip you.

Another myth is often stated like this: "If I file for bankruptcy, I'll lose everything." True enough, some bankruptcies require you (or a trustee) to sell your assets, but other types of bankruptcies assume precisely the reverse: they anticipate you will not sell but will rehabilitate yourself by negotiating your way out of burdensome debt, including tax debt.

And many a person considering bankruptcy has thought: "If I file for bankruptcy, the IRS will get everything, including my home and pension." Not so. In fact, in many cases, the IRS gets very little on its tax claim. Sometimes you can even save a pension or a home in the aftermath of a bankruptcy.

These are just some of the common misconceptions that surround taxes in bankruptcy.

The good news is this: Bankruptcy is a powerful, effective instrument you can often use to manage an otherwise impossible tax collection problem. It always stops the IRS in its tracks for at least some period of time, giving you much needed breathing room. It sometimes stops the IRS completely and forever.

The bad news is: You won't always be able to discharge your taxes. Bankruptcy also can trigger other financial problems, and a bankruptcy on your credit record is like a scarlet letter *B* you wear for years.

HOW BANKRUPTCIES WORK

Individuals and businesses normally file one of three types of bankruptcies: Chapter 7, Chapter 11, or Chapter 13. In a Chapter 7 case, you are throwing in the towel: it's a liquidation. A court-appointed trustee takes title to your assets, sells them, and pays your creditors with the proceeds. So you're cleaned out; but in return, you get a fresh start from your debts, paid or not. At least, that's what Chapter 7 is supposed to do. It doesn't always work out that way, especially for taxes.

Chapter 11 and Chapter 13 are the converse of Chapter 7. They are not liquidations; they are rehabilitations, or "reorganizations" in the language of the Bankruptcy Code. Both of these chapters presume that you intend to continue on in business (whether as a corporation, partnership, proprietor, or wage earner), that you want to compromise some of your debts and stretch out others, but that you intend to pay something on your debts without liquidating all of your assets.

When you file a petition in bankruptcy, no matter which chapter you use, the mere act of filing puts an immediate, automatic stop to all your creditors' collection efforts. That includes everyone from the phone company to credit card companies to the IRS. From the instant you file, the IRS and other creditors are forbidden from seizing assets, filing liens, making assessments, and taking most other creditor-type actions. They know this rule and obey it in most cases. But you have to let them know you have filed!

The IRS does have special rules that allow it to perform a few tax-related actions even after a bankruptcy filing. For instance, it may mail a Notice of Tax Deficiency (see chapters 15 and 21), investigate some claims, and conduct some audits. But if you are really afraid for your assets and you fear the IRS is about to lower the boom, any bankruptcy filing will stop collection at least for a while. You can let the agency know you filed by fax, letter, or phone.

This "automatic stay" of creditors' attempts to collect is the strongest weapon you have as a taxpayer. In fact, it's usually the only legal weapon *you* have the power to exercise. In other cases, when the IRS forbears from collecting against you, it's because the agency chose to forbear—its decision, not yours.

So, filing for bankruptcy calls a big "time out" to the creditor versus debtor contest. You have breathing room, time to think, time to plan. For taxes, you also need to plan *before* you file because the timing of bankruptcy as an instrument to handle your tax problem is absolutely critical.

DISCHARGING TAXES IN BANKRUPTCY

Only a few types of taxes are dischargeable at all (if you meet certain rules), but two are big ones: federal and state income taxes. Also dischargeable are gross receipts taxes and certain excise taxes. Some taxes are never dischargeable: employment taxes, Trust Fund Recovery Penalty taxes (see chapter 10), and others.

Let's say you want to discharge a federal or state income tax. You can't just file for bankruptcy and have the tax declared "discharged," even if the bankruptcy court grants you a general discharge from your debts. You have to meet certain other rules. First, the bankruptcy petition must be filed more than three years after the due date of the tax return involved. For example, if you filed your return on

April 15, 1992 (for 1991), you must file bankruptcy petition April 16, 1995, or later. If you went on extension to file, measure the three years from the extended date. That doesn't mean the date you actually filed, but the true extended date.

> *Example:* In one court case, a taxpayer extended his filing date to October 15, 1990 (for 1989), and filed his bankruptcy petition October 10, 1993, five days too soon. He missed the three-year rule and could not get a discharge.

The second rule is: If your return was filed late, file the bankruptcy petition more than two years after you actually filed your return. Again, this rule is ironclad: either you meet it or you don't. If you are planning for this rule, it's usually wise to find out from the IRS when it received your return so you don't get into a dispute as to when you actually filed.

Third, file the bankruptcy petition more than 240 days after the IRS' assessment of the taxes you want to discharge.

> *Example:* Nina Nopay filed her 1992 tax return on April 15, 1993. She owed $10,000 on the return, which the IRS assessed against her on April 17, 1993. Nina must wait until December 16, 1993 (the 241st day), to file her petition.

Now, let's say she files on December 16 but the IRS audits her return on December 18, 1993, and finds she owes another $5,000. Nina's discharge won't extend to the new $5,000 bill.

Watch out for offers in compromise. If you filed one, this 240-day time period is suspended while the offer is being considered, plus thirty days.

Fourth, you cannot have evaded your taxes. That means you can't have filed a fraudulent return or evaded the payment of the taxes.

Fifth, you cannot discharge a tax that is "still assessable" when you file. For example, if your return is under examination and the IRS proposes more taxes, those taxes can't be discharged (the Tina Nopay example above). But the taxes you reported on the return are dischargeable if you meet the other rules described above.

Penalties and interest can also be dischargeable, though not always. A good rule of thumb is: A late-filing, late-payment, or negligence penalty (the most common penalties the IRS imposes) is dischargeable if the underlying tax is dischargeable. Even if this is not the case, the penalty is dischargeable if it relates to conduct that is more than three years old.

> *Example:* In 1990, Thaddeus Thumbnose committed civil tax fraud by failing to include $100,000 in gross income on his tax return. He filed the return promptly on April 15, 1991. The IRS caught him in 1993 and assessed $30,000 in tax and a $22,500 civil fraud penalty (75 percent). Thaddeus filed for Chapter 7 (liquidating bankruptcy) on April 16, 1994. The taxes were not dischargeable because of the tax fraud, but the fraud *penalty* was dischargeable because Thaddeus committed the fraud more than three years before he filed his bankruptcy petition.

GETTING THE DISCHARGE FROM TAXES

Here's how it works. Let's say you have satisfied all the rules and have carefully planned for your Chapter 7 liquidating bankruptcy. You then file your Chapter 7 petition. A "bankruptcy estate" springs into being automatically when you file the petition. It's an artificial entity, something like a trust in which you might put assets. In a Chapter 7 case, by law everything you own (with a few exceptions) automatically becomes part of this bankruptcy estate. The assets are not yours anymore. They belong to the estate. A trustee is assigned to handle your case. The trustee's job is to sell any assets that might raise cash, distribute these to your creditors, and close the estate. The trustee may decide that some assets can't be sold for cash, or would not yield enough after paying off the prebankruptcy liens. The trustee will abandon such assets back to you. The trustee might also abandon a home if it has no equity. (All states also have a homestead exception that varies in amount.)

What about the taxes? The IRS is often at the top of the food chain in bankruptcies. In such cases, the IRS may get paid first, or it might be paid after other, prior secured creditors. But if there's not enough to go around, the unpaid taxes are discharged by law. If the IRS has filed a notice of lien, you still get the discharge of taxes, but the lien remains attached to the assets in your bankruptcy estate.

Usually, the bankruptcy court will not specifically rule that your taxes (or any debt) have been discharged. It will simply grant a "general discharge," a one-page document. That document is your legal "fresh start" as to any debt that was legally dischargeable, including taxes. The IRS then decides on its own whether your particular taxes have in fact been discharged.

The IRS office that handles bankruptcy cases is the Special Procedures Section. When you file your case, this office gets the case file and looks over the assessments, the due dates of the returns, the liens on file, and the rules described above. If you meet all the rules, in almost every case the agent will note the file for discharge and close it. You will never hear from them again. Your account in the IRS computers will be adjusted to "zero" tax for each tax year involved.

Sometimes the IRS determines that your taxes are not dischargeable, or the computer makes a mistake and continues to try to collect against you. Then you have to convince the agency that it made a computer mistake (if that is what it was), or that your taxes were in fact legally discharged.

If worst comes to worst, you can always reopen your bankruptcy and ask the bankruptcy court to declare formally that your taxes have been discharged.

HOW CHAPTER 11 AND CHAPTER 13 WORK

Since these are not liquidations but rehabilitations, you handle taxes a little differently. In both types of cases, you propose a "plan of reorganization." This is a written plan that tells the court how much you want to pay all of your creditors.

As with any type of bankruptcy, in Chapters 11 and 13 you file your petition and make a complete statement of assets and liabilities. Then, you propose a plan to pay your debts. In such a plan, some debts are more "equal" than others. At the top of the heap in any bankruptcy are secured creditors. These are creditors who have a valid, perfected lien against one or more of your assets. A good example would be the bank that loaned you money for your home mortgage. Another might be a receivables financier for a business. The IRS becomes a secured creditor in a bankruptcy whenever it files a Notice of Federal Tax Lien. As chapter 4 explains, that Notice of Federal Tax Lien ties up all your property and rights to property, wherever located. As against real estate, the lien is valid if it is filed in the place state law requires, usually the county land records. When it is filed, all the equity in your property is tied up by this federal tax lien.

If the agency has not filed a notice of lien, the taxes are unsecured. They may be "priority" taxes or "general unsecured" taxes, depending on how old they are and whether they met the discharge rules described earlier in this chapter.

Priority taxes must also be paid in full according to the plan, unless the IRS compromises them. General unsecured taxes have the same low standing as any other unsecured debt. You must propose a plan that will pay as much or more as would be received if the case were a Chapter 7 liquidation.

Chapter 13 plans are particularly useful to wage earners and other persons with periodic income. Basically, you propose a plan to pay your priority taxes (and other debts) over three years according to the rules of the Bankruptcy Code. Courts can approve plans that stretch an additional two years. Once you are finished with your plan payments, that's it. You receive a discharge from all the debts that are provided for in the plan. In most cases, the tax debts are all "provided for," because the IRS has filed a proof of claim in your case. But that's not universally true. Sometimes it fails to file a proof of claim, often losing its claim because of this failure.

Chapter 13 plans are specifically geared toward paying your debts out of future income. Moreover, you can be very flexible in designing a Chapter 13 plan (or Chapter 11 plan). Payments must start "as soon as practicable" after confirmation of the plan, but nothing in the code says they have to be equal. So, debtors have designed plans that deferred some debts for awhile, and paid others that were in arrears. The most common example is a mortgage in arrears. Even tax debts can be deferred until later years this way. The IRS doesn't like it, and it often opposes these postponements, arguing that it should be paid equally and evenly along with everyone else. But the courts are lenient about approving Chapter 13 plans that defer some types of creditors, including the IRS.

What if things don't work out, and you lose your job or suffer other "hardship" during the five years you had proposed in your confirmed plan? You can apply for a hardship discharge. The result? You get your discharge even though you have not paid for the full three to five years.

The bankruptcy laws can be important tools in other respects as well. Let's say you dispute a tax, such as an income tax or even the Trust Fund Recovery Penalty (see chapter 10). The bankruptcy courts have wide discretion to try many types of tax cases. You don't have to go to tax court or federal district court if you think you can do as well or better in bankruptcy court. Traditionally, bankruptcy courts are pro-debtor, though you should not count on any particular bias in your favor from the bankruptcy judge simply because you have come to him or her for help. Still, the bankruptcy courts are open and available to adjudicate your tax disputes in most cases.

To be eligible for Chapter 13, you must have regular income, unsecured debts of less than $250,000, and secured debts of less than $750,000. Wage earners, pensioners, sole proprietors, and other types of earners are eligible to file Chapter 13. Chapter 13 plans are simpler than those in Chapter 11, and less expensive as well. They have other advantages over Chapters 7 and 11 that your bankruptcy attorney can review with you.

PUTTING THESE CONCEPTS INTO PRACTICE

Always seek professional help when planning for a bankruptcy. A bankruptcy attorney, especially one familiar with the tax rules, should plan your bankruptcy, file it, and advise you as it goes along. Preplanning is absolutely essential: the casebooks are littered with the financial corpses of people who thought they were getting a fresh start from their taxes by filing bankruptcy, only to awake the next day to tax liens and levies.

But if you plan it well, a bankruptcy can be a satisfactory solution to your tax problems, either through discharge or reorganization.

Chapter 13
"HELP!!"—THE PROBLEM RESOLUTION PROGRAM

About twenty years ago, the Swedish word "ombudsman" came into our language. This ombudsman had a license to seek out and destroy bureaucratic red tape and snafus and other incomprehensible messes wherever they existed in government agencies. Many private corporations now use ombudsmen, too. The IRS has had an ombudsman for eighteen years. It's even in the name—the Office of Ombudsman (changed in 1996 to the Office of Taxpayer Advocate). The national ombudsman has charge of thirty-three suboffices, one in each of the IRS' districts around the country. Appendix II contains a list of them. This local branch, called the Problem Resolution Office (PRO), exists for one purpose: to untangle the mess you are in because some part of the IRS has shut the steel trap of bureaucracy on you. The PRO's job description actually includes taking your side over the IRS' when the bureaucracy overwhelms you. If that means the IRS will get less money, so be it.

In 1988, Congress gave the problem resolution offices a huge new club to subdue the bureaucracy: the Taxpayer Assistance Order. This part of the PRO's authority is so important that it can be viewed as a distinct service. That is, the PRO handles (1) applications for taxpayer assistance orders, plus (2) all other bureaucratic snafus.

ARE YOU IN COLLECTION TROUBLE? FILE "911"

When you truly have the IRS blues, when collection officers threaten your business, when you just can't pay but the revenue officer insists on it despite the hardship it will create, the Problem Resolution Office can come to the rescue. PROs have wide authority to intervene and stop all collection action when you file an Application for a Taxpayer Assistance Order. The halt is usually short, but it gives you a chance to work things out with the Collection Division. The PROs in fact grant some measure of relief in about half of all cases.

An Application for a Taxpayer Assistance Order has only one drawback. It suspends the period of limitations on collection for the time the application is pending. Usually that suspension is very short, and well worth it, especially if you get the relief you want.

That relief from a too-harsh tax collector is spelled "Form 911." Yes, it is true, they actually have Form 911, intentionally so numbered, for situations of "undue hardship" in the collection of taxes. Form 911 is a one-page form in which you tell the IRS what hardship the collection officer is causing or threatening and the relief you want.

Strictly speaking, the law authorizes the PRO to intervene when the IRS' action would "offend the sense of fairness of taxpayers in general under all the surrounding facts and circumstances." In practice, the PROs interpret this rule more narrowly, but still come to your rescue in many cases. The Application for a Taxpayer Assistance Order is a legal remedy you can invoke, reserved for true collection emergencies where you've tried your best through the normal channels.

Example: Roger and Rosetta have been married for twenty-five years. For the last three years, Roger has been clinically depressed, in and out of hospitals, on and off medications. He also has terminal cancer. As a result, he did not file tax returns for those three years. The IRS filed substitute returns for each year and assessed the taxes. Then it levied on the couple's bank account for a much larger amount than they actually owed. They needed time while another branch of the service considered their request for abatement of tax and penalty. They filed Form 911, claiming undue hardship. The Problem Resolution Office moved to release the levy. But it also ensured that Roger and Rosetta filed tax returns of their own.

Example: Your restaurant is behind on payroll taxes for six months. It's now summer, the slow season. You know you can catch up in the fall, but cash is even tighter now than usual. The revenue officer demands immediate payment and threatens to close your business or seize your bank accounts. Suppliers may get wind of this. Customers may flee, and the whole enterprise may come crashing down. You file Form 911, asking for a delay of three months on collection of the back taxes while you stay current on present taxes. The Problem Resolution Office has the authority to grant your request over the opposition of the Collection Division.

Example: You owe $10,000 in back taxes on last year's return. The Automated Collection System representative calls you. She is abusive and threatening. She demands you stay on the phone, even after you ask for a time-out to consult a professional. She demands information from you upon penalty of immediate collection. After you hang up, you are nervous and shaky. You file Form 911. The Problem Resolution Office should again intervene to help get you courteous treatment and a reasonable time to respond.

The "hardship" the PROs look for in this type of case must be "undue," a standard that leaves plenty of room for discretion. This means they won't intervene just because you are upset at the revenue officer—her job is to get the money, not to make you feel good. But the revenue officer crosses the line in such areas as depriving you of necessary living expenses (for example, rent, utilities, groceries, and other necessities). Hardship may be undue if she threatens to file a Notice of Federal Tax Lien, which could ruin your credit, cause a default on loans, or force a bankruptcy, all without giving you a fair chance to pay. The revenue officer also could cross the hardship line by threatening to levy your business or personal accounts, depriving you of the necessary cash flow to continue, when you could easily pay in large installments.

The problem resolution officer will also look at every category of necessary living expense to determine whether the collection action threatens those necessities. This would include food, clothing, housing, medical supplies, utilities, even education. She will take notice if the collection action will threaten your job or business, if the action is imminent, even if you become "so overwhelmed" or overcome by the pressure from the revenue officer that you begin crying. In theory, she is not supposed to "blame" you if you are the one whose intransigence or fault caused the problem. In practice, PROs are human beings; they take that into account.

HOW TO FILE 911

You can get the form from any local IRS office, download it from the IRS' address on the Internet (see chapter 26), or obtain a copy from many libraries. You can even call the local IRS office, whose representative will send or fax you a copy. Also, you may get the form by dialing 1-800-TAX-FORM, but be prepared to wait seven to ten days. A copy of Form 911 is found at the end of this chapter. Form 911 also can be "filed" by telephone.

Before you file Form 911, you are required to exhaust at least one level of review. So if the revenue officer was nasty to you or threatened to levy your business accounts, appeal to her immediate boss, the group manager. Usually, this is a waste of time; the boss will nearly always back her revenue officer. In some IRS districts, you must make one more appeal, to the branch chief. All of this takes time, but it can be done by phone. Take notes on all the calls you make. If hours count, call the group manager directly, or ask the revenue officer if she has cleared the levy, lien, or other seizure action with her group manager. If so, you have "exhausted" your appeal responsibilities, and you can now go to the PRO.

If the group manager is absent, ask for the acting group manager. If that person is unavailable, immediately call the Problem Resolution Office and explain that the internal appeal was futile because everyone was absent or unavailable. That is usually enough to give the PROs jurisdiction. They will see you have tried to work it out, but the bureaucracy stood in the way.

Once the PRO will listen, the next step is to send, mail, or fax your Application for Taxpayer Assistance Order (Form 911) to the Problem Resolution Office. (You can file the application by phone, but you're usually better off doing it in writing.) Most of the form is self-explanatory. The most critical sections are blocks 12 and 13, though all parts must be completed. Part 12 asks what the problem is. Be clear, concise, and detailed. State facts, not opinions. Tell what the revenue officer did or threatened to do. Start with a summary paragraph such as, "The revenue officer is threatening to levy on my retirement account when I need this money for the care of my elderly parents, who are otherwise without support." Then start a new paragraph. Begin at the beginning and tell what happened. Your story need not be more than one typewritten page, though many good applications are longer. Sacrifice no detail, but do not ramble. This is not the place to state your candid opinion of the revenue officer or to editorialize about the tax system. Just state what she did or is threatening that you believe to be unduly harsh.

Part 13 is equally critical. Tell the Problem Resolution Office what relief you want. Do you want the Collection Division to stop collection forever? For a time? Do you want the revenue officer to release or withdraw a lien (nearly impossible)? To release a levy (easier)? Do not be concerned about legalisms or fancy language. State in plain English what you want the PRO to do.

If the PRO officer accepts the application, she immediately calls the revenue officer's group manager and tells her to stop everything. This halt-in-place is like a bolt of lightning: it strikes fast and hard, but it lasts for only a short time. It's a temporary hold on collection, for no more than forty-eight hours. But it gives you, the PRO, and the Collection Division time to work things out. At this point, the Problem Resolution Office becomes a mediator. Experience shows that this mediation helps in many cases, though not all. In some IRS districts, the problem resolution officers interpret "undue hardship" very narrowly, almost always taking the side of the revenue officer. So be careful to use this weapon sparingly.

At the end of the process, with any luck you will have worked out a livable deal with the Collection Division. If not, there is nothing more the PRO can do for you, and you are on your own once again.

This Application for Taxpayer Assistance Order is a fantastic weapon at your command when it is truly merited. Everyone hopes that things never get that hot between you and the Collection Division, but it happens. The Service's own statistics show 125,000 applications for taxpayer assistance orders in fiscal 1994, and 90,000 in which relief was granted in one form or another (though an actual TAO is rarely granted).

THE OFFICE OF TAXPAYER ADVOCATE

The 1996 Taxpayer Bill of Rights strengthened the old Office of Ombudsman and renamed it the Office of Taxpayer Advocate. In theory, Congress gave this advocate new powers to take your side in tax disputes. The office will also report directly to Congress, rather than through the IRS bureaucracy. Whether this new office will project new strength and commitment down to the problem resolution offices remains to be seen.

OTHER RED-TAPE ISSUES

The Problem Resolution Office also helps you slash red tape in every other area where it threatens strangulation.

By and large, the PROs do this extremely well. The types of problems and snafus they encounter are dizzying in their variety. After all, the IRS is so big and complex that things can go wrong almost anywhere. And once a problem occurs, it's hard to fix. But the majority of these cases fall into several classes.

The first is your tax refund. The IRS usually sends your refund within six weeks after you file your return, faster if you file electronically. But sometimes refunds are lost or delayed. Other times, when you file a separate claim for refund after your return has been filed, the claim can get lost. If you get no action after your second request, or ninety days pass, the PROs have jurisdiction to help.

Second, if you make any other request for information to the IRS and forty-five days pass without action, it's now a job for the PRO. Many people do not realize they can ask for help in virtually any procedural IRS matter after this forty-five-day period. Often they make call after frustrating call through normal channels, or write letter after unanswered letter, getting nowhere for months or years at a time.

Third, if you receive two collection notices from the Automated Collection System, or two other notices that you owe taxes from an IRS service center, and you answer them but the Service fails to respond to you, the PRO can take action. It can stop the notices, conduct a "prayer session" with the collection agent who is harassing you, and take other helpful action.

Beyond these examples, the PRO can help with a wide variety of bureaucratic problems. These are too varied to be described, so recall the basic rule: When all else fails, call the PROs. In fact, call them before all else fails; they will help you through the worst of IRS gridlock.

Form **911**

(Rev. January 1994)

Department of the Treasury – Internal Revenue Service

Application for Taxpayer Assistance Order *(ATAO)*

(Taxpayer's Application for Relief from Hardship)

If sending Form 911 with another form or letter, put Form 911 on top.

Note: If you have not tried to obtain relief from the IRS office that contacted you, use of this form may not be necessary. Use this form only after reading the instructions for When To Use This Form. Filing this application may affect the statutory period of limitations. (See instructions for line 14.)

Section I.   Taxpayer Information

1. Name(s) as shown on tax return

2. Your Social Security Number

4. Tax form

3. Social Security of Spouse Shown in 1.

5. Tax period ended

6. Current mailing address (number & street). For P.O. Box, see instructions   Apt. No.

8. Employer identification number, if applicable.

7. City, town or post office, state and ZIP Code

9. Person to contact

If the above address is different from that shown on latest filed tax return and you want us to update our records with this new address, check here.........☐

10. Daytime telephone number   (   )

11. Best time to call

12. Description of significant hardship *(If more space is needed, attach additional sheets.)*

13. Description of relief requested *(If more space is needed, attach additional sheets.)*

A

T

A

O

14. Signature of taxpayer or Corporate Officer *(See instructions.)*

15. Date

16. Signature of spouse shown in block 1

17. Date

Section II.   Representative Information *(If applicable)*

18. Name of authorized representative (Must be same as on Form 2848 or 8821)

22. Firm name

19. Centralized Authorization File (CAF) number

23. Mailing address

20. Daytime telephone number   (   )

21. Best time to call

24. Representative Signature

25. Date

Section III.   (For Internal Revenue Service only)

26. Name of initiating employee

27.
☐   IRS Identified
☐   Taxpayer request

28. Telephone   (   )

29. Function

30. Office

31. Date

Cat. No. 16965S

19

Form **911** (Rev. 1-94)

Instructions

When To Use This Form: Use this form to apply for relief from a **significant hardship** which may have already occurred or is about to occur if the IRS takes or fails to take certain actions. A significant hardship normally means not being able to provide the necessities of life for you or your family. Examples of such necessities include, but are not limited to: food, shelter, clothing, or medical care. You may use this form at any time. Instead of using this form, **however, the IRS prefers that requests for relief first be made with the IRS office that most recently contacted you.** In most cases, the relief needed can be secured directly from the appropriate IRS employee. For example, Collection employees handle requests for payment arrangements on late taxes or releases of levy on wages, salaries, or bank accounts; Taxpayer Service employees handle requests for immediate refunds of overpaid taxes; Examination employees handle requests for review of additional tax assessments when the taxpayer has had no opportunity to present proof of claimed deductions.

If an IRS office will not grant the relief requested, or will not grant the relief in time to avoid the significant hardship, you may submit this form. No enforcement action will be taken while we are reviewing your application.

Note: Do not use this application to change the amount of any tax you owe. If you disagree with the amount of tax assessed, see **Publication 1, Your Rights as a Taxpayer.**

Where To Submit This Form: Submit this application to the Internal Revenue Service, Problem Resolution Office, in the district where you live. For the address of the Problem Resolution Office in your district or for more information, call the local Taxpayer Assistance number in your local telephone directory or 1-800-829-1040.

Overseas Taxpayers: Taxpayers residing overseas should submit this application to the Internal Revenue Service., Problem Resolution Office, Assistant Commissioner (International), P.O. Box 44817, L'Enfant Plaza Station, Washington, D.C. 20026-4817.

Caution: Incomplete applications or applications submitted to the incorrect office may result in delays. If you do not hear from us within one week of submitting Form 911, please contact the Problem Resolution Office where you sent your application.

Section I. Taxpayer Information

1. Name(s) as shown on tax return. Enter your name as it appeared on the tax return for each period you are asking for help even if your name has changed since the return was submitted. If you filed a joint return, enter both names.

4. Tax form. Enter the tax form number of the form for which you are requesting assistance. For example, if you are requesting assistance for a problem involving an individual income tax return, enter "1040." If your problem involves more than one tax form, include the information in block 12.

5. Tax period ended. If you are requesting assistance on an annually filed return, enter the calendar year or the ending date of the fiscal year for that return. If the problem concerns a return filed quarterly, enter the ending date of the quarter involved. File only one Form 911 even if multiple tax periods are involved. If the problem involves more than one tax period, include the information in block 12.

6. Current mailing address (number and street). If your post office does not deliver mail to your street address and you have a P.O. box, show your box number instead of your street address.

8. Employer Identification Number. Enter the employer identification number (*EIN*) of the business, corporation, trust, etc., for the name you showed in block 1.

9. Person to contact. Enter the name of the person to contact about the problem. In the case of businesses, corporations, trusts, estates, etc., enter the name of a responsible official.

10. Daytime telephone number. Enter the daytime telephone number, including area code, of the person to contact.

12. Description of significant hardship. Describe the action(s) being taken (or not being taken) by the Internal Revenue Service that are causing you significant hardship. If you know it, include the name of the person, office, telephone number, and/or address of the last contact you had with IRS regarding this problem.

13. Description of relief requested. Be specific. If your remaining income after paying expenses is too little to meet an IRS payment, give the details. Describe the action you want the IRS to take.

14. and 16. Signature(s) If you filed a joint return it is not necessary for both you and your spouse to sign this application for your account to be reviewed. If you sign the application the IRS **may** suspend applicable statutory periods of limitations for the assessment of additional taxes and for the collection of taxes. If the taxpayer is your dependent child who cannot sign this application because of age, **or someone incapable of signing the application because of some other reason,** you may sign the taxpayer's name in the space provided followed by the words "By (your signature), parent (or guardian)." If the application is being made for other than the individual taxpayer, a person having authority to sign the return should sign this form. Enter the date Form 911 is signed.

Section II. Representative Information

Taxpayers: If you wish to have a representative act in your behalf, you must give your representative power of attorney or tax information authorization for the tax form(s) and period(s) involved. (*See Form 2848, Power of Attorney and Declaration of Representative and Instructions or Form 8821, Tax Information Authorization, for more information.*)

Representatives: If you are an authorized representative submitting this request on behalf of the taxpayer identified in Section I, complete blocks 18 through 25, attach a copy of Form 2848, Form 8821, or the power of attorney. Enter your Centralized Authorization File (*CAF*) number in block 19. The CAF number is the unique number that Internal Revenue Service assigns to a representative after a valid Form 2848 or Form 8821 is filed with an IRS office.

(For IRS Use Only)

ATAO Code	How received	Date of Determination	PRO signature

Form **911** (Rev. 1-94)

Chapter 14

———✦———

THE TAXPAYER BILLS OF RIGHTS

A popular myth has pervaded the country for years: People have few if any rights against the IRS. In fact, you have plenty of rights. The myth persists because the IRS' powers sometimes seem arbitrary and overwhelming. Other times people may not appreciate the powers, legal rights, and procedures they can exercise to defend themselves.

Congress tried to help in 1988 by passing the Taxpayer Bill of Rights. That name does a disservice to the real Bill of Rights, the first ten amendments to the Constitution. The Taxpayer Bill of Rights does not define your relationship to the federal government or the IRS. But it does have a few useful features, and one in particular that can be a blockbuster—the Taxpayer Assistance Order. That one provision can be so important when you need it in a tax collection emergency that everyone should know how and when to use it. Chapter 13 discusses this right in detail.

To supplement the 1988 act, in 1996 Congress enacted the Taxpayer Bill of Rights 2.

Let's review the 1988 Taxpayer Bill of Rights and the most important parts of its 1996 supplement.

WHEN YOU ARE AUDITED

1. *Right to an explanation.* The IRS must explain its audit procedures and findings in simple, nontechnical language. This right applies to the taxes and penalties it proposes and to your audit and appeal rights. By and large, the Service succeeds in this obligation. True enough, audit notices can sometimes confuse. But generally, the IRS' notices are now more clear, simple, understandable, and complete than at any time in the past.

2. *Right to interest abatement.* The Service can also abate interest if it unreasonably delays your case. Let's say you are audited, and the IRS concludes you owe $1,000. What if they don't send a bill for four months ("Sorry, it fell through the cracks.")? For many years, the Service has been able to abate interest if it made such a "ministeral" error. Now, with the 1996 act, the agency can also abate interest if it makes a "managerial" error, that is, if one of its agents or managers unreasonably delays a computation or a bill. On top of that, if the Service refuses your request for abatement, you can now take it to court. Before the 1996 act, you were stuck with the fact that the IRS got to judge itself; no one could judge the IRS. But now, if your case is strong enough for interest abatement, you can ask a United States Tax Court judge for an independent ruling. And, those tax court judges are *very* independent. They call cases as they see them.

3. *Right to abate penalty and interest if you rely on IRS.* The IRS is required to abate tax and penalty if you reasonably relied on advice from the IRS in preparing an item on your return. Of course, there are several catches. The advice has to be in writing. The IRS agent has to have acted in his official capacity (verbal or informal advice doesn't count). And you must have given adequate and accurate information to the IRS about your transaction. If the tax and penalty are abated, the computers will automatically abate all of the associated interest.

4. *Right to tape-record interview.* It's hard to believe anyone actually uses this right, and for the most part it's unnecessary and counterproductive. Congress put it in the law for that occasional audit where the revenue agent or tax auditor truly misunderstands your position or misquotes it (either deliberately or inadvertently). As a matter of strategy, its normally unwise to record an interview with an IRS agent. Think how you would feel. Recording hardens attitudes, stiffens and formalizes communication, and therefore undermines your ability to get the best result. The IRS has no statistics on how many people ask to record interviews.

WHEN THE IRS COMES TO COLLECT YOUR TAXES

5. *Right to a clear explanation.* The IRS must give you a clear and complete explanation of its enforcement procedures and your rights against them. Its vehicle is Publication No. 1 "Your Rights as a Taxpayer," reprinted at the end of chapter 1. This is an excellent publication, clearly written, fair, and informative. If you follow its advice and exercise all your rights, you will rarely have an IRS problem you cannot solve. The explanation of rights in Publication No. 1 covers four topics: (1) your rights and the IRS' duties in an audit, (2) appeal rights within the IRS and to the courts, (3) procedures for filing refund claims and taxpayer complaints, and (4) the IRS' enforcement powers to collect a tax that is past due. The publication explains the right to negotiate with the revenue officer, the availability of an appeal to her boss, the right to legal and accounting representation, the right to appeal within the IRS, and your right to contest some matters in court. The IRS sends this flyer with almost every collection notice, and if you read nothing else, read this publication.

6. *Installment agreement.* The IRS now has explicit legal authority to let you pay your taxes in installments. It's not a right—you cannot force the IRS to accept such an agreement, but at least the authority is now clearly part of the law. In fact, the Service enters into more than a million installment agreements every year. Chapter 7 tells you how and when to ask for one, and how to negotiate a livable payment plan. The 1996 Taxpayer Bill of Rights requires the IRS to notify you thirty days before terminating your installment agreement. The agency had come around to doing this anyway, but now the law requires it. The Service can end an installment agreement if you don't pay, if the information you based the agreement on turns out to be wrong, or if you strike it rich and the IRS thinks you can pay more. Now, this thirty-day window gives you a chance to renegotiate. You can also ask for an independent review of that termination, but so far the Service has not established any review procedure.

7. *Right to thirty-day cooling-off period before a levy.* By law, the IRS has to tell you in advance that it is about to seize your assets. Ten days used to be all the notice it had to give; now it's thirty days. That may not sound like a lot, but it's an eternity if you are moving fast to convince the IRS to lift a wage or other levy.

WHEN YOU SUE THE IRS

8.   *Right to attorneys' fees and other costs.* If you beat the IRS in court, you can sometimes win attorneys' fees, accountants' fees, and other costs and fees. Not all the time, but sometimes. Naturally, the IRS fights these attorney fee requests with all its strength, heart, and soul. It's a hard fight to win, and you are not even eligible unless you actually hire attorneys and accountants. (You can't get fees if you act as your own attorney.)   However, experience shows that courts award attorneys' fees in about one-third of cases the taxpayer wins.

The 1996 Taxpayer Bill of Rights makes your job easier. Now, the burden is shifted to the IRS to show that its position in your case was "substantially justified." This provision will likely result in more awards to taxpayers of their attorneys' fees.

9.   *Right to sue for damages.* If the IRS abuses its authority by publicly disclosing information about you it should not, failing to release a lien when it should, or otherwise not following the collection laws, you now can sue for damages. Most of these suits are thrown out, but a few succeed. To win, you have to show the IRS agent acted recklessly or intentionally outside the law. Also, you can now recover your actual, direct economic damages, or $1,000,000, whichever is less. On top of that, you normally have to bring your claim to the IRS first (but the court can waive this), and you must try to minimize your damages. If you sue, the limitations period is two years after the IRS' violation, whether you knew of it or not. These are high hurdles to jump, so it's no wonder most of these suits fail. Still, everyone needs to know of this right for the rare case where the IRS greatly oversteps its authority.

10.   *Right to representation.* You have the right to ask a tax practitioner or other representative to do battle on your behalf with the IRS. It can be a lawyer, accountant, enrolled agent, enrolled actuary, or other type of representative. Chapter 31 discusses these IRS-qualified representatives in detail. People were aware of this right even before the Taxpayer Bill of Rights, but sometimes the IRS worked around the representative. Either it ignored her or required the taxpayer personally to attend one or more meetings with the IRS agent. Now, the agent can require that you attend an interview only by issuing an administrative summons. This rejuvenated right to representation has made agents more respectful of taxpayer representatives, and the agents generally allow the full range of representation the law permits and encourages.

11. *Right to twenty-one-day wait.* Banks must now wait twenty-one days after receiving an IRS levy before sending the money. They used to jump the gun all the time, often even before you knew a levy had been served. As a courtesy, many banks now notify you if an IRS levy or other garnishment or judgment is served, but the law does not require this. So, when you learn of a bank levy, you have twenty-one days to try to get the levy released. See chapter 5. This doesn't mean your account is useless, because, in theory, any money you deposit after the levy is served is not subject to it. Some banks understand that rule, others do not. It is best to call your bank to be sure it understands how the levy is supposed to work.

The IRS must also now send you simple, nontechnical explanations of how the levy works. The Service routinely does this. Its explanation is clear and concise.

12. *Right to quick appeal for some property seizures.* Sometimes the IRS will seize a business to stop the business from bleeding away payroll taxes or simply to collect the past-due taxes. Under the Taxpayer Bill of Rights, if property is essential to your trade or business, the IRS must grant an accelerated appeal to determine whether the levy should be released. It is hard to think of any business property as unessential, but that is the way the new rule reads. Appeals, even quick ones, are not often successful. Where they are, the IRS can extract major concessions or big payments in exchange for releasing the property. In other words, this provision of the Taxpayer Bill of Rights does not give you quick relief; it just gives you a quick appeal. The only way you can *force* the IRS to give back your business property is by filing for bankruptcy. (See chapter 12.) Short of that, you can appeal by telephone right up the chain of command and at least get a quick answer. Sometimes the IRS' middle or upper management is more sympathetic to working a deal than the agent who is intent on collecting the tax. So after you speak with the agent and his group manager, consider calling the branch chief, the division chief, or sometimes even the district director, the highest official in the district. You may even consider another right under the Taxpayer Bill of Rights, the Application for a Taxpayer Assistance Order. This right is a flanking movement around the chain of command and often works extremely well. Chapter 13 discusses this provision in detail.

13. *Right to review of liens.* The IRS is supposed to release a lien against you if the lien has expired or the tax has been paid. In the past, the agency often delayed, but now you have a legal right to a quick release. The idea is to let you begin repairing your credit as quickly as possible. You can't use this new law to "unpay" your taxes, only to finish the lien release process if the IRS has balked for

some bureaucratic reason. This new right to review the lien simply forces the IRS to file the release. You can sue for damages in federal court if the IRS fails to release a lien when it should. What type of damages? Let's say you're on the verge of a big business deal, but closure depends on a lien release. If the deal falls through because the IRS delayed, you might have damages and be able to sue.

1996 SUPPLEMENT

In 1996, the IRS supplemented the Taxpayer Bill of Rights by administrative action in a number of areas. The most important of these is the right to appeal liens, levies, and seizures *before* the IRS makes them. This doesn't mean the IRS will stop collecting, but at least you can appeal before it strikes. Form 9423, Collection Appeal Request, and Publication 1660, "Collection Appeal Rights for Liens, Levies, and Seizures," are intended to guide you through this process. Nationally, most of these appeals are rejected, but give it a try if you feel the revenue officer has gone beyond his or her authority.

MORE RIGHTS FROM THE 1996 ACT

14.   *Office of Taxpayer Advocate.* For years the IRS has had a watchdog—the Office of the Taxpayer Ombudsman. This office supervised the problem resolution offices around the country and generally tried to help cut through IRS red tape. This was especially the case in hardship situations. Now, the Office of the Taxpayer Advocate replaces the ombudsman. Congress wants the taxpayer advocate to have more power to fight for taxpayers' interests before the Service and, importantly, before Congress. In effect, this office will report to Congress directly on how the IRS is doing. But don't expect that office to come charging to your rescue every time a revenue officer looks at you cross-eyed. It's a "big picture" office, not one you will encounter every day. Still, its suboffices, the problem resolution offices, will now have more authority to issue taxpayer assistance orders. Of course, they always did, but the idea of the 1996 act is to reinforce that authority and for Congress to say, "We really mean it."

15.   *"But my ex promised to pay!"* How many times do we hear that one spouse of a broken marriage has fled to parts unknown, leaving the other squarely in the gun sights of the Collection Division? The revenue officer may be sympathetic,

but he or she still must get the money from whatever source is available. Often your protests that "my divorce agreement requires my ex to pay these taxes" go unheeded. The 1996 act changes this situation—but only a little. You may now find out from the IRS what efforts it has made to collect from your ex, and how much. That can be very helpful when you press the right to payment in divorce court as well.

16. *Withdrawing a public notice of lien.* Filing a Notice of Federal Tax Lien used to be a permanent, irrevocable act, even if the revenue officer acknowledged that it was wrong. That Notice of Federal Tax Lien also had a tendency to frighten lenders and buyers away from your real estate. True enough, with much pushing and shoving, you might be able to discharge property from the lien, or subordinate the lien (see chapter 4), but you could not *remove* the lien (unless you paid in full). Now, you can. You must convince the IRS that the withdrawal of the lien will facilitate collection or would be in the best interests of you (the taxpayer) and the IRS. You may also try to persuade the IRS that the lien should be removed because you have entered into an installment agreement.

17. *Trust fund taxes.* When a corporation fails to pay its employment taxes, the IRS can go after its officers as well as the corporation. Chapter 10 discusses this concept in detail. The 1996 Taxpayer Bill of Rights makes no change in that rule, but does give a few more protections. You can ask the IRS to tell you what it has done to recover the taxes from other officers. Also, you can now sue those other officers in federal court for "contribution." Also, the new law protects volunteer, unpaid members of the boards of directors of tax-exempt organizations, but only if they did not participate in the day-to-day financial operations of the organization and did not know of that charity's failure to pay the taxes.

All in all, the 1988 Taxpayer Bill of Rights and its 1996 supplement are of modest utility to most people who face IRS pressure. But their two most important features—the Application for a Taxpayer Assistance Order and the general right to stand up for and fully exercise other procedural rights—are very important to help ease undue IRS pressure.

Part II

AUDITS

Chapter 15

⚊⚋∽⚋⚊

"YOUR TAX RETURN HAS BEEN SELECTED FOR EXAMINATION"—audits, Audits, AND AUDITS

One of the most unnerving letters you can receive is the tan envelope with the return address "Internal Revenue Service" and the government stamp ("Penalty for Private Use—$300"). Then you open the letter—carefully, slowly. You unfold it. It begins innocently enough, "Dear Taxpayer." Then it hits: you have lost the audit lottery. You are one of the lucky 1 percent of individuals or 5 percent of businesses whose tax return will now be examined. (Despite these low percentages, they amount to more than one million audits per year.) How do people react? There is a range, from, "Oh my gosh—get my toothbrush, kiss the kids, I am going to jail," to, "Oh no, not again," to, "Those so and sos—into the trash you go."

Probably the more useful reaction would be, "What's this all about? What type of audit is this?"

WHY ME?

Why are *you* the lucky one? In most cases, it goes back to the return you filed. The IRS has a scoring system known as DIF—short for Discriminant Information Function. Your tax return is scored and earns point according to DIF criteria when you send it in.

The details of the DIF scoring system are nearly as secret as our nuclear strike command codes or an aging starlet's birth date. Few people know all the items on the scorecard, or how many points a return earns for each. But educated guesses abound; after all, the score sheet is intended to make the IRS money. So, the scoring system likely assigns points for your occupation, the types of income you earn (whether wages or independent contractor income), and your deductions in type and amount. Your tax return may earn DIF points for your being a doctor, for gross income of $50,000 or $100,000, for being in a business that deals in cash. Even common types of deductions such as mortgage interest or real estate taxes can yield a high score if the amounts you deduct are high. Your return probably also scores high if you've been a good customer in the past, that is, if the IRS has made money from past audits. (Everyone likes repeat business.) Higher income individuals such as doctors, lawyers, and other professionals probably merit higher scores. Unusual occupations are on the list, also occupations that deal in cash: jewelers, car dealers, boatyards, and junkyards. Remember also that the IRS is out to make money, so almost any type of loss is likely to earn DIF scores: casualty losses, business losses, losses on sales of non-publicly traded stock. Also, it stands to reason that the most commonly used and abused deductions will stand out from the crowd: home office deduction, noncash charitable deductions, travel and entertainment expenses, and legally unallowable deductions.

If your return scores high enough, the computer selects it for a closer look, and off it goes to an office in your area of the country. But DIF doesn't exclude Joe Sixpack from its clutches. A certain number of low or moderate income, plain vanilla returns also are examined, just so people don't get *too* complacent. The IRS also has a "classification handbook." Agents use this handbook to classify DIF-selected returns for a closer look.

The returns that are selected are then screened according to the importance of the DIF score and the items in question on the return. The IRS will look to the size of the item, its character, and any evidence that you were trying to confuse or mislead the Service in how you reported the item. It will check whether you put it on a schedule that would lead to lesser tax (for instance, Schedule C versus an itemized deduction) and the relationship between the questioned item and others on the return. This is a judgment call, depending on the experience of the reviewer.

The IRS recently gave birth to a close cousin of DIF known as DORA, short for District Office Research and Analysis. This program targets areas of the country, by zip code and specific taxpayer groups, to find areas of noncompliance. It also focuses on specific tax issues. Recent statistics show that the IRS made adjustments (usually in the IRS' favor) in 95 percent of cases it examined under the DORA system.

Finally, there is the Coordinated Examination Program (CEP), an in-depth, labor-intensive, multiagent inquisition once reserved for major corporations but now expanded to about thirty thousand companies.

That covers the great majority of audits. Others get started for a variety of reasons. Maybe you suffered through one audit and the revenue agent thinks the same issues will recur in other tax years. Maybe someone who holds a big-time grudge has told the IRS about hidden assets or hidden income. Informers can earn rewards of up to 10 percent of the amount the IRS collects. Maybe your corporation has been examined, and as a result the IRS now wants to look at your related personal return.

Whatever the source, whatever the reason, once you get that notice, you're stuck with an audit until it is finished.

NOT ALL AUDITS ARE CREATED EQUAL

The IRS conducts only three basic types of audits: the correspondence audit, the office audit, and the field audit. Every three years, the IRS inflicts a special, research-purpose audit on about 50,000 to 150,000 taxpayers, called the Taxpayer Compliance Measurement Program. One was scheduled for 1996 until people got so upset that Congress stepped in to call a halt.

The Correspondence Audit. This type of audit is simple, straightforward, and usually painless—like an injection. The IRS finds an apparent error in your return and writes you a letter. In most cases, there is absolutely nothing to fear from a correspondence audit. Did you put down the wrong number from your W-2? Forget income from Form 1099 (for nonwage income such as interest and dividends)? The correspondence audit clears this up. Did you take a clearly unallowable deduction? File using the wrong filing status? Make a mistake on your IRA contribution? Claim a questionable refund? Relatively simple questions like these are easily handled by mail. The IRS writes you, notes the issue, and asks for a response. Heed its deadline or get an extension. If you don't, the tax machine will grind on, sending you a follow-up request, then a "thirty-day letter," and finally a Notice of Deficiency. If you fail to respond to the Notice of

Deficiency, the IRS will assess the error as it sees it. You then have a legal bill you usually cannot fight except by paying it first and going to court.

Even a lowly correspondence audit can hide nasty traps. For example, the IRS watches out for alimony compliance, child support refunds that should be paid to another spouse, erroneous refunds, tax credits, and a host of other errors that its computers can detect electronically. Some of these can balloon into big fights, between you and the IRS or between ex-spouses. So the rule is, pay attention and respond to these correspondences audits.

Since these audits are conducted almost entirely by mail, you won't see an IRS representative. But you may speak to one by telephone in a few cases. That's not the usual rule, but sometimes a phone call helps to clear up the issues. Do not hesitate to call the IRS, even in a correspondence audit, if that phone call will solve the problem.

Office Audit and Field Audit. Now let's escalate. Your return has a bigger error. It contains an issue the computers can't handle. You have unreported income, or you simply scored too high in the IRS' audit lottery. Then your return is selected. Someone in the service center where you filed it physically mails that return (along with the returns of many other lucky taxpayers) and the usual cover sheets to the local IRS district office that will handle your case.

Then the fun begins. An officer in that district office has to decide which returns to examine, and whether you get "office audit" treatment or the royal attention of a revenue agent (field audit). The local office can't audit every return it receives, or even those it selects for a closer examination. Many of these are therefore "closed on survey." Someone looked at the return and decided it lacked sufficient dollar or issue appeal to bother with.

As to the rest, well, they have won/lost the audit lottery.

An examiner assigns some returns for office audit. This is an audit conducted in the IRS' office. It is usually reserved for issues the selecting officer deems complicated or significant enough to look at, but not so heavy-duty as to merit a full field audit. It's a judgment call.

Usually a tax auditor conducts an office audit. She sends you a letter asking for or making an appointment, noting the questionable items and requesting certain records. You gather the records, bring them into the office, and discuss the issues.

Office audits have their own perils. On the income side, tax auditors are trained to spot unreported income by performing indirect checks on the amount of income you reported on your return. They love to dive into cash businesses, and they salivate at the mere mention of "gross receipts." They will ask you many questions: "How did you get your gross receipts number? Have you checked it against other records? Does it square with your checking accounts, personal and business?" They ask you where you got your money—from gifts, loans, or inheritances? They ask about your lifestyle. They check your personal return against your main assets and liabilities. If you lifestyle is Jaguar but your income is Volkswagen, you had better be prepared to explain.

Tax auditors also question unusual or very large deductions. Since many taxpayers are poor record keepers, auditors have a turkey shoot with many business and personal deductions. In fact, the poorest record keepers are usually people who say or think, "I can keep sloppy records. The IRS can never prove my figures are wrong." That taxpayer is in for a nasty surprise when he finds that the burden of proof is on him, not the IRS. So if you have very sloppy records, the IRS will often disallow your deductions for "lack of substantiation," then penalize you for negligence because you kept sloppy records. People who run cash businesses are especially at risk in this type of audit.

The field audit is the final type of common audit the IRS conducts. This is a full-blown examination of any and all items on a taxpayer's business and/or personal return. The revenue agents who conduct these audits are often certified public accountants. Even when they're not, they've had years of training inside or outside the IRS.

Revenue agents focus on many of the same issues that an office audit might address, but they are far more thorough. Also, the dollar amounts at stake and the complexity of the issues are usually higher both on the income and the deduction side. Examples might be home office deductions, hobby losses, or complicated business deductions. They might also address capital gains and losses, income from the sale of residences, and pension and retirement issues. Here is a recent list of fourteen of the most commonly audited and appealed issues, on a nationwide basis:

- gross income

- trade or business deductions

- deductions for losses

- bad debts

- depreciation

- net operating losses

- capital expenditures

- taxability of a corporation on distribution (of assets)

- taxable year of inclusion (that is, in what year is an item of income properly taxed?)

- taxable year of deductions

- last-in, first-out inventories

- allocation of income and deductions among taxpayers

- taxes of foreign countries and U.S. possessions

- definition of gross estate

In the last reporting year, these issues accounted for $56 billion in proposed new taxes, 57 percent of the total of $98 billion involved in all audits. These items also represented 45 percent of the number of cases.

The revenue agent normally selects the site of the audit. Unless the choice is unreasonable in time or place, his choice prevails. Still, if the presence of a revenue agent would harm your business, the agent normally makes alternative arrangements, such as an isolated room or an off-site location. Quite often, the taxpayer's accountant is the buffer between the taxpayer and the auditor, and the accountant can usually work out an acceptable time and place of examination.

HOW THE REVENUE AGENT WORKS

Revenue agents operate from groups of six to eight, usually one or two groups in each local office. Their boss is a group manager. The group manager's boss is a branch chief. If you don't like the agent you get, you can't request another. But if you have a communication problem or personality conflict, don't hesitate to call the group manager. You have the right to fair and courteous treatment, and if you are not getting it, like a true American you should complain.

The revenue agent works steadily and methodically. He often prepares a list of documents he wants to examine, using a IRS form called an Information Document Request. IDRs can go on for two to three pages (in simple audits) and can ask for five to fifty items. Agents often freely discuss the issues they are focusing on if you ask them. You can tell a lot about what the agent is thinking just by looking at the documents he wants.

Having the records available and in good shape is a good idea. Taxpayers who keep sloppy records usually wind up paying more in taxes.

But records carry their own perils. You, the taxpayer, know where the bodies are buried: the unreported income, the erroneous deductions. The agent does not. So the agent's questions may range widely. Many taxpayers then panic because their returns contain ordinary, garden-variety mistakes. Still, there is no reason to be afraid unless you have truly evaded your taxes and the agent's documentary net threatens to expose your crime. If you have something to hide, discuss that issue with a tax professional before responding to the IDR.

The revenue agent also has specialists available to him. Examples might be art appraisers and industry specialists. He can request help in any specialized area where he does not feel completely comfortable.

CAN THE AGENT REALLY GET ALL THOSE RECORDS?

Current law says yes. The agent's authority to examine is almost unlimited. Chapter 2 discusses this authority in more detail, but a quick rule is that the agent can get any record that is or may be relevant to the examination. That agent has the authority to assure himself that the law has not been violated, as well as to find out where it has.

Revenue agents wield other powers, too. They can expand the audit to other years, both before and after the year at issue. Revenue agents can examine any related returns, including especially partnership returns and corporation returns. Those inquiries can open more issues for the corporation, partnership, shareholders, and partners. The agent can refer a case to the Criminal Investigation Division if he suspects fraud. He can propose increases in your taxes and thereby thrust the burden on you to prove him wrong. He can also propose penalties, as to which you again have the burden of proof. Although these seem like very powerful tools, each is fully authorized by law.

OTHER TYPES OF AUDITS

One special type of audit is called the Taxpayer Compliance Measurement Program (TCMP) audit. Every three years or so, the IRS selects about 50,000 to

150,000 returns for a line-by-line, item-by-item examination. These TCMP audits are excruciating for taxpayer and auditor alike. In such an audit, you may be asked to verify every item on your return. For example, you may have to bring in birth certificates to verify the existence of children you claim as exemptions. The agent can demand a copy of your marriage license to show "married, filing jointly" status. The agent can require you to show every mortgage payment, every receipt for a charitable deduction, every telephone bill for your business. The IRS uses these audits for research purposes to refine the DIF scoring system.

How else can the Service bother you? In many interesting ways that are technically not audits but feel like them anyway. A common example is an employment tax investigation. The IRS may claim that the people you employ as independent contractors are really your employees, making you liable for their employment taxes.

If your business fails to pay its payroll taxes, you as an officer or director might be liable personally for a portion of these taxes. See chapter 10. That tax results from an investigation as well.

Or, one of the worst nightmares: concluding you have committed tax fraud, the agent refers your case to the Criminal Investigation Division. That's in part an audit, too, but it is also a high-level criminal investigation extremely different from a normal audit because the special agent wants to throw you in jail. Chapter 11 explains the ground rules.

These days, the IRS is abandoning TCMP audits in favor of what it calls "lifestyle audits," or "economic reality audits." Agents look at your lifestyle to see whether you live beyond your means. They look at net worth, significant assets, net equity, and business affairs. They search for other assets such as boats and fancy cars. They often perform an analysis called a "cash T" to see whether you are spending more than you are apparently bringing in. Someone who lives well beyond his means can often explain the discrepancy (inheritances, loans, and so on), but in many cases, the lavish or visible lifestyle means the taxpayer has been evading taxes by failing to report all income. So, if your spending habits are too lavish, watch out. High-profile people like this tend to become visible targets.

Here are some of the topics from a recent lifestyle audit list:

SELECTED IRS "ECONOMIC REALITY" QUESTIONS

1. What real estate do you own and when was it acquired? Monthly rent? Do you manage or do you have a management company?

2. Did you make any improvements to any of your real estate? What was done, how much was it, and how was it paid for?

3. How many autos do you own? What are they? What is the payment?

4. Do you own any large assets (over $10,000) besides auto and real estate? What is it, where is it kept? Is it paid for? If not, what is the payment?

5. Did you sell any assets? If so, what, to whom, and how much?

6. Do you ever take cash advances from credit cards or lines of credit? How much and how often?

7. What cash did you have on hand in the audited year, personally or for business, not in a bank—at your home, in a safe deposit box, hidden somewhere?

8. What is the largest amount of cash you had at any one time in the audited year?

9. Did you deposit all paychecks into the bank? What account?

10. Do you have a safe deposit box? Where? What is in it?

11. Were you involved in any cash transactions of $10,000 or more?

12. Employee business expenses: What meals are being deducted? Provide appointment calendar receipts, business purpose, business relationship for all expenses.

And these questions are just the start. The agents have wide discretion, so far uncurbed by courts, to ask questions about your lifestyle. You must respond unless you invoke the privilege against self-incrimination.

REQUESTING AUDIT RECONSIDERATION

What if you simply can't get your act together during the audit and the IRS machine grinds out an assessment? You may request "audit reconsideration." Audit reconsideration is like stopping a train after it has left the station because you just found your ticket. It's a great way to have your case reconsidered, even when you've been given an opportunity once or twice already.

You are entitled to audit reconsideration in many cases, though not all. For instance, you can ask the examination division to reconsider your case if you have new information suggesting the IRS' assessment is excessive. Reconsideration may be available if the IRS made a computational error, you didn't get notice of the proposed adjustment in time, or you simply didn't have enough time to substantiate your position. Ask for reconsideration if you didn't receive the IRS' audit report or the follow-up statutory Notice of Deficiency. Finally, if you have one or more unfiled returns, you can automatically get audit reconsideration by filing true original returns. The Service has broad discretion to reconsider and abate any assessment that is too high (or increase one that is too low) even after an audit has been closed.

The mechanics of your request are simple. Address a letter to the local service center, the Collection Division, or even the Problem Resolution Office. State that you are requesting audit reconsideration. An amended return with a cover letter will do. In your letter or amended return, note the issues you are questioning and the grounds for abatement or adjustment. Attach a copy of the affected tax return and the IRS' audit report if it is available. Also enclose all documentation you can find to support your position.

The IRS has a long list of required information, depending upon what issue you select. For example, if you ask for an additional exemption for a dependent, the Service wants to see items such as school, medical, or other records to determine residence, a record of income, or a copy of the birth certificate. The IRS publishes "substantiation requirements" for many other items, such as retirement accounts, alimony payments, medical and dental expenses, auto expenses, and entertainment.

The request is routed to the local service center. If it is accepted, the service center sends it to your local IRS office, where your friendly revenue agent or tax auditor reopens your case. Then, you're back in the IRS audit loop.

WHAT'S ON THE HORIZON

The IRS is always looking for new and different ways to audit the American public. Over the past few years, it has invented something called the Market Segment Specialization Program (MSSP), a fancy name for audits of entire industries at a time. So far, the Service has identified ninety-eight industries or issues for this special audit status. These include law firms, accounting practices, bed-and-breakfasts, the construction industry, and many others. Then, the agency devises an entire audit strategy that applies to every audit it conducts in each of these groups. It's no mystery; the IRS publishes these Market Segment Specialization Program guides from time to time. So you'll always know what the revenue agent is thinking if you fall in that group. These guides tend to be long, complex, and detailed.

To go along with MSSP guides, the IRS is training industry specialists in the Audit Specialization Program. The typical revenue agent is a generalist; she'll take whatever case is assigned, from verifying your mortgage interest to measuring unreported income. Industry specialists concentrate on one type of business, such as restaurants, auto dealerships, or landscape services. They know these industries inside and out. They know how much business you should be doing, what your expenses are likely to be, and where the holes in your records usually are. In short, they usually know whether you've been naughty or nice.

The Service is also testing something called the Automated Issue Identification System. This system uses computerized artificial intelligence to spot possible audit issues on your tax returns. It can also classify returns for examination. For example, suppose that you run a bed-and-breakfast. Your costs are 10 percent higher than normal for your size and location, according to the IRS computer. You might have run afoul of the IRS' Automated Issue Identification System. It's not Big Brother, but it begins to come close.

Finally, the IRS is neck-deep in the age of computerization. It has computer audit specialists, particularly useful for big cases and big taxpayers. Naturally, the goal of all of this is maximum dollars and maximum compliance.

WHAT CAN THE AGENT DO TO YOU?

When the agent finishes his audit, what happens? Actually, nothing. Strictly speaking, the agent can only *recommend* some action, really a choice of four possibilities:

1. *No change.* The agent found no errors, or only minor ones not worth pursuing. He writes a No Change Report, and sends you a letter advising you that the examination resulted in no change to your return.

2. *Agreed case.* The agent found errors and proposed more taxes (or a refund), possibly penalties. (Interest is added automatically by law.) You agree with all the changes or choose not fight them. The agent writes a Revenue Agent's Report and asks you to sign it. In this report you agree to the immediate assessment of the taxes. If you agree and sign, you soon get a bill from the IRS for the extra taxes, penalties, and interest.

3. *Unagreed case.* You and the agent could not resolve any of the issues. He reports the entire audit as "unagreed." He sends this Revenue Agent's Report to you or your tax representative. It has a cover sheet, a summary page reciting exactly what items the agent is increasing or decreasing, and by how much. The report explains each item.

   The summary sheet sets out how much tax the agent proposes. Often it has a calculation of penalties and sometimes of interest.

4. *Partially agreed case.* You agree with the agent on some issues, but not all. This hybrid case is split. The agent prepares a partial agreement form, and writes the remaining issues as unagreed.

If all or part of the audit is unagreed, the agent then sends you a "thirty-day letter." This formal letter advises you of the proposed changes and gives you thirty days to agree or disagree. If you don't agree, you may want to appeal. Nothing in the law grants you the right to an appeal within the IRS, but the agency found a long time ago that internal appeals often settle cases. In fact, it has an entire branch devoted to these appeals, the Office of Appeals.

People often ask whether the agent has the authority to settle an issue that is in conflict over the facts or law. Usually, he does not. His job is to call an issue one way or another, not to settle an issue based on litigating hazards. Appeals officers have this authority.

If you write the IRS that you want to appeal within the thirty-day deadline, the agency will not assess the tax. Instead, it sends the case to the Office of Appeals. Chapter 17 explains how appeals should be handled.

If you do nothing? Remember one of the rules of IRS survival: Doing nothing usually hurts you. In this case, the IRS sends you a formal letter called a Notice of Deficiency. Unlike the thirty-day letter, this Notice of Deficiency is required by law before the IRS can assess a tax. The notice is a formal proposal that you owe more taxes. It gives you ninety days (not three months) to file suit in the United States Tax Court to contest the notice. See chapter 21. Filing suit in the tax court stops the IRS from assessing the tax it had proposed, at least until the case is resolved. But if you miss the ninety-day deadline by a day, an hour, or a minute, the IRS makes the assessment against you several weeks later and sends a bill. At that point, there is little you can do but pay the bill. (If the bill is wrong but you simply missed the deadline, you can still file a claim for refund. See chapter 22).

The court case, an agreed assessment, or an unagreed assessment ends the audit process that started when your return was "selected for examination."

Chapter 16

MAKING YOUR RETURN AUDIT-PROOF—
OR NEARLY SO

Would you like to ensure that the IRS never selects your return for audit? Who wouldn't. There is one surefire way: Don't file one. Since that is not an option for most, the next best thing is to file one with average gross income (subject to withholding), average deductions or standard deductions, no partnerships, no fancy shelters, and no tax losses. Even returns like that have *some* chance of audit, though small.

At the opposite extreme, would you like to ensure that your return is in fact selected? Take big tax losses, operate a business in cash, and keep sloppy records. Don't report income you earn from third-party payers (who report it to the IRS), and take unusual or extremely large deductions.

Most returns fall between these two extremes. We don't want to sacrifice a valid deduction, even if it's large or unusual. But we're concerned that taking such a deduction waves the audit flag. The fact is that no magic formula can make a return audit-proof. And, like it or not, much of our economic life—like paying deductible mortgage interest, earning income, and so on—finds its way to a tax return no matter what the numbers turn out to be. All income and deductions must be reported, and reported truthfully. If those facts mean you have a higher chance of audit, there is usually little you can do.

Still, there is some room for maneuver even within these confines.

1. *Keep deductions within the averages.* Each year, the IRS publishes the average deductions (depending on income) people claim for each major category on Schedule A of the individual tax return: mortgage interest, charitable contributions, state and local taxes, medical expenses, and miscellaneous deductions. You probably won't earn many audit selection score points if your deductions are within these averages. True enough, you spend what you spend, and if you are entitled to the deduction, you should take it. Moreover, you risk the charge of filing a false return if you omit a valid deduction for the purpose of evasion. A missed deduction also costs you money.

Still, you can legally time some deductions or arrange your affairs to bring yours within the averages. For example, sometimes you can delay payment of a state income tax until January 1 of a new year. If it helps keep your deduction within the average, you may accelerate the payment to the current year. You might decide to prepay some interest on a mortgage, defer paying some interest, pay down principal to obtain a lower rate, or refinance to obtain an adjustable rate mortgage with its lower interest payments in the first year. You may decide to accelerate or delay medical expense payments, or do the same with charitable contributions and miscellaneous expenses.

Bear in mind that all of these timing strategies may cost you money; a deduction delayed to a later tax year means you pay more tax this year (though less in a later year).

2. *Report all third-party payor income.* Report all W-2 wages and Form 1099 income, no matter how small, on page 1 of the return and Schedule B, respectively. If your bank sends you a Form 1099 for interest income of $1,000, but you really only earned $500, try to convince the bank to issue a corrected form *before* you file your return. If that's not possible, file using the $500 but attach an explanation. Similarly, report income from every other third-party payor: your employer, union, state tax department (for an income tax refund), and a host of others. One way to check whether you have actually received all 1099 forms is to go through your bank account at the end of the year. Identify all deposits as wages, dividends, interest, rebates or refunds, insurance reimbursements. Then decide whether each is required to be reported as gross income.

3. *Use the right forms.* The IRS loves forms. It has hundreds from which to choose each year. New ones are devised all the time. Using the wrong form often results in at least a notice inquiry. The notice inquiry asks about your income or deduction item. If you put it on the wrong form, normally you need only put it on

the right form or send an explanation, and that is the end of the matter. But sometimes using the wrong form triggers the interest of an agent. For example, Schedule F is used by farmers. You may get audit selection points if you use this schedule. If you suffered a loss, perhaps the agent may conclude your farming activity was only a hobby, causing disallowance of the loss. Similarly, Schedule C, for sole proprietors, and Schedule E, for partnership income (among other types), probably attract more attention.

In particular, Schedule C attracts IRS interest. Sole proprietors often deal in cash. If yours is a cash-intensive business such as jewelry dealer, car salesperson, boat dealer, pawnbroker, dry cleaner, or restaurant operator, you probably earn more audit selection points for that occupation alone. Such occupations make it more likely that you or your employees are part of the underground economy, a $100 billion per year shadow economy that escapes federal taxation. So the choice of how to characterize and name your business is important. But the name must be accurate; using a misleading name to avoid audit scrutiny could be a criminal false statement. If you run a pawnshop, you can't call it a bank.

4. *Operate a noncash business.* Since cash-based businesses are inherently subject to abuse, they invariably attract more than the usual IRS attention. Use checks, credit cards, bank deposits, and anything else that generates a true record of your income and expenses. After all, in a tax audit, you, not the IRS, have the burden of proof.

Some cash businesses try to have it both ways. They keep meticulous records reporting *some* of their cash, but other cash slips mysteriously through their fingers and into someone's wallet. The IRS has ways of finding this, including using industry averages, net worth examinations, and undercover techniques in criminal investigations. So reporting less than the average for businesses of your type may well trigger an audit. For example, if dry cleaners usually report gross income of $500,000 per year and yours reports $250,000 in a high volume area, this may be an audit trigger. In any case, it may cause an agent to look more closely if your return is selected for some other reason. The same can happen if you claim too much by way of deductions in a cash business.

5. *Use only employees, not independent contractors.* For years, the IRS has fought a running battle with many industries over the tax classification of subcontractor workers. Are they employees, making the owner liable for their payroll taxes? Or are they independent contractors, responsible for their own income and self-employment taxes? From an audit selection standpoint, it's probably safer to classify your workers as employees despite the extra burden of withholding and

filing larger payroll tax returns. This issue might arise if you have a large deduction for "subcontract labor" or a similar category of expense.

> *Example:* The Great Big Construction Company is in the business of building residential and commercial buildings. It grosses $4 million per year. It pays wages to employees of $100,000 and subcontract labor of $2 million. The IRS may have a program to compare these two amounts, or to compare both amounts to industry averages, and thereby spot the issue. Or, if the company is audited for some other reason and the agent looks at business deductions, he can easily spot the big disparity between subcontract labor and regular employees. Still, for competitive reasons, or paperwork-burden reasons, many businesses continue to use subcontract labor.

6. *Use a corporation or partnership, not a proprietorship.* Choosing a corporate or partnership form of doing business, instead of a proprietorship, may lessen your chances of being selected for audit. Proprietors tend to be more lax in their record keeping and more cash-intensive, and do other things that might attract the interest of the IRS. The disadvantage of incorporating or using a partnership is that it doubles your paperwork and reporting requirements, but the net amount of tax should generally be the same unless you use a "C" corporation. Even then, tax planning can cut down or eliminate the double taxation that that form of corporate life normally entails.

7. *Watch cosmetics and arithmetic.* Commonsense steps: file on time, check your income and deductions, and check your arithmetic. A clean, neat return is a return that avoids at least one extra pair of eyes.

8. *Avoid unusual deductions or exclusions from income.* Millions of people claim unusual deductions or unusually large deductions. For example, some might try to deduct the cost of a small in-ground swimming pool as a medical necessity (shown by doctors' statements). Such a deduction is extremely unusual and is quite likely to be audited.

An unusually large deduction might be one for mortgage interest of twice or three times the national average. Other examples of unusual deductions the IRS loves to hate are home office deductions, hobby losses, casualty losses, and business operating losses. These are not "unusual," in the sense that millions of people take them every year. But agents tend to see these types of deductions as subject to abuse. They examine them carefully and often. Other times you might receive money during the year that is not reportable gross income. Examples would be loans, gifts, inheritance, or awards from some lawsuits.

In these cases, the issue is always whether to claim the deduction or omit the income, and whether to disclose your choice. The IRS' most common sanction is to penalize you for negligence or for substantially understating your tax liability. You can immunize against these penalties by disclosing the item on Form 8275 attached to your return. You don't have to use this form if your deduction appears on Schedule A or on certain other schedules.

The IRS claims publicly that filing Form 8275 does not increase your chances of an audit. Still, filing such a form is bound to make people nervous. They may feel the form flags the issue for the IRS or that audit selection points are awarded for the act of filing this form. Whether to use the form is a judgment call, depending on the circumstances of your own case.

9. *Check your lifestyle.* Truly rich people who flaunt their wealth need not worry here. But if you seem to be living beyond your means and an agent suspects you are overspending your income, you may be subjected to an IRS "lifestyle" audit. The basic idea is that you had to get the extra money from somewhere. If the agent looks long and hard, you may not be able to show where you obtained your evident riches. This alone can bring you under the IRS' audit microscope.

10. *Hire a pro.* Using a professional return preparer by no means reduces your audit selection score, but it can help in a number of ways. First, the professional may spot a troublesome deduction or omission of income that could have triggered an audit. Since the professional also does this for a living, common mistakes on the return are less likely. If for no other reason, a second pair of eyes that are not your own (or Aunt Alice's) can objectively review the tax return for errors and trouble spots.

Many businesses use professional return preparers as a matter of routine. They also make frequent use of payroll services to pay payroll taxes and prepare payroll tax returns. Both of these techniques are well-advised. While quality among commercial payroll services varies, the competent ones can be a godsend to a busy executive. Payroll tax compliance, a soft spot in many businesses, is often the first place the IRS looks. Once it looks there, it has a license to look elsewhere. So using a payroll service can often avoid that first inquiry from a curious agent.

11. *Keep your evidence.* Audits don't always escalate from zero to one hundred in less than thirty seconds. An agent may question only one or two items on a return and be satisfied you have your evidence lined up and ready to go. By contrast, nothing tweaks an agent's curiosity more than evasive answers, sloppy

records, or inconsistent and unpersuasive evidence. So, if you are tempted to take an unusual deduction, keep all of your records and evidence together, ready to go in case they're needed.

Tax audits are a fact of life and always will be, even if for only a small percentage of taxpayers. So the goal of minimizing your chances of audit should not lead to extreme conservatism on your tax returns. Even the IRS encourages you to take every deduction to which you are entitled. While you don't want the nagging threat of an audit to rule your life, taking care to keep records and prepare your return carefully can minimize the chances of your becoming personally acquainted with an IRS revenue agent.

Chapter 17

APPEALING A BAD AUDIT RESULT

Tax audits and other tax investigations can often be frustrating or futile. By training, IRS agents see many issues in black-and-white terms. Either you can support your deduction, or you cannot. It's therefore reassuring to know there is an appeal you can file without having to go to court. This is the function of the Office of Appeals. Founded in 1925, this office exists for the sole purpose of settling your tax case, if at all possible. Its mission is to craft the right settlement based on the chance the IRS might lose in court. Appeals officers have the authority to concede issues, to sustain the case agent's findings, or to split issues. Only in rare cases involving issues of widespread impact and importance will the appeals officer lack discretion to seek a good settlement.

The overall statistical chances of your obtaining a settlement at appeals are 50 percent. Those are encouraging odds, especially considering how easy and inexpensive it is to file an appeal.

WHERE THE CASES COME FROM

Each of the IRS' thirty-three districts has one Office of Appeals staffed by five to fifteen appeals officers. Sometimes there are satellite or branch offices. Six main types of cases filter up to the Office of Appeals.

First is the income tax audit. Chapter 15 discusses the process in detail. If you and the revenue agent (or tax auditor) can't agree on every issue in your case, the agent writes a report on the unagreed issues and sends it to you. That report is known formally as a "thirty-day letter." You have thirty days to agree, disagree, or do nothing. If you agree, you sign it, date it, and send it back. Doing nothing allows the IRS to conclude the agent was correct and bill you accordingly. If you disagree, you appeal to the Office of Appeals simply by filing a "protest." Appeal rights apply to any item the revenue agent adjusts, whether tax or penalty. File the protest within the thirty days or any extension you obtain before the thirty days run out. Ask for this extension from the IRS office that issued the thirty-day letter, usually the revenue agent's office. Once you file the protest, the audit machinery grinds to a halt until your appeal is considered and resolved. That could be a minimum of two months, but appeals lasting a year or more are common. Of course, you take a calculated risk. Interest on your eventual tax bill continues to accrue.

The second main source of cases is employment tax investigations of two types: Trust Fund Recovery Penalty and employee-independent contractor cases. In a Trust Fund Recovery Penalty investigation, the revenue officer investigates who is responsible for a corporation's failure to pay its payroll taxes and recommends an assessment against the officers as a personal liability. Each officer has the right to appeal the recommendation to the Office of Appeals before the assessment can be made official.

In employee-independent contractor investigations, the revenue officer examines corporations that classify workers as independent contractors. These corporations don't withhold taxes; instead, they furnish 1099 forms at the end of the year. Quite often the IRS concludes these workers are employees, making the corporation liable for the workers' payroll taxes. The corporation has the right to protest such a finding to the Office of Appeals before the IRS assesses the tax.

The third main source of cases is penalty appeals. A late return, an insufficient estimated tax payment, a late payment, and many other types of penalties are assessed directly by the IRS' seven regional service centers. See chapter 18. You may contest these penalties at whatever level the IRS recommends or imposes them. If you get no relief, you can appeal the denial to the Office of Appeals.

Fourth, if your offer in compromise to settle a big back tax bill (see chapter 6) is rejected, you may appeal the rejection to the Office of Appeals.

Fifth, you may file a refund claim for taxes you overpaid in the past. (See chapter 22). If it's rejected, an appeal lies to the Office of Appeals.

Finally, if you decide to sue the IRS in tax court (see chapter 21), you can sometimes still get appeals office consideration. This can happen when the auditing agent proposes more taxes and you petition the tax court right away rather than first taking your case to appeals. Bypassing an appeal by going directly to tax court results in the case being transferred back to appeals.

PREPARING YOUR PROTEST AND YOUR CASE

An appeal is filed by preparing a protest. There's no official, complicated form; it's just a letter you send to the office that proposed your tax. The protest has seven parts. You'll find a sample at the end of this chapter. Of the seven parts, four are of the fill-in-the-blank variety: your name, other identifying information, the office that issued the letter, and the tax periods. The heart and soul of the protest are parts five, six, and seven. In these three sections, the task is to tell the appeals officer the findings with which you disagree (part five), the facts (part six), and why the agent was wrong based on the law and the facts (part seven).

Keep part five brief. Consider stating, "The revenue agent erred in disallowing my deduction of $1,000 for a wheelchair for my dependent aging mother." Or, "The revenue agent erred in characterizing a loan from my Aunt Josephine as unreported income." Number each such summary point so as to negate, point by point, the same items in the Revenue Agent's Report.

In the next part (six), tell all the facts underlying the issues you are protesting. You need not protest every issue; in fact, often people change their minds after reading the Revenue Agent's Report and decide not to protest even though they disagreed. But as to the issues you wish to fight, recite all the facts in detail, and prepare to prove them.

> *Hint:* Some practitioners disagree with this general strategy, preferring to hold their fire until they meet face-to-face with the appeals officer. They file a bare-bones protest, reciting enough to preserve your right to appeal the issues but not so much to show all your cards. This strategy may be appropriate in some cases, but in general, taking a strong, well-supported stand right away has a better chance of achieving a good settlement.

State the facts logically and cogently. Stay away from opinion and hyperbole. Assume the appeals officer knows nothing about your case but learns quickly from a cogent presentation. (The officer will in fact have read the Revenue

Agent's Report in advance.) So, begin at the beginning if that will make your factual statement complete and understandable within its four corners.

Next, prove your facts. Most people assume they already did that at the agent's level, so they'll use the same proof at appeals. But be on the lookout for even more evidence. In fact, new evidence at the appeals level often gives the appeals officer the justification she needs to settle your case. Appeals officers can and do consider evidence that would never make it past the front door of a courtroom: hearsay, third-party information, and anything else that appears to be relevant. In fact, the more third-party information you can bring to the table, the more credible your case. Above all, include and rely on your own testimony. After all, you, the taxpayer, have the most intimate knowledge of the tax-relevant facts. Whenever you can, put the evidence in writing, under oath.

Sometimes an agent or appeals officer objects to your statements of fact as "self-serving." Of course they are; that's the whole idea—to help *you*. What the agent really means is that your statements lack credibility because you have a natural bias in your own favor. That also may be true. However, your statements under oath are subject to the penalties of perjury and are fully admissible in any court. That's good enough for a judge or jury; it should be good enough for the IRS. So don't be reluctant to use your own statement, bolstered by your oath.

Part seven is the statement of law. Here, your tax representative can help or write the section for you if she is familiar with the law. If you represent yourself, a statement of the law is still required, so consider performing your own legal research. Still, the process is very informal. You need not file a Supreme Court-style brief with citations to cases, rulings, and other authority, though solid research like that adds credibility. But you do have to say what the law is. Bear in mind that the appeals officer is always well-versed in the law governing your issues. In fact, she will sometimes assist you in your research if you ask and indicate a willingness to do copying, legwork, and other tasks.

When you have the law firmly in mind, write it in this section as best you can, and then apply the facts to those legal rules. An example might be something like this.

> *Example:* My Aunt Rose is seventy-five years old, barely ambulatory, and lives with me. I am her sole support. I provide more than one-half of her support in terms of food, clothing, shelter, and other necessities. She has no income of her own. She is not married. Last year, she underwent total hip replacement on the right side and needs a wheelchair to get around the house. Since I work for a living, she needs the wheelchair to feed herself and stay out of bed.

Dr. Smith Jones prescribed a wheelchair for her last year, and I bought it. A letter from Dr. Jones and a copy of his prescription are enclosed. The wheelchair cost $2,000. Of that cost, I deducted $1,600 because of the 7.5 percent floor on medical expense deductions. However, the agent disallowed this deduction.

The rule on medical expense deductions is that such an expense is deductible if medically necessary for a dependent's condition. Here, the facts show that the wheelchair was in fact medically necessary for my aunt. Therefore, the agent's conclusion to the contrary was in error.

At the end of the protest, include the following statement *above* you signature: "Under the penalty of perjury, I have examined the foregoing statement of facts in the foregoing protest, together with all exhibits, statements, and other documents referenced therein, and to the best of my knowledge and belief, it is true, correct, and complete."

THE APPEALS CONFERENCE

Your next stop is the conference. The appeals officer normally sends a preliminary letter letting you know she has the case, will review it, and will call you for a conference. Sometimes these letters set a conference date, which you should confirm or change immediately (a phone call will do).

To prepare for the conference, review your protest throughly. Also review the Revenue Agent's Report and all your files, to have them firmly in mind. Keep looking for other evidence. In fact, appeals officers will give you ample opportunity to gather more evidence even after the conference.

Then, on the appointed day, you go to the Office of Appeals. Appeals conferences are very informal. You simply enter the appeals officer's office, sit across the desk from her, and begin to talk about the case. No one records the conference. You may take notes, as will the appeals officer, where appropriate. Your task is to convince the officer that the agent's mistake should result in a full or partial concession by the government. In theory, the appeals officer's role is to be neutral. She weighs the evidence for and against the revenue agent's position and comes to some compromise based on the hazards of litigation. Many appeals officers try to act with neutrality; others unintentionally slide into defending the revenue agent against your attacks. This slippage is a danger and one major reason why your protest and demeanor at the conference should be unemotional, businesslike, and firm. Moreover, the appeals officer has heard it all before—all the facts, all the law, all the name-calling. This does not mean you should downplay the agent's mistakes. Hit them all. Showing how wrong the agent was, and how contrary to the facts, goes a long way toward obtaining a good result.

The appeals conference proceeds issue by issue until there is no more left to say. The appeals officer might indicate she is willing to concede some issues. On yet others, she may say the agent was right and she will sustain the finding. On others, she may need more information. It often helps to ask what additional facts she would need to accept your position. She may suggest evidence you might be able to gather, and, if so, she will give you ample opportunity. Then go get that evidence and send it to the appeals officer as quickly as possible. She will give you a deadline and reasonable extensions if you ask for them in advance.

The end of the process is the appeals officer's report. If all has gone well, she writes an "agreed report," formalizing the final settlement on all issues. She then sends it to you for signature. A tax bill or tax refund follows. If you can't agree on all issues, try to agree on most.

"Unagreed" issues are written in a "ninety-day letter." This is the formal letter the law requires the IRS to send you before it assesses your tax. You then have two choices. If you do nothing, the bill soon arrives. To forestall that bill, you may file a petition in the United States Tax Court to contest the remaining unagreed items. Chapter 21 discusses this course of action.

The appeals process can be lengthy, but it's usually fairly simple to get through. Moreover, it's your one chance at reasonable expense to get a better result than you obtained from the revenue agent. There's little harm in trying and much to be gained.

Tel:_____

Date:_____

Internal Revenue Service
Collection Division
500 N. Capitol Street, N.W., Room 3207
Washington, D.C. 20221
Att: Ms. Jones

Re: Penny Pencil, 000-00-0000; Wonder Widgets, Inc., EIN 00-0000000

Dear Ms. Jones:

PROTEST

Protest is hereby made of the proposed assessment of Trust Fund Recovery Penalty with respect to Penny Pencil. The following information is submitted in support of this protest.

1. *Name, Address, Social Security No.*
   Penny Pencil
   1 Main Street
   Anytown, USA 11111
   SSN: 000-00-0000

2. *Conference.* A conference relating to this protest is hereby requested.

3. *Date and Number of Letter.*
   Letter dated July 26, 1995; Letter 1153(DO)(Rev. 3-93)

4 *Tax Periods.*
   3rd quarter 1993; 4th quarter 1993; 1st quarter 1994

5. *Findings Disagreed With.*

The revenue officer erred in determining that Penny Pencil was a person responsible for the failure of Wonder Widgets, Inc., to collect, account for, and pay over the withholding and Social Security/Medicare taxes of the employees of Wonder Widgets, Inc., for the above periods, and that Penny Pencil willfully failed to ensure that these amounts were paid over.

6. *Statement of Facts.*

[Here state all facts to support your case.]

7. *Statement of Law.*

The Trust Fund Recovery Penalty may be imposed under IRC § 6672 only if two separate requirements are fulfilled. First, the person must be under a duty to "collect, truthfully account for, and pay over" the withheld taxes, that is, he or she must be a "responsible person." IRC § 6672 imposes liability only upon the person or persons who are actually responsible for an employer's failure to withhold and pay the government, that is, the person who is under the duty to perform the act, and not necessarily the individual who is nominally charged with disbursement of the funds. *White v. United States*, 372 F.2d 513 (Ct. Cl. 1967); *Turner v. United States*, 423 F.2d 448 (9th Cir. 1970).

The second element, willfulness, requires that the responsible person shall have intentionally, deliberately, voluntarily, or knowingly failed to pay over the withheld taxes. *White v. United States, supra.* Mere negligence in failing to ascertain facts regarding the tax delinquency is insufficient to constitute willfulness under IRC § 6672. *Bauer v. United States*, 543 F.2d 142 (Ct. Cl. 1976).

Under these standards, I am neither responsible nor willful for the following reasons. [State additional grounds.]

In view of these cases, I should not be deemed a responsible person. By contrast, the evidence in this case shows that others may have been the responsible persons. Also, I had no knowledge that the taxes were unpaid until the time period when the business closed.

For the foregoing reasons, the proposed assessment of the Trust Fund Recovery Penalty against me should not be sustained.

Under the penalties of perjury, I have examined the foregoing statement of facts in the foregoing protest, together with all schedules, exhibits, and attachments, and to the best of my knowledge it is true, correct, and complete.

Sincerely yours,

Penny Pencil

Chapter 18

PENALTIES

Over the past decade, Congress has asked the IRS to preside over a virtual explosion in penalties—more than 150 and counting. Sometimes it seems there is a penalty for everything, whether you are right or wrong, whether you look left or right, up or down. In 1994, the Service assessed nearly thirty-four million penalties for $13 million. It abated only five million of these penalties.

In this chapter, we'll explore only nine of these penalties, the most common ones people see year after year. We'll see how they arise, how you can fight them, when they can be abated, and how you can appeal if you don't get satisfaction the first time around. It might be helpful to glance at the following handy summary to get an idea of how these common penalties arise and may be handled.

Personal Penalties	How Much	When Does IRS Impose or Recommend it?	When Can You Appeal it?	This Penalty Can be Excused if You Show:	What Form do I Use?	Where do I Send an Appeal?
Late filing of a tax return	5% of amount due per month; 25% maximum	• When you file your return • During audit • After assessment of tax	• When you file return • When IRS bills you • During audit • After payment, in claim for refund • In bankruptcy	"Reasonable cause" and no willful neglect	• Form 2751 or letter • Form 843 • Bank-ruptcy	• Service Center • Office of Appeals • Bankruptcy Court • IRS Auditor • Federal Court
Late payment of a balance due	0.5% per month of amount due, escalating to 1%; 25% maximum	• When you file your return • After an additional assessment of tax	• When you file return • When IRS bills you • After payment, in claim for refund • In bankruptcy	Reasonable cause and no willful neglect	• Form 2751 or letter • Form 843 • Bank-ruptcy	• Service Center • Office of Appeals • Bankruptcy Court • IRS Auditor • Federal Court
Fraudulent failure to file	15% per month; 75% maximum	• When you file your return • During audit	• When you file return • When IRS bills you • During audit • After payment, in claim for refund • In bankruptcy	No intent to evade the filing requirement	• Form 2751 or letter • Form 843 • Bank-ruptcy	• Service Center • Office of Appeals • Bankruptcy Court • IRS Auditor • Federal Court

Personal Penalties	How Much	When Does IRS Impose or Recommend it?	When Can You Appeal it?	This Penalty Can be Excused if You Show:	What Form do I Use?	Where do I Send My Evidence or an Appeal?
Fraud	75% of amount due to fraud	• When you file your return • During audit	• When you file return • When IRS bills you • During audit • After payment, in claim for refund • In bankruptcy	No intent to evade tax; reasonable cause	• Form 2751 or letter • Form 843 • Bank-ruptcy	• Service Center • Office of Appeals • Bankruptcy Court • IRS Auditor • Federal Court
Estimated tax penalty	Penalty rate × amount under-paid × period of underpayment	• During audit • When you file your return	• When you file return • When IRS bills you • During audit • After payment, in claim for refund • In bankruptcy	Casualty, disaster, or unusual circumstances so that penalty is against equity and good conscience	• Form 2751 or letter • Form 843 • Bank-ruptcy • Form 2210, 2210F	• Service Center • Office of Appeals • Bankruptcy Court • Federal Court • IRS Auditor
Bad-check penalty	2% of the check; if check is under $750, lesser of $150 or amount of check	• When you bounce a check to IRS	• When you send the check in • After payment, in claim for refund • In bankruptcy	Reasonable cause and good-faith belief that check was good	• Form 2751 or letter • Bank-ruptcy	• Service Center • Office of Appeals • Bankruptcy Court • Federal Court • IRS Agent

Personal Penalties	How Much	When Does IRS Impose or Recommend it?	When Can You Appeal it?	This Penalty Can be Excused if You Show:	What Form do I Use?	Where do I Send My Evidence or an Appeal?
Negligence	20% of additional tax due	• During audit	• During audit • At appeals • In claim for refund • In bankruptcy	• Good-faith and reasonable cause, or no intentional disregard of IRS rules or regulations • Adequate disclosure of nonfrivolous position	• Protest • Form 843 • Bankruptcy	• Office of Appeals • Bankruptcy Court • IRS Auditor • Federal Court
Substantial understatement of tax in your return	In general, 20% of the understatement of tax	• During audit	• During audit • At appeals • In claim for refund • In bankruptcy	• Good-faith and reasonable cause, or no intentional disregard of IRS rules or regulations • Disclosure of the nonfrivolous item on the return • Substantial authority for your position	• Protest • Form 843 • Letter • Bankruptcy	• Office of Appeals • Bankruptcy Court • IRS Auditor • Federal Court
Failure to deposit payroll taxes	Up to 10%	When you make the deposit or file the quarterly return	• When you make the deposit or file the quarterly return • After payment, in claim for refund • In bankruptcy	Reasonable cause and no willful neglect; ordinary business care and prudence	• Form 2751 or letter • Form 843	• Service Center • Office of Appeals • Federal Court • Bankruptcy Court
Trust Fund Recovery	See chapter 10	See chapter 10	See chapter 10	See chapter 10	See chapter 10	See chapter 10

HOW THE IRS LOOKS AT PENALTIES

As an institution, the IRS has the overall goal to impose and administer penalties fairly. Since the penalty program was revised in 1992, agents are supposed to treat similarly situated taxpayers alike, to allow them an opportunity to be heard, to be fair and impartial, and to make the right decision. Whether that translates into real understanding at the agent's level is another matter entirely. Results vary widely around the country. The imposition of most of these penalties depends greatly on the agent's discretion, or on the judgment of an appeals officer when the agent sustains the penalty. For this reason, you cannot count on the general "feel good" objectives of the Internal Revenue manual. To avoid or overturn these penalties, you must have facts and proof at your command showing "reasonable cause" or similar standard. The IRS approach must be consistent, accurate, impartial, and correct, with adequate opportunity for you to be heard. In fact, if you present anything resembling reasonable cause to the agent, he is required to advise you of the reasonable cause provisions even if you don't know about them.

For all of these penalties, your reasonable cause explanation will be examined quite closely. The IRS will ask many questions, including these (all drawn from the Internal Revenue manual):

- Does your reason truly address the penalty imposed? Do the dates and explanations clearly correspond to the events on which the penalties are based?

- Is this the first time the penalty has been imposed, or are you a repeater?

- What is the length of time between the reasonable cause events and your repair of the problem? If you took too long, and failed to try to correct the problem, you may lose your reasonable cause.

- Could you have anticipated the events that caused your noncompliance? Were these events truly beyond your control?

ASSERTING OR ASSESSING THE PENALTIES

The IRS can assess or assert a penalty in many different ways. It depends on the type of penalty and, in part, on how you trigger the penalty.

For instance, sending a late return to an IRS service center will automatically attract the 5 percent per month late-filing penalty if the return reflects a balance due. But you can still suffer this penalty later, even if the return reflects a refund. Let's say the IRS audits the late return and assesses more taxes (you thought you had a refund) . Suddenly, your return becomes a balance due return, subject to the late-filing penalty. The same is true of the late-payment penalty and the estimated-tax penalty.

The negligence, substantial understatement, and fraud penalties are normally asserted as a result of an audit, rather than automatically at the IRS service center where you file your return. That's because someone must look at your facts and affirmatively determine that you acted negligently, committed civil fraud, or substantially understated your taxes.

The bad-check penalty is simple; the IRS asserts it anytime you bounce a tax check. The penalty for failure to deposit payroll taxes starts at 2 percent on the first day and escalates to 10 percent depending on how late you are and how often the IRS has to nudge you by formal notices. Finally, the IRS imposes the Trust Fund Recovery Penalty on corporate officers and employees who were responsible for their company's failure to pay withholding taxes. This special penalty is a world unto itself. Chapter 10 discusses it in detail.

THE SCOPE OF THESE PENALTIES

Late-filing penalty. The late-filing penalty is extremely high—5 percent per month (or any part of a month) for each month a return is late, up to a maximum of 25 percent. The stiffness of this penalty shows how serious the IRS is about having returns filed on time. Of course, the Service also wants you to pay on time, but that penalty is lower. In 1994, the IRS imposed the late-filing penalty more than five million times.

It's important to watch the due date of your return when you have applied for an extension to file. The first extension, to August 15, is automatic. The second, to October 15, is discretionary, but usually granted if you have anything resembling a good reason. Also, the IRS sometimes disallows even the August 15 automatic extension if you have not paid enough taxes with the extension form. While this harsh rule is changing in 1996, people who thought they had an extension to file until August 15 can sometimes find their extensions invalidated by the IRS. The courts consistently uphold the IRS on this point.

Late-payment penalty. The late-payment penalty is the little cousin of the late-filing penalty. The IRS assessed this penalty more than seventeen million times in 1994. It's also imposed automatically by computer when you send a return without full payment. This penalty is .5 percent per month, up to 25 percent. It increases to 1 percent per month after the IRS sends you a "final notice" that your payment is overdue. The IRS may not simultaneously impose the late-filing and the late-payment penalties, so if you filed more than five months late, you get a free ride on the late-payment penalty for those five months. That's the good news. The bad news is that the maximum for both penalties, put together, is 47.5 percent of the tax due. And that does not include interest, which accrues in the penalty as well as the tax.

Estimated-tax penalty. The estimated tax penalty is the third penalty relating to return filing. This penalty normally arises when you have income that is not subject to withholding, such as interest or dividends, but you haven't paid enough tax on it during the year. As with other penalties, it is asserted by the IRS automatically when you file your return. This penalty even has a worksheet you can send with your return showing the amount of the penalty.

Accuracy-related penalty. The next group of penalties relate to the accuracy of your return. These penalties range from 20 percent to 75 percent, so, in theory, a taxpayer who *really* messes up by filing late, paying late, and filing an inaccurate return can rack up penalties from 77 percent to 132 percent of the tax due, plus interest. It doesn't often happen, but surprisingly the law allows such a result.

> *Example:* Sudden Sam filed his 1991 federal income tax return three years late. The tax due was $10,000. He had no reasonable cause for this delinquency so the IRS assessed the maximum late-filing penalty (25 percent) and a late-payment penalty (22.5 percent). Then Revenue Agent Ronnie Rushmore audited the return, finding that Sam committed civil fraud. (Sam had left out income from a stock sale on purpose, that is, with intent to evade the tax laws.) So another $5,000 in tax was asserted, plus a 75 percent civil fraud penalty on this item. If the whole return was fraudulent, the penalties could have totalled 132.5 percent of the tax due.

Negligence. The negligence component of the accuracy penalty can be asserted following an audit. In the real world, some revenue agents assert it as a matter of routine. The penalty is 20 percent of the additional tax due. It applies where the IRS concludes you have negligently disregarded tax rules and regulations. (Some revenue agents think that if you made a mistake they catch, you must have intentionally disregarded the rules.)

Substantial understatement. Instead of the negligence penalty, the agent can assert the "substantial understatement" penalty, also 20 percent of the additional tax due. The details of imposing this penalty are complex, but as a rule of thumb, if you owe $5,000 more tax after an audit, the revenue agent can assert this penalty.

Civil fraud. The civil fraud penalty is imposed where the revenue agent concludes you have intentionally evaded the tax laws. This is the big one, 75 percent of the amount of tax due to fraud. It is routinely asserted after any criminal conviction for evasion.

What is civil fraud? It differs from criminal fraud only in that criminal fraud requires proof of fraud beyond a reasonable doubt. For civil fraud, proof need only be "clear and convincing." According to the IRS manual, civil fraud requires that the IRS show you materially misrepresented facts, that you knew of their falsity and intended the IRS to rely on them and act as if they were the truth. For evidence, the IRS will generally look for badges of fraud. These might include specific items you understated, fictitious or improper deductions, or false entries or double sets of books. Other badges are destroyed records, false or inconsistent statements, transfers of assets, consistent underreporting of taxable income over many years. Anything you say or do that looks dishonest, misleading, or evasive could be a badge of fraud. And, remember, if the agent finds enough of these badges of fraud, he or she *must* suspend the investigation and refer the case to the Criminal Investigation Division. Only if CID refuses the case will it come back for civil action. In that time, you will live in suspended animation, never knowing whether the criminal investigators will take the case and send you to jail. But even if you are "relieved" by the case remaining civil, you will undoubtedly be subject to the 75 percent fraud penalty on the underreported tax.

Fraudulent failure to file. People who fail to file returns can't incur the civil fraud penalty—they haven't filed a fraudulent return in the first place. So Congress invented the "fraudulent failure to file" penalty, also up to a whopping 75 percent of the tax due.

> *Example:* Daniel and Diane lived in Spokane, Washington. They made a living through bookmaking. Unfortunately for them, this was illegal. The police paid them a surprise house call. Among the things discovered in the raid were wagering records such as "pay and collect" sheets, other bet sheets, cash, bookmaking books, and other gambling paraphernalia. There was also a phone bank that attracted the interest of the police, and eleven audio cassette tapes that made for interesting listening. All of this led to raids on several safe deposit boxes plus the seizure of $50,000 in currency.

Daniel and Diane were of course convicted of gambling under state law. But their problems didn't stop. They had not filed federal income tax returns when the raids took place. The IRS added the fraudulent failure to file penalty and the court sustained it. The same "badges of fraud" that apply to tax evasion also apply to this new penalty. These include failing to file returns, engaging in an illegal occupation, concealing assets, failing to cooperate with the tax authorities, dealing in cash, failing to make estimated payments, keeping inadequate records, and understating income.

These are by far the most common penalties normally encountered. There are more than one hundred others that are more rare, or that apply to other types of taxpayers such as return preparers, banks, mortgage companies, and other reporting institutions. These are beyond the scope of this book.

FIGHTING THESE PENALTIES ON THE FRONT LINES

The tax laws and IRS procedures fortunately give you many ways to fight these penalties, at least nine in most cases. That's the good news. The bad news is that while you may have up to nine paths to choose from, they are all uphill.

The first principle in fighting a penalty is preemption. Convince the IRS not to assert the penalty in the first place. With the late-filing, late-payment and estimated-tax penalties, the most common way is to send your return to the IRS service center with a written request to "nonassert" these penalties due to reasonable cause.

You can do the same thing by walking into a local IRS office, speaking to the taxpayer service representative, filing your returns with her, and requesting nonassertion of these penalties.

The third path is to let the IRS assess the penalties, then file your "request for abatement." You may also request nonassertion to any revenue officer on an assessed penalty (but not if your return is still in audit).

A fourth way is to assert reasonable cause or other grounds for nonassertion during an audit if the penalties are asserted for the first time at that stage. With negligence, substantial understatement, and fraud, the revenue agent's level is normally the place to start. You may also appeal to the revenue agent's boss, the group manager. But the chances of a reversal at this level are somewhere between "slim" and "none."

Fifth, you can wait for the Collection Division to begin collecting the assessment, and then request abatement due to reasonable cause.

Sixth, you can pay the penalties and file a claim for refund, asserting reasonable cause in your claim or in a later lawsuit for refund of the penalties.

Seventh, you can make an offer in compromise (see generally chapter 6) on the grounds that you don't owe the penalty because you have reasonable cause. This type of offer is known as an offer based on "doubt as to liability."

Eighth, you can file for bankruptcy. A bankruptcy can often discharge a penalty that is more than three years old, but the technicalities of this rule are complex. In fact, it is unwise ever to file bankruptcy without sound legal advice, especially if you are filing to discharge a tax penalty. As with strong medicine, you need to proceed with caution in using bankruptcy, and only after full consideration of all side effects. Still, bankruptcy promises to deal usefully and effectively with many penalties. Chapter 12 discusses how to manage taxes and penalties in bankruptcy.

Finally, you may fight any of these penalties in court. When the IRS asserts them after an audit, you may go to United States Tax Court first, that is, without having to pay the penalty. (See chapter 21.) If you prefer, you can pay the tax and penalty, then file a claim for refund. If the claim is denied or six months pass without action, you can file suit in federal district court or the United States Court of Federal Claims to contest the penalty. Chapter 22 discusses these procedures in more detail. In particular, the Trust Fund Recovery Penalty (see chapter 10) may be contested, and often is, in federal court suits.

With all of these paths to choose from, how to guide your choice? Generally, it's best to fight the penalties at the earliest possible stage and the lowest possible level. This could be when you first file your return if it's a balance due return, or at the audit stage if that's where the penalty is first asserted. Generally, the later you launch your claim for abatement or nonassertion, the less likely the IRS will be to abate it. Besides, in the tax business, its usually better to know bad news as quickly as possible. It helps in your tax and business planning.

APPEALING DENIAL OF PENALTY ABATEMENT

All of these paths converge when you appeal. You may appeal the denial of your abatement claim after most of these stages. The appeal goes to the Office of Appeals, the same office that considers income tax appeals following an audit. Appeals officers have full authority to abate or compromise penalties, wherever the appeal comes from within the system.

If you are denied at audit, or at the service center when you file a return, you will usually receive a polite denial letter explaining your rights to appeal. The IRS normally gives thirty days to file a protest. Then, the revenue agent or taxpayer service representative packages your file and ships it to the Office of Appeals. The appeals officer reviews the case, contacts you, asks for more information if you have it, and schedules either a phone call or an in-person conference to review your appeal.

Now let's say the appeals officer denies your request for abatement of the penalty. Are you out of luck? Of course not. You can still fight some penalties in court. The tax court has jurisdiction if you haven't paid the penalties. The U.S. district courts or U.S. Court of Federal Claims can hear the case if you have. Chapters 21 and 22 discuss these procedures in more detail.

You can see that you have many chances to contest these penalties, at least three and sometimes four or five depending on how often you appeal within the court system. Moreover, there is usually no reason not to appeal. These penalties are add-ons, which can be frightening, maddening, and onerous, especially when you were just trying to do your best.

PROVING YOUR CASE

You, not the IRS, have the burden to prove your case to abate these penalties except for fraudulent failure to file and civil fraud. To avoid the late-filing, late-payment, estimated-tax, and bad-check penalties, you must show "reasonable cause," or something conceptually similar. The casebooks and professional literature are littered with thousands of cases interpreting what these two little words mean. It all boils down to this: If you have a pretty good excuse, the mistake wasn't your fault, you tried to prevent it, and you corrected it as best you could, *that's* reasonable cause. Even then, you don't always win; remember that thousands of taxpayers who thought their cases were airtight went to court and lost. Even the winners wound up in court in the first place because the IRS rejected their statement of reasonable cause.

The Internal Revenue manual spells out what the agency considers reasonable cause. All winning arguments in penalty excusal cases are variations of these. Here are the eleven "official" reasonable causes.

1. *Death, serious illness, or unavoidable absence.*

A death, serious illness, or unavoidable absence of you or a member of your immediate family may be reasonable cause. Of all the official excuses, this is probably the most common, measured by paper used and litigation filed. "Serious illness" appears to be epidemic among nonfilers, that is, people who are so late with their returns that they haven't filed at all. The Service's own studies of nonfilers have shown that a pattern of nonfiling often results from a serious physical or mental illness. It could be a bitter divorce; a business disaster; mental illness; drug, alcohol, mental, physical, or sexual abuse; or other personal tragedy lasting for years at a time. Combinations of two or more of these disasters are common. The tale of personal woe has to be serious and credible. If it is, the IRS often listens with a sympathetic ear and grants the request for abatement. Many are the cases in which a mental illness has prevented someone from filing for three, four, or five years. Often a downward slide into drug abuse or alcoholism caused an otherwise diligent taxpayer to fail in filing and payment obligations.

> *Example:* The "mental illness" card can, however, be played too much. Consider the story of Zachary, who hired a tax attorney and accountant to file returns, but somehow failed to file for ten years. He even received an IRS refund check but didn't cash it, and didn't sign one return his wife had prepared. He also failed to answer IRS correspondence. What was the problem? He saw a psychiatrist one month before his tax court trial. The doctor diagnosed a phobia: a phobia of preparing tax returns. Yes, that's right, "tax return phobia." Imagine the consequences if this proposition had been accepted by the court. But it was not.

> *Example:* Another case occurred some years ago when Joseph, a professional, failed to file tax returns for five years. His reasonable cause was alcoholism. While the court was sympathetic, the facts just weren't there. In particular, he was shown to be fully capable in other aspects of his life, including service as president of a corporation for some of the years involved. (Apparently even a drunken return is better than none at all.)

> *Example:* If not this reason, then possibly something else outside your control might work. How about the following: I couldn't prepare the return in time because I was having a baby. Noah and Hannah tried that one. They had an extension to file their return to August 15. But Hannah gave birth on August 14. They didn't file the return until September 20. Not good enough, said the court.

But, in other cases, if you can prove mental or physical illness, you should be relieved of the penalty. For example, Sam was a partner in a professional firm when he got into tax trouble. He had omitted a large amount of income from his tax return. The IRS assessed the tax and a penalty, but the tax court rejected the penalty. It seems that Sam suffered from severe depression, anxiety, and paranoia, causing him to be hospitalized for many months. The court believed his testimony, and he was relieved of the penalty.

A regular illness also will do. In one case, John couldn't file tax returns because his arms and legs became paralyzed. He was hospitalized and diagnosed with a condition with an extremely long, unpronounceable name. He saw a number of physicians and underwent many tests, all to no avail. He tried experimental therapy, which didn't work. Essentially, he was unable to take care of himself. Nor was his wife familiar enough with return preparation to do the job. That was reasonable cause.

Also, the nature of the particular syndrome, such as alcoholism, depression, or abuse, often has roots in childhood or at least stretches back many years. The more you elaborate on how the illness got started, how it culminated in your late filing or late payment, the more likely an IRS employee will be inclined to believe you and find you have shown reasonable cause. A full statement of reasonable cause can sometimes run to ten single-spaced, typewritten pages, with a half an inch or more of medical, social, or psychiatric documentation.

To request abatement of these reasonable cause penalties due to illness, write the IRS a letter, include Form 2751, and tell the full story. Include the dates and nature of your illness or absence, show how the illness or absence prevented compliance, and note whether other things you did in life, such as running your business, also suffered as a result.

It is impossible to overstate how important good documentation is for this type of reasonable cause (and for others as well). The IRS treats your statement of reasonable cause very seriously; its agents also diligently guard the privacy of the information you submit. Painful as it is to recount the details, a compelling story causes the IRS to listen, hear, and, in many cases, give you the benefit of the doubt.

   2.   *Fire, casualty, natural disaster, or other disturbance.*

Believe it or not, some people succeed in abating penalties by claiming, "There was a flood in my basement," or, "A fire burned my records." Of course, it's one thing to say, another to prove. You have to show how and why. Address whether you could have gotten your tax return or payment together by other means. Again, documentation always helps. Enclose fire, police, or insurance reports. If these are not available (or even if they are), attach any other supportive documentation. Notarized statements from disinterested third persons are always credible and helpful. Pictures also are worth thousands of words.

3.   *Unable to obtain necessary records.*

If your records are unavailable, you may have reasonable cause. When your records are missing, the "reasonableness" of your cause depends on whether you exercised "ordinary business care and prudence" but your records nevertheless disappeared because of circumstances beyond your control. In your request for abatement, specify the nature of the records, why they were unavailable, how you tried to fix the situation, whether you called the Service about the missing information, and why you couldn't use estimates and still comply.

> *Example:* Sal was divorced from his wife Mona. She moved out and took all records of income and expense of Sal's profession. He went to court to get the records back, but failed. He met with the IRS before the due date, told them he was at his wit's end trying to get his records, and signed an extension until July 15 to file the return. Before that deadline, he went again to the IRS and told them he still couldn't get all of his records together. So the IRS told him to do the best he could, which he did. Naturally, the IRS penalized him. But the court rejected this penalty. He had done all he could to reconstruct his records, and even asked for professional help, so his conduct should not be penalized.

4.   *Lack of funds.*

"I can't pay" is not usually reasonable cause, but if you couldn't pay despite your best efforts or due to circumstances beyond your control, that might be reasonable cause for late payment. For example, if you were about to pay a tax bill but someone stole or embezzled the money you had set aside, that might be reasonable cause if you had no way of preventing or foreseeing it. If undue hardship, bankruptcy, or insolvency might have resulted if you paid the taxes on time, you might have reasonable cause. An example might be a sudden, totally unexpected bill, or a sudden downturn in business. Not many people succeed with this cause, but if you have a good reason, it's worth a try.

Example: This happened in a case involving a company that was building ships for the Navy. The Navy and the builder had the usual fights over performance of the contract, but nothing horrible happened until the Navy stopped progress payments. Eventually, the taxpayer-contractor could pay only certain subcontractors and suppliers, and as a result failed to deposit payroll taxes. The Navy then terminated the contract, owing the company more than $165,000. "Reasonable cause," said the court. The company did the best it could, and it had a right to rely on the Navy's promise to pay. It was the government's own fault that the contractor couldn't pay its taxes.

Example: An electrical and mechanical contractor ran into the same problem in another case, though not with the government. The contractor had decided to finish a number of large jobs, relying on the owner's promise to pay right after completion. Of course, the promise was empty. The contractor tried his best to pay some of the taxes, but could not pay all. If the contractor had paid the taxes, he would not have been able to finish the jobs and would have gone out of business. That was enough, said the court, to show reasonable cause for late payment. Payment would have caused "undue hardship."

5. *Ignorance of the law.*

This one is especially tough. We've all heard that ignorance of the law is no excuse, a principle that applies doubly when it come to taxes. Still, there's a bit of wiggle room in this principle. The IRS' manual says that ignorance of the law, combined with other facts and circumstances such as limited education or lack of previous tax penalty experience, may support reasonable cause. For instance, where you confront a difficult or complex tax issue and the Service doesn't give you guidance, the IRS may concede that reasonable people might differ as to how to treat the issue. Also, if ignorance is based on a recent tax law change unavailable to people generally, that might qualify.

6. *You or a subordinate made a mistake or were forgetful.*

Again, not usually an excuse, but some court cases have held that a subordinate's error was excusable. An example might be when you tell your trusty assistant, "Now, Dr. Watson, I want you to take this tax return and immediately go to the post office to mail it." When Dr. Watson fails to mail the return because he forgot or stuck it in the drawer, that might be reasonable cause. Of course, if Dr. Watson had a reputation for forgetting things, you'd be out of luck.

> *Example:* But what if your trusted employee makes the mistake? Even that may not be reasonable cause, as one physicians' group found out. The long-employed, trusted secretary was supposed to make tax deposits and file returns, but did not. The doctors could not delegate this ministerial responsibility to someone else, then avoid responsibility for that employee's failure.

> *Example:* In another example, a supply company filed its tax return late and applied for an extension only after the deadline had run out. "But I relied on my attorneys, accountants, and pension adviser," said the president. Not good enough, said the court. You can't rely on your adviser to do what the law requires of *you.* That's not what reasonable cause means. These kinds of deadlines may not be delegated, so the penalty was proper.

7.   *Relied on the advice of a competent tax adviser.*

If your accountant or lawyer made a mistake in advising you, you shouldn't be blamed for it. Of course, you are in the awkward position of proving that an adviser *you* selected made the mistake. Also required is proof the auditor was otherwise competent, and that you gave complete information and cooperation. If your accountant says you don't have to file on October 15, that might not be reasonable cause, because everyone is held to know that October 15 is the last date. But if she said, "Your $100,000 court award is not taxable," and it really was, that might be reasonable cause because this is a gray area of the law.

> *Example:* One corporation tried to blame the accountant when it failed to file payroll tax returns on time and failed to pay the taxes. The problem was with one customer, who delayed paying invoices for up to four months. "Not a problem," said the accountant. "You don't have to file until you have enough money to pay. In fact, if you don't file, the IRS will not close the business, and you can catch up on your payments when your customer pays." Clearly, such misplaced reliance will not be reasonable cause.

> *Example:* But in another case, "blaming the accountant" worked. Oliver had a high school education. Anita, his wife, quit school before finishing

the tenth grade. Neither had any other formal education. Oliver had other problems: diabetes, hearing loss, and impaired eyesight. They joined forces with Oliver's brother to open other businesses. They also bought real estate. Things got complex, so they hired a CPA. Everything went fine until Oliver threw caution to the wind by investing in foreign speculative ventures. He made a killing. But the CPA said Oliver did not have to pay U.S. taxes since Oliver and Anita were paying taxes overseas. Not so, said the IRS. And the agency was right, so Oliver had to pay a hefty tax. But the tax court threw out the penalty. Why? Oliver and Anita had limited education. They relied on a competent CPA who turned out to be wrong. But that doesn't mean they should pay the extra burden of a penalty.

8. *Erroneous oral advice from IRS.*

Where the IRS gives you bad advice, you would expect to have reasonable cause, and indeed that is so. But, again, you must jump through hoops. You must show you gave the IRS accurate and complete information, and you exercised ordinary business care and prudence when you relied on the advice. Because this relates to oral advice, proving these elements is difficult, but even your detailed handwritten notes of your conversations with the IRS may suffice. Note in particular what office you called, to whom you spoke, and the date the IRS gave you the advice.

Example: To appreciate how difficult the "erroneous oral advice" case is to prove, consider the case of a law firm that failed to file employment tax returns for most of two years. Naturally, this minor omission attracted the IRS' attention. Marilyn, a revenue officer, got the case, and the firm asked for her help. She helped fill out the returns, and the firm sent in payment of more than $100,000, which the law firm claimed was all that was due. Not so, said the IRS' computers. So a large penalty was assessed. Could the law firm get out of it? No. Even if the law firm relied on Marilyn, she had access only to the taxes shown on the computer. The computer was wrong because the law firm had filed an incorrect return in the past.

9. *Erroneous written advice from IRS.*

The same idea is at work here, and your proof is a little easier. In fact, there's even a law on this one, requiring the IRS to abate any penalty attributable to its own erroneous written advice. But that advice must refer to your specific written request. Also, you must have given the IRS complete and accurate information about your situation, and you have to have relied on the advice. In the real world, the IRS is fairly liberal about granting relief here, giving the taxpayer the benefit of the doubt if the advice was written.

10. *Failure to deposit due to no coupons.*

Employers deposit payroll taxes using a coupon, Form 8109. If you don't have these coupons, you may have reasonable cause for failure to deposit, but you need to show you used ordinary business care and prudence. This includes requesting the books five to six weeks in advance but not receiving them in time. Also, over-the-counter federal tax deposit coupons, Form 8109-B, are available. Try to demonstrate you didn't have them and couldn't get them in time.

11. *Embezzlement.*

Employees and officers who embezzle company money are becoming an increasingly common fact of business life. However, blaming a late-filing or late-payment penalty on embezzlers seldom works.

> *Example:* For almost thirty years, Hartley worked long and hard in his leather importing business. Then he suffered a heart attack. So his vice president and controller took over. And "take over" they did. They embezzled more than $150,000 and tried to hide their offense by failing to file payroll tax returns. The accountant for the company sounded general quarters. Hartley returned to find the disaster. Could his company get out of the penalty? No, said the judge.

The same thing happened to another company that performed medical research and manufacturing. The chief executive officer/chairman of the board and the chief financial officer embezzled so much money that the company had to file for bankruptcy. Of course, the top echelon were indicted and convicted of embezzlement. In this case, that was enough to relieve the company of the penalty, that is, to avoid the normal rule that a company is liable for the acts of its agents. But the company still had to show that it did everything else right, including maintaining adequate internal controls that the embezzlers were able to circumvent.

12. *Bad-check penalty.*

This one is tough to have abated, but there are some times when the IRS will do so. If the bank made a mistake or the IRS made a mistake in handling the check, that's probably reasonable cause. If the check was lost in the mail and you replaced it, stopping payment on the first check, the IRS should abate the bad-check penalty if it later receives your first check and tries to cash it. Also, sometimes a freeze can be placed on your bank account for other reasons, such as another creditor's judgment or the death of a signatory. The Service will usually consider these to be reasonable cause as well, but, again, you have to show you tried to prevent the bad check or did your best to make it good afterward.

13. *Negligence penalty.*

When you omit an income item from your return or your deductions are disallowed, you may have acted "negligently." Negligence means you failed to make a reasonable attempt to comply with the revenue laws or failed to exercise ordinary and reasonable care in preparing your tax return. Negligence also includes a failure to keep adequate books and records or to substantiate items of income or deduction properly. Finally, an item on your return is attributable to negligence if it lacks a reasonable basis but falls short of outright fraud.

These standards don't mean that every dollar a revenue agent adds to your tax bill is due to negligence. But in the real world, revenue agents often take that position. They sometimes reason that if you had not been negligent, you would not have taken a disallowed deduction, or you would have included an extra item of income. So they deem any mistake to be negligent by the fact it was made. This circular reasoning is not the law, but sometimes you may need to fight long and hard to convince them.

Still, some actions are clearly negligent. Failing to include an income item as to which an information return (for example, Form 1099) has been filed (example, bank interest), or taking a deduction or credit that seems too good to be true, are examples. If you are careless or reckless, or if you intentionally disregard IRS rules or regulations, that's negligence.

To overcome the negligence penalty, you need to show that you did your best and acted reasonably and prudently in taking the deduction. Check for such things as prior audits where your position was allowed. Prove you examined your return carefully. Show you relied on the advice of an accountant or an attorney, that you reasonably interpreted IRS publications in taking the deduction, or that the law changed. Demonstrate that your position was justified, even if it turned out to be incorrect. In particular, proving an honest misunderstanding of the facts or the law may overcome the negligence penalty.

Example: In one case, a taxpayer we'll call Jack liked to buy insurance. Jack's life insurance agent proposed a scheme under which Jack took out whole life policies, paid the premiums, and received the same amount from the agent as a kickback. Then he allowed the policy to lapse. The agent, not Jack, was indicted and convicted of several crimes. Jack was taxed on the kickbacks. But was he negligent? No, said the court. The kickbacks may have been "improper," even illegal, but that didn't mean Jack negligently failed to report them. After all, Jack's returns were prepared by a professional preparer, and Jack promptly paid the tax once the IRS declared that the payments were taxable. Since Jack's position on the tax issue was "not frivolous," the negligence penalty didn't apply.

This type of case, and hundreds like it, highlight the rules of the road to avoid the negligence penalty: Take a good-faith position, stick to it, and make full disclosure to your advisers and the IRS.

14. *"Substantial understatement" penalty.*

Another component of the accuracy penalty is the "substantial understatement" of taxes. Even if you weren't negligent, the IRS can penalize you 20 percent if the changes to your return result in a "substantial" understatement. You avoid this aspect of the accuracy-related penalty if (1) you disclosed the item on the return or (2) you had substantial legal authority for reporting it the way you did. Disclosing an item on a return normally requires a special form, Form 8275. But for some common items, merely listing them on the return in the right place is adequate disclosure. These include all Schedule A items (medical expenses, real estate interest, state taxes, charity, and miscellaneous) and other items as well. Every year, the IRS publishes a list of the items that are "adequately disclosed" just by reporting them on the return. As to every other item, consider filing Form 8275 if the item is questionable.

You may also avert the substantial understatement penalty by finding substantial authority for the position you took on the return. This requires researching the law, including the statutes, regulations, court cases, and other tax authority. Of course, assembling this authority before taking the deduction also satisfies the negligence standard.

All these grounds for penalty relief have an additional common element: do everything you can to fix the problem, catch up, or get duplicate records. You can't sit back thinking, "Oh well, I got sick (or I lost my records), I don't have to file or pay until I get around to it." Show the IRS that you scrambled in every reasonable way to avoid or fix the problem once your learned of it, or to correct it after the failure occurred.

15. *Estimated-tax penalty.*

To earn relief from the estimated-tax penalty, you must generally show that your failure to pay the right amount of estimated tax was caused by casualty, disaster, or unusual circumstances, and that imposing the penalty would be against equity and good conscience. This is not the same as the reasonable cause you may use for other penalties. The Internal Revenue manual itself describes that reliance on a competent tax adviser, or erroneous advice from the IRS, would not be enough to waive the estimated tax penalty. You must show circumstances such as that your records were destroyed by fire, flood, or other natural disaster, you became seriously ill or injured, or that your estimated-tax payments were offset against past-due child support or other federal debts. There are other waivers available for newly retired or disabled individuals, but, again, these must be shown to include reasonable cause and an absence of willful neglect.

MECHANICS OF MAKING YOUR ABATEMENT REQUEST

The chart at the beginning of this chapter shows the forms to use or letters to write. Try to use these forms, since IRS employees are familiar with them. The supporting documentation for your reasonable cause request need not follow any particular form. Letters, affidavits, or statements will suffice.

When you appeal from a denial, you likewise need no particular form; a letter is sufficient. Also, the IRS' denial letters often contain specific instructions on how to frame the appeal letter, whom to send it to, and when.

Above all, don't give up. These penalties can be your profit margin or your discretionary budget. They are sometimes quite high, and interest is charged on them. Sometimes you'll have success at the second or third level where the first was a disaster. Take advantage of every chance the law and the IRS give you to contest and protest these penalties.

Chapter 19

"BUT I JUST SIGNED WHERE HE TOLD ME": THE INNOCENT SPOUSE AND THE INJURED SPOUSE.

Example: Emily and Ernest were married in 1940. Emily had only a high school education. Ernest handled all of the family's finances. Emily took care of the house, using the couple's joint checking account to pay for groceries, utilities, and the mortgage. Emily also raised two daughters. Of course, the couple filed joint federal income tax returns.

Meanwhile, Ernest and his brother formed a partnership to open a store. He never discussed the store's business with Emily, nor did Emily visit. To prepare the couple's joint tax return, Emily gave their reliable accountant a list of household expenses, then simply signed on the dotted line.

Things went well for years, then Ernest passed away. The IRS audited the couple's joint returns and assessed more than $40,000 in taxes for three years. Without Ernest, Emily found herself alone: solely and completely liable for all of these taxes. They did not live lavishly; there were no expensive fur coats, luxury yachts, trips to Bermuda, or private schools. Emily always did as Ernest asked, keeping faith with her husband and his professional accountant-advisers. Yet, because she signed the joint returns, she was held liable for all of the tax.

Congress felt there ought to be some remedy for situations like this, so in 1969 it passed the "innocent spouse" statute, a part of the Internal Revenue Code. If you meet the tests, you get complete absolution from all tax, penalties, and interest that you otherwise guaranteed by signing a joint return. Meeting the tests of the innocent spouse law is difficult. Still, it can be done; many do it each year. You can go it alone, but you are almost always better off having professional help to prove this issue.

WHEN YOU MAY CLAIM TO BE INNOCENT

You may raise the innocent spouse defense almost anytime in the tax process, but the issue usually arises during an audit. The agent finds a hidden bank account, or one spouse is arrested for drugs or gambling. A corporation's president is charged with extra income because the corporation paid personal expenses, or the couple takes an unallowable deduction. These events and myriad others could result in an increase in taxes. Then the "innocent" spouse claims, "I had no idea my husband [or wife] had all this extra income [or had taken unallowable deductions]." The defense also can arise during a divorce. In the divorce decree, the husband (or wife) commits to pay the taxes for past years when the couple filed a joint return. The IRS audits those returns, or finds some other reason to propose more taxes. The wife (or husband) can claim innocent spouse at that time.

Finally, we also see the issue in garden-variety collection situations. Here, the IRS is trying to collect on past-due taxes from joint returns. Often one spouse will raise the innocent spouse defense.

Note that the innocent spouse defense is not available unless the IRS proposes more tax than what you reported on the joint return.

PROVING YOU ARE INNOCENT

Proving innocent spouse status is arduous even under the best of circumstances, and sometimes a spouse is not eligible no matter how unfair the overall situation. Let's explore how a spouse can establish "innocence."

The proof has four elements, the first two easy, the second two difficult. First, you must have filed a joint return for the tax year involved. This item seems simple enough—either you signed or you didn't. But sometimes a wife denies the genuineness of her signature on the return. Then the fight starts. The husband claims she in fact signed, or that he signed her name with her permission. Even where one spouse doesn't sign the return at all, the IRS sometimes argues that the facts show the spouse intended to file a joint return. If so, by law it's a joint return.

The second requirement is that there be an understatement of tax that is substantial. That's defined as $500 or more. Again, not much confusion here, but watch the details: there must be an understatement of tax *on the return*. This means that you are stuck with anything you reported on the return as the true tax. You may be innocent, if at all, only as to extra taxes the IRS proposes.

> *Example:* Jack and Jill were married for ten years. When Jill signed their joint returns, Jack said, "Don't worry, dear, I'll pay the taxes." He always promised he would, but the IRS never knocked on the door. When they divorced in 1995, Jack promised again to pay all taxes due on past returns, $50,000 in total. The divorce became final. Jack moved to Kodiak, Alaska, and Jill was left in the IRS' target zone, struggling as a single mother to support three children, all under the age of five.
>
> Innocent spouse? No! Maybe Jill can get relief in other ways, such as urging that collection would be a hardship. Chapter 13 discusses these options. But she is not an innocent spouse under the law. She signed all the returns, and there was no understatement of tax. The return stated exactly how much tax was owed. It simply was not paid.

The third requirement is that the understatement must be caused by a "grossly erroneous" item. Omitted income qualifies as grossly erroneous, as does any deduction or credit that lacks a basis in fact or law. Also, these deductions or credits have to be big, typically more than 10 percent of the spouse's gross income. That number moves to 25 percent if the spouse makes more than $40,000.

Grossly erroneous deductions might include items such as deducting twice the allowable amount for a home office; deducting a plane trip to where you conducted little or no business; or claiming a large, nondeductable loss. It could mean deducting interest you paid on an unsecured loan that was personal, not business, in nature; or deducting state taxes you owe but didn't pay.

Notice what you are trying to prove: the deduction you took in the first place is so totally and clearly wrong that it has no basis whatsoever. The agent would naturally ask, "Then why did you sign your name? Didn't you know the deduction was off the wall?"

In fact, this third legal requirement also requires that the spouse must not have known of the understatement of tax. This rule does not mean you can sign the return in blank or not read it all. You can't hide your head in the sand and expect to get tax relief. Instead, the requirement is to show you acted with "reasonable prudence." For example, if you reviewed the return but relied on your husband, wife, CPA, or lawyer to prepare it correctly, that would be reasonable prudence. But if you put your left hand over your eyes and scribbled your signature with your right, that's not. It's also not reasonable prudence if you ignore obvious warning signs that something is wrong or too good to be true. A spouse who lives in a million dollar home knowing her husband earns $20,000 a year cannot be "innocent." Maybe a spouse's suspicious behavior could put you on notice; maybe your lifestyle is way above your earnings. Possibly there are unusual or inconsistent warning signs, such as long, unexplained absences from home, lavish gifts, erratic behavior, or sudden changes in lifestyle or net worth. The agent and the IRS will seize on any of these to show you should have known that there was something wrong with the tax return you signed.

The fourth requirement is that, under all the circumstances, it would be inequitable to hold you liable for the taxes. "Inequitable" means "unfair." This is a catchall requirement that limits relief to the truly needy. The rich and famous of the world do not usually qualify. Even if life was hard when you signed the return, if life is great now, there's no unfairness in holding you responsible for past taxes. Still, the law makes an explicit exception for normal support. So, if your spouse supports you with food, clothing, and shelter within normal amounts, not lavishly or extravagantly, the government cannot claim you failed the "inequitable" test by that fact alone.

Example: One recent case shows how far this argument will stretch. Lucy and Larry were married. Larry started a business raising and selling radishes. He was so successful that he built a house on ten acres, complete with swimming pool, tennis court, clubhouse, and airplane landing strip. Thirty years later, Lucy and Larry divorced. She got $225,000 each year as guaranteed income, plus the house, clubhouse, swimming pool, and tennis court (apparently, Larry kept the landing strip). Two years later, the couple remarried each other. For three years, Larry gave his wife $15,000 per month, plus two Mercedeses and trips in the airplane. Naturally, they had a getaway in Florida during the winter growing season.

However, the winds of love blow hot and cold. They divorced a second time, this time permanently. As a parting gift, Lucy got $4.28 million as alimony.

Of course, the IRS then came into the picture, proposing massive taxes on the couple's jointly filed returns. Lucy said, "I am an innocent spouse." The IRS said, "You've got to be kidding. Just look at your lavish lifestyle, including your $15,000 a month allowance, new cars, European vacations, race horses, a full-time maid and gardener, two homes, and a clubhouse, swimming pool, and tennis court. You must have known that Larry was underreporting his taxes, and besides, it's certainly not unfair to hold you liable."

Believe it or not, the court sided with Lucy. "One person's luxury may be another's necessity," said the court. She was rich before the returns were filed, she was rich during the years in question, and she was rich afterward. Nothing in her lifestyle would have put her on notice that anything had changed.

Despite occasional wins like the Lucy case, in the real world agents are extremely reluctant to believe your claims of innocence, or even to credit sworn testimony to that effect. Often, you must prepare to go to court to prove innocent spouse status. Even there, the courts are quite skeptical about granting relief. Your case must be excellent to prevail.

The best way to prove you're an innocent spouse is to assemble a catalog of evidence and present it to the IRS or to a court if necessary.

First, prepare your own affidavit. Tell your life story, focusing especially on the years of trouble with your spouse. Common to these cases are long, sad stories of spouse abuse, psychological and physical domination, alcoholism, drug abuse, and other dysfunctional behavior. Wives who are abused and dominated by their husbands can often be innocent spouses. It is common sense that if one spouse dominates the relationship, he or she can take charge of the taxes, and the return comes out wrong without the other spouse's knowledge or consent.

It's also very common for innocent spouse cases to arise out of family businesses. One spouse (usually the husband in case law), runs the business with an iron hand. The other spouse minds the home and children, participates in community activity, and has minimal involvement in the business. Then, when the IRS proposes more tax, the wife claims innocence because the husband ran the business and refused to keep her informed of income or tax-related matters. It's common to hear, "My husband ran the business. He refused to let me participate in it. I trusted him to file the returns, and we had the accountant to help get it right. When I asked him about the return, he would just say to sign and not ask any questions." While sometimes this can be a convenient excuse, quite often it is the truth.

Your "life history" affidavit should be long and detailed. Include everything. Show how the other spouse's personality, bad habits, or ways of doing business meant that you could not know that the taxes were understated. Demonstrate the unfairness of holding you liable for the other spouse's errors.

Second, begin to assemble third-party witness statements. Evidence from people with no ax to grind on your issue is always credible with the IRS and the courts. If your three best friends knew of your spouse's alcoholism, drug abuse, or domineering nature, have them write affidavits. Bankers may have known of his secretive business habits. Counselors and friends can testify about the personalities and financial habits they observed.

Third, gather objective evidence. This would include bank statements, notices, business records, and anything else on paper that supports your case. You will be amazed at how much support you can find once you start to look with this issue squarely in mind.

Fourth, get help. Find a friend or ask a professional whether your case is good and how it can be improved. Then follow up. Ask the revenue agent or tax auditor for as much time as you need to put the evidence together. Cite helpful court cases. These are available in the professional literature, but you may need some help finding them.

Fifth, don't give up. Statistically, you will lose your claim at the agent's level. You may then appeal to the Office of Appeals or go to court. If the case comes up after the assessments have been made, consider requesting audit reconsideration.

Finally, ask the Problem Resolution Office (PRO) for help. Make your innocent spouse case to that office if you never had sufficient opportunity to prove your case to the agent. Even if the Problem Resolution Office does not sustain your innocent spouse claim, it may refer your case back to the examination division for reaudit. The PRO also may decide that your case is so worthy, and enforced collection would be so unfair, that it will stop the Collection Division anyway under the "hardship" rules. Chapter 13 discusses how the Problem Resolution Office comes to your rescue in cases of clear hardship.

There is no form for claiming innocent spouse relief. So assemble and organize your evidence in any way that makes sense. You may choose separate exhibits with exhibit numbers, or simply bundle it all altogether. Write a cover letter to the agent setting forth all the facts and asking for innocent spouse relief. Be sure to keep a copy, which you will surely need.

The 1996 Taxpayer Bill of Rights also helps a bit on the collection side. Let's say you can't prove innocent spouse status, or you've settled your innocent spouse claim somewhere in the middle. You therefore still owe taxes, but, in the meantime, what has the IRS been doing to collect against your ex? Now, an agent must tell you whether she has tried to collect, the general nature of her efforts, and how much has been collected. These facts may put some pressure on the agency to spread the burden of these joint taxes. Congress also has required the Treasury Department to study the whole problem of unfairness in charging an "innocent" spouse with joint liability. That report is due in early 1997.

THE INJURED SPOUSE

The "injured spouse" concept has nothing to do with "innocent spouse" status. It is a fancy name for a spouse who did not receive his or her fair share of a joint refund. These cases arise quite often, particularly in the aftermath of a divorce or separation. One spouse has two-thirds of the income and has paid two-thirds of the taxes through payroll withholding, but does not receive two-thirds of the refund. In fact, the injured spouse may receive nothing.

So, the IRS devised a form to file by which you can receive your proportionate share. Form 8375 and its detailed instructions explain how to file your claim. Basically, you are entitled to get back your share of a joint refund, based on your proportionate share of the tax you and your spouse paid together.

You can file an injured spouse claim anytime before the IRS issues a refund. It's usually best to do so with the tax return itself, or right afterward. Sometimes you can get back money from years past if the IRS has not issued the refund. But once the refund has been issued, you can't get it back except from the other spouse.

Chapter 20

———⊶⊷———

THE STATE TAX IMPACT OF AN IRS AUDIT

These days, it's fashionable to pay increasing attention to state governments. By ambush and attrition, states are slowing recapturing the powers they once possessed but had ceded to the federal government. As this trend accelerates, the states need ever more money to run their programs. They also need stronger enforcement mechanisms to ensure they reap the fields of green within their borders.

Everyone who owes a federal tax should consider whether he will end up owing a state tax as well. States are no longer paper tigers when it comes to tax enforcement. They also gain strength every day.

YOU CAN'T KEEP SECRETS

State-federal cooperation has been a feature of our federal system since the first days of the republic. The states and federal government continue to cooperate very closely when it comes to taxes.

One area they share is information, and lots of it. The IRS and many (in some areas, all) state governments have signed a series of protocols, called Information Sharing Agreements, of which the public is largely unaware.

The first sharing agreement is for tax information. The exchange goes both ways. The IRS tells states what you earn. States tell the IRS what you have reported to them. They also share refund information, and, of course, states are required to send you an IRS Form 1099 when you get a state tax refund.

The states and the IRS also share employment and sales tax information. The reporting cycle is every eighteen months to three years. For example, the federal government wants to know how much your business is reporting to the state for sales tax purposes so it can check this against the amount you reported on your federal return. Cheating usually shows up when you report more gross sales on your state sales tax returns than gross income on your federal income tax return.

The states and the IRS also share employment information. They exchange data on your employees, so you can't tell the state you have "employees" and call them "independent contractors" for federal tax withholding purposes.

The IRS shares the results of income tax audits with your state's department of taxation. State laws require that you amend your state income tax return if you owe more after a federal audit. The same laws also suspend the statute of limitations on assessment if you owe more state taxes as a result of a federal audit. So, even though more than three years have passed, the state can still assess more state tax as a result of your federal audit. Often, the states have computer programs to generate a bill to you whether or not you file an amended state tax return after your federal audit.

Some states also cooperate with the IRS to investigate or audit you, the taxpayer. For instance, suppose a state investigates your business to see whether your workers are employees or independent contractors. The choice makes a big difference in your state unemployment tax. It makes an even bigger difference to the withholding and Social Security taxes you must pay to the IRS. The state will share the results of this investigation with the IRS. As electronic filing and computerization of federal and state tax records become more common, we'll be seeing much more of joint audits and joint collection.

Nonfilers need to be hyperalert to these features of state-federal cooperation. The nonfiler who owes taxes to the federal government almost always owes state taxes as well. The state taxes may be only 1 percent to 10 percent of the federal total, but they are still important. So the nonfiler should file state tax returns when he files delinquent federal tax returns.

All states with tax laws have vigorous enforcement provisions as well. These laws prescribe criminal penalties for violating state tax statutes of all varieties—income, employment, sales, and so on. Moreover, states are enforcing these statutes more diligently and regularly than at any time in the past. Their methods include arresting people for failing to pay taxes, prosecuting for evasion or nonfiling, closing delinquent businesses, and similar strong medicine. The criminal investigation divisions of the states and the IRS also share information after they complete their investigations. States have civil seizure powers comparable to those of the IRS, including levying on wages and seizing bank accounts.

Tax refunds are also a prime target. Each year, states seize $20 million to $30 million in state tax refunds to send to the IRS. The states have asked the IRS to return the favor with federal refunds, though so far it has not. Still, the IRS does collect child-support payments from tax refunds. It sends those monies to the states that have signed up for this program.

So, if you owe a federal tax, always think through whether you also owe comparable state tax. If so, make arrangements to pay or compromise that tax as well.

On the happier side, states are working ever more closely with the IRS to make tax life simpler. For example, there is a big push toward joint federal-state electronic filing, that is, filing both federal and state returns at one time and in one place. This idea has been tested since 1990. Eventually, it will become standard practice.

States also have authority to compromise a tax you owe. The leniency or strictness of these programs runs the gamut from reasonable to impossible, but the authority is there. Call your state tax department for information. Often the states don't publicize their compromise authority out of fear people will flood them with requests and stop trying to pay their current and past-due taxes.

Each state is a sovereign when it comes to taxes; you must act accordingly. The key to survival is to anticipate the state tax liability. Check whether it can be reduced or compromised and then address the state tax problem before it surprises you.

Part III

TAX LITIGATION

Chapter 21

HANDLING YOUR OWN CASE IN TAX
COURT—IF YOU DARE

Have you ever pictured yourself a giant killer in the courtroom? Have you ever thought, "Wait 'til I get those IRS so-and-sos in court. I'll slash them from ear to ear." Lots of people have this vision. For about twenty thousand people each year, it's no fantasy—they sue the IRS in the U.S. Tax Court to contest a proposed tax bill. Tax court litigation is a perilous, sometimes high-stakes contest; and if there is one theme to remember, it's this: Do not try this experiment at home if you can help it. Find a competent lawyer or other qualified representative to help with your case in tax court.

If you absolutely must act as your own lawyer in tax court, this chapter may help you emerge with your skin mostly intact.

For one reason or another, thousands of people try their own cases in tax court. They are called *pro se* petitioners, from the Latin phrase meaning "by yourself." In fact, fully one-half of all tax court cases are handled by nonlawyers, the taxpayers themselves or in rare cases certain nonlawyer representatives. Since the IRS consistently wins 70 percent to 80 percent of cases that are not settled, it's hard enough for tax court petitioners to win even when they are represented, harder still when they go it alone. The procedures, the standard of proof, the rules of evidence, and other factors always stand in the way.

The tax court rules make available a "small case" procedure for matters involving less than $10,000 in controversy for any one tax year. These are usually handled by taxpayers themselves. The rules and procedures in "S" cases are similar to those of regular cases, but here, you get a break. The judges operate more informally; the process of trial preparation and trial itself is less cumbersome. Still, the chances of winning are no greater. You don't have to elect this small-case track, but it's there if you want it. Since all of the tax court rules still apply, the trial phases described below are still important, but the judges conduct proceedings quite informally.

THE UNITED STATES TAX COURT

It's well known that our nation has many different court systems. Every state has at least one trial-level court in each county or city, sometimes more than one. States also have courts of appeal to at least one intermediate level, and then a state supreme court.

The federal government also has a court system, totally separate from but parallel to the state system. The federal district courts try cases in ninety-six districts, one or more for each state. Appeals are made to the courts of appeals, thirteen in total (one or more for groupings of states, territories, commonwealths; one for the District of Columbia; and one for a special federal circuit). Appeals from the courts of appeals are to the United States Supreme Court.

After 1913, when the permanent income tax was enacted, it became clear that tax disputes should not be funneled routinely to these court systems. Litigation was very expensive, and the judges tended to be unfamiliar with the intricacies of tax law. So, in 1924, the IRS created a board within itself, called the Board of Tax Appeals, to which you could bring a tax dispute you could not resolve with the agents or the Office of Appeals. The idea was to channel disputes to an expert neutral panel that heard nothing but tax cases. If you wanted to sue in federal district court, you could still do so. But you had to pay the whole tax in advance. Most people didn't have the money, so the Board of Tax Appeals was the place to contest their proposed tax bill without first paying.

In 1969, Congress made this Board of Tax Appeals a separate, freestanding court, the United States Tax Court. Today, this court resolves more than twenty thousand cases a year. An additional twenty thousand are filed each year. In the 1970s, when tax shelters were hot, the tax court's inventory was doubled.

The tax court has nineteen judges to handle this litigation. The president nominates these judges; the Senate confirms them. They serve for fifteen years.

They are paid the same as federal district judges, about $125,000 a year. The court's headquarters is in Washington, D.C., but the judges travel all around the country, holding two-week sessions in many major cities. This makes it very convenient for many people to file their cases in tax court; trial time is almost a judicial "house call."

The "S" cases are handled by special trial judges. Procedures are informal. Rules of evidence are relaxed. Everyone bends over backward to let you tell your story without too much lawyering or legalese getting in the way. About 10,000 "S" cases are filed each year. There are nineteen special trial judges, all appointed by the chief judge of the tax court.

GETTING YOUR CASE TO TAX COURT

The road to the United States Tax Court starts with an audit. Any type of audit will do. If you can't agree with the revenue agent on all issues, he or she writes a report called a Revenue Agent's Report and slaps on a cover letter called a "thirty-day letter." This letter states that you can appeal the revenue agent's proposed findings within thirty days. If you appeal, the case is transferred to the Office of Appeals, where appeals officers review it with an eye toward settlement. Appeals officers have wide authority and discretion to settle cases based on the possibility the IRS might lose in court. They can split issues, trade issues, and generally compromise cases. For this reason, many taxpayers choose to appeal rather than to settle at the audit level.

If you can't agree at that level, the IRS issues a statutory Notice of Deficiency, or, informally, the "ninety-day letter." By law, the IRS must send you this letter (by certified mail) when it formally proposes a deficiency in your tax that was not resolved at the audit level or appeals. The attachments to the Notice of Deficiency are schedules setting out in detail taxes, penalties, and interest the IRS proposes. You'll be familiar with all the issues because you worked with them at the audit or appeals level.

The law allows 90 days from the date stamped on the notice to file a petition in the United States Tax Court (150 days if the notice is addressed outside the United States). That's how you get to the United States Tax Court.

A statutory Notice of Deficiency has a cover letter, and the heart of this document is a table of adjustments. Let's say the table shows two issues, making this a "two-issue case." For example, the IRS proposes to increase your income by

$5,000 for the tax year 1994 because you received a $5,000 loan from your rich and very nice Uncle Gaston. You told the IRS that it was a loan, but you had no evidence such as an IOU or Uncle Gaston's check marked "loan."

The second issue may be a "deduction" issue. Here, the IRS proposes to disallow your medical expense deduction for $2,000 because you couldn't prove to the agency's satisfaction that the stair climber you installed in your home was medically necessary for your aging, dependent mother.

The rest of the table goes on to make the tax and penalty calculations that result from these changes.

These are just two simple examples. Sometimes deficiency notices are very thick, with dozens of issues. Most of the time they are confined to about five or fewer issues. But they all have the same pattern.

REPRESENTING YOURSELF IN TAX COURT

Anyone can represent himself in tax court. In most cases, it's wiser to have some-one represent you, but thousands of people choose the *pro se* alternative either because they want to or because financially they have no other choice.

If you want someone to represent you, that person must be specially admitted to practice before the tax court. The right to represent people in tax court follows almost automatically for lawyers. Anyone else must pass a rigorous examination the tax court administers once a year. Not many pass, so your choice is usually between yourself and a lawyer.

On the other side are the IRS' lawyers. Every IRS district has a legal arm called the Office of District Counsel. That office employs from one to thirty-five lawyers, depending on the size of the district. Offices are located in all major cities. The IRS' lawyers handle many types of matters, including representing the IRS in the United States Tax Court. So, if you try your own case, you're going up against experienced lawyers who work with the tax code and tax court rules every day and understand them thoroughly. They probably forget more tax procedure between breakfast and lunch than most *pro se* petitioners will ever know. Still, all is not lost. Remember that you have only one case to try; they have dozens. Also, the tax court judges look to the IRS to bend over backward in your favor, espe-cially in "S" cases. Often IRS lawyers will give you a bit of help with your case, trying to go the extra mile and tell you what you need to do before you get to court. Knowing that *pro se* petitioners will not be familiar with tax court procedures, the judges encourage this. Judges are also somewhat more lenient with you, expecting more from government lawyers who are supposed to know their business inside out.

Despite these courtesies, remember that you, the taxpayer, bear the burden of proof except in rare cases. This means the IRS lawyer can sit back and do nothing, coolly watching you struggle to prove your case. If you don't, the IRS wins without lifting a legal finger.

All in all, you do not have a level playing field. While you may be David and the IRS Goliath, you're not at all guaranteed to win every fight or hit the mark with your first stone.

TRYING YOUR TAX COURT CASE

Think of a tax court case as encompassing seven main phases. The time line for normal cases is six months to a year, so you'll have plenty of time for each phase. Each main phase also has subdivisions.

The phases are these:

1. petition

2. discovery

3. preparation for trial

4. pretrial order and memorandum

5. calendar call

6. trial

7. decision

PHASE 1—PETITION

To get started, file a petition within 90 days of the date on your Notice of Deficiency (150 days if the notice is addressed outside the United States). If you miss this deadline, the tax court lacks jurisdiction of your case and it will be quickly dismissed. A dismissal means you have lost your right to contest the proposed taxes in the tax court, and the IRS will soon issue a bill.

This ninety-day deadline is as strict a deadline as exists in all of recorded history. It doesn't mean three months, nor ninety-one days, nor ninety days and one hour. It means ninety days. Sometimes people actually receive their statutory notice forty-five or more days into this period. That makes no difference. It's ninety days from the date stamped on the statutory notice. In fact, even if you *never* receive this notice, the ninety-day deadline holds as long as the IRS sent it to your last known address.

The safest way to ensure you meet the ninety-day deadline is to send your petition by certified or registered mail, return receipt requested. A special law says "mailing is filing" if you do it this way. Since you will have proof of mailing, you'll be able to prove you filed your petition on time. Private delivery services such as Federal Express, DHL, and carrier pigeon don't count, although the 1996 Taxpayer Bill of Rights is in the process of changing this rule. You can send your petition on the eighty-ninth day by personal messenger, but if it arrives on the ninety-first day, you are out of luck. But if you mail your petition on the eighty-ninth day by certified or registered mail, it can arrive a year later and still be considered "on time." Don't despair if you're miles away from the court on the ninetieth day. You can mail your petition, and, as long as it's timely mailed by certified or registered mail, return receipt requested, it's "timely." The IRS now also has the authority to designate private delivery services to qualify for this rule, but, so far, it has not yet done so. So, the safest way is still to use the U.S. mail. Every day, people file their petitions late for one reason or another. Every day, those petitions are routinely dismissed.

At the end of this chapter, you will find two sample forms for petitions, one for regular tax court cases, the other for the informal "S" case, where less than $10,000 is at stake. The tax court provides these sample petitions to make sure everyone knows what to say. They are easy to follow. You need no formal language, and the court interprets them liberally. Just be sure to include all the issues and facts.

The heart of the petition is paragraphs four and five. In paragraph four, state which items the IRS got wrong. Usually you can take these straight from the Notice of Deficiency. You do not have to contest every issue, only the ones where you feel the IRS erred.

Paragraph five of the petition requires you to state all the facts on which you base your case. Here, it is wise to proceed issue by issue, with a headline for each issue. The recitation of facts need not be lengthy. In fact, it's best to be short, sharp, and to the point. Above all, be clear. This is your first chance to convince the judge. The clearer your story, the more credibility you have as the case proceeds.

After you file the petition and pay a $60 filing fee, the clerk of court sends copies to the IRS. Court rules require the IRS to respond within sixty days. If the IRS thinks your case should be dismissed, its lawyer will make a motion to dismiss it. But if you have pleaded correctly and on time, the IRS answers your allegations. Usually the answer is a point-by-point admission or denial of your facts, with a request at the end for the court to sustain the Notice of Deficiency.

That ends phase 1. You've told the IRS, "Let's fight." The IRS has said, "OK. Let's fight." Now you move on to phase 2.

PHASE 2—DISCOVERY

It's now time to gather your stones and make your arrows. This is the "discovery" phase. Here, ask yourself, "If this case goes to trial, what must I prove, and how do I prove it by admissible evidence?" You therefore need the legal standards for each issue, and to assemble all the facts, witnesses, and documents to meet those legal standards. In our example, the burden is on you to prove that the $5,000 Uncle Gaston gave you was a loan, not omitted gross income. If you can't prove it was a loan or gift, it automatically becomes taxable as unreported income.

If you are not sure of the legal tests and standards you must meet, seek help. Ask your accountant, lawyer, or anyone else who knows the law. You can even ask the IRS' lawyer, and hope that she is willing to educate you on the applicable tests or standards.

Next assemble your proof. Recall two key words: witnesses and documents. You need people to testify for you. You also need any documents you can find that support your case. Your main witness is probably yourself, but try to convince Uncle Gaston to testify that he intended to have you pay back the money. You may bring your aging mother and her doctor to court to say that she is disabled and needs a stair climber in your narrow three-floor apartment.

Also, look for documents. Paper is probably the most important single source of proof. Examples might include medical reports, notes, minutes, and just about anything else that supports your case.

None of this should surprise you. You have massaged this case at the audit level and possibly in the Office of Appeals. During that time, the revenue agent and the appeals officer have asked you for the same documents and witness statements you are now required to produce in court. Still, always look for more in this second phase of the case.

The IRS is also in its second phase. Upon request, you must give the IRS lawyer any evidence she does not already have, a process called "informal discovery." She also must give you anything in the government's files that helps or hurts your case.

This process can go on for several months, but it's best to conduct all informal discovery and evidence-gathering as quickly as possible. That trial date creeps up on you, and before you know it, it's tomorrow. The judges also expect you to be ready for trial when the trial calendar is called. Finally, informal discovery exposes the weaknesses in your case. The sooner you know these, the better. If one witness is unavailable, maybe you can find another. If a document is missing, it may take time to get a replacement. You won't get much sympathy from the judge if you start asking for bank documents the day before trial, or complain that Dr. Smith wasn't available but Dr. Jones might be, except you can't find her. The best attitude is to treat your case as if it were going to trial next week. Then you, rather than the IRS, will be in control.

In this phase, the court's procedures also strongly emphasize the stipulation of facts. You are required to agree with the IRS on as many facts as the two sides possibly can, and to put those stipulated facts in writing. Examples would include stipulating to the Notice of Deficiency, the tax returns, background facts about you and your deductions, and any other facts that all agree are true.

Phase 2 is also the time you or the IRS may make motions to the court. People make motions for a number of reasons. These include asking for enlargements of time for some deadlines, motions to compel answers to formal discovery, requests for admission of facts, consolidating trials, and many other procedural matters. The tax court rules spell out the types of allowable motions. The function of these motions is to get the case in shape, procedurally, for development and for trial, so that nothing stands in the way when trial time comes.

Either side also can file a "dispositive motion." This is a motion the granting of which decides ("disposes of") the case completely one way or another without a trial. One example of a dispositive motion is a motion to dismiss where the petition is filed late. Another occurs if your case is so good that the material facts and the law are all on your side. Then there is no need for a trial, so you may decide to file a "motion for summary judgment." Few tax court cases fit this category, but they are not unheard of. Again, the tax court rules spell out what motions the court can consider.

PHASE 3—PREPARATION FOR TRIAL

In this phase, prepare your witnesses, facts, and documents for a logical presentation to the court. Some of this can be done in phase 2 as well. There is no magic formula for preparing your case for trial. Whatever is logical and whatever works is, by definition, the way to do it. Some people "have it all in their heads." Others will map their case, issue by issue, on paper. On the left side of the page, they list the issue and the elements of proof needed to satisfy their contentions. On the right side, they list the witnesses and documents that prove each element, and what they expect those witnesses and documents to prove. Telephone your witnesses to inform them they might be called for trial. Advise them of the court's subpoena procedures. It is critical to interview adverse witnesses as well. This avoids surprise at trial, usually a fatal error. Study the IRS' documents, which its lawyer has sent to you through informal or formal discovery.

Preparing a case for trial in the tax court can be complicated even for simple issues. As with everything else in such a court, the wise litigant gets help from a trial lawyer, even if he intends to try the case by himself.

"S" cases tend to be less complex in this phase. Often there are only one or two witnesses, or only a few documents, which the judge will be lenient about admitting into evidence.

PHASE 4—PRETRIAL ORDER AND MEMORANDUM

At some time three to six months after the IRS answers your petition, the tax court judges and clerks get together to schedule calendar calls and trials. They gather all the cases to be tried in your city and list them on a huge calendar. Sometimes these calendars run two hundred to three hundred cases. The court finalizes the calendar, and the clerk publishes it. You know this is happening because you'll get a notice of calendar call about three to six months after the IRS answers your case, together with a standard pretrial order. The notice tells you when your case will be called for trial, usually three to six months after the first notice is issued. So again, you'll have plenty of time. If you have been taking a long vacation, treat this notice as a wake-up call. The judges rarely allow postponements of your case from the calendar call. Be ready.

This pretrial order also requires you to file a pretrial memorandum. This fill-in memorandum tells the court all about your case. Include your witnesses, documents, and anything else you need to bring to the court's attention. In fact, you can use this pretrial memorandum as a checklist to test your case for readiness. Of course, the IRS must reveal its case to you as well.

The judges take these pretrial memoranda seriously. Many a sad taxpayer has found this by failing to file one, only to have the case dismissed as a result. Other times the judge punishes you, such as by excluding certain key evidence, even if she does not dismiss the case. So begin to write the pretrial memorandum as soon as you get the notice. By their nature, the items in the memorandum also gently nudge you to continue preparation for trial; they tell you what the court expects to see when the case is called.

At some point in phase 4 or earlier, you can also ask the judge to hold a pretrial conference. This conference can help narrow the issues, encourage a stipulation of facts, or simplify the presentation of evidence. It may also resolve issues of the burden of proof and otherwise help to ready the case for trial or possible disposition without trial. Pretrial conferences are not required, but either side can ask for one. If the judge agrees, she will usually set it during the calendar call.

Phase 4 is also the time to confer informally with the IRS' lawyer. Discuss such matters as the stipulation of facts, discovery, evidence (including particularly documents), and settlement. At the calendar call, the judge will ask about these and many other aspects of the case.

PHASE 5—CALENDAR CALL

On the appointed day, everyone comes to court for the calendar call. By now, the two hundred to three hundred cases originally on the calendar have been whittled down to a manageable load. The rest have been dismissed or settled and have been marked off the calendar.

The judge proceeds to "call the calendar." In open court, the clerk recites the number of the case and the petitioner's name. When yours is called, you are expected to stand at a central lectern and tell the judge whether you are ready for trial. If you have not settled the case, be ready to try it or give the judge a very good reason why not. The same expectations hold for the IRS. Quite often cases don't need to be tried, or they are close to settlement and the parties just need a little more time or effort. The tax court judges understand this; they always help if settlement prospects are real.

When your case is called, the IRS lawyer might say, "Your honor, this case is for trial. We could not settle it despite our best efforts. We anticipate the trial will last one day." Then the judge will turn to you. You might say something like, "Your honor, I agree. But I think the case will last two days, not one." The judge asks many other questions, all with a view toward efficiency: there are many cases to try; the judge wants to schedule them as efficiently as possible. So the judge might say, "Your trial date is two days from now, for two days." Or, the judge might ask you to wait until the end of the calendar so she can schedule other cases for trial. Sometimes the judge will schedule a special trial date outside the usual two-week window, a procedure usually reserved for more complex cases. Some cases take only an hour or two, especially if they are one-issue or simple cases. "S" cases tend to be tried quickly, often in less than a few hours. It all depends on the number of issues, their complexity, the number of witnesses, and your estimate and that of the IRS on how long the trial will take.

The calendar call usually lasts two to three hours if it's a long calendar. At the end, the judge has whittled down the calendar even further, ideally to a list of cases that can be tried within the two-week period of the calendar call. Once you have been scheduled, you are free to go. You then reappear for trial on the appointed day and hour.

PHASE 6—TRIAL

Now comes the actual fighting. Here's where you stand up, tell the judge what you intend to prove, and then prove it. You call witnesses (including yourself). You ask that documents be admitted into evidence. If you've done your homework, you have worked out the admissibility of most documents before trial by agreement with the IRS. If not, you must prove the admissibility of any documents you want the judge to consider. In *pro se* cases, the judges are usually lenient on admitting contested documents. But don't count on it. *Pro se* petitioners, untrained in the rules of evidence, are at a great disadvantage. This is one of the main reasons not to try your own case if you can possibly avoid it.

After you present witnesses and move the admission of documents, your part of the case is over. Then the IRS presents its case. Then you can rebut, as can the IRS, until both sides have nothing more to say. The judge then decides, either in open court or after calling for posttrial briefs from both sides. In *pro se* or "S" cases, posttrial briefs are not the norm, but the judge can ask you to research the issues if your position is not completely clear. Also, the IRS usually files a brief. Since judges are trained to read briefs, you could be at a disadvantage if you don't file one. Still, a bad brief is worse than no brief at all. If the judge knows your position and your evidence, she may not ask for a brief but simply announce that the case is ready for decision and that you will be notified when the decision is made.

PHASE 7—DECISION

The judge is required to decide your case, but there is no formal deadline. It could be weeks, months, or sometimes years. *Pro se* cases are usually decided quickly, either right there in court or soon after in a written opinion. The fight is then over. You have either won, lost, or come out somewhere in between on each of the issues. The judge then enters a one-page decision, the formal end of the case.

You can appeal an adverse decision, but such appeals are rarely successful. Again, consult professional help before considering any such appeal.

OTHER TRAPS AND RULES

These seven phases of a tax court case are the bare bones of what you need to know. Many questions will arise. How do you subpoena witnesses? Is arbitration or mediation available? Can you take depositions? In fact, the tax court's thick book of rules, running to 174 pages and 274 rules, governs all its proceedings. Buy a copy from the clerk of court. It will answer most of your questions, and the clerk is often available for others. The clerk won't try your case for you, but is often willing to be helpful on procedural matters.

Once you read the rules, you'll see what a difficult time any *pro se* petitioner will have in tax court. But if you must represent yourself, it's still possible to win. If your case is good on the facts and the law, the chances for a win or good settlement are high.

Above all, when you handle a case in tax court, recall the words of a famous tax court judge, who said: "[T]he trial of a case is a human process and . . . judges, as well as litigants, are human beings with all the concomitant attributes, both good and bad."

In short, judges bring their own lifelong experiences and wisdom to the trial of any case. If you present your case to address the commonsense and human aspects as well as the legalities, you will have done the best you can.

Internal Revenue Service

Date: JUN 2 2 1995

Department of the Treasury

Taxpayer Identification Number

Form: 1040
Person to Contact:

Telephone Number:

DUPLICATE ORIGINAL
CERTIFIED MAIL

Tax Year Ended: December 31, 1989

Deficiency:
Increase in tax $ 16,000
Penalties
  IRC 6651(a)(1) $ 4,000
  IRC 6662(a) $ 3,200

Dear Mr. _

--NOTICE OF DEFICIENCY--

We determined that you owe an additional amount, as shown above. This letter is your NOTICE OF DEFICIENCY, as required by law. The enclosed statement shows how we figured the deficiency.

If you want to contest this deficiency in court before making any payment, you have 90 days from the above mailing date of this letter (150 days is addressed to you outside the United States) to file a petition with the United States Tax Court for a redetermination of the deficiency. To get a petition form and the rules for filing a petition, write to: United States Tax Court, 400 Second Street, NW, Washington, DC 20217.

Send the completed petition form, a copy of this letter and a copy of all statements and schedules you received with this letter to the Tax Court at the same address.

The time you have to file a petition with the Court (90 or 150 days) is fixed by law. The Court cannot consider your case if you file the petition late.

If this letter is addressed to both husband and wife, and both want to petition the Tax Court, both must sign and file the petition or each must file

(continued next page)

2727 Enterprise Parkway, Suite 100
Richmond, Virginia 23294

Letter 894(RO) (Rev. 4-93

- 2 -

a separate, signed petition. If only one of you petitions the Tax Court, the full amount of the deficiency will be assessed against the non-petitioning spouse.

Small Tax Cases
The Tax Court has a simplified procedure for small tax cases, when the amount in dispute is $10,000 or less for any one tax year. You can get information about this procedure, as well as a petition form, by writing to the Clerk of the United States Tax Court at the court address shown in the second paragraph above. You should write promptly if you intend to file a petition with the court.

If you decide not to file a petition with the Tax Court, please sign and return the enclosed waiver form. This will permit us to assess the deficiency quickly and will limit the accumulation of interest. The enclosed envelope is for your convenience.

If you are a "C" corporation, under Internal Revenue Code Section 6621(c), large corporate underpayments may be subject to a higher rate of interest than the normal rate of interest for underpayments.

If you decide not to sign and return the waiver, and you don't file a petition with the Tax Court within the time limit, the law requires us to assess and bill you for the deficiency after 90 days from the above mailing date (150 days if this letter is addressed to you outside the United States).

If you have questions about this letter, you may call or write to the person whose name is shown above. If the telephone number is outside your local calling area, you will be charged for a long distance call. If you write, please attach a copy of this letter to help us identify your account. Also, include your daytime telephone number so we can call you if necessary.

Sincerely,

Margaret Milner Richardson
Commissioner
By

Associate Chief

Enclosures:
Copy of this letter
Waiver
Statement
Envelope

Letter 894(RO) (Rev. 4-93)

FORM 4089	Department of the Treasury - Internal Revenue Service NOTICE OF DEFICIENCY - WAIVER	Symbols RCH:AP:
	Name, SSN or EIN, and Address of Taxpayer(s)	

Kind of Tax INCOME	[ ] Copy to Authorized Representative

DEFICIENCY - Increase in Tax and Penalties

Tax Year Ended: December 31, 1989

Deficiency:
Increase in tax $16,000
Penalties
  IRC 6651(a)(1) $ 4,000
  IRC 6662(a) $ 3,200

See the attached explanation for the above deficiencies

I consent to the immediate assessment and collection of the deficiencies (increase in tax and penalties) shown above, plus any interest provided by law.

Your Signature	Date signed
Spouse's Signature, If A Joint Return Was Filed	Date signed
Taxpayer's Representative Sign Here	Date signed

Corporate Name:

Corporate Officers Sign Below

Signature	Title	Date signed
Signature	Title	Date signed

(For instructions, see next page)
If you agree, please sign one copy and return it.
Keep the other copy for your records.

Form 4089 (Rev. 1-83)

– 2 –

Instructions for Form 4089

te:

If you consent to the assessment of the amounts shown in this waiver, please sign and return it in order to limit the accumulation of interest and expedite our bill to you. Your consent will not prevent you from filing a claim for refund (after you have paid the tax) if you later believe you are entitled to a refund. It will not prevent us from later determining, if necessary, that you owe additional tax; nor will it extend the time provided by law for either action.

If you later file a claim and the Internal Revenue Service disallows it, you may file suit for refund in a district court or in the United States Claims Court, but you may not file a petition with the United States Tax Court.

Who Must Sign

If this waiver is for any year(s) for which you filed a joint return, both you and your spouse must sign the original and duplicate of this form. Sign your name exactly as it appears on the return. If you are acting under power of attorney for your spouse, you may sign as agent for him or her.

For an agent or attorney acting under a power of attorney, a power of attorney must be sent with this form if not previously filed.

For a person acting in a fiduciary capacity (executor, administrator, trustee) file Form 56, Notice Concerning Fiduciary Relationship, with this form if not previously filed.

For a corporation, enter the name of the corporation followed by the signature and title of the officer(s) authorized to sign.

CONTINUATION SHEET

	Page
Mr.	TIN:

...terest on Deficiencies

Interest on deficiencies will accrue from the due date of the return until paid.

Delinquency Penalty IRC section 6651(a)(1) and 6601(e)(2)

Since your income tax return(s) for the taxable year(s) ended December 31, 1989,   were not filed within the time prescribed by law, and you have not shown that such failur to timely file your return(s) was due to reasonable cause, a penalty of fi (5) percent is added to the tax for each month or part of a month (but not to exceed a total of twenty-five (25) percent) for which your return was late. If your return was filed after December 31, 1982 and was more than 6 days late, the minimum penalty is the lesser of $100 or the tax due. In addition, interest is figured on this penalty from the later of the due da of the return (including any extensions) or July 18, 1984.

Accuracy-related Penalty IRC section 6662(a) and 6601(e)(2)

Since all or part of the underpayment of tax for the taxable year(s) ended December 31, 1989,   is attributable to one or more of (1) negligence or disregard of rules or regulations, (2) any substantial understatement of income tax, or (3) any substantial valuation overstatement, an addition to the tax is charged as provided by section 6662(a) of the Internal Revenue Code. The penalty is twenty (20) cent of the portion of the underpayment of tax attributable to each component of this penalty. In addition, interest is computed on this penal from the due date of the return (including any extensions).

| Dep 'ment of the Treasury - Internal Revenue Serv' | 1. Office Symbols |
| Statement - Income Tax Change | CC:MA:RCH:AP: |

2. Name and Address of Taxpayer	3.
	x Notice of Deficiency _____ Other (specify)
	_____ Settlement Computation

| 4. Social security number | 5. Form number | 6. Court docket number |
| | 1040 | |

7. Adjustments to income	Year End: 12/31/89
A. See adjustments listed on page 2	49,100
B.	
C.	
D.	
E.	
F.	
G.	
H.	
8. Total adjustments	49,100
9. Taxable income as shown in:	
_____ Preliminary letter dated _____	
_____ Notice of deficiency dated _____	
X Return as filed	1,000
10. Taxable income as revised	50,100
Tax Method	Tax Table
Filing Status	Head of Household
11. Tax	12,000
12.	0
13. Corrected tax liability	12,000
14. Less A.	
Credits B.	
C.	
D.	
15. Balance (line 13 less total of lines 14A thru 14D)	12,000
16. Plus A. SELF-EMPLOYMENT TAX	6,000
B.	
C.	
D.	
17. Total corrected income tax liability (line 15 plus amounts on lines 16A through 16D)	18,000
18. Total tax shown on return or as previously adjusted	2,000
19. Adjustments to EIC/Fuels Credit - Increase (decrease)	0
20. Increase in Tax or (Overassessment - Decrease in Tax) (line 17 less line 18 adjusted by line 19)	16,000
21. Additions/Adjustments to the Tax (listed below)	

De 'ment of the Treasury - Internal Revenue Ser		1. Office Symbols
S...tement - Income Tax Change.		

Name of Taxpayer	Social Security or Employer Identification Number	Return Form No.
		1040

1. Adjustments to income	Year End: 12/31/89
A. Interest Income	$ 800
B. Schedule C Expenses	2700
Schedule C - COGS	3600
D. Award	17000
E. Schedule C Activity	25000
F. Schedule C Income -	-75
G. Other Income	75
H. SELF-EMPLOYMENT TAX DEDUCTION	
I.	
J.	
K.	
L.	
M.	
N.	
O.	
P.	
Q.	
R.	
S.	
T.	
U.	
V.	
W.	
X.	
Y.	
Z.	
2. Total adjustments to page 1	$ 49,100

Name of Taxpayer	Social Security or Employer Identification Number	Return Form No.
		1040

1. Additions to the tax	Year End: 12/31/89	
A. Delinquency IRC 6651(a)(1)		4,000
B. Accuracy-related IRC 6662(a)		3,200
C.		
D.		
E.		
F.		
G.		
H.		
I.		
J.		
K.		
L.		
M.		
N.		
2. Total additions to the tax		7,200
Summary of Taxes, Additions to Tax, and Interest:		
A. Increase or (decrease) in tax (line 20, Form 5278)		16,000
B. Additions to tax (line 2, above)		7,200
C. Interest (IRC 6601)		
D. Amount due or refund (sum of lines A, B, and C)		23,200

Note: Line D does not include interest.

FORM 1

PETITION (Other Than In Small Tax Case)

(See Rules 30 through 34)

UNITED STATES TAX COURT

....
Petitioner(s)

v.

COMMISSIONER OF INTERNAL REVENUE,

Respondent

Docket No.

PETITION

The petitioner hereby petitions for a redetermination of the deficiency (or liability) set forth by the Commissioner of Internal Revenue in the Commissioner's notice of deficiency (or liability) [Service symbols] dated ...., 19 ...., and as the basis for the petitioner's case alleges as follows:

1. The petitioner is [set forth whether an individual, fiduciary, corporation, etc., as provided in Rule 60] with mailing address now at

....
      Street   City   State   Zip Code

and with legal residence (or principal office) now at [if different from the mailing address]

....
      Street   City   State   Zip Code

Petitioner's taxpayer identification number (e.g., Social Security or employer identification number) is ....

The return for the period here involved was filed with the Office of the Internal Revenue Service at...
                             City   State

2. The notice of deficiency (or liability) (a copy of which, including so much of the statement and schedules accompanying the notice as is material, is attached and marked Exhibit A) was mailed to the petitioner on ...., 19 ...., and was issued by the Office of the Internal Revenue Service at...
                                      City   State

3. The deficiencies (or liabilities) as determined by the Commissioner are in income (estate, gift, or certain excise) taxes for the calendar (or fiscal) year 19 ...., in the amount of $.............., of which $.............., is in dispute.

4. The determination of the tax set forth in the said notice of deficiency (or liability) is based upon the following errors: [Here set forth specifically in lettered subparagraphs the assignments of error in a concise manner. Do not plead facts, which properly belong in the succeeding paragraph.]

5. The facts upon which the petitioner relies, as the basis of the petitioner's case, are as follows: [Here set forth allegations of fact, but not the evidence, sufficient to inform the Court and the Commissioner of the positions taken and the bases therefor. Set forth the allegations in orderly and logical sequence, with subparagraphs lettered, so as to enable the Commissioner to admit or deny each allegation. See Rules 31(a) and 34(b)(5).]

WHEREFORE, petitioner prays that [here set forth the relief desired].

(Signed) ....

Petitioner or Counsel

....

Post office address

Dated: ...., 19 ....

....

Telephone (include area code)

....

Counsel's Tax Court Bar Number

178   (7/1/90)

FORM 2

PETITION (Small Tax Case)
(Available—Ask for Form 2)

(See Rules 170 through 179)

UNITED STATES TAX COURT

....

Petitioner(s)

v.

COMMISSIONER OF INTERNAL REVENUE,
Respondent   } Docket No.

PETITION

1. Petitioner(s) disagree(s) with the tax deficiency(ies) for the year(s) ...., as set forth in the NOTICE OF DEFICIENCY dated ...., 19........ A COPY OF WHICH IS ATTACHED. The notice was issued by the Office of the Internal Revenue Service at...

City   State

2. Petitioner(s)' taxpayer identification (e.g., Social Security) number(s) is (are) ....

3. Petitioner(s) dispute(s) the following:

Year	Amount of deficiency disputed	Addition to tax (penalty), if any, disputed	Amount of overpayment claimed
....	....	....	....
....	....	....	....

4. Set forth those adjustments, i.e., changes, in the NOTICE OF DEFICIENCY with which you disagree and why you disagree.

....

....

....

....

Petitioner(s) request(s) that this case be conducted under the "small tax case" procedures authorized by Congress to provide the taxpayer(s) with an informal, prompt, and inexpensive hearing at a reasonably convenient location. Consistent with these objectives, a decision in a "small tax case" is final and cannot be appealed to higher Courts (the Courts of Appeals and the Supreme Court) by the Internal Revenue Service or the Petitioner(s).*

Signature of Petitioner	Date	Present Address—Street, City, State, Zip Code, Telephone (include area code)
Signature of Petitioner (Spouse)	Date	Present Address—Street, City, State, Zip Code, Telephone (include area code)

Signature, name, address, telephone number, and Tax Court Bar Number of counsel, if retained by petitioner(s)

*If you do not want to make this request, you should place an "X" in the following box. ☐

Chapter 22

―⦅⦆―

CAN YOU "SUE THE FEDS"? YES.

Some people think you can always sue the government over taxes; others believe you never can. The answer lies in between. In colonial times, people used self-help to resolve tax disputes with the government, as by dumping tea into Boston Harbor when they didn't like the king's tax. These days, we take our tax disputes to court. But even an accessible court system is not open to tax suits whenever the mood strikes. You may sue the government over taxes (or anything else) only when Congress gives you permission, a concept called "sovereign immunity." This prohibition dates back to medieval England, when you could not sue the king (the "sovereign") without his consent because "the king can do no wrong."

Nowadays, Congress has granted permission for people to sue the federal government in a wide variety of cases, including many types of tax cases. But your case must fit within the bounds of that permission, strictly construed, or the court will dismiss it. Thousands of tax cases are filed every year on behalf of individuals, corporations, and partnerships. Of those not dismissed, the government wins many, but taxpayers also win a healthy percentage. Many are also settled short of trial.

A wise litigant finds a lawyer to sue the government over taxes. Lawsuits of any type are rarely successful when handled on your own; in tax cases, representing yourself is even more perilous. Still, no law forbids you from representing yourself in a tax case. Even if you do not engage a lawyer, it's helpful to be able to spot a possible case on your own and bring it to a lawyer's attention. This chapter will help you keep a close eye on your rights to sue over taxes.

Here are the most common types of tax cases people bring.

1. *Suit for tax refund.* If you've paid your tax, filed a timely claim for a tax refund with the IRS, and the claim has been denied (or six months elapse without action), you can sue the United States for a tax refund. A tax refund suit may be filed in one of two federal courts. The first is federal district court, usually the one where you live or where you filed your tax return. It joins all other suits over which the federal courts have jurisdiction, including cases involving securities, environmental litigation, criminal cases, and civil rights, among others. The other forum is the United States Court of Federal Claims, located in Washington, D.C. This is a special court that handles tax cases and a few other types of claims.

In a tax refund suit, you, the taxpayer who overpaid your taxes, are the plaintiff. Until 1995, the courts routinely dismissed cases in which someone other than the taxpayer tried to sue. Then the Supreme Court carved an exception to this rule, allowing an ex-wife who paid her ex-husband's tax (so she could sell their house) to sue the government. These types of nontaxpayer refund suits are rare, though its likely we'll see more in the future.

You may base a tax refund suit on just about any provision of the entire Internal Revenue Code. It could be a disallowed deduction or an assessment that is barred by the statute of limitations. It might be a bank deposit the IRS concluded was unreported income, or a penalty abatement claim. Your case can be based on any events that, you contend, caused an overpayment of the proper amount of your taxes.

For most tax refund suits to proceed, you must have first paid the full amount of the taxes, penalties, and interest. Other requirements are to file a timely claim for refund with the IRS and wait six months, or wait for the IRS to disallow the claim.

Consider undertaking this type of refund claim or suit only with the help of a qualified professional. Many a valid claim has been lost through violations of the technical rules governing refunds.

2. *Civil damages for unauthorized disclosure.* Congress takes the sanctity of tax returns and tax information very seriously. After Watergate, it passed a law strictly limiting the IRS' authority to make tax information public. In general, IRS

employees scrupulously observe it. If they don't, the government can be sued for unauthorized disclosure. Every once in a while a case like this is filed. Most fail, but there are some spectacular examples of real messes caused by overzealous IRS employees. Here's one true tale.

> *Example:* Roland was a professional. The IRS audited his tax returns and found a $100,000 error in his records. The Criminal Investigation Division was called in. The special agent sent a circular letter to hundreds of his clients, informing them that Roland was being investigated by the Criminal Investigation Division and asking for information about the fees they paid to Roland. Before the agent sent the letters, he had not reviewed the law forbidding unnecessary disclosures, nor had he asked the approval of his chief. The clients were furious. "Our pro, under *criminal* investigation? How could that be?" Many deserted Roland's practice. The fact that the Criminal Investigation Division was involved, and had made unauthorized, unnecessary disclosures, meant that the government had to answer in damages.

3. *Civil damages for failure to release a tax lien.* For many years, people complained bitterly to Congress that the IRS was slow to release tax liens even after the tax had been paid. Suffering a tax lien was hard enough in the first place; it ruined credit and sabotaged the sale of property. So Congress passed a law requiring the IRS to release a lien within thirty days after a request, if the tax was paid or was no longer legally collectible. If the Service fails to release the lien and the failure causes damages, you may sue the government to recover. Not many suits like this are filed even today, if for no other reason than it is sometimes hard to prove the extent of your actual damages. But the right of action is there. The IRS, aware of it, usually releases liens quickly.

> *Example:* Albert and Jeanne, husband and wife, made a terrible mistake. They invested in a tax shelter to earn a big tax break. Of course, in the 1970s the IRS declared World War III on tax shelters. Albert and Jeanne's case went to tax court, with the result that no tax was due, nor any refund payable. In other words, all their hard work earned them nothing and lost them nothing. But that didn't dissuade the IRS, which proceeded to make big assessments against them for six more years. On top of that, the revenue officer filed a notice of tax lien, seized their home, and

put it up for sale. Albert and Jeanne's accountant asked the revenue officer to stop. Even an appeals officer got into the action, instructing the
revenue officer to stop. Did he stop? No. He sold their home for $8,600
at auction. Albert and Jeanne were unhappy. They sued because the revenue officer had failed to remove the tax lien when it had been filed in
error. "That's right," said the court. Now the IRS will have to answer in
damages.

4. *Civil damages for unauthorized collection actions.* This type of suit has been
authorized since 1989. You have the right to sue in federal court for damages
when an IRS employee recklessly or intentionally violates the tax laws, usually in
connection with collecting taxes assessed against you. Once again, many procedural roadblocks stand between you and a suit like this. These include filing your
claim first with the IRS (or else the court may reduce your damage award), mitigating your damages, and suing within two years after the violation occurs. As
usual, the burden is on you to prove damages, which are limited anyway to the
lower of actual damages or $1,000,000. But suppose there are multiple violations.
That happened in one case, where a court found the IRS had made eighty-four
separate illegal disclosures.

> *Example:* Remember Albert and Jeanne? Their suit included a count for
> unauthorized collection action. The IRS tried to defend by claiming that
> only the "assessment" was incorrect, not the subsequent "collection." Too
> cute, said the court. Such a narrow interpretation of the law would thwart
> Congress's intent to have the IRS answer for its unauthorized actions. So
> again, the IRS had to pay.

5. *Suit to contest a summons.* You can sue the government to contest the
enforceability of an IRS summons. The IRS has broad authority to look into your
tax affairs. For this reason, it's rare to find an IRS summons that exceeds the
Service's authority. But an occasional summons may do so, for example, by
requesting attorney-client privileged information or information irrelevant to the
tax investigation. Possibly the summons is overbroad, or procedurally its issuance
may harbor other defects. The law gives you the right to have a federal judge
review the legality of that summons.

6. *The constitutional tort.* There is a type of suit that is not authorized by any
statute but by the Constitution itself. It's called a "Bivens" action, named after the

1967 Supreme Court case that established this right. In a Bivens-type case, you sue individual IRS agents on the ground that they have personally violated your constitutional rights and must answer personally in damages. Again, this is not something you do every day. There are many defenses to Bivens suits. Very few ever proceed to trial, much less result in a taxpayer victory. But where the agent has truly overstepped his authority and violated your constitutional rights, the Bivens-type suit is available.

> *Example:* Harry promoted tax shelters, many of them, whether they made any economic sense or not. Of course, the IRS said they did not and sued him for an injunction to stop this activity. They also assessed taxes against him. Harry protested long and hard because the IRS filed notices of federal lien and levied on his many bank accounts. One of Harry's allegations was that by suing him, filing notices of lien, and levying, the IRS had unconstitutionally interfered with his freedom of speech, liberty, and property rights. Specifically, it abrogated his right to engage in a chosen profession. He claimed the IRS issued the levies and liens only to punish him for criticizing the IRS. That's enough, said the court, for the lawsuit to survive. Of course, Harry would have to prove his allegations, but if the agent did as Harry claimed, the agent would not be immune from the suit.

7.   *Suit for wrongful levy.* Sometimes an IRS seizure injures the property rights of third parties who have claims superior to that of the IRS. An example would be the IRS' seizure and sale of a tax delinquent's truck on which a bank holds the first lien. The law calls such a levy "wrongful" because it takes property subject to a better claim. You, the delinquent taxpayer, can never sue for wrongful levy. But a third party with a superior lien or claim can sue and often win. The claimant files this suit in federal district court and tries to prove its superior claim to the property the IRS seized. Here are two examples from cases.

> *Example 1:* Big Bank made a number of loans to Carl, who signed a promissory note pledging his deposits as security. What Carl knew, but the bank didn't, was that Carl also owed federal taxes. So the IRS naturally filed notices of federal tax lien and levied on Carl's bank deposits. The bank dutifully sent the money to the IRS and then sued for "wrongful levy." The bank said it had a perfected security interest in the accounts, an interest that arose before the IRS' liens and was therefore superior to

it. By taking the money, the bank argued, the IRS destroyed the bank's superior interest. "That's right," said the court. The levy was wrongful.

Example 2: Daniel and David had a similar story. Daniel bought a car on a promissory note, listing the car as security. He never made any payments, but instead sold the car to David. Meanwhile, the IRS filed a notice of lien and seized the car. That levy was wrongful because Daniel never had an ownership interest in the car at the time the notice of lien was filed; he had already sold it.

The IRS also wrongfully levies when it seizes a bank account that in fact belongs to a nondelinquent taxpayer. This happens often in parent-child situations where only the parent owes taxes. If the parent can prove the money really belongs to the child, was held in trust for the child, or represented money someone else had contributed, to that extent the levy is wrongful and should be remedied.

The wrongful levy suit has a major trap: the filing deadline is a mere nine months after the IRS seizes the property (sometimes extendable to twelve months). The court must dismiss any case filed after this short deadline. Many a lienholder has filed such a wrongful levy suit, only to find to his surprise that he acted a day, a month, or a year too late.

8. *Suits for surplus proceeds.* The IRS often seizes and sells property that belongs to both a delinquent taxpayer and someone else. One example might be a friend who has loaned you money secured by your home, but only after the IRS filed a notice of lien against you for taxes. Another example might be a piece of land you own as joint tenants with a friend.

The nondelinquent owner is entitled to his share if the IRS sells the property. The law gives that owner the right to sue the government to claim that share. It's not always necessary to sue; usually rights are fairly clear and the IRS honors them. But since tax life is not perfect and disputes do arise, it's nice to know a "suit for surplus proceeds" is available. Even where rights are clear, there can often be a dispute about interest and penalties on taxes. These take the same priority as the underlying tax claim.

9. *Suit for substituted sale proceeds.* Sometimes you may need to sell real or personal property, but the IRS and others have claims against it. You've got a hot buyer, so you need to discharge the federal tax lien quickly to give clear title. You can enter into an agreement with the IRS to sell the property free of the tax lien. The IRS' lien and all other claims then attach to the proceeds. If everyone cannot

agree on who is entitled to the proceeds, anyone who claims them can sue the United States to enforce the claim.

10. *Suits to adjudicate rights to property.* The government gets involved as a defendant in a variety of state and federal court lawsuits in which people fight over entitlement to property. One such case is called an "interpleader" suit. The basic idea is this: If some third party is holding money or property that you and the IRS are fighting over, that third party should have to pay it once—to either you or the IRS, but not both. The stakeholder's remedy is to sue you and the IRS, throw the money into court, get out of the lawsuit, and let you and the IRS fight it out. People file interpleader suits in all kinds of cases. A common example comes from the construction industry. Suppose a general contractor owes money to a subcontractor, who owes it to plumbers and electricians. The subcontractor also owes payroll taxes to the government. The general contractor does not know whom to pay, so it sues everybody: the IRS, the subcontractor, the plumbers and the electricians, and throws the money into court. The claimants then fight it out. The entity with the superior legal claim will win. And, despite the conventional wisdom, the IRS does not always win. Quite often, particularly in construction cases and other cases involving real estate, the IRS has the inferior claim. It's all determined by a combination of state and federal law.

A second type of property case is a suit to "quiet title" to property. When real estate such as land, a building, or a home is sold, sometimes the chain of title is ambiguous. Other times, the IRS has filed a notice of lien, which itself puts a "cloud on title." The buyer needs to be absolutely certain he got what he paid for. So the buyer, a title insurance company, or any of the parties can sue the government in state court to quiet title to the property.

A third example is a suit to partition property. A property owner may wish to divide his property, but an IRS tax lien stands in the way. The government may be sued to participate as a defendant in that type of case.

A fourth type of property suit is a condemnation suit where the IRS has a federal tax lien on file. Finally, the government may be named as a defendant in a suit to foreclose a mortgage or other lien on property. This includes both real property and personal property, because the federal tax lien attaches to everything the taxpayer owns, real and personal.

These five types of cases make it relatively easy and convenient to sort out everyone's priorities and property rights. This goal would be impossible if the government's lien could stand on the sidelines, creating uncertainty for everyone else.

11. *Declaratory judgment.* A "declaratory judgment" case is a lawsuit in which the court declares the rights and legal relations of the parties. This suit requests

no damages, injunction, or other relief. The law prohibits anyone from suing the government for a declaratory judgment over taxes, with one exception. You can sue to declare that a charity or private foundation is tax exempt. Again, you must exhaust the remedies within the IRS before filing such a suit, and certain time limits govern, but the suit is available if all else fails.

12.   *Suit to contest jeopardy levy or assessment.* Among the most devastating of IRS weapons is the jeopardy or termination assessment. This type of assessment, followed immediately by a seizure of property (cash, bank accounts, cars, drugs, and anything else lying around), can come so swiftly that you have little if any time to react. That's the whole idea. Though giving the IRS immediate levy powers, Congress did not want to leave people without a remedy. So it enacted a law that allows you to sue the government to contest a jeopardy or termination assessment, but only *after* it has been made. It's not a full-scale trial, but a quick look by a federal court to rule whether the making of the assessment was reasonable and the amount assessed was appropriate. Start to finish, the whole case normally takes less than forty days. In most circumstances, neither side can appeal. The government wins most of these cases, but taxpayers win a few. This type of suit is at least somewhat of a check on the government's jeopardy assessment practices.

That's it. That's the list of common tax suits that may be brought against the government. Any attempt to sue outside the allowed types of cases will be dismissed. In fact, Congress has passed several laws explicitly stating that you *cannot* bring certain types of lawsuits. For example, you cannot sue the government for an injunction against collection action. This would include suing the IRS when it levies on assets, files a notice of lien, or takes most other collection actions. (In fact, the only injunction available against the collection of taxes is the automatic injunction of a petition in bankruptcy. Chapter 12 discusses how this works.)

People normally think of suing the government only as a last resort, usually a wise attitude. Tax litigation can be expensive. Moreover, several types of cases that *are* available require that you go to the IRS for relief first. Lawsuits over taxes can be viewed as the top section of a tax claim pyramid; only a few claims eventually rise to the summit.

If you have a tax claim or dispute, you need to understand and evaluate your right to sue, even if it may never be used. Your lawyer should be in a position to discuss this "menu choice" along with other alternatives.

Chapter 23

$\diamond\!\!\diamond\!\!\diamond$

DEFENDING SUITS BY THE GOVERNMENT

The IRS collects most taxes through its administrative enforcement powers—assessment, liens, levies, and other weapons described in part 1 of this book. But sometimes, the IRS resorts to the courts when its agency powers don't get the job done. In such cases, the government sues *you*, the taxpayer, rather than the reverse. The IRS' litigating arms are part of the Department of Justice, specifically, the Tax Division, and the United States Attorneys' offices. Just as you may go to court only as a last resort, so too the IRS normally goes to court only when all else fails.

You'll certainly know when the government has sued you. A complaint will be filed. The United States Marshal will serve a copy on you. In these types of suits, help from a lawyer is critical, particularly a tax lawyer experienced in tax litigation. Don't try to go it alone; defending these suits is complicated and expensive. Few nonlawyers are familiar with the rules governing federal court litigation. Few others have enough skill with these rules to make informed decisions on how to defend against IRS suits. Moreover, federal district courts are reluctant to help with procedure and substance if you represent yourself. So if you face a suit by the government to collect your taxes or otherwise enforce the tax laws, it's almost mandatory to get help from a lawyer. This chapter provides an opening acquaintance with the types of suits people may have to defend from time to time.

Congress has authorized the government to file eight main types of cases relating to taxes.

1. *Suit to reduce a tax assessment to judgment.* Despite the IRS' firepower to collect taxes, sometimes people manage to dodge the bullet. For instance, some try to outwait the tax collection period, which normally lasts ten years after assessment. But just when you thought you were home free, the IRS drags out a little-known weapon to prolong the agony for at least another ten. It asks the Justice Department to file a federal lawsuit against you to reduce the tax assessment to a judgment. Usually, the Department of Justice files suit close to the ten-year deadline. Also, the Service often chooses high-dollar or high-profile cases; it will not sue on every assessment that otherwise would lapse. But think how you would feel if, on the last or next-to-last day before the ten-year collection period expires, the Justice Department files suit against you. It could ruin your whole decade.

If the government wins, it has a court judgment on which it can collect. That judgment also gives the IRS some extra authority to put assets up for sale. The tax lien is also extended for however long state law provides for these types of judgment liens, often ten years or more.

The legal issue in a suit to reduce an assessment to judgment is always whether you owe the tax. The court presumes the IRS' assessment is correct. You have the burden to show it's not. That's a hard burden to bear, one you would have gladly shouldered in the previous ten years if you had adequate proof. Still, a few people shoulder that burden and win.

> *Example:* In one case, Oscar owed taxes dating back to 1981. The government made timely assessments of these taxes in 1984, and sued him in 1994, within the ten-year time limit. Oscar's defense: "I don't owe the taxes because you didn't give me credit for many deductions." Fortunately for Oscar, he actually had the proof. Granted, he had to dig it out from among trash bags full of records, but he found it, proved his case, and eliminated the assessments.

2. *Suit to enforce a lien or to subject property to the payment of tax.* The Justice Department can sue to foreclose the federal tax lien on specific property such as your house, business equipment, or any other property subject to the federal tax lien.

The Justice Department often combines one count to reduce the tax assessment to judgment with one to foreclose the federal tax lien (if it knows of property you own). The government's assessment and lien are again presumed valid and enforceable absent your proof to the contrary. If the government wins, it asks the court to appoint a United States Marshal to sell your property. In difficult cases involving many items of property or hidden assets, it may ask the court to appoint a receiver to take charge of the property and sell it over time. This happens often with homes the IRS wants to sell, where a nondelinquent third party such as a spouse or a coowner claims legal interest in the property. Getting a federal court involved means that everyone will be forced to have their claims resolved in one case, once and for all.

> *Example:* Lance and Lisa owned farmland. Since they also owed taxes, the government sued them to reduce the assessment to judgment and to foreclose the federal tax lien on their farm. Lance and Lisa had no real defense against the tax bill, but they said the government should not be allowed to sell because they each had a "homestead" interest that state law granted to them. This type of state law could not stop the IRS, ruled the court, because federal law allowing a tax sale was superior to any state exemptions. So they lost their farm in a foreclosure sale. Owning a home as "tenants by the entirety" also did not help, since Lance and Lisa jointly owed federal taxes. But if only one owed taxes, the government would not have been able to sell their farm.

3. *Suit for erroneous refund.* If the government sends you a refund and later figures out that you really owed the tax, it can sue you within two years of the payment to recapture the erroneous refund. This type of case might arise where you filed an amended return to get a refund, but the IRS later adjusted your return (such as after an audit).

A variation of this scenario occurs where you get a refund out of the blue. You know you are not entitled to it, but you got it because the computer skipped a beat and issued you a lottery-size refund. Should you keep it, hoping the IRS will miss the two-year deadline for filing an erroneous refund suit? No! The government can sue you simply for taking money that doesn't belong to you, a fraudulent act. The better course is to send the check back to the IRS with a cover letter explaining the circumstances.

4. *Suit to enforce an IRS levy.* If the IRS serves a tax levy on you, common sense and the law dictate you have to surrender the taxpayer's money or property that you possess. For example, an employer served with a levy pays a delinquent taxpayer's wages to the IRS, not the taxpayer. A bank drains the taxpayer's account

for the IRS. If you owe the taxpayer money and the IRS levies on you, you pay the IRS, not the taxpayer.

When someone refuses, the IRS can sue for the amount not surrendered, *plus a 50 percent penalty*. Banks suffer headaches over this rule, because they can't possibly police all the business loans they make. All of a sudden, when one of their borrowers gets into tax trouble, the first thing they see is a levy that hits the borrower's account. The bank desperately wants to call the loan and offset the borrower's bank deposits against the loan, but legally it cannot. It's too late *after* the levy hits. Many banks have suffered the wrong end of a suit for failure to honor a levy when they've taken the borrower's money and applied it against the loan instead of sending it to the IRS.

5. *Suit to enforce estate taxes.* The government has special authority to sue to collect estate taxes. Such suits are rare because the estate typically will pay the applicable tax, or the IRS collects it administratively by seizures and sales. But failing that, the government can sue to subject the decedent's property to sale by court order.

6. *Suits for fraudulent conveyance and transferee liability, and other state law suits.* The federal government has the same rights as any other creditor to sue under state laws. One of the most important of these is the right to rescind a fraudulent transfer of property, a cause of action in every state. With the IRS hot on their heels, many taxpayers make the mistake of transferring property. They make a "gift" of a car, house, pension, bank accounts, jewelry, or anything else of value. It's perfectly fine for someone to buy these things from you, even if it's a close friend or relative, but it's not OK simply to transfer them without any payment to avoid taxes, or to sell them after the tax lien attaches. Also, if you shed assets or put them in someone else's name, becoming insolvent as a result, that too is a badge of a "fraudulent transfer" which the IRS can undo by suing you. It happens all the time, and the courts take a dim view of such fraudulent transfers.

In some cases, the government also can sue your *transferees* and impose liability on them for the value of the property you transferred.

> *Example:* In one such case, the government sued William and Zack, his son. Apparently, William hadn't filed a few federal tax returns, so the government began investigating him. This is a good time, thought William, to transfer my country inn with its land to my son, Zack. And I can still run the place.
>
> Thereafter, William was indicted and convicted for willful failure to

file tax returns. The government then sued him and his son to get the inn. William had transferred the property by gift (that is, without fair consideration) to a blood relative, with intent to hinder or defraud the IRS. The transfer was fraudulent. So the government's tax lien attached to the property, which was sold for taxes.

7. *Suit against third-party lenders of wages.* When a bank makes a business loan to a shaky employer, sometimes it stipulates that the loan be used to pay wages. The bank figures that if workers' wages are assured, the project will go to completion. For example, sometimes general contractors designate subcontractor payments to go directly to workers. But even these stipulations don't ensure that the wages will be paid; the borrower sometimes defaults on payroll taxes. Under these circumstances, the government can sue the bank or general contractor for the money that was designated to pay wages. These types of suits are not that common these days, but they are still filed from time to time.

8. *Suit to enforce an IRS summons.* Most IRS summonses are self-enforcing. If you, the summoned person, take no action to contest it, the summons is presumed valid. The government can then haul you into court for contempt if you don't surrender the records. But not all summonses are self-enforcing. For the exceptions, the government must sue to enforce the summons. All it takes is a quick trip to federal court, where the government asks the judge to issue an order to you. The order says, "Appear in court to show cause" why the summons should not be enforced. On the hearing date, if you or the summoned person fails to respond or cannot mount a substantial defense, the judge will order the summons enforced, with the penalty of contempt or criminal prosecution if the summoned person fails to obey.

These are the main lawsuits that the government can file against delinquent taxpayers and third parties. It files thousands of them every year, in every federal district. Defending them is hazardous and expensive, but if you think you have a defense, the best course is to let a lawyer experienced in tax matters evaluate the case and advise you.

Part IV

THE IRS IN YOUR EVERYDAY LIFE

Chapter 24

⚬⚬⚬

TURNING THE TABLES:
GETTING INFORMATION FROM THE IRS

Sometimes it seems that the information flow between you and the IRS is one-way: it asks, you tell; it demands, you produce. But in fact, the IRS is a gold mine of information *you* can get—about yourself, about corporations in which you have some ownership, and much else. In fact, you are probably entitled to learn 90 percent or more of the information that the IRS has about you.

The Service maintains vast databases and stockpiles of electronic and paper records. As a general rule, very little of this mountain of data is publicly available, that is, yours or anyone's for the asking. Tax returns and return information are exempt from disclosure except to people who have a legal right or need to know, that is, a legal interest the law recognizes. A legal interest means that the information is about you, a client of yours, or a partnership, corporation, or other business entity in which you have an interest such as by ownership, directorship, or corporate office.

Knowing how to get these data can be useful or even vital in many ways. You may need to know when the statute of limitations on collection against you expires, or when your deadline runs out for filing a refund claim. You may need a back tax return, or to learn how much someone in your family paid to the IRS in withholding taxes, and when. You may need third-party information such as 1099 or W-2 forms, or other income information. The list of potential needs is lengthy. And, when the Service investigates *you*, you can usually find reams of information helpful for your case that the IRS is not legally entitled to withhold.

Method 1: Call the agency. There is a tremendous amount of information about you available with a simple telephone call to the toll-free number, 1-800-829-1040. All you need is to be on the telephone, Social Security number or employer identification number handy. The IRS will quiz you on certain other identifying data, such as address or possibly telephone number to make sure you are not an imposter. But once satisfied, the agent tells you many things about your own tax affairs, using a highly computerized search mechanism that retrieves much of your tax history with the push of a button.

For example, the agent can tell you when the IRS received your last return (or returns from many prior years), how much you earned, and your itemized deductions. The computer knows your withholding. It knows whether the IRS added penalties and interest, and how much; whether adjustments were made to your taxes by audit or otherwise; and how much you owe as of a recent date. The agent can tell whether and when the Service filed a tax lien against you, whether levies were issued, when you filed an offer in compromise, and many, many other details of your account. In fact, you may request a plain-English transcript of your entire account for any tax year, a process that usually takes about fifteen days. If you want only information on your income, useful for credit or other financial reasons, request Letter 1722, again taking about fifteen days. Both options are available by telephone request.

To get a copy of a tax return you must use Form 4506, pay a $12 fee for each return, and wait six to eight weeks.

Method 2: Ask the agent. If your return is audited or a Collection Division agent is assigned to your case, use this opportunity to ask for information. Within limits, the agent will accommodate you. Among the things you can ask for are tax account information (such as the information you can get by telephone call described above), the case history sheets, and affidavits and other statements (sometimes from third parties, with the names deleted). You may also request tax returns, other witness statements, and many other types of documents. Even the Criminal Investigation Division (CID), secretive as it is, still discloses some information as long as the investigation is not undermined. For example, CID agents often tell you the specific transactions they are examining for criminal purposes and by how much they think you have evaded your taxes.

You can also ask these agents to provide a copy of the sections of the

Internal Revenue manual that apply to your case. The manual itself is a huge, multithousand-page book divided into major subparts according to IRS function ("Examination," "Collection," and "Criminal Investigation," among others). It's so big partly because it tells agents in great detail how to audit, investigate, and collect. The agents will not give you the whole collection or examination section of that manual, but they might point you to a reading room where the manual can be found. Except for the section on the Criminal Investigation Division, the book is public record, available at all principal IRS offices around the country and many satellite offices. Soon it will reach the Internet.

Method 3: Find and analyze the tax rules. This is a daunting task for anyone, but for those so motivated, studying the tax laws and rules can be useful. Generally, you will be searching three sources for these tax rules: libraries, the IRS itself, and sources available electronically such as through the Internet.

Square one in beginning any such search is the Internal Revenue Code. This code can be found in all law libraries, many public libraries, in Fedworld on the Internet, and through commercial publishing companies that specialize in legal products. The code is complicated, intricate, and obscurely written, but we're all stuck with it. It is still the basic source of authority for all tax law. Of course, no law Congress passes would be complete without regulations. The regulations that interpret the Internal Revenue Code are three times the length of the code itself. These are also available from the same sources.

The *Internal Revenue Bulletin* is a weekly IRS publication that covers many topics. Among other things, the bulletin publishes notices, announcements (for example, "The interest rates for the next quarter will be 9 percent," or, "Hurricane Andrew victims will have longer to file their returns"), and interpretations of the Internal Revenue Code known as Revenue Rulings and Revenue Procedures. This bulletin is available from law libraries, commercial tax publishing services, and Fedworld on the Internet.

IRS publications. The Service has long maintained a publications program that attempts to explain discreet segments of the tax law in plain English. For the most part, it succeeds. IRS publications are well written, thorough, and useful. Appendix I contains an indexed list of publications that apply to audits, collection, and other tax procedure topics. Getting one is easy. Just call 1-800-TAX-FORM and ask for it. Expect to receive it within fourteen days. You can also access all publications and forms through Fedworld on the Internet.

Teletax. The IRS has about 150 tax topics on its Teletax system. Each is a three- to five-minute recording on a tax topic. You simply call and listen.

Examples of topics covered include "filing your payroll tax returns," and "mortgage interest deductions." To access Teletax, call 1-800-829-4477.

Private-letter rulings, technical advice. Sometimes you are thinking about a business or personal transaction that you hope will have favorable tax treatment, but you are not sure. Or, you are fairly sure but you want the IRS' stamp of approval in advance. That's what the "private letter ruling" is for. In many, but not all, areas of tax law, the IRS will officially rule, in advance, on the tax effect of your proposed transaction. It could be a business merger, the sale of some property, the sale of assets, or many other business or personal transactions. When issued, private letter rulings become public record, though names and other identifying data are deleted. You can find these rulings from commercial publishers in the tax field, from the IRS itself, or through Fedworld on the Internet. They are not precedent; you can't cite them in court even if they favor your case, but they tell you what the IRS is thinking and often help you plan.

"Technical advice" is given during a tax audit when you and the agent cannot agree on a particularly complex or unsettled tax question. It's usually an important tax question, so either you or the agent can ask a special IRS office for "technical advice" on how the issue should be resolved. The IRS then publishes the technical advice in a memorandum available through the *Internal Revenue Bulletin,* commercial publishers, and Fedworld. Again, the names are deleted.

The Office of Appeals. If your tax return is audited but you and the agent cannot agree on all issues, you may appeal within the IRS to the Office of Appeals. Chapter 17 discusses the function of the appeals office in more detail. This office is another good source of information about you and your case. Simply ask the appeals officer for information in the file, and he will give it to you. For example, he might show you portions of the revenue agent's files, her notes, transmittal letters, letters from third parties, and much other information the revenue agent did not feel free to reveal. The appeals officer is not required to reveal all of this, but often he will, just to get the case moving.

Method 4: The Freedom of Information Act and the Privacy Act. Congress passed these two acts twenty years ago in reaction to Watergate. Both have proved extremely useful for people who want tax information from the IRS. (Of course, these acts apply governmentwide to the entire executive branch.) People make so many requests under both acts that most agencies, including the IRS, have special offices detailed for them, plus reams of regulations on how requests must be made and what can be disclosed.

The Freedom of Information Act (FOIA) aims to make government records widely available, with a number of important exemptions. Through it, you can get such things as your own tax file, transmittal letters, and third-party statements (with names and other identifying data blocked out). The act permits some limited access to the revenue officer's or revenue agent's history sheets, narratives, and other notes of your case, sometimes the agent's legal analysis, and third-party statements such as those of other witnesses. All of this can be extremely useful in any tax case. For instance, such information is often critical in defending against the Trust Fund Recovery Penalty, discussed in chapter 10.

Through the Freedom of Information Act, you also can obtain some staff manuals, statements about the agency's operations, and descriptions of its organization and addresses. Of course, much of this information is available elsewhere, but it is certainly accessible through the FOIA.

To make a request under the Freedom of Information Act or the Privacy Act, write to the disclosure officer in your IRS district. A list of the thirty-three Internal Revenue districts and their addresses is contained in appendix II. At the end of this chapter, you will also find a sample request under the Freedom of Information Act.

Your letter should ask for a "record," that is, something that already exists on paper or electronically. You may not ask the IRS to perform research. Describe as clearly and specifically as possible what you are asking for. Include your name, address, and telephone number. You may wish to limit the copying and search fees the IRS can incur without your prior approval. For example, "You are authorized to incur $250 of research and copying fees without my prior authorization. Costs in excess of this amount should be discussed with me in advance at the telephone number listed above."

But even the FOIA won't get you everything. Important exemptions include classified documents, Criminal Investigation Division files, internal personnel rules and practices, confidential business information, and all information about third parties. That's why the names and identifying data of third parties, such as other officers in a corporation and third-party witnesses, are deleted from some records you get. But often you can guess enough to fill in the blanks. Even if you can't, it's better to know what the third-party affidavit states even if you don't know who gave it.

The Privacy Act overlaps the coverage of the FOIA in many respects. People often make requests under both statutes just to be sure they have covered everything. But the Privacy Act was intended for a different purpose: to enable you to learn what the agency has on record about you and to correct any errors.

So, under the Privacy Act, the IRS must allow you to see and copy its records about you and to change or amend them if they are incorrect.

To make a request under the Privacy Act, write a letter to the district disclosure officer stating that the request is made under the Privacy Act. Include your name, address, signature, and telephone number, and a description of the records as specifically as possible. Sometimes people simply ask for "all records pertaining to or relevant to the undersigned," which is usually sufficient. The agency has a fee structure for copying, but does not charge for search time. Like the FOIA, the Privacy Act contains exemptions, such as for classified information and investigatory materials.

Once you obtain your Privacy Act information, you can ask to amend it. To do this, send a letter stating that it is a request to amend a record under the Privacy Act of 1974. Identify the specific record or information, state the reasons why the information is not accurate, relevant, timely, or complete, and why (with supporting documentation or evidence). Finally, correct the information by stating what you believe should be included.

The IRS acknowledges your request under either the FOIA or the Privacy Act (or both), usually within ten to sixty days, and responds with the information or requests an extension. If the Service withholds information, it so advises you, citing the specific statutory exemption on which it relies.

With all of these tools at your disposal, information gathering should be a two-way street. The IRS expects that you will ask for information; it is geared up to respond. Getting information from the agency in these ways can never hurt your case, and often it can spell the difference between failure and success.

Tel:_____

Date:_____

Director, Baltimore District
Internal Revenue Service
P.O. Box 1018
Baltimore, Maryland 21203

Re: Freedom of Information Act Request
       Wonder Widgits, Inc.
       EIN 00-0000000

Ladies/Gentlemen:

Pursuant to the Freedom of Information Act, 5 U.S.C. § 552, as amended, I hereby request copies of the following records of the Internal Revenue Service:

1. All original documents and files created or maintained by any person or division of the Internal Revenue Service or any other agency or department of the United States government that relate to the tax liability of Wonder Widgits, Inc., EIN 00-0000000, and/or relating to the Trust Fund Recovery Penalty assessment that is proposed against Penny Pencil, SSN 000-00-0000.

2. All documents relating to the above request, including but not limited to the following: IRS forms 4180, 433, 433-A, 433-B, 2848, 2973, 2275 (Collection Support Unit check sheet), Requests for Quick or Prompt Assessment (Form 2859), Trust Fund Recovery Penalty file transmittal, Form 4183 (Trust Fund Recovery Penalty Data), forms 941, 1120 or 1120S, Internal Revenue Service Memoranda, Appeals Transmittal Memoranda and supporting statements, routing slips, correspondence, transcripts of account, correspondence from the Internal Revenue Service to any person, case history sheets, revenue officer notes, bank account statements, canceled checks, bank signature cards, bank corporate resolutions, affidavits, declarations, corporate minutes, any documents pertaining to Wonder Widgets, Inc., copies of notices of federal tax lien (IRS Form 668), and all other papers, documents, forms, letters, or documents of whatever description located in the Trust Fund Recovery Penalty file of the Internal Revenue Service with respect to the above-named individual.

The Internal Revenue Service is authorized to charge me for searching the records, for making deletions from them, and for making the requested copies, up to $250 in charges without further authorization. If the total charges are estimated to exceed that amount, please provide me with an estimate of the charges and seek further authorization from me.

If it is determined that any requested record or portion thereof will not be disclosed, please provide the nonexempt records and the nonexempt portions of the remaining records. If any requested record or a portion thereof is not disclosed, please also provide an index and a detailed description of each record or portion thereof not disclosed, and a statement describing the statutory basis for not disclosing each record or portion thereof.

Please address the requested material to me at the address set forth above. If you have any questions concerning this request, please contact me by telephone at the number set forth above.

Sincerely yours,

Penny Pencil

Chapter 25

TURNING THE TABLES: MAKE THE IRS GIVE YOU MONEY

Because the IRS is so aggressive about keeping the money it collects, many people believe the expression, "Once gone, always gone." There is truth in that expression, but it's helpful to know the exceptions. In fact, you can get money back from the IRS in at least four ways.

1. *Claim for refund.* By far the most common way people get money back from the IRS is by filing a claim for refund. Your tax return automatically functions as such a claim when you end up with a credit due to you (an "overpayment") on the return. You need only send in the return (or file it electronically), and your refund will follow absent any unusual circumstances. In 1994, the IRS issued eighty-five million refunds totaling more than $108 *billion*. Of these, individuals obtained eighty-two million refunds for $87 billion, or more than $1,000 for the average refund.

You also may file a claim for income tax refund using Form 1040X, the Amended Return. This must be filed within the later of three years from the date you filed the original return or two years from the date you paid the tax. Thousands of forms 1040X are filed every year. For other types of taxes, such as excise, employment, and penalty, use Form 843, Claim for Refund. The procedures and deadlines are the same. Fill out the return, send it in, and wait. Every claim for refund is reviewed at least once, sometimes at two or three levels, for accuracy and legality. If all is correct, a refund request is processed and the money comes your way.

Refund claims come in all shapes and sizes. Here are just some examples of actions or events that might result in a refund:

- *Your business suffers an operating loss.* The tax laws allow you to offset that loss against your future income or past income, starting three years back. If you choose the latter course, a refund commonly results. If you carry the loss forward, you may get a refund in a future year.

- *You forgot about a deduction, or you reported income that wasn't taxable.* Either type of event can result in a refund if you amend a past return to claim the deduction or exclude the income.

- *A husband and wife filed jointly and were due a refund, but the next year they divorced.* If one spouse's income and tax payments were disproportionately larger than the other's, that spouse can claim a refund under the "injured spouse" principle. Chapter 19 discusses this in more detail.

- *Your tax return is audited.* You've been so meticulous and scrupulous that the agent finds nothing wrong, but actually spots a deduction you didn't take. That agent is duty-bound to give you that deduction and the resulting refund.

- *You're an "innocent spouse."* Signing a joint return means you guarantee to pay all the taxes on that return, including tax increases from audits. But sometimes one spouse is innocent and should not be held liable for the extra. Chapter 19 discusses this issue. Proving innocent spouse status can be difficult. But if you succeed, you are entitled to a refund.

2. *Rewards.* Want to feel real, deep-down satisfaction, reduce the federal deficit, and get paid to boot? Turn in a tax cheat. Yes, it's true, the IRS pays bounties to people who turn in delinquent taxpayers. The reward is generally up to 10 percent of the amount the IRS eventually collects (excluding interest). But before you go rushing off to the telephone, bear in mind that the IRS has discretion as to how much and even whether it grants an award. Form 211 and Policy Statement P-4-86 explain this in more detail.

Under the 1996 Taxpayer Bill of Rights, the IRS may now grant rewards in civil tax collection cases. Previously, only criminal cases could generate rewards. It's a bounty system: the amount of the reward is paid from the amount the IRS collects from the delinquent taxpayer, a true whistleblowers' reward in the right case. True enough, the IRS will take into account the value of the information, and the amount is what the IRS considers "adequate compensation" under the circumstances. Still, there are some numeric guidelines. These are generally 10 percent of the first $75,000 recovered, 5 percent of the next $25,000, and 1 percent of additional recovery. The total maximum award is usually not more than $100,000. There are other monetary guidelines that depend on the value of the information the informant supplies.

3. *Attorneys' fees.* In the last ten years, the door has opened slightly to awards of attorneys' fees where you beat the IRS in court. Progress is slow but steady. Generally, to earn such an award of attorneys' fees, you must first hire a lawyer to defend or prosecute your tax case. If you win and the court rules the IRS' position was not "substantially justified," the courts often award attorneys' fees. The 1996 Taxpayer Bill of Rights shifted the burden of proof; now it's on the government to prove that its litigating position was "substantially justified" even though it lost the case.

4. *Suits for damages.* For several years, the law has authorized anyone who is injured by the IRS' collection activity to sue for damages. To earn such damages, you must show in general that the IRS acted illegally and recklessly. Moreover, you also need to prove the extent of your damages and give the IRS the opportunity to pay damages in advance of any lawsuit. See chapter 22.

These are the main ways in which you can obtain money back from the IRS. If they seem too few, that's intentional on the part of Congress. The revenue stream was intended to run one way—away from you and to the IRS. Still, these are good ways to reclaim some of your hard-earned funds.

Chapter 26

THE IRS IN THE ELECTRONIC AGE

IRS Electronic Address

1. World Wide Web Home Page: **http://www.irs.ustreas.gov/prod/**.

2. a) Internal Revenue Information System (IRIS) is on FedWorld's bulletin board or the IRS Home Page on the World Wide Web.

   b) By modem: (i) set modem parity at "none," data bits to 8, stop bit to 1; (ii) dial 703-321-8020; (iii) enter "guest."

The Internal Revenue Service has both feet planted firmly in cyberspace. So swift are the electronic changes the Service is making that by the time you read this chapter, it will be out of date. Thousands more documents, publications, and forms will be on the government's World Wide Web site. Millions more people will file electronically.

Those who are computer savvy will find much happiness in those aspects of the IRS that bow down in praise of the electron.

FILING AND PAYMENT OPTIONS

EZ Telefile. Since 1992, the IRS has experimented with paperless filing of Form 1040EZ by telephone. For 1994, almost seven hundred thousand people in ten states filed by phone. The Service expected twenty-three million people with gross incomes of less than $50,000 would be eligible to file this way for 1995. Starting in 1996 (for 1995), people who want to file by telephone need do nothing. The IRS notifies you, by letter/packet, that you might be eligible. The packet will include detailed directions, a personal identification number (PIN) that serves as a "signature," and all necessary worksheets. Only those who are so notified will be eligible. An IRS fact sheet gives the following additional requirements:

- you are single with no dependents

- you have taxable income of less than $50,000

- you filed a tax return in some prior year

- you have W-2 forms for all wages and taxable scholarships or fellowships, but not more than five W-2s

- you have taxable interest income of $400 or less

- you have no income from unemployment compensation

- you owe no employment taxes on wages paid to a household worker

- you are at the same address as last year

The instructions guide you through entering the information, and the IRS automatically computes the tax and the refund. In theory, you may expect to receive the refund within three weeks, or to be notified of any balance due. The paperless filing phone call is expected to take about ten minutes. In actual experience, this program got off to a rocky start, but the future is brighter.

Electronic refunds. Starting in 1996 for the 1995 tax year, most people can have refunds directly deposited into a bank account, and *you need not file electronically* to take advantage of this program. This is a major change from the past, when only those who filed electronically or used Form 1040PC could obtain this direct deposit. To get your refund by direct deposit, fill out Form 8888, Direct Deposit of Refund, and attach it to your tax return. Long form and short form filers will be eligible.

Form 1040PC. Millions now take advantage of this form of electronic filing. You buy the Form 1040PC software from a commercial vendor (most have it), install, and then answer the questions. Form 1040PC is electronically sent to the IRS via your modem. This package shortens your form to include only the lines you answer; blank lines and "zero" lines are excluded. You can also have your refund deposited directly this way. If you owe tax, the software prints a voucher for the balance due.

Other electronic filing. Since 1989, when electronic filing became available, the IRS has seen a thirteenfold increase in its use, from about one million to about thirteen million in 1994. The IRS now also accepts electronic filing for nonindividual returns such as fiduciary, partnership, and employee plan returns. Even quarterly payroll tax returns (forms 941) are now electronically fileable, the IRS' pilot program having begun in October 1994 (one hundred thousand employment tax returns filed electronically).

Unlike telephone filing, electronic return filing is available only through providers, called Electronic Return Originators. These providers include tax preparation services, accountants, financial planners, and others. All of them apply to the IRS for a special identifying number and for the software that allows the provider to transmit returns electronically to the IRS.

You can easily find these providers by canvassing the yellow pages or newspapers, or by asking your tax preparer or other financial adviser. The IRS' Home Page on the World Wide Web also has a list of On-Line Filing Program companies.

For the 1996 filing season, the Service somewhat tightened the requirements. You are not able to file Form 1040, Form 1040A, or Form 1040EZ electronically after October 15, 1996, even if you have an extension beyond that date. According to the IRS, Electronic Return Originators must not have a foreign address, and must take corrective action within twenty-four hours of receiving acknowledgment that a return has been rejected.

Electronic filing and tax assistance are also available for the VITA (Volunteer Income Tax Assistance) and TCE (Tax Counseling for the Elderly) programs.

Internet filing. Don't want to use an Electronic Return Originator? Beginning in 1996, you can file via the Internet or by using your home PC and modem to call a toll-free number. By the year 2001, the IRS expects eighty million electronic returns to be filed this way. The returns will be received by FedWorld, a site the Department of Commerce manages through its National Technical Information Service. There is no fee for this electronic filing.

Filing on-line starts with a return you prepare electronically on your own personal computer. You then transmit this return to an on-line service or transmitter. This service converts your data to the IRS' format and transmits the information to the IRS. The IRS then notifies you whether the return has been accepted. The program had growing pains in 1996.

Paying electronically. You can now pay electronically, too. The Service has a program called TAX LINK available to businesses to make payroll and estimated-tax payments. Many large companies use it, but it's available to anyone. Electronic paying is now mandatory for companies with more than $50,000 in annual payroll.

Telephone help. You can call a toll-free number, 1-800-829-1040, for tax help anytime during the year. Almost twenty million people make one or more calls during each filing season. You can ask any question, ranging from tax advice to account information. Naturally, these call sites get very busy during filing season, so be patient. The earlier in filing season you call, the more likely you are to get through and to get the correct answer. According to the IRS, its accuracy rate in answering questions is about 90 percent.

Teletax. This is a prerecorded announcement service that gives you information on about 150 tax topics, and always growing. You need a push-button phone to call, 1-800-829-4477. Nearly seven million people used this service in 1995.

The Internet. The IRS has a Web site and plenty of other presence on the Internet. Its World Wide Web address is **http://www.irs.ustreas.gov.** The IRS uses FedWorld as its Internet home, available at **fed world.gov.FTP-ftp.fed world. gov.** In 1995, FedWorld received more than twenty-five thousand requests *every day.*

Internet users can access and download a tremendous amount of information. In fact, the 1994 filing season saw three million forms downloaded to personal computers, and at one point, a form or publication was downloaded every 1.5 seconds.

The IRS updates its site on FedWorld daily. The Home Page lists these subpages.

- *Tax Stats:* Tax tables, Earned Income Tax Credit tables, and rate schedules. This sets the stage for a second phase later on—a full database application where a taxpayer can input adjusted gross income and marital status to get the correct tax.

- *Tax Info For You:* Hypertext versions of publications 334 and 17. Users can move from one section to a reference with a click of the mouse. "Tax Trails" is an interactive program that leads you through basic tax questions and answers.

The Home Page also contains the following options:

- *Electronic Services:* This topic leads to electronic filing options and other items on the Internet.

- *Taxpayer Help and Education:* In this section, the IRS has listed summaries of 150 tax topics and frequently asked questions.

- *Tax Info for Business:* Access to business information, forms, and publications.

- *Tax Regs in English:* Plain-English summaries of tax regulations, and a library of the actual regulations.

- *IRS Newsstand:* This contains a full library of tax news and press releases, as well as all Teletax topics.

- *Forms and Pubs:* Electronic versions of IRS forms, sometimes issued even before the paper forms are available.

- *What's Hot:* The newest options, items, publications, rules, and laws.

- *Meet the Commissioner*

- *Comments and Help*

- *Site Tree*

Within the FedWorld on the Internet you will find the Internal Revenue Information System (IRIS). You can also find this service on the IRS' Home Page in the World Wide Web. The IRIS main menu options are these:

IRIS Main Menu Options
A   About IRIS at FedWorld
B   Tax Forms and Publications

C   Individual Income Tax Information
D   Business Tax Information
E   Tax Information for the Media
F   IRS Regulations and Plain Language Summaries
G   Goodbye
H   Help
I   Dear IRIS
T   IRS Statistics of Income

You may download forms and publications from IRIS. This requires a personal computer, a modem, and a printer.

Fax. In 1996, the IRS will conduct a pilot program of "Fax on Demand." With this service, taxpayers can call from their fax machines and get tax information they need fast; a one-page menu of items will be available simply by pressing a button.

Tax forms. There are now four ways to get tax forms, all in addition to walking down to your local IRS office. You can 1-800-TAX-FORM, Monday through Friday during regular hours. You may also have most tax forms faxed to you at any time from the National Technical Information Service, maintained by the Department of Commerce. Use the voice portion of your fax machine and dial 703-487-4160. Finally, the IRS has issued a CD-ROM with more than six hundred tax forms and publications, which you can search, view, and print out any time. This is available at $46 through the Superintendent of Documents of the Government Printing Office. This CD-ROM is set up for Windows 3.1 or higher, or through Macintosh System 7.5 using Adobe's Acrobat Exchange—LE Software.

In the future, you will be able to get virtually any IRS item that is public record. This includes all regulations, proposed regulations, possibly even the Internal Revenue manual. Cases, notices, announcements, and other items that interpret the tax law are already available electronically from other sources on the Internet, such as law libraries. The IRS is also exploring the use of paperless imaging, which will let you keep "paper" records electronically. For an agency that handles more than two billion pieces of paper each year, this may be the biggest blessing of all.

From here on, the user must browse and click. The potential for information availability is unlimited.

Chapter 27

~~~~~~~~~~

IF YOU OWN A BUSINESS; IF YOU WORK
FOR YOURSELF

The American dream often includes owning a business or working for yourself. Millions make this dream a reality every year. In fact, most American business is small business, not big corporations. Upwards of four out of every five jobs exist in nonpublic corporations, from street vendors to multibillion-dollar family-owned enterprises.

But the American dream can turn into a nightmare over taxes. Even successful small businesses can trip over the many tax rules they must all obey, not to mention the dozens of nontax laws and rules. And, by neglect and inadvertence, a failing business can multiply its tax problems beyond saving.

This chapter alerts you to the most common IRS problems that businesses encounter, and shows how to avoid them. Prevention is the most important principle.

CHOOSING YOUR BUSINESS FORM

When you start or take over a business, you get to choose the legal form in which you want to operate. You can be a sole proprietor (working for yourself only), a proprietor (you own the business and have employees), a partnership, or a corporation. "Limited liability" companies are now also becoming more common. There is no one right answer, but the corporation has a major advantage over the others. The owners are not personally liable for the corporation's debts. So, if the corporate car runs someone down, or the corporate machine injures an employee, your personal assets are protected. Only the business assets are at risk.

The proprietorship is the simplest form of business organization. In fact, in 1992 some fifteen million people formed proprietorships, more than 70 percent of the total of all businesses. With a proprietorship, you and your business are legally inseparable. You own it all. You receive all the profits or suffer the losses. These features have the advantage of simplicity, but there are disadvantages as well. The biggest is unlimited liability. You are personally liable for all debts of the business. And, all debts means taxes, too. So, if you have employees and fail to pay employment taxes, you are personally liable for all the payroll taxes, plus penalties, plus interest.

A partnership is formed when two or more people unite for the purpose of sharing profits and losses, but they don't incorporate. Again, it's easy to organize, in most states requiring no particular forms (limited partnerships usually require more formalities). The profits are taxed to the partners individually in proportion to their ownership shares; the partnership itself pays no tax. However, the partnership does have a separate legal status and filing and reporting requirements, and so is more cumbersome to manage than a proprietorship. Also, except in limited partnerships, the general partners are totally exposed to personal liability for the partnership's debts. They also are liable to each other for breaches of the duty of loyalty.

A corporation is the most formal type of business organization. Every state has laws permitting corporations to be formed and regulating how they operate. Corporations are complex, with many formalities and forms to be completed each year. Regular corporations, called "C" corporations in the tax law, pay taxes on their profits. A special type of corporation, called the "S" corporation, does not. Instead, like partnerships, "S" corporations flow profits through to the owners in proportion to their ownership shares. An "S" corporation is still a real state-authorized corporation, with limited liability, but it has simply chosen to take advantage of the special status the federal tax laws allow for such companies.

THE TAX TRAPS FOR SMALL BUSINESSES

1. *Employment taxes.* No matter what form of business entity you choose, you will be subject to filing many different types of business and personal tax

returns: federal, state, and sometimes local. The most common are employment tax returns. Every business entity files payroll tax returns, such as forms 941 and 940, if it has employees. Sole proprietors, partners, and corporate shareholders also file estimated-tax returns based on their anticipated profit in the business.

Businesses that lose money usually run into trouble over payroll taxes more than any other type. The owners or managers pay the employees' net wages, recording on the books the business tax liability for withholding, Social Security tax, Medicare, and state income tax. Then they don't pay these taxes to the federal and state governments. The reasons vary. Often cash flow is tight. Managers may figure that a big payment will come in the next week or next month, or that they can "work it out" with the IRS. They have to keep the doors open, so employees and suppliers get paid, but the IRS doesn't come calling until later—weeks, months, sometimes years later. The Service sounds the payroll tax alarm more quickly these days, but there is still two to six weeks of delay, at a minimum, after its computers detect nondeposit of taxes or the company sends in a quarterly tax return without full payment.

This failure to pay payroll taxes is a ticking time bomb. The corporation, as a separate legal entity, is of course always liable for the full amount of tax, penalties, and interest it fails to pay. But on top of this, the owners and managers who were in control of the company's finances are *personally* liable for a portion of those taxes, the portion withheld from employees' paychecks. This liability is known as the Trust Fund Recovery Penalty. Chapter 10 discusses it in detail.

This danger of personal liability points to the single most important reason why you may wish to incorporate your business. As a rule, the personal liability component of the corporation's tax bill is 67 percent to 75 percent of the total tax bill. Moreover, the owners and managers are not personally liable for the penalties and interest. The IRS makes the Trust Fund Recovery Penalty assessment fifty thousand times a year, with a total of more than $1 billion in assessed tax liability. If your business is not incorporated, you are personally liable for everything—all taxes, withheld or not, all penalties, and all interest. So, using a corporation has the major advantage of shielding the owners and managers from one-third of the personal liability for payroll taxes if the business fails. True enough, a corporation is more cumbersome in terms of paperwork. But many a proprietor and general partner have sadly wished in retrospect that they had simply incorporated their business.

The other single most important practice tip is to keep up the corporate formalities. Being a corporation is not a "file and forget" proposition; the corporation must act like one. That means it maintains its existence separate and apart from that of its owners. The shareholders and directors hold meetings and record minutes. They advertise, write checks, and make contracts in the corporate name. If not, the IRS, like any other creditor, can hold the owners personally liable for every ounce of tax the "corporation" owed because it wasn't really a corporation. Maintaining these corporate formalities is like getting a dull headache once a year. It nags at you to pay attention and do something, but it's easily done. Yet thousands of corporations are lax in keeping up their corporate records to some extent. The owners are too busy keeping up with business to worry about "the paperwork." When a crisis hits, they wish they had.

2. *Employee-independent contractors disputes.* The other major payroll problem some companies encounter arises out of treating workers as independent contractors rather than employees. A business must pay its "employees'" withheld payroll taxes (plus the employer's share of Social Security/Medicare), but not if the workers are "independent contractors." The problem arises when the IRS thinks you had so much control over your independent contractors that they should be considered your employees. All of a sudden, your business is liable for a ton of payroll taxes, sometimes going back years. For thirty years, the IRS has conducted a nationwide running battle with the business community over this issue. The courts have ruled in dozens of cases involving nurses, drywall installers, insurance agents, teachers, doctors, and other worker classes. Even Congress gets into the fight from time to time, usually granting some measure of relief to businesses that are stuck with these types of investigations. It continues to be a nagging problem.

The easiest way to solve it is to give in: treat all your workers as employees, subject to withholding. But many businesses cannot do this because competitors refuse to go along. Others simply see more profit in using independent contractors. These businesses run the risk of an IRS investigation. If you treat your workers as independent contractors, consider several steps to help your case in advance.

   a) Use a written contract that addresses the factors the IRS considers in deciding whether your workers are independent contractors or employees. Then, be sure your business practices conform to the contract. Among the most important factors are the degree of control you exert over the workers' methods, including your instructions and training. The IRS also looks at whether the workers are free to work for others, whether they furnish their own tools, how they are supervised and paid, where the work is done, who pays the expenses, and who bears the risk of loss.

b) Collect information as you go along about how your competitors treat their workers. If a substantial portion of your industry consistently treats workers as independent contractors, assemble that evidence. It may help if you are investigated.

c) Treat your workers consistently as independent contractors, from Day One. You will have at least a few real employees, so your payroll tax returns will reflect the withholdings from employees' wages. Exclude independent contractors from those returns; instead issue forms 1099 to them.

d) Find a way to ensure that the independent contractors have paid their income and self-employment taxes. In the real world, this is easier said than done. But if you can conveniently police their tax behavior, the IRS gives you credit for each worker whose taxes have been paid, even if that worker ends up being your "employee."

KEEPING BUSINESS RECORDS

These days, there is truly no excuse for keeping sloppy or incomplete business records. Even small, start-up businesses can and need to keep their accounting and other records by computer. Hardware and software are so inexpensive, so easily available, and such a great help to bookkeepers and executives alike that record keeping should be smooth and easy. The biggest advantage of computerization of business records is that you enter data once, and from that entry you may generate accurate income and expense reports, profit and loss statements, balance sheets, and many other reports. Today's computers can manipulate the accounting data to any form that seems convenient to you. Using computers avoids losing deductions and averts unreported income problems. Tax software will keep you abreast of all deductions, including depreciation. Software is also available to remind you of tax-sensitive dates such as filing deadlines and payroll tax payment deadlines. The computer will catch any arithmetic mistake as well.

Another big advantage of computerization is to enable you to separate your accounts. Any business and its owner should be separate (even if the owner is an unincorporated proprietor), and this is easily maintained using a computer system.

Every month, quarter, or year, print a hard copy of your financial statements. Keep a back-up disk of all your data off site, and maintain the integrity of your business's computer systems by having an accountant who can check behind you.

THE IRS EDUCATION PROGRAM

The IRS publishes a number of excellent items to help you start your business. Publication 583, Taxpayers Starting a Business, contains a detailed analysis of the records that are required, a suggested record system, comments on bookkeeping and record-keeping systems, and explanations of accounting methods.

The IRS also publishes a small business education kit, Publication 1466, an eight-part, six-inch presentation of the following aspects of starting a business:

1. business assets

2. business use of the home

3. employment taxes

4. excise taxes

5. starting a business/record keeping

6. Schedule C and ES and Form 1040-ES

7. self-employed retirement plans

8. the small business as a partnership

9. tip reporting and allocation rules

10. "S" corporation/"C" corporation

This publication, several hundred pages long, is a gold mine of information about small businesses and is particularly helpful to the new, start-up business where the owner may not have previous experience.

Finally, the IRS is deep into small business on its Web site on the Internet.

With so much help available from the IRS and from commercial publishers, including computer hardware and software makers, starting a business these days is relatively easy. True enough, it's up to you to make the sales and service the customers. But at least the compliance portion has been made easier.

Chapter 28

"THEY DON'T EAT MUCH"— KEEPING AND ORGANIZING YOUR TAX RECORDS IN THE '90s

Here's a quick game of "Answer Person." (The Answer Person gives the answer; you guess the question.)

1. *Answer Person:*

   "three years"
   "four years"
   "six years"
   "ten years"
   "forever"

The question: "How long should I keep tax records?"

2. *Answer Person:*

   "none"

The question: "What specific records does the law require that I keep?"

Surprising as it may seem, with a few narrow exceptions that do not apply to most people, there is absolutely no legal requirement to keep any specific types of tax records. Of course, you will certainly want to. The IRS encourages accurate record keeping, and good records are essential to know how you're doing financially. But the only law is to keep records the tax *regulations* require. And, strictly speaking, for most people those regulations require only that you keep records that are "sufficient to establish the amount of gross income, deductions, credits" for your tax returns. Translation: Keep whatever records you need to support your tax return. At the end of this chapter is a handy guide showing suggested record-retention periods.

How long to keep them? Again, the law specifies no time period to retain checks, receipts, or other records. The only hint is to keep records "so long as the contents thereof may become material in the administration of any Internal Revenue law." Translation: Keep them as long as you or the IRS may need them.

What good would a tax rule be without exceptions? Some specific requirements apply to farmers, certain types of wage earners, corporations that use computerized records extensively, and exempt organizations (mostly charities). Also, if you've been a poor record keeper in the past, the IRS can specify in writing that you have to keep checks, receipts, or other specific types of records.

Even when the tax regulations are more specific, such as the requirement to keep books of account, they are also vague, stating only that the books of account must be kept accurately but in no particular form. Your books just have to be organized well enough to enable an IRS agent to examine them and make sense of them.

This vagueness is understandable. The IRS cannot possibly keep up with even the known types of records that people generate, much less new ones periodically invented. The agency has enough trouble keeping up with its *own* records. And a regulation that spelled out exactly what records to keep would be self-defeating—so quickly outdated it would be impossible to administer. (Actually, it would be a windfall for taxpayers if the agency tried. You could argue that since the IRS didn't tell you to keep a check for this or a receipt for that, you don't have to.)

So, instead, the IRS says, "Let's not get into that. You keep whatever records are necessary to allow us to examine you if we want to." And, of course, the burden of proof in tax examinations and most tax cases in court is on you, the taxpayer. So although the regulations don't say you *must* keep specific records, it is wise to do so.

THE IMPORTANCE OF KEEPING GOOD RECORDS

Many businesspeople look on record keeping as a necessary evil, a chore to be avoided or delegated. Thousands adopt the attitude, "I must be making money, just look at my sales" just before their ship sinks. If businesspeople who hold their noses at record keeping realized how critical good records are, they would treat them with the same importance as making the next sale.

For example, you can never know accurately whether you are making money, and how much, unless you know your income, receipts, payables, and receivables.

> *Example:* In one case, Marshall, owner of a small business, was in a cash crunch at the end of the year. It seemed impossible; sales had doubled and expenses had certainly not come anywhere near doubling. His internal bookkeeper had recently left, so one Monday he decided to take a look at her work. By Friday, he needed $150,000 to meet payroll, tax payments, and other expenses. The bank balance was $5,000. He looked at the bookkeeper's accounts receivable files. To his horror, the bookkeeper had failed through ignorance or oversight to bill $200,000 of work. Some was never billed, some was marked as "paid" when it was not; other files were too confusing to understand.
>
> Marshall painstakingly reconstructed every file, called his customers, and saved the day. But it cost him countless hours of agony, some tax penalties, and plenty of interest on undeposited receipts that were overdue.

A second reason to keep good records is that it avoids costly penalties and allows you to take normal business discounts vendors often allow for quick payment. You can also avoid late-payment penalties, interest charges, and IRS charges for late payment of payroll taxes. Many other tax penalties also can be avoided. This kind of control is impossible without good record keeping.

Third, in the '90s your business must be lean and mean. No one has extra money to throw around at unnecessary expenses. You can't have an accurate picture of expenses—where to cut or where to add—without accurate and timely records. It is no exaggeration to say that for many businesses the difference between profit and loss is the control over expenses and income that comes with good record keeping.

Fourth, if you need more money, lenders are impressed with accurate long-range (over three years) record keeping. It shows a mastery of your business; it implies accuracy; it instills confidence. In fact, institutional lenders such as investment bankers and commercial banks will *demand* not only good records, but also audited records. Your CPA cannot start to audit your records unless you give her an accurate set and a system for keeping records that works into the future.

Fifth, good record keeping builds credibility in every area of your business. It shows you are on top of things. If that's so, customers and vendors have more confidence in everything else you say about your business.

Sixth, if you want to sell your business, you'll certainly need accurate financial statements. It's hard to play catch-up after five or six years of neglect. Many buyers want audited financial statements, or at least ones that are reviewed by a certified public accountant.

Seventh, think about going public. It's the dream of many business-people. You become instantly rich and retire to the beach of your choice. You have no hope of taking a company public without audited financial statements, which means they must be well organized and accurate from the start.

WHAT RECORDS, FOR HOW LONG?

In the absence of detailed requirements, be guided by common sense and good judgment. Here are some guidelines for the most common types of records that people create and use.

1. *In general.* A good rule of thumb is to keep any tax-related paper a minimum of four years. These records would include proof of Schedule A items: medical expenses, taxes, interest, contributions, and miscellaneous deductions including unreimbursed employee expenses. For example, if you claimed deductions on your individual return, keep the receipts, canceled checks, check registers, and so on, at least four years. That's because a deduction taken on January 1, 1996, is not reported to the IRS until April 15, 1997 (at the earliest). The IRS then has at least three years to audit the return and assess more taxes. But people who trash their records at 12:01 A.M. on April 16 three years after they file their return take an unwise, needless tax risk. Many events, some totally unexpected, can extend the normal three-year period of limitations, and then you are stuck—unable to meet your burden of proof—if the IRS audits your return.

What are some of these events? It may sound strange, but, from time to time, strictly by accident, the IRS loses tax returns. The IRS sends a polite letter: "We don't have any record of your return." After picking yourself up off the floor, you write back, "What do you mean? I sent it in!" The IRS responds: "Prove it." Since you didn't send the return by certified mail, return receipt requested, you can't prove you filed it. But, you have a copy! It's even dated, and it bears your signature. "Not enough," says the IRS. "Re-sign and redate the copy, and send it in." So you send in a copy of the return you *did* file, signed and dated anew. The IRS audits that return and proposes more taxes. There you are, more than three years after you filed your original return—without records.

Another example: You trash your records at the three-year mark, confident to a moral certainty that the return is totally correct. But you forgot about some income you earned because you never got a Form 1099. That extra income was more than 25 percent of your gross income. The law says if you omitted 25 percent of your income, the IRS has six years, not three, to audit your return.

If the IRS accuses you of civil fraud, there's no statute of limitations on assessment at all! It may assess a new tax at any time.

2. *Your home.* Keep records on your home, such as purchase documents and improvement records, until four years after you sell it, or until you die, whichever comes first. Be able to prove what you paid for the home, purchase expenses, improvement costs, and any other adjustments to your cost basis.

Many people never really "sell" their home for tax purposes. If you're lucky, you'll buy two, three, or more homes during your lifetime, keeping the last one until death does you part. Each time you sell a home and roll over the paper profit (the "gain"), you report that transaction on your tax return even though you don't pay tax. Your heirs later inherit the home at its market value. In such a case, your earlier records won't be necessary, though some fix-up records could show a higher market value.

But many people stray off the roll-over track. Some sell their homes and pay tax on the gain. Others can't qualify for full deferral when they roll over the gain from one sale. Some taxpayers sell other real estate such as investment property. Still others go through a divorce and divide the marital properties, including the home. Here it's crucial to keep all records relating to your purchase, as well as records for any additional money you put in over time.

3. *Stocks, bonds, and other investments.* Keep records on these until you sell them, plus four years.

When you sell a stock, bond, other security, or real estate, you have to report the profit or loss on your next tax return. Profit or loss is the sales price minus the cost, so you need to know the cost of the property, known in the trade as "basis." You also need to report when you bought and sold the stock, the expenses of sale, and whether it is a capital asset. Let's say you bought one hundred shares of Consolidated Widgets, Inc., in 1970. You sell them in 1990. You report that sale on April 15, 1991, and pay tax on the profit. If the IRS ever questions what you paid for the stock, you'll need your twenty-year-old records to prove the basis. Then add four years to April 15, 1991, to get to April 15, 1995. That's a total of twenty-five years of record keeping. Still, records don't eat much, so storing them costs little.

If you own investment property such as real estate, keep records of capital improvements (big-ticket items or repairs that can't be deducted right away). These add to your basis, decreasing your profit and therefore your tax when you sell. They also serve as a record of your basis for depreciation.

4. *Business records.* The technical requirements for keeping records on travel and transportation expenses, entertainment, meals, gifts, and lodging are so extensive that they virtually defy description. Entire forests have been decimated to make the paper on which these requirements are printed. Despite the volume of rules, we're all required to follow them. How long to keep records? Again, the rule of thumb is four years at a minimum because the statute of limitations on business audits is generally three years after the return is filed. This rule applies whether you report your business profits on an individual return (Schedule C) or whether you are a shareholder in a small corporation and receive dividends from that corporation.

5. *Tax returns.* Keep your tax returns forever. True enough, their usefulness may diminish after four or more years, but you'd be surprised how many unanticipated needs you will have for old tax returns. And don't count on the IRS to find an old return for you. The agency keeps these returns for only about six years. To get a copy of your return, use Form 4506, Request for Copy or Transcript of Tax Form. There is a charge, but no charge for a copy of Form W-2.

If you have not kept your tax returns, it is worth the investment to get copies of all that are available. Then simply keep them in a file marked, "Tax Returns." This goes for all kinds of tax returns, including personal property, gift tax, and estate tax returns.

6. *Gifts.* Keep records of gifts you receive for as long as you hold the gift, plus four years. When you sell the gift, you many need to prove the giver's basis (or cost), as well as the market value and any gift tax the giver paid on it.

ORGANIZING YOUR RECORDS DURING THE YEAR

By far the biggest problem tax practitioners face when dealing with the IRS is the failure of clients to act like pack rats. If people would only save paper, they would save millions in taxes and professional fees. Life would be easier for the audited taxpayer, and, believe it or not, the IRS would also be happier, or more inclined to give you a break on your audit or collection problem. A few simple rules will help in most situations.

RULE 1: SAVE PAPER

Unfortunately, people throw away valuable documents every day. Receipts, checks, notices, bills, you name it. Billions of dollars of tax-saving evidence winds up in landfills or incinerators, much of it impossible to reconstruct. Even when you can reconstruct it, for example a bank statement from the bank's microfilm, it's expensive, time-consuming, and frustrating.

So, why not just keep the records you may need? It's easy, and you need not be the world's most organized person to keep your records in good enough shape so that preparing for tax season or an audit is a breeze.

Many people use the "shoebox" approach. They throw everything in a big pile and hope to sort it out at the end of the year. (Some people actually use a shoebox.) Actually, the shoebox approach is a good method if you don't end up with a room full of them at the end of the year. If you have that many records, you'll have to be more organized during the year.

You might try the "modified shoebox" approach. At the beginning of the year, take an envelope or file and mark it "Taxes 1997." Into that folder go all tax-related documents, *as you get them during the year.* That means you decide as you get a document whether to keep it and put it in the file. Use this test: "Is it possible that I might need this piece of paper at the end of the year for taxes?" For example, you'll need your check register; most people keep this with their checkbook. Medical records, real estate tax bills, records of charitable deductions, possibly bank statements, receipts for other deductions—all of these can go into your "modified shoebox."

As you write checks during the year, note on the check and the check register what the payment is for and whether it may be deductible. Use some type of memory aide, like an asterisk, a check mark, or "deduct" to remind you at the end of the year that the checks for doctor visits or the contribution to the church are deductible. Do the same even with the more obvious ones like mortgage, real estate taxes, state income taxes, and unreimbursed business expenses.

That's really all most of us need to do. Records won't be so voluminous or complex *during* the year that you will need to organize them any better than this. Then, at tax time, it's only a short step to separate your expenses to prepare your return.

RULE 2: BUSINESS AND PERSONAL—NEVER THE TWAIN SHALL MEET

Sole proprietors (unincorporated business) report their business income and expenses on Schedule C of their individual Form 1040. For proprietors, an absolute, hard-and-fast rule is never to mix business and personal expenses. Use two checking accounts: one business, one personal. When you need personal money during the year, write a check from the business account to the personal account. Cumbersome? Somewhat, but well worth the pain and suffering if the IRS ever questions your Schedule C deductions. Also, it saves monumental efforts when tax return preparation time comes around. You'll be certain all your business expenses are in fact business-related and deductible on Schedule C. Of course, keep *all* business records for at least the four years discussed above.

For corporations and partnerships, the "separation" rule is usually less of a problem because these entities have a separate legal existence, and therefore are required to maintain separate bank accounts and records.

RULE 3: THE COMPUTER IS YOUR FRIEND

Nowadays, superb software is available for people who computerize their personal and business lives. There are programs for calendars, scheduling, tax return preparation, organizing records, filing, you name it. These programs can be a good discipline tool. Any good one will feature "one entry" to generate a cash receipts and disbursements journal, general ledger, balance sheet, income statement, bank reconciliation, or other financial report. Probably the best advice for the '90s is to keep your business and personal finances on computer, not on paper done by hand. And back up your data onto a disk, storing the disk off-site.

Also, remember the computer adage, "Garbage in, garbage out." The data you enter should be complete and accurate for the computer to do any good. A printout that looks pretty is not necessarily accurate. Some people sit at a computer every day to log in their business or personal expenses, receipts, and checks. Others do it on a weekly or monthly basis. But if you have the discipline, by all means go ahead and use that computer. At the end of the year, a push of the button generates your financial history and tax life.

PREPARING FOR TAX SEASON

Now the year is over; it's January 2. You've recovered from New Year's parties (and you'll deduct the allowable expenses). The faster you file your return, the faster you'll get that tax refund.

Let's explore some easy steps on what to do if you don't use a computer. These guidelines apply whether you use a paid return preparer or prepare the return yourself.

What to do with the inch-thick pile of records you've been keeping all the past year? A good rule is: Use the "envelope" method. Start out with about twenty empty envelopes for your personal return and your business return (Schedule C). Use last year's return as a guide, checking to see you haven't missed any category. Mark the backs of these envelopes with your tax categories, taken from the lines and categories you will use on the return itself. For example, one envelope could be marked "W-2 Income." Another could be marked "Form 1099 Income." On the deduction side, mark envelopes such as "Medical," "Taxes," "Contributions," and so forth. Make sure no paper is an orphan.

What about your checks and check registers? Again, there are many ways to separate these expenses for tax purposes, and any method that works for you and is traceable will do. One method is to go through the check register and make a list of the check amounts for all deductible expenses. Then separate the items on that list into their respective "envelopes." Tally them on a tape, then transfer the totals to your return.

If you use a home computer, the software available today will quickly separate all of your deductible expenses. Tax return software practically does everything. All you do is enter the number and select an expense category.

The final rule is: Start early. Start on January 2 if you can. You'll have most of your tax records available even then because you've been filing them in the "modified shoebox" all year. You'll have to wait for your W-2, Form 1099, or Schedule K-1, but at least your other records will be in good shape and available.

A tax-related record-keeping guide can be another big help. Many excellent guides are available in bookstores and office supply stores, or are included in software programs. Some focus on personal records, others on financial records, yet others on tax records. Tax record guides will likely be more comprehensive than you need; they try to cover *everyone's* case. Don't be deterred. Instead, select the categories or organizational aids from those books that apply to you. You'll find that the same categories recur, year after year.

A word of hope: Keeping and organizing your tax records for a painless tax day does not involve much lifting. Once you get the hang of it, it's easy, though rarely fun. You'll find yourself designing variations of a record-keeping program, personal hints that make record keeping and reporting easy for you. Customizing is the key. And once your methods are in place, they'll keep you tax-comfortable year after year.

This chart suggests how long you might wish to retain tax-relevant records. There is no hard-and-fast rule. Opinions differ among practitioners, but you will generally find broad agreement on the following items.

1. *Keep these records forever:*

    - tax returns, federal and state

    - all home purchase and improvement records

    - records of gifts (cash or noncash) by and to you

    - deeds

    - birth certificates

    - financial statements and business accounting records such as general journals, general ledgers, balance sheets, and cash receipts and disbursement journals

2. *Keep for seven years:*

    - canceled checks

    - deductible expense records

    - receipts

    - contracts of employment and other contracts

    - other tax-related records such as forms 1099 and W-2 and credit card statements

3. *Retain until sold, plus four years:*

    - stock certificates

- brokerage statements reflecting sales of securities

- purchase and sale documents for any other large asset, such as a car

4. *Keep for four years:*

- all other tax-related documents

Chapter 29

DIVORCE AND SEPARATION

With half of all marriages ending in divorce and many divorcing couples owing back taxes, it's no wonder the IRS is the "third partner" in many divorces. In fact, divorce taxation is a field of study in itself. Divorce lawyers routinely work the tax issues in their cases, planning for them and taking advantage of the breaks the Internal Revenue Code gives to such couples.

People bargain over many tax-related items in a divorce: who gets the house, who gets the insurance and retirement accounts, how much alimony and child support are to be paid. The Internal Revenue Code has rules covering each of these issues. But while those helpful rules may smooth the way toward understanding the tax results of property transfers incident to divorce and separation, they have no effect whatsoever on what happens when taxes have to be collected.

For instance, special rules allow couples to fix alimony and child support so these items are deductible by one spouse and reportable as gross income by the other. The code also allows very liberal transfers of property, such as of homes or retirement accounts, without any current tax. These rules, however, do not bind the Collection Division when it goes out to collect delinquent taxes. Divorcing couples, and unfortunately sometimes their professional advisers, often overlook many tax traps in the often rocky road to a divorce or separation.

HOW THE PROBLEM ARISES

Every tax collection problem in a divorce tracks back to one basic fact: When you and your spouse sign a joint federal income tax return, you are each "jointly and severally liable" for the taxes on that return. By your signatures each of you agrees to pay the entire tax due. This means the IRS can collect the whole amount from either one, or some from one and some from the other. This is true even if one spouse earned no income and the other earned it all.

The other major principle that causes tax collection problems after a divorce or separation is this: The IRS is not bound by clauses in a divorce or separation agreement that allocate the tax liability between the divorcing spouses.

These two principles play themselves out in a number of very common situations.

1. We'll call the first one, "But he promised to pay." John and Jane's divorce decree makes John liable to pay the taxes on their past returns and any taxes that might become due if the IRS audits those returns. Two years after the divorce, the dreaded audit takes place. The result is a $10,000 bill. Jane waves the divorce decree in the IRS' face, but the agent scoffs. "You signed the joint return; you get to pay the extra tax." This agent would be entirely within his or her rights to demand payment from Jane (unless she is an "innocent spouse"— see chapter 19).

This scenario and its many permutations are common in the world of divorce and separation. You can beg and plead all you want, but the IRS still has the right to come after either spouse. To make matters worse, the more irresponsible spouse has probably moved to Moose Breath, Minnesota, leaving the wage-earning, responsible spouse exposed to the Collection Division. Sometimes, agents will have mercy and try to find the wandering spouse, but until the 1996 Taxpayer Bill of Rights, there was no such legal requirement. Now, agents must tell you of their efforts to collect from the other spouse if you ask.

2. The issue also can be built into property transfers. A major part of many divorces are property transfers of assets such as bank accounts, retirement accounts, insurance policies, and the big one, the "marital home." Generally, the tax laws allow these to be transferred tax-deferred, even if the profit in them has been building over time. That built-in profit makes these assets even more exposed to the Collection Division's outstretched hand. And if any has to be sold or if the IRS sells them, there is often a huge tax to be paid on top of everything else.

Example: John and Jane divorce. Jane receives the couple's one thousand shares of Megaplex Corporation, worth $50,000. The shares cost $10,000. There is no tax on the transfer of these shares to Jane. After the divorce, the IRS comes after Jane for taxes on the joint return, even though John had earned all the money. The IRS seizes the stock, sells it for $50,000, and goes away satisfied. Jane has not only lost her stock, but also, because of the IRS' forced sale, been made liable for the tax on $40,000 profit.

Sometimes a divorce gives the more exposed spouse other valuable assets the IRS may want to seize. An example would be if Jane got the house from John in the divorce. Since the divorce gave Jane sole title, the house is no longer protected by the joint ownership rules of most states. Such laws normally protect a home owned by a married couple from the clutches of creditors, including the IRS. So, in addition to having to pay John's taxes, Jane must do so with the equity in her only asset, the home.

NEGOTIATING WITH THE COLLECTION DIVISION AFTER A DIVORCE

If you are the "innocent" victim after a divorce, you can still take a number of steps to help your collection situation.

First, go to the source. Find your ex-spouse, demand that he or she live up to the divorce decree, and let the IRS know you have done that. In some cases, of course, this is easy to say but hard to do. Still, most states have laws allowing a spouse to haul the delinquent into court for contempt if he or she violates a divorce decree or property settlement agreement. A clause in Jane's divorce decree that requires John to pay back taxes won't bind the IRS, but it will bind *John* on pain of contempt of court if Jane enforces it. This contempt power is a potent weapon, and if you exercise it, often the IRS will hold off and allow some time to straighten things out with your ex-spouse.

If that does not work, all is not lost. Granted, you are in the position of trying to convince the Collection Division that you can't pay, or can't pay much, but here your divorce decree can still help. Sometimes the decree calls upon you to pay money to your ex-spouse, such as for maintenance, child support, or other "health and welfare" expenses. So, when you fill out the IRS' financial statement

(Form 433-A—see chapter 7), cite the divorce decree as authority that those hefty payments have collection priority over the claim of the IRS. If the payments are ordered by a court and are reasonable in amount, the IRS should allow them as "necessary living expenses" ahead of its claim. If so, the amount you have to pay to the IRS might well be reduced.

You also can try to negotiate an offer in compromise. Chapter 6 discusses this technique. The general idea is: With all your expenses and payments under the divorce decree, you will never be able to pay the full tax bill. So the IRS should take a reduced amount.

PROTECTING YOURSELF, ANTICIPATING PROBLEMS

Most of these problems can be avoided by some careful planning. When you review a divorce or separation agreement, it's wise to think in "what if" terms. What if the spouse who promises to pay the taxes does not? What if you no longer can find him or her? By asking these questions in advance and assuring yourself of reasonable answers, you go a long way toward protecting yourself, your family, and your assets from the "third partner" lurking outside the divorce court, the IRS.

Chapter 30

—∞∞∞—

TIME IS (NOT) ON YOUR SIDE—
STATUTES OF LIMITATION IN TAX MATTERS

Anyone who has ever missed a deadline—and that's most of us—knows you can lose valuable rights you would otherwise have exercised. That principle holds true ten times over in tax matters. Statutes of limitation in tax cases destroy millions of tax claims each year, on the taxpayer's side and the government's. In most cases, there is nothing you can do about a missed deadline. The law is that hard-and-fast. This chapter will guide you through the most common deadlines and their extenders, and give a few hints on how to avoid missing them.

DEADLINES WHEN THE IRS COMES AFTER YOU

The most common statutes of limitation the IRS must obey are those dealing with the assessment and collection of taxes.

When you file your return. Filing your federal income tax return triggers the well-known three-year rule. The IRS has three years to assess more taxes, whether by audit or other adjustment on its computer system. But audits often last beyond the three years. Some do not even start until two years into the limitations period. So the IRS often asks for extensions. Give careful thought to each one. The downside of refusing is that the IRS will simply stop its audit and immediately assess the tax or send you a Notice of Deficiency. That action will force you to go to tax court to prevent a proposed assessment from becoming a formal bill. The IRS sometimes, but rarely, misses these deadlines. So you are usually better off agreeing to the extension. In most cases, in reality you have no other good choice. But try to limit that extension, possibly to one tax year, or to certain issues the IRS has already examined. Try to avoid giving an open-ended extension. Read the extension language carefully. Ask the agent to explain its fine print.

If you file an amended tax return within sixty days before the three years runs out, the IRS legally gets more time to audit, an additional sixty days after receiving the amended return. For instance, if you file an amended return on the last day within the three-year period, the new deadline would be sixty-one days later.

The basic three-year rule on assessments is subject to many exceptions. Two are mentioned above: (1) you extend by agreement and (2) the IRS issues a formal Notice of Deficiency proposing more taxes. That Notice of Deficiency is not a bill; it is only a formal proposal. Issuing that notice suspends the period of limitations on assessment until ninety days runs or you file a petition within the ninety days and the tax court resolves your case. Some other exceptions to the three-year rule are as follows.

The six-year rule. The IRS has six years to assess a tax if you omitted 25 percent of gross income from a tax return. This rule protects the Service in these high-dollar cases. It also alerts the Service to be very thorough about other tax years in which you may have omitted income.

The "forever" rule. Some taxes are forever, that is, subject to no statute of limitations. Such is the case with civil tax fraud. Tax fraud consists of filing a false return with intent to evade the tax, or willfully attempting to evade the tax. (Criminal tax fraud must be prosecuted within six years from the date the crime was committed—usually the date the fraudulent return was signed.)

There is also no statute of limitations on assessment where you do not file a return at all.

Ten-year rule. After the assessment is made, the IRS collects it. Normally, the agency has ten years from the date of the assessment to collect the tax. The deadline used to be six years, but Congress extended that period to ten in 1989. Note the big difference between *assessment* and *collection.* Let's say the IRS assesses your tax on the deadline three years after you file your return. The collection period starts then and lasts ten years from that date. So you may be living with this IRS problem for thirteen years, or even longer if the period of limitations for assessment or collection is extended.

The ten-year collection statute can be extended. For instance, if you file an offer in compromise, the statute of limitations on collection is extended for the time the offer is pending, plus one year. So you may decide not to file an offer if you are already close to the deadline.

The ten-year collection statute is also suspended anytime you or your assets are in the custody of a court, plus six months. This concept includes bankruptcy or receivership. So filing for bankruptcy stops the tax collection period until the bankruptcy is over, plus six months. That's the trade-off the law exacts for keeping the IRS at bay under the bankruptcy laws.

You also extend the collection period when you file an emergency Application for a Taxpayer Assistance Order (Form 911). (See chapter 13.) The extension is the price you pay for quick intervention to avoid a harsh collection result.

If you stay outside the United States for a continuous period of six months, that action also suspends the collection period. It starts running again when you return to the United States.

Many times taxpayers extend the collection period by written agreement, called a waiver (Form 900). The Service requires this waiver for many installment agreements that would otherwise last past the ten-year deadline.

Finally, the government can also take legal action to extend the ten-year period by suing you in federal district court to reduce the tax assessment to a judgment (chapter 23). If the government wins, the tax lien is extended for more years, depending on your state's law governing such judgments.

DEADLINES WHEN YOU WANT MONEY FROM THE IRS

Now change hats. You are seeking money from the IRS, either through a refund, a credit, or a lawsuit.

Claims for credit or refund. You must file a refund or credit claim within three years from the date you file your return, or two years from the date you pay, whichever is later. If the government owes you a refund on your original return, no need to worry. The return is the claim for refund. But if you file an amended return later, claiming a refund, you must do so within three years. For this purpose, returns filed early (before April 15) are considered filed on the due date. Late returns are considered filed on the date you mail the return.

Now, let's say you pay a tax three years after you file your return, but you really do not owe it. Can you get it back? Yes. You have another two years from the date of payment to file a claim for refund.

Suits against the government. People sue the government over taxes all the time. For example, about twenty thousand people file tax court petitions each year. Thousands of others file suits in federal district court or in the United States Court of Federal Claims. Certain deadlines apply, or else your suit will be thrown out of court.

Tax court. You must file suit in the United States Tax Court to contest the IRS' formal Notice of Deficiency within ninety days from the date stamped on the notice. That's not three months; it's ninety days, counting from the day after the date on the notice. Sometimes people get the notice well into the ninety-day period; some receive it *after* the ninety days have run. Some people never get the notice even though it was mailed. In these disasters, the issue is always whether the IRS mailed the notice to your "last known address." If so, you're out of luck if you file your tax court case too late.

Federal district court. People also sue the government in the federal district courts. The deadlines there depend on what kind of suit you file. The shortest is for a suit to contest a jeopardy assessment. That deadline is thirty days after the IRS sends you the notice of jeopardy determination. Chapters 8 and 22 discuss this issue.

The next deadline is nine months. This deadline applies when the IRS has levied or seized property that really belongs to a nondelinquent taxpayer with a claim superior to that of the IRS. For example, if the IRS seizes a car and you have a first lien on it, it has "wrongfully levied" the car. But you have only nine months to sue, sometimes extendable to twelve.

The next deadline is two years. This deadline applies to suits for refund of taxes. Thousands of these suits are filed every year. They must be filed within two years of the date the IRS disallows your claim for refund.

OTHER DEADLINES

Other deadlines pervade the tax laws. Some are formal, others informal. Many are obscure and relate to very few taxpayers. But the common thread is that all are strictly construed, either against the government or against the taxpayer. Sometimes, the law allows exceptions from these harsh deadlines, but not often and only in narrow cases.

Chapter 31

——— ∞∞∞ ———

DO I NEED A TAX LAWYER (OR OTHER TAX PROFESSIONAL)?

There's an old expression, "One who acts as his own lawyer has a fool for a client." This motto holds doubly true in tax matters. The tax laws, regulations, and the IRS' internal procedures abound with detail after thorny detail and deadline after hidden deadline. But every day, taxpayers who try to "go it alone" miss these deadlines, requirements, and rules. As a result, they undercut or sabotage their own cases. They may not realize they are committing legal suicide. Even when they do, it's often too late for a tax professional to step in and rescue the situation. You don't always need a tax professional; many taxpayers in fact handle their own matters successfully. But your chances of getting the best result are greatly increased if you either know what you're doing or you hire someone who does.

DO YOU NEED A TAX PROFESSIONAL AT ALL?

Criminal investigations. In some types of IRS matters, the answer is unmistakably, unequivocally "yes." The best example is the criminal investigation. The moment you find out you are the subject of a criminal investigation, STOP! Call a tax lawyer. Although this seems like common sense, the IRS counts on taxpayers *not* to do this. When its criminal investigators, the special agents, come knocking at your door, the only thing they have in mind is to interview you or, sometimes, to seize your records under a search warrant. They already believe you have committed a tax crime; they now want you to confess the essential facts under questioning. Consenting is equivalent to signing your own guilty plea. Feeling intimidated, many taxpayers consent to these interviews, often spending two to ten hours with a special agent cataloging their crimes (though often they don't think of it as a confession). After such an interview, a lawyer's role may be reduced to arguing about how much jail time you should get, not whether you should go to jail at all.

You have an absolute right to seek legal advice when the special agents come calling, or any other agents for that matter. They understand this right and will not press the point if you insist on getting legal advice. No one can imprison you for seeking legal advice; but the IRS can and will prosecute after you consent to an interview in which you "make their day."

You may not always know when a criminal investigation is under way. The first sign might be special agents who come knocking at the door. They identify themselves as "special agents of the Criminal Investigation Division" of the Internal Revenue Service, often flashing a gold badge like Sergeant Joe Friday on *Dragnet*. Then they ask to interview you and inspect your records. Well before they show up at the door, they've done plenty of homework. You may get wind of that investigation by the trail that homework leaves. For instance, they may telephone third-party witnesses, who then call you. They sometimes send canvassing letters to your customers or friends, who notify you. Or they may send out IRS summonses to banks, of which you will get notice.

In any case, no matter how busy you are, *stop* what you are doing and immediately call a lawyer. Not just any lawyer, but a criminal defense attorney experienced in defending IRS investigations.

Bankruptcy. Filing for bankruptcy should be done with the assistance of an attorney, preferably one knowledgeable about the tax aspects of bankruptcy. Many attorneys are well versed in the bankruptcy laws and the practices of their local bankruptcy courts, but often they lack expertise in tax matters, including bankruptcy tax matters. Since that's the reason you're going to them—to get relief from or manage your tax problem—you need a bankruptcy lawyer who is familiar with the many rules governing how taxes are treated in bankruptcy. Chapter 12 reviews some of these rules.

Civil suits. If the government sues you or you want to sue the government, consult a lawyer experienced in tax litigation. This would be true whether you are contesting a statutory Notice of Deficiency in the United States Tax Court (see chapter 21) or your case proceeds in a federal district court (see chapters 22 and 23). It's not absolutely essential that this lawyer be versed in tax matters and procedures, but it certainly helps. Many fine litigators feel uncomfortable handling tax cases. Besides, if you make the right phone calls, you can usually find a tax litigator. The Department of Justice and the Internal Revenue Service graduate dozens of such litigators each year into private practice.

OTHER CIVIL MATTERS

Aside from these cases, it's not always obvious that you need a tax professional, or even what *type* of tax professional. To decide, consider some of the following tax-related tasks and questions.

Tax professionals are asked to provide a multitude of services. Among these are the following:

1. *Prepare tax return.* Clearly, this is the most common service accountants, enrolled agents, and some tax lawyers offer. In fact, you need no college degree, nor do you have to pass any test, to be a paid return preparer. The only requirements are that you prepare the return and be paid for it. Millions of people prepare their own returns each year; other millions rely on paid preparers. If you are a procrastinator (and who isn't, from time to time?), you're unsure of your work, or you just don't have the time, find a qualified, well-trained tax preparer.

2. *Tax advice on a pending transaction.* Thinking about selling a business? Selling a house and reinvesting the proceeds? Collecting disability payments or damages from lawsuits? The tax impact of these and hundreds of other questions may not be completely clear. You may need competent professional advice about their tax implications.

3. *Getting information from the IRS.* You may need a copy of your tax return from a past year. Or, you may need a transcript of your account. A tax professional can help you cut through the red tape.

4. *Other disputes.* You may get into a fight with the IRS over someone else's taxes. It could be about an employee, a customer, or client. Priority contests between the IRS and builders, merchants, and financiers are extremely common. A professional's help is often critical in such a case.

5. *IRS audit.* Do you need a tax professional to help you survive an audit? The answer depends on the type of audit, the amount involved, and other factors. Consider engaging a tax professional for a full-scale field audit or a Taxpayer

Compliance Measurement Program audit, as contrasted with a simple correspondence or office audit that you might handle by yourself. If you have been cheating on your taxes, this would be an excellent time to consult an experienced criminal tax attorney.

6. *Error on past return.* You made a mistake on a prior return, such as overstating a deduction or failing to report income. How should you handle this? Should you do nothing? Amend your returns?

The list of issues and questions where a tax professional's help may come in handy could go on and on. These are only some of the most common.

Should you then handle the matter yourself? To decide, consider a few more questions.

How comfortable do you feel handling this matter by yourself? The range of answers varies from "completely at ease" to "scared to death." Even if you think you know what you are doing, arcane rules can trip you. Some are so obscure few people know they exist. So it's wise to check in with an expert, even if only to verify your own judgment as to whether you can handle the matter. People who are nervous about their own tax matter, whether out of fear of the IRS or uncertainty about their own knowledge of the tax laws, often exercise clouded judgment, a fatal error in the tax business.

Is your regular tax representative qualified to handle your matter? If you have an accountant, enrolled agent, or tax attorney already on board, is she qualified and comfortable with representing you on this matter? Not all tax professionals can handle every type of tax case. Lawyers may feel uncomfortable preparing returns. Accountants may decline to handle a complex audit where evidence is hard to assemble. You will usually know your representative's comfort level from the start, and if not, it's certainly fair to ask. Tax professionals have an informal referral network, so if yours does not feel up to handling the matter for whatever reason, she usually has people to call for help. Sometimes the help may be a simple "Let me run this one by you." Other times the professional may recommend transferring your case. But you, the client, should never hesitate to pick up the phone and call your own tax professional to ask if she can handle your particular case.

WHO ARE THE TAX PROFESSIONALS?

There are five main types of tax professionals and, beyond these, others who can represent you before the Internal Revenue Service under some circumstances.

1. *Tax attorneys.* These are lawyers who have made tax their specialty.

Almost all are graduates of law schools, and all have taken and passed the bar exam of at least one state. (Some states allow people to sit for the bar exam and obtain a law license even without having gone to law school.) The law license alone entitles them to practice before the Internal Revenue Service in tax matters. Many tax attorneys are former IRS or Justice Department Tax Division attorneys.

2. *Certified public accountants.* CPAs have studied accounting in school, and have taken and passed a rigorous certified public accountant examination that each state society of CPAs administers. Certified public accountants are trained in all aspects of financial and tax accounting, as well as in tax return preparation. They often represent their clients before the Internal Revenue Service.

3. *Noncertified accountants.* Like certified public accountants, noncertified accountants have long and rigorous training in all aspects of accounting and tax return preparation. For one reason or another, they have chosen not to take all parts of the certification examination. In some cases, they have taken the examination, but have not passed all parts, and therefore cannot hold themselves out as CPAs.

4. *Enrolled agents.* Enrolled agents have taken and passed a tough IRS examination on all aspects of tax law and tax administration, thereby qualifying them to practice before the Internal Revenue Service. You don't have to be a lawyer or an accountant to take the enrolled agent's examination, though many enrolled agents in fact have an accounting or legal background or degree.

5. *Enrolled actuaries.* Like enrolled agents, enrolled actuaries have taken and passed an IRS examination. Their field of expertise is limited to actuarial matters. This generally includes the mathematical computations underlying retirement plans, pension plans, and deferred compensation plans. It also encompasses estates and trusts and other topics where sophisticated mathematics (actuarial calculations) must be made and defended.

Most tax professionals, whatever their expertise, will be called upon to perform one or more of the following tasks.

- *Tax audits and tax collection.* The professional will need to meet with you or at least confer by phone, analyze your case, and perform any necessary legal research. She will need to gather the facts and advise you of your rights under the law, IRS regulations, the Internal Revenue manual, and the vast array of unwritten IRS procedures that permeate the tax audit and collection culture. Sometimes she will need to call a revenue agent or revenue officer one or more times, write to him to state your position in the audit, or defend you against collection actions. She will need to document your position legally and factually.

- *Protest.* The tax professional who files a "protest" (see chapter 17) needs to meet with you, analyze the facts and the law, develop any more facts required to prove your case, and file a formal document known as a protest. He will need to follow this protest with more research, fact gathering, and finally a meeting with an appeals officer at which he will argue your case. Then, he may need to follow this meeting with more work. Finally, he will counsel you on whether to accept a proposed settlement or litigate the matter.

- *Litigation.* A tax litigator is usually (but not always) engaged when all else fails and a case must be tried in court. A tax litigator has many tasks, the most important being meeting with you, the client, and your CPA or other tax professional; interviewing you and gathering facts; performing legal research; interviewing witnesses; and preparing for trial. The tax litigator will have to respond to the IRS' requests for pretrial discovery, including depositions, and prepare to try the case. She will also need to discuss settlement with you and the IRS and, depending upon the outcome of the case, file or defend an appeal.

FINDING A TAX PROFESSIONAL

The best way to locate a competent tax professional is by recommendation. Ask around. If you have a regular family or business lawyer, ask her. Inquire of the accountant or an enrolled agent who regularly does your work whether he feels comfortable representing you, or whether you need representation in the first place. If he is not comfortable, maybe he can suggest someone to call. Sometimes it takes two, three, or more calls before you find the right person to handle your case. Ask other lawyers whom they would consult for a tax problem, including their own.

Some tax professionals advertise. They place these advertisements in accounting journals, in legal periodicals, sometimes in the newspaper, in the yellow pages, and sometimes over the airwaves.

Some tax representatives will even seek you out. They do this by checking the public records, such as at county courthouses, for filed notices of federal tax lien or IRS or state court judgments for taxes. Then they send advertisements or canvassing letters suggesting that you might need their services.

Bar associations also maintain lawyer referral services and lists. Some tax groups also maintain lists of recommended professionals.

Regardless of how you come upon a tax professional, the critical issue is whether she can handle the matter at a cost that you can bear. Moreover, in most cases, your tax representative cannot guarantee the outcome. After all, you are dealing with the IRS or a court, which have wide discretion whether to grant you relief.

CHOOSING AN ETHICAL PROFESSIONAL

All tax professionals are subject to a strict code of ethics and practice. The formal name is *Circular 230,* which the IRS publishes. Among other things, this code requires tax professionals to be truthful with the IRS, not to misrepresent the facts, and to be prompt in meeting deadlines. *Circular 230* also requires practitioners to submit records or information to the IRS promptly upon request and not to interfere or attempt to interfere with the IRS' efforts to gather information. Practitioners must also exercise "due diligence" in preparing papers for the IRS and in ensuring that whatever they say or write to the IRS is correct. Finally, practitioners must not engage in any "incompetent or disreputable" conduct. And, of course, lawyers, accountants, enrolled agents, and all others must avoid conflicts of interest among their clients.

Lawyers, accountants, and enrolled agents are also subject to other codes of ethics, including those of state bar associations, ethical codes of state CPA societies, and their own, hopefully well developed, sense of right and wrong.

None of these codes of ethics requires tax professionals to take positions that are against your interest. In fact, most specifically require the tax professional to represent your interests zealously, but within the bounds of the law.

The IRS, state bar associations, and state CPA societies receive many ethical complaints every year. Most are not well founded, but some are pursued to the ultimate conclusion of sanctions such as fines or suspensions from practice. Always be alert to any unethical practice that a tax professional may suggest. Never hesitate to ask, "Is what you're suggesting within the bounds of your ethical codes?" If you get an equivocal answer, it's time to look elsewhere.

CHOOSING A TAX PROFESSIONAL

Your search proceeds in stages. First, once you have someone in mind, give her a call. Explain your problem in as much detail as you can, and answer any questions the tax professional may ask. For instance, you may tell her you own and operate Joe's Bar and Grill, which is delinquent in paying six quarters of payroll taxes. The IRS is knocking at the door, asking questions, threatening seizure. Or, you may be under IRS audit and be completely lost as to what the issues are and how you should handle the audit.

At the very least, ask the following questions, either by phone or when you first meet the representative.

1. *Do you need more facts to understand exactly what my problem is?* A good tax professional will spot all the issues, check deadlines and statutes of limitation, ask a dozen other questions you hadn't thought to ask, and spot dangers of which you may be only vaguely aware. For example, suppose you own Joe's Bar and Grill and you have been paying the IRS on a monthly installment agreement for close to two years. You may not realize that you could be eligible for abatement of some of the penalties, but the statute of limitations on claiming a refund of those penalties may expire after two years.

Another example: You operate Alice's Restaurant. You receive an IRS levy for wages payable to John, your employee. So far, John has begged you not to pay, and you've gone along with this. The IRS has sent you a "final demand." The tax professional should realize and advise you that you can be liable for not only paying John's wages to the IRS, but also a 50 percent penalty. Remember: There can be a big difference between answering your specific tax question and solving your overall tax problem. Hire the professional who will solve your problem.

2. *The tax professional must know much more than taxes.* The best tax professionals know the Internal Revenue Code as a bare minimum requirement. They are also knowledgeable in commercial transactions, financing, loans, real estate, and bankruptcy, among other legal areas. The IRS' rights and yours often implicate these areas of the law. For instance, your tax professional can't suggest you file for bankruptcy unless she knows whether bankruptcy will discharge the taxes or enable you to propose a viable plan of reorganization.

3. *Experience.* No tax professional should take offense if you ask about his experience. For example, does he only represent people in court? Handle only audits? Collection matters? How long has the professional been in practice? Ask what percentage of the professional's time is devoted to dealing with the

IRS. Find out whether he knows the agents in the local office, and how long he's been dealing with them. Don't be afraid to ask whether he enjoys a good reputation with them. You can be sure that every professional who has one or two cases in the local IRS office has some reputation. You need to know whether it's good or bad.

4. *Ask the basic game plan the professional has in mind for your situation.* Be prepared with the facts when you interview the professional. Above all, gather the paperwork—yours and the IRS'. The professional will be able to save hours simply by reviewing the papers. This would include all IRS notices. With some exceptions, a thorough tax professional usually can explore your goals and how she plans to achieve them even if there are detours along the way. For instance, if you come in with a tax audit problem, you are entitled to be advised of the possible outcomes at each stage: the revenue agent's level, an appeal within the IRS, and possibly tax court. If you come in owing $100,000 in taxes, the professional may guide you on what you can expect at each stage, and what the best and worst outcomes might be. All possible outcomes may not be knowable at the first meeting. Inevitably, legal and factual questions arise that must be filled in, but the *goals* can usually be spelled out. In short, at the end of this meeting, expect to know at least generally where you are going and how you are to get there. In many cases you may come out with a realistic, step-by-step game plan, including the strengths and weaknesses of your matter.

5. *Ask yourself whether you have understood what the professional is talking about, in general and in many of the details.* If not, question whether that professional is the right one for you. The tax law can be frighteningly complex, but it's not Sanskrit. A good tax professional can explain it to anyone. Albert Einstein once explained the theory of relativity to nonscientists in a short book entitled *Relativity.* A tax professional should be able to explain your IRS rights and options.

Above all, the tax professional will become your legal confidant and your moral confessor. You need to enjoy complete comfort with the relationship.

THE COST

Most tax professionals charge by the hour; some charge a contingency fee; some a combination. (Criminal cases cannot ethically be charged on a contingent fee basis.) While hourly rates are important, it's actually more important to know how much the engagement as a whole will cost, from start to finish, and at each stage. Ask yourself whether you are getting value for your money. Is the expected recovery worth the cost? Remember that tax professionals usually cannot guarantee the outcome of an IRS fight, so you may be faced with spending a certain amount of money without the absolute assurance of a good result.

Among types of tax professionals, fees vary widely. Lawyers can charge between $50 and $500 per hour, depending upon their experience, their firm's practices, their location, and other factors. A lawyer who charges a high hourly rate is not necessarily "too expensive." Maybe that lawyer can accomplish in two hours what another, lower-priced lawyer could not accomplish in ten. So, try not to go into sticker shock at a lawyer's hourly rate. The cost for the overall engagement may be modest compared with the quality of the result.

Accountants and enrolled agents often charge lower hourly rates than do attorneys, but, again, the range can vary considerably. There's no hard-and-fast rule, but accountants and enrolled agents' fees often are between $50 and $200 per hour, sometimes higher.

These fee structures may sound high, but even if you are going to handle the matter yourself, you may need just a little guidance or hand-holding, not very expensive even at high hourly rates. It's all a cost-benefit analysis: What are you spending and what can you expect to get in return? With these principles as your guide, choosing a tax professional with satisfying results becomes easier.

Above all, don't delay. The absolute worst course is to stick your head in the sand. Fighting the IRS properly takes time. Moreover, you will surely pass a number of deadlines, whether known to you or not, if you delay.

RELATING TO THE PROFESSIONAL

An incredible amount of trust is taken for granted whenever you hire a tax professional to help with an IRS problem. Often it's a person whom you don't know, or perhaps whom you have just met. Sometimes the professional comes recommended by someone you trust; other times not. You are about to hand this person both money and a good deal of responsibility for your financial life. Always remember that the trust factor is there for your benefit. In some ways the tax professional involved in a difficult collection or audit matter is like a father confessor. You can and should tell that person anything and everything that might conceivably bear on your tax problem; let the professional sort out what is relevant and what is not. The professional needs to know you, your personality, your tolerance for controversy and difficulty, and many other things before he or she can guide you successfully through the IRS maze. Relate to him or her as a human being as well. After all, they've heard many stories. You may think yours is unique, and perhaps it is. But you may be assured that your lawyer, accountant, or enrolled agent has heard similar ones. The professional you hire is and should be a friend as well as an adviser. Viewing them in this way can almost always be to your benefit. You'll give them more of yourself and get more in return by way of a good result.

Chapter 32

—⊗⊗⊗—

CONCLUSION: IS THERE A "NEW" IRS?

For the last five years, the IRS has advertised a new way of doing business. To the agency, or at least to its headquarters in Washington, D.C., the "revolution" is as sweeping as any in its history. It represents a change in attitude, style, and method that will affect every one of us. Some of these ways live up to their promise. As to others, there is more promise than results.

THE "OLD" IRS

A measure of respect or a stab of fear always follows the IRS. This is the agency that sent Al Capone to jail when no one else could. This is the agency that seizes your salary, puts a lien on your home, disallows your deductions. But it is also the agency that loses paper, mishandles your return, makes you wait years for refunds, and gives you bad tax advice.

In the past, the IRS made only modest efforts to correct its "tough guy" image. The IRS was an *enforcement* agency; it wanted us to know that.

Things began to change about five years ago. The tax system started to break down. The IRS was being crushed under mountains of paper. It was losing returns, misfiling documents, mistreating taxpayers. Horror stories began to surface. Congress held the usual hearings and the media publicized the worst stories. Moreover, the agency had to admit that some of those stories were true.

WHAT HAS CHANGED?

The "new" IRS wants us to see it as a business, not a bully. Some of its new "businesslike" ways will translate into real dollars, true savings, and refreshing changes in the way we deal with the agency every day. But other changes will make life harsher for some people.

THE ELECTRONIC AGE

The first part of the agency's change is to join (or catch up with) the electronic age. The IRS has embarked on a ten-year program to modernize the entire tax system. Some parts of the program are already in place and functioning, and are a welcome change. For example, millions can now file their returns electronically, resulting in quicker refunds. When you move around the country, the IRS has more and better information, more quickly available "on line" in your new location. Correspondence with the agency is getting easier, though it still has a long way to go.

Another good side of the electronic revolution is that our paperwork burden will abate. From electronic filing, to "one-stop reporting" of wages and wage information, to cutting down on letter-writing blizzards between taxpayers and the agency in favor of telephone calls—all of this will eventually make a big difference, though it has only just begun.

But the electronic age in taxes also means that Uncle Sam will watch you more accurately and closely. The government will know where you live and when you move, so hiding will be more difficult. The IRS is always exchanging information about your taxes with state governments and is becoming more efficient all the time. So even if the agency can't track you, your new state of residence can, and it will send electrons to the IRS telling where you are.

For nonfilers, that is, people who have dropped out of the tax system, the chances have gone way up that the IRS will now find you and get you back on to the system. For the rest who do file, audits will become more scientific. Using sophisticated computer programs, the agency will eventually "know" whether your business is likely to produce more taxes—and then go after those taxes. Its computers will "sense" where the dollars are and where the cash is hidden.

COME IN FROM THE COLD

The second big change is in the way the IRS collects taxes. The welcome mat is now out for the millions who owe money to the IRS. Four years ago, the agency decided to write off its uncollectible accounts and get what it could from the rest. To settle over $100 billion of accounts receivable, the IRS liberalized the offer in compromise program, under which the IRS will settle for less than the full amount owed. And, true to promise, the IRS now accepts about half of all offers made, up from less than 20 percent only four years ago.

But watch out for the teeth behind the sweet talk. If you ducked the system for years and have now been persuaded that the IRS will be a "nice guy" about your old taxes, be careful. Once you are back on the system, they know where you are, and if your offer is not accepted, you're now a new customer.

There is also real change for people who can't qualify for an offer but have to pay all they owe. The liberalized installment agreement program means that about 97 percent of delinquent taxpayers will qualify to pay over time. Again, this is both carrot and stick. Most people default their agreements to pay taxes over time. Then it is back to square one—full collection by force.

Finally, the IRS wants to entice five million to ten million tax system dropouts to come in from the cold. These are people who have not filed federal income tax returns in one or more years. Sometimes the default can be six years, ten years, or longer. To get these people back into the system, the IRS promises some leniency if they come in voluntarily. Those who do, however, can look forward to dealing with local IRS tax collectors if they owe money on those returns—and most do.

All in all, the new IRS will be more efficient, with all that "efficiency" implies. Efficiency may mean more prosecutions, sharper audits, and better collections. But everyday tax life may become somewhat simpler. Efficiency will ease many everyday burdens, reduce paperwork, speed refunds, and result in fewer errors.

APPENDIX I

———⚬⚬⚬———

PUBLICATIONS AND FORMS USEFUL
IN IRS AUDIT AND COLLECTION MATTERS

PUBLICATIONS

FORMS

668-B	Levy
668-C	Final Demand
668-D	Release of Levy/Release of Property from Levy
668-W(c)(DO)	Notice of Levy on Wages, Salary, and Other Income
668(Y)	Notice of Federal Tax Lien Under Internal Revenue Laws
669-A	Certificate of Discharge of Property from Federal Tax Lien (Sec. 6325(b)(1))
669-B	Certificate of Discharge of Property from Federal Tax Lien (Sec. 6325(b)(2)(A))
669-C	Certificate of Discharge of Property from Federal Tax Lien (Sec. 6325(b)(2)(B))
669-D	Certificate of Subordination of Federal Tax Lien (Sec. 6325(d)(1))
669-E	Certificate of Subordination of Federal Tax Lien (Sec. 6325(d)(2))
669-F	Certificate of Subordination of Federal Estate Tax Lien (Sec. 6325(d)(3))
792	United States Certificate Discharging Property Subject to Estate Tax Lien
843	Claim for Refund and Request for Abatement
866	Agreement as to Final Determination of Tax Liability
870	Waiver of Restrictions on Assessment and Collection of Deficiency in Tax and Acceptance of Overassessment
870-AD	Offer to Waive Restrictions on Assessment and Collection of Tax Deficiency to Accept Overassessment
870-E	Waiver of Restrictions on Assessment and Collection of Deficiency and Acceptance of Overassessment
872	Consent to Extend the Time to Assess Tax
872-A	Special Consent to Extend the Time to Assess Tax
872-A(C)	Special Consent to Extend the Time to Assess Tax
900	Tax Collection Waiver
906	Closing Agreement on Final Determination Covering Specific Matters
907	Agreement to Extend the Time to Bring Suit
911	Application for Taxpayer Assistance Order (ATAO) to Relieve Hardship
921	Consent to Extend the Time to Assess Income Tax
945	Annual Return of Withheld Federal Income Tax
945-A	Annual Record of Federal Tax Liability
952	Consent to Extend Period of Limitation on Assessment of Income Taxes

1117	Income Tax Surety Bond
1127	Application for Extension of Time for Payment of Tax
1128	Application to Adopt, Change, or Retain a Tax Year
1902-B	Report of Individual Income Tax Examination Changes
2039	Summons
2045	Transferee Agreement
2063	U.S. Departing Alien Income Tax Statement
2222	Sealed Bid for Purchase of Seized Property
2261	Collateral Agreement
2261-A	Collateral Agreement
2261-B	Collateral Agreement
2261-C	Collateral Agreement
2270	Demand to Exhibit Books and Records
2297	Waiver of Statutory Notification of Claim Disallowance
2433	Notice of Seizure
2434-A	Notice of Sealed Bid Sale
2435	Certificate of Sale of Seized Property
2436	Seized Property Sale Report
2504	Agreement to Assessment and Collection of Additional Tax and Acceptance of Overassessment (Excise or Employment Tax)
2688	Application for Additional Extension of Time to File U.S. Individual Income Tax Return
2725	Document Receipt
2750	Waiver Extending Statutory Period for Assessment of Trust Fund Recovery Penalty
2751	Proposed Assessment of Trust Fund Recovery Penalty
2751-AD	Trust Fund Recovery Penalty—Offer of Agreement to Assessment and Collection
2769	Computation of Deposit Penalty
2797	Referral Report for Potential Fraud Cases
2848	Power of Attorney and Declaration of Representative
3040	Authorization to Apply Offer in Compromise Deposit to Liability
3242	Request for Information from Employer
3363	Acceptance of Proposed Disallowance of Claim for Refund or Credit
3439	Statement of Annual Income (Individual)
3439-A	Statement of Annual Income (Corporation)
3610	Audit Statement

3623	Statement of Account
3911	Taxpayer Statement Regarding Refund
3913	Request for Refund Check Cancellation
4089	Notice of Deficiency-Waiver
4089-A	Notice of Deficiency Statement
4180	Report of Interview with Individual Relative to Trust Fund Recovery Penalty or Personal Liability for Excise Tax
4183	Recommendation re Trust Fund Recovery Penalty Assessment
4219	Statement of Liability of Lender, Surety, or Other Person for Withholding Taxes
4417-A	Request for Federal Tax Deposit Coupon Books
4419	Application for Filing Information Returns Magnetically/Electronically
4422	Application for Certificate Discharging Property Subject to Estate Tax Lien
4490	Proof of Claim for Internal Revenue Taxes
4491-A	Proof of Claim for Internal Revenue Taxes (Bankruptcy Act Proceedings—Administrative Claims)
4506	Request for Copy or Transcript of Tax Form
4549-E	Income Tax Discrepancy Adjustments
4571	Explanation for Filing Return Late or Paying Tax Late
4585	Minimum Bid Worksheet
4669	Statement of Payments Received
4670	Request for Relief from Payment of Income Tax Withholding
4700	Examination Workpapers
4789	Currency Transaction Report
4789-T	Currency Transaction Report
4822	Statement of Annual Estimated Personal and Family Expenses
4862	Statement of Income Tax Changes
4868	Application for Automatic Extension of Time to File U.S. Individual Income Tax Return
5318	Penalties for Failure to File Tax Return and Pay Tax
5495	Request for Discharge from Personal Liability Under Internal Revenue Code Section 6905
6014	Authorization—Access to Third Party Records for Internal Revenue Service Employees
6018	Consent to Proposed Adverse Action
6112	Prior Years' Tax Forms Order
6166	Certification of Filing a Tax Return

APPENDIX II

———— ✺✺✺ ————

TELEPHONE NUMBERS AND ADDRESSES OF IRS PROBLEM RESOLUTION OFFICES, AND OTHER USEFUL NUMBERS

Nationwide General IRS Number 1-800-829-1040

PRO Sites
(Source: Pub. 1320 (Rev. 11-94))

SERVICE CENTER PROBLEM RESOLUTION OFFICES

Correspondence and facsimile transmissions should be addressed to:

Problem Resolution Office
Internal Revenue Service

with the appropriate address from the following list. Street addresses are provided if you wish to send correspondence by courier. FAX numbers are also listed if you prefer to send information by facsimile transmission.

Andover Service Center
310 Lowell Street (Stop 120)
Andover, MA 05501
FAX: (508) 474-5640

Atlanta Service Center
P.O. Box 48-549 (Stop 29A)
Doraville, GA 30362
or
4800 Buford Highway (Stop 29-A)
Chamblee, GA 30341
FAX: (404) 455-2527

Austin Compliance Center
P.O. Box 2986 (Stop 1005 AUCC)
Austin, TX 78768
FAX: (512) 460-1930

Austin Service Center
P.O. Box 934 (Stop 1005 AUSC)
Austin, TX 78767
or
3651 S. Interregional Hwy.
(Stop 1005 AUSC)
Austin, TX 78741
FAX: (512) 462-7961

Brookhaven Service Center
P.O. Box 960 (Stop 102)
Holtsville, NY 11742
or
1040 Waverly Avenue (Stop 102)
Holtsville, NY 11742
FAX: (516) 447-4879

Cincinnati Service Center
P.O. Box 12267 (Stop 11)
Covington, KY 41019
or
201 West Second Street (Stop 11)
Covington, KY 41019
FAX: (606) 292-5405

Fresno Service Center
P.O. Box 12161
Fresno, CA 93776
or
5045 East Butler Avenue
Fresno, CA 93888
FAX: (209) 456-5272

Kansas City Service Center
P.O. Box 24551 (Stop 2)
Kansas City, MO 64131
or
7720 W. 119 Street.
Annex 5, (Stop 2)
Overland Park, KS 66213
FAX: (913) 344-7986

Memphis Service Center
P.O. Box 30309 AMF (Stop 77)
Memphis, TN 38130
or
3131 Democrat Road (Stop 77)
Memphis, TN 38101
FAX: (901) 365-5025

Ogden Service Center
P.O. Box 9941 (Stop 1005 OSC)
Ogden, UT 84409
or
1160 W. 1200 South Street (Stop 1005
OSC)
Ogden, UT 84201
FAX: (801) 620-6319

Philadelphia Service Center
P.O. Box 16053, DP 111
Philadelphia, PA 19114
or
11601 Roosevelt Blvd., DP 111
Philadelphia, PA 19154
FAX: (215) 516-2677

DISTRICT PROBLEM RESOLUTION OFFICES

Correspondence and facsimile transmissions should be addressed to:

Problem Resolution Office
Internal Revenue Service

with the appropriate address from the following list.

ALABAMA
500 22nd Street South (Stop 316)
Birmingham, AL 35233
(205) 731-1177
FAX: (205) 731-0017

ALASKA
P.O. Box 101500
Anchorage, AK 99510
or
949 East 36th Ave.
Anchorage, AK 99508
(907) 271-6877
FAX: (907) 271-6413

ARIZONA
210 E. Earll Dr. (Stop 1005 PX)
Phoenix, AZ 85012-2623
(602) 207-8240
FAX: 602 207-8250

ARKANSAS
700 West Capital St. (Stop D:P)
Little Rock, AR 72201
(501) 324-6260
FAX: (501) 324-5109

CALIFORNIA
Laguna Niguel District
P.O. Box 30207
Laguna Niguel, CA 92607-0207

or
24000 Avila Rd.
Laguna Niguel, CA 92656
(714) 643-4182
FAX: (714) 643-4705

Los Angeles District
P.O. Box 1791
Los Angeles, CA 90053
or
300 N. Los Angeles St.
Room 4352
Los Angeles, CA 90012
(213) 894-6111
FAX: (213) 894-6365

Sacramento District
P.O. Box 2900 (Stop SA 5043)
Sacramento, CA 95812
or
4330 Watt Ave.
North Highlands, CA 95660
(916) 974-5007
FAX: (916) 974-5902

San Francisco District
1301 Clay St., Suite 1540 S
Oakland, CA 94612-5210
(510) 637-2703
FAX: (510) 637-2715

San Jose District
P.O. Box 100 (Stop HQ0004)
San Jose, CA 95103
or
55 S. Market St., Room 900
San Jose, CA 95113
(408) 494-8210
FAX: (408) 494-8065

COLORADO
600 17th St. (Stop 1005 DEN)
Denver, CO 80202-2490
(303) 446-1012
FAX: (303) 446-1010

CONNECTICUT
135 High St. (Stop 219)
Hartford, CT 06103
(203) 240-4179
FAX: (203) 240-4023

DELAWARE
409 Silverside Rd., Room 152
Wilmington, DE 19809
(302) 791-4502
FAX: (302) 791-4511

DISTRICT OF COLUMBIA
P.O. Box 1553, Room 620A
Baltimore, MD 21203
or
31 Hopkins Plaza, Room 620A
Baltimore, MD 21201
(410) 962-2082
FAX: (410) 962-9572

FLORIDA
Ft. Lauderdale District
P.O. Box 17167
Plantation, FL 33318
or

One North University Dr.
Room A-312
Plantation, FL 33324
(305) 424-2388
FAX: (305) 424-2483

Jacksonville District
P.O. Box 35045 (Stop D:PRO)
Jacksonville, FL 32202
or
400 West Bay Street, Room 116
Jacksonville, FL 32202
(904) 232-3440
FAX: (904) 232-2266

GEORGIA
P.O. Box 1065 (Stop 202-D)
Room 1520
Atlanta, GA 30370
or
401 West Peachtreet Street, N.W.
Summit Bldg., Room 1520
(Stop 202-D)
Atlanta, GA 30365
(404) 331-5232
FAX: (404) 730-3438

HAWAII
300 Ala Moana Blvd.
Room 21004
Box 50089
Honolulu, HI 96850-4992
(808) 541-3300
FAX: (808) 541-3379

IDAHO
550 West Fort Street
Box 041
Boise, ID 83724-0041
(208) 334-9153
FAX: (208) 334-9663

ILLINOIS
Chicago District
230 S. Dearborn Street
Room 3214
Chicago, IL 60604
(312) 886-9183
FAX: (312) 886-1564

Springfield District
P.O. Box 19201 (Stop 22)
Springfield, IL 62794-9201
or
320 West Washington Street
Springfield, IL 62701
(217) 527-6382
FAX: (217) 527-6332

INDIANA
P.O. Box 44687 (Stop 11)
Indianapolis, IN 46244
or
575 N. Pennsylvania Street
D:PRO (Stop 11)
Indianapolis, IN 46204
(317) 226-6332
FAX: (317) 226-6222

IOWA
210 Walnut Street (Stop 2)
Des Moines, IA 50309-2109
(515) 284-4780
FAX: (515) 284-6645

KANSAS
P.O. Box 2907
(Stop 1005 WIC)
Wichita, KS 67201
or
271 W. 3rd Street, North
(Stop 1005 WIC)

Wichita, KS 67202
(316) 352-7506
FAX: (316) 352-7212

KENTUCKY
P.O. Box 1735 (Stop 120)
Louisville, KY 40201
or
601 West Broadway
Louisville, KY 40202
(502) 582-6030
FAX: (502) 582-5280

LOUISIANA
600 South Maestri Place
(Stop 12)
New Orleans, LA 70130
(504) 558-3001
FAX: (504) 558-3200

MAINE
68 Sewall Street (Stop 110)
Augusta, ME 04330
(207) 622-8528
FAX: (207) 622-8458

MARYLAND
P.O. Box 1553
Room 620A
Baltimore, MD 21203
or
31 Hopkins Plaza
Room 620A
Baltimore, MD 21201
(410) 962-2082
FAX: (410) 962-9572

MASSACHUSETTS
JFK P.O. Box 9103
Boston, MA 02203
or

JFK Federal Bldg., E-211
Government Center Plaza
Boston, MA 02203
(617) 565-1857
FAX: (617) 565-4959

MICHIGAN
P.O. Box 330500 (Stop 7)
Detroit, MI 48232
or
477 Michigan Avenue (Stop 7)
Detroit, MI 48226-2597
(313) 226-7899
FAX: (313) 226-3502

MINNESOTA
P.O. Box 64599
St. Paul, MN 55164
or
316 N. Robert Street
Room 381
St. Paul, MN 55101
(612) 290-3077
FAX: (612) 290-4236

MISSISSIPPI
100 W. Capitol Street
(Stop 31)
Jackson, MS 39269
(601) 965-4800
FAX: (601) 965-5251

MISSOURI
P.O. Box 66776 (Stop 002)
St. Louis, MO 63166
or
Robert A. Young Bldg.
1222 Spruce Street
(Stop 002)
St. Louis, MO 63103
(314) 539-6770
FAX (314) 539-2190

MONTANA
Federal Building
301 S. Park
Helena, MT 59626-0016
(406) 449-5244
FAX: (406) 449-5342

NEBRASKA
106 S. 15th Street (Stop 2)
Omaha, NE 68102
(402) 221-4181
FAX: (402) 221-4030

NEVADA
4750 W. Oakey Blvd.
Room 303
Las Vegas, NV 89102
(702) 455-1096
FAX: (702) 455-1216

NEW HAMPSHIRE
P.O. Box 720
Portsmouth, NH 03802
or
Federal Office Bldg.
80 Daniel Street
Portsmouth, NH 03801
(603) 433-0571
FAX: (603) 433-0739

NEW JERSEY
P.O. Box 1143
Newark, NJ 07101
or
970 Broad Street
Newark, NJ 07102
(201) 645-6698
FAX: (201) 645-3323

NEW MEXICO
P.O. Box 1040
(Stop 1005 ALB)
Albuquerque, NM 87103

or
5338 Montgomery Blvd., N.E.
(Stop 1005 ALB)
Albuquerque, NM 87109-1311
(505) 837-5505
FAX: (505) 837-5647

NEW YORK
Albany District
Leo O'Brien Federal Bldg.
Room 617
Clinton Ave. & N. Pearl Street
Albany, NY 12207
(518) 431-4554
FAX: (518) 431-4490

Brooklyn District
G.P.O. Box R
Brooklyn, NY 11202
or
10 Metro Tech Center
625 Fulton Street
Brooklyn, NY 11201
(718) 488-2080
FAX: (718) 488-3100

Buffalo District
P.O. Box 500
Niagara Square Station
Buffalo, NY 14201
or
111 West Huron Street
Thaddeus J. Dulski FOB
Buffalo, NY 14202
(716) 846-4574
FAX: (716) 846-5473

Manhattan District
P.O. Box 408
Church Street Station
New York, NY 10008

or
290 Broadway, 7th Floor
New York, NY 10007
(212) 436-1011
FAX: (212) 436-1900

NORTH CAROLINA
320 Federal Place
Room 125
Greensboro, NC 27401
(910) 378-2180
FAX: (910) 378-2485

NORTH DAKOTA
P.O. Box 8
Fargo, ND 58107
or
657 Second Avenue, N.
Fargo, ND 58102
(701) 239-5141
FAX: (701) 239-5644

OHIO
Cincinnati District
550 Main Street, Room 5504
Cincinnati, OH 45202
(513) 684-3094
FAX: (513) 684-6417

Cleveland District
P.O. Box 99709
Cleveland, OH 44199
or
1240 E. Ninth Avenue
Cleveland, OH 44199
(216) 522-7134
FAX: (216) 522-7419

OKLAHOMA
55 N. Robinson
(Stop 1005 OKC)
Oklahoma City, OK 73102-9229
(405) 297-4055
FAX (405) 297-4056

OREGON
P.O. Box 3341
Portland, OR 97208
or
1220 S.W. 3rd Avenue
Room 681
Portland, OR 97204
(503) 326-2333
FAX: (503) 326-5453

PENNSYLVANIA
Philadelphia District
P.O. Box 12010
Philadelphia, PA 19106
or
600 Arch Street, Room 7214
Philadelphia, PA 19106
(215) 597-3377
FAX: (215) 597-7341

Pittsburg District
P.O. Box 705
Pittsburgh, PA 15230
or
1000 Liberty Avenue
Room 1102
Pittsburgh, PA 15222
(412) 644-5987
FAX (412) 644-2769

RHODE ISLAND
380 Westminster Mall
Providence, RI 02903

(401) 528-4492
FAX: (401) 528-4646

SOUTH CAROLINA
P.O. Box 386 MDP 03
Columbia, SC 29202
or
1835 Assembly Street
Room 571, MDP 03
Columbia, SC 29201
(803) 765-5939
FAX: (803) 253-3910

SOUTH DAKOTA
115 4th Avenue, Southeast
Aberdeen, SD 57401
(605) 226-7248
FAX: (605) 226-7270

TENNESSEE
P.O. Box 1107 (Stop 22)
Nashville, TN 37202
or
801 Broadway (Stop 22)
Nashville, TN 37203
(615) 736-5219
FAX: (615) 736-7489

TEXAS
Austin District
300 E. 8th Street
(Stop 1005 AUS)
Austin, TX 78701
(512) 499-5875
FAX: (512) 499-5367

Dallas District
P.O. Box 50008
(Stop 1005 DAL)
Dallas, TX 75250

or
1100 Commerce Street
(Stop 1005 DAL)
Dallas, TX 75242
(214) 767-1289
FAX: (214) 767-0040

Houston District
1919 Smith Street
(Stop 1005-HOU)
Houston, TX 77002
(713) 653-3660
FAX: (713) 653-3708

UTAH
P.O. Box 2069
(Stop 1005 SLC)
Salt Lake City, UT 84110
or
465 South 400 East
(Stop 1005 SLC)
Salt Lake City, UT 84111
(801) 524-6287
FAX: (801) 524-5164

VERMONT
Courthouse Plaza
199 Main Street
Burlington, VT 05401
(802) 860-2008
FAX: (802) 860-2006

VIRGINIA
P.O. Box 10113
Room 5502
Richmond, VA 23240
or
400 N. 8th Street
Richmond, VA 23240
(804) 771-2643
FAX: (804) 771-2008

WASHINGTON
P.O. Box 2207
(Stop 405)
Seattle, WA 98111
or
915 Second Avenue (Stop 405)
Seattle, WA 98174
(206) 220-6037
FAX: (206) 220-5651

WEST VIRGINIA
P.O. Box 1040, Room 1004
Parkersburg, WV 26102
or
425 Juliana Street
Parkersburg, WV 26101
(304) 420-6616
FAX: (304) 420-6682

WISCONSIN
310 W. Wisconsin Avenue
Room M-28
Milwaukee, WI 53203
(414) 297-3046
FAX: (414) 297-1640

WYOMING
308 W. 21st Street
(Stop 1005 CHE)
Cheyenne, WY 82001
(307) 772-2489
FAX: (307) 772-2488

NATIONAL OFFICE
1111 Constitution Avenue, N.W.
Room 3107 C:PRP
Washington, D.C. 20224
(202) 622-6100
FAX: (202) 622-4318

Taxpayers residing overseas or in the U.S. territories should write to:

Problem Resolution Office
Internal Revenue Service
Assistant Commissioner
(International)
P.O. Box 44817
L'Enfant Plaza Station
Washington, D.C. 20026-4817
or
950 L'Enfant Plaza, S.W.
Washington, D.C. 20224
(202) 874-1930
FAX: (202) 874-1782

Index

bankruptcy and, 179-80, 238
civil fraud, 236
estimated-tax, 233, 235, 249
fighting, 237-38
fraud, 234
fraudulent failure to file, 135, 236-37
late-filing, 179, 233, 234
late-payment. *See* Late-payment penalty
negligence, 179-80, 234, 235, 247-48
proving case against, 239-49
reasonable cause for contesting, 239-46
scope of, 234-37
substantial understatement, 234, 235,
    248-49
Trust Fund Recovery. *See* Trust Fund
    Recovery Penalty
Penalty abatement, 193, 237. *See also* Penalties
appealing denial of, 238-39
mechanics of making request for, 249
Pensions, 56
Perjury, 120
Petitions, 267-69
other than in small tax case, *283-84*
in small tax cases, *285*
Policy Statement P-4-86, 310
Powers of the IRS, 12-19
Pretrial memorandum, 271-72
Pretrial order, 271-72
Priority taxes, 181-82
Privacy Act, 304-6
Private-letter rulings, 304
Problem Resolution Office (PRO), 6, 9, 25,
    184-91
functions of, 15
functions of officers, 19
innocent spouse and, 255
levies and, 49, 58
liens and, 109
purpose of, 184
red-tape issues and, 189
telephone numbers for, 365-74
undue hardship criteria and, 186
Property partition suits, 292
Property rights adjudication, 291-92
Property sales

lawsuits for substituted sale proceeds, 291
lawsuits for surplus proceeds, 291
levies and, 58-60
liens and, 30, 35-36
Property seizures, 7, 18, 21. *See also* Levies
sale of property and, 58-60
statutes of limitation and, 343
Taxpayer Bill of Rights on, 196
Property transfers, 337-38
Proprietorships, 217, 318, 319. *See also* Sole
    proprietorships
Pro se petitioners, 263-85. *See also* Litigation
Protests
of audit results, 221, 222-24, *226-28*
professional assistance for, 349
of Trust Fund Recovery Penalty, 153-55
Publications of the IRS, 303, 359-60

Quiet title to property suit, 292

Railroad Retirement act, 56
Railroad Unemployment Insurance Act, 56
Real property
installment agreements and, 111, 112-13
offers in compromise and, 74, 76-77, 85
Reasonable cause
for contesting penalties, 239-46
for nonfilers, 131-32, 137-38
Reasonable prudence, 253
Recommendations for Trust Fund Recovery
    Penalty Assessment, 149-50
Records, 205, 325-35
computerization of, 322-23, 332
importance of proper, 327-28
length of time to maintain, 328-30,
    334-35
organizing during the year, 331-32
preparing for tax season with, 333-35
separation of business and personal, 332
types of to maintain, 328-30
Refunds, 21, 238
assistance in obtaining, 189, 221
electronic, 313
filing claims for, 309-10
for injured spouse, 256